FIFTH EDITION

Forms of Writing

KAY L. STEWART
MARIAN ALLEN
SHELLEY GALLIAH
Grant MacEwan Community College

A RHETORIC, HANDBOOK, AND READER

PEARSON
Prentice
Hall

Toronto

To Adam, who runs, laughs, and argues with me—thank you for under-standing the value of bad sci-fi movies and for keeping me sane, yet silly.

Library and Archives Canada Cataloguing in Publication

Stewart, Kay L. (Kay Lanette), 1942–
    Forms of writing : a brief guide and handbook / Kay L. Stewart, Marian Allen, Shelley Galliah.—5th Canadian ed.

Includes index.
ISBN 978-0-13-206850-5

    1. English language—Rhetoric—Textbooks.   2. English language—Rhetoric—Problems, exercises, etc.   I. Allen, Marian, 1945–   II. Galliah, Shelley Anne, 1968–
III. Title.

PE1408.S762 2009   808'.042   C2007-905325-4

ISBN-13: 978-0-13-206850-5
ISBN-10: 0-13-206850-8

Vice President, Editorial Director: Gary Bennett
Acquisitions Editor: Chris Helsby
Marketing Manager: Sally Aspinall
Supervising Developmental Editor: Suzanne Schaan
Production Editor: Amanda Wesson
Copy Editor: Ann McInnis
Proofreader: Elizabeth Phinney
Production Coordinator: Janis Raisen
Composition: Integra
Art Director: Julia Hall
Cover and Interior Design: Anthony Leung
Cover Image: Veer Inc.

1 2 3 4 5   12 11 10 09 08

Printed and bound in Canada.

Credits
Page 102: "Fast Relief for You and Your Dog" by Erin Zier. Used with permission of the author.
Page 116: "The Ties That Bind" by Toni Williams. Used with permission of the author.
Page 125: "A $55-Million Ride—Worth Every Cent" by Paul Sullivan as printed in the *Globe and Mail*, July 7, 2003, A13. Paul Sullivan is the President of Sullivan Media, a communications consultant, journalist, and teacher.

Brief Contents

Contents

PART 2: DEVELOPING YOUR WRITING STRATEGIES

PART 3: WRITING ESSAYS

PART 4: REVISING YOUR ESSAY

PART 5: PROOFREADING: THE FINAL TOUCHES

PART 6: READINGS

APPENDICES

Appendix 1: Essay and Citation Format

Preface to the Fifth Edition

OUR APPROACH

The approach in *Forms of Writing* rests on this assumption: good writing results when you know your purpose, your audience, your subject, and the conventions of your chosen form. We focus on three main purposes for writing—sharing personal experience, explaining, and persuading—to show how your purpose influences the strategies you choose and the forms you use in writing for a particular audience.

Because this book covers a wide variety of writing forms, such as personal essays, summaries, and research essays, it is suitable for communications courses, introductory writing courses, and English courses with a strong writing component. The appendices, which contain a grammar glossary as well as advice on assignment format and business writing, also extend beyond English courses: students continuing to write in their discipline and on the job will find these materials useful.

Although this edition retains the basic material of the previous editions, new content has been added and some chapters have been expanded and reorganized.

ORGANIZATION OF THE TEXT

- Part 1, The Writing Process, gives you an overview of all the steps in completing a writing assignment, from defining your purpose and audience to revising and proofreading.
- Part 2, Developing Your Writing Strategies, introduces you to principles of paragraph structure and methods of developing paragraphs—such as analysis, definition, and evaluation—that you may use in many forms of writing.
- Part 3, Writing Essays, provides guidelines for the types of writing you are most likely to do in college and university courses, including essays on literature and research papers.
- Part 4, Revising Your Essay, gives guidelines for revising the structure, language, and style of your essay.
- Part 5, Proofreading: The Final Touches, explains accepted practices in grammar and punctuation so that you can meet your readers' expectations for clarity and precision in language.
- Part 6, Readings, contains readings by Canadian authors for further study.
- The appendices cover material you may need to consult frequently when you write: guidelines for formatting, using quotations, and

documenting sources (Appendix 1). There is also an appendix on business writing (Appendix 2), which covers the kinds of business writing that most people do, whatever their occupation—letters of application and résumés, memos, emails, brief reports, and promotional material. A Glossary of Grammatical Terms and Answer Keys for exercises are also included (Appendix 3).

- Updated weblinks at the end of each part direct you to online resources offered, in most cases, by Canadian and US colleges and universities.

CHANGES IN THE FIFTH EDITION

- New examples, several from the sciences, illustrate the types of paragraphs and essays discussed in Parts 2 and 3.
- Part 1, The Writing Process, contains more information on defining your audience as well as some guidelines for writing within your discipline.
- Chapters 2 and 3 have been combined into a single chapter that takes you through the entire writing process, from planning to proofreading.
- Part 2, Developing Your Writing Strategies, contains new information on paragraph unity and coherence, and on paragraph divisions.
- The chapters on expository writing have been reorganized so that there is a separate chapter on writing about literature and new expository examples (Chapters 10 and 11).
- Chapter 13, Research Papers, has been revised to provide more information on searching within electronic databases and using Boolean connectors.
- Chapter 14, a new chapter, contains new advice on revising your essay.
- The new Part 6, Readings, contains readings by Canadian authors.

OTHER RESOURCES

- *Instructor's Manual* includes suggested course outlines, classroom activities and exercises, teaching tips, and suggestions for further reading. The Instructor's Manual is available for downloading from a password-protected section of Pearson Education Canada's online catalogue (vig.pearsoned.ca). Navigate to your book's catalogue page to view a list of those supplements that are available. See your local sales representative for details and access.

Good writing!

Shelley Galliah

Acknowledgments

I wish to thank Marian Allen and Kay Stewart, who generously entrusted me with taking over this project, one of their babies, and whose hard work and practical advice still form much of the foundation of this textbook. This edition also owes much to Susan Leiberman, whose extensive knowledge of business communications informs Appendix 2: Business Writing; and Ilona Ryder, whose earlier work on research papers and documentation made the revision of Chapter 13 much easier.

Like earlier editions, this textbook depends on the work of students who entrusted their writing to Kay, Marian, and me. Extended thanks also go to these students who provided papers: Sharon Cornelius, Erin Zier, and Tony Williams.

I would also like express gratitude to my colleagues. David Annandale and Carolyn Ives deserve special recognition for taking time from their busy academic schedules to contribute essays for Part 6. I also owe much to Anna Ford and Arlene Davis-Fuhr for their creative advice and enthusiastic approach to writing and teaching. The following instructors reviewed the previous edition and/or parts of the new edition: Trevor Arkell, Humber College; Christina Decarie, St. Lawrence College; Heather Gosein, Georgian College; Chandra Hodgson, Humber College; Richard Leighton, Sheridan College: Corinne Marshall, Fanshawe College: Patricia Morgan, Humber College; Julia Sparrow, St. Lawrence College; and Angela Woollam, Algonquin College.

I am immensely grateful to developmental editor Shelley Murchison, who showed a combination of professionalism, friendliness, and patience when replying to my almost one hundred emails. She promptly answered all my questions, even the foolish ones, always encouraging me to keep on track and to complete the project on time.

I owe much to Adam Wellstead, who, in the last few months, has been immensely patient and has done more than his fair share of cleaning, barbecuing, and dog-walking. A heartfelt hug goes to Memphis, my rescued greyhound and my four-legged running and walking partner, and to Mom and Leslie for tolerating, once again, my stress and my lack of long-distance phone calls.

Shelley Galliah

PART 1

THE WRITING PROCESS
AN OVERVIEW

As the Industrial Revolution marked the nineteenth century, the Communication Revolution marked the twentieth. We can now pop a DVD into a player, download documents from a computer, retrieve articles from an electronic database, and send a text message to a cell phone. Instead of reducing the need for good writing skills, these new technologies have actually increased this need. Someone, somewhere, must write the script for the DVD, the entries in the database, the text on the webpage. In the twenty-first century, that person may be you.

You can more easily meet the varied and changing demands made on your writing skills and adjust to these new technologies if you understand the basic steps many successful writers take in planning and completing a piece of writing.

What we offer in this text is only a blueprint; you may find your own writing process much less clearcut and tidy. For instance, you may discover that you spend more time and energy on some steps than on others, depending on the writing project and your creative style. Understand that the writing process we describe is not a rigid structure for you to impose on your writing, but a general plan to help you shape an idea into a written piece. Use our steps to guide you, but please make the process your own.

Also understand that in this text, we move from discussing types of paragraphs to types of essays. This organization has two main purposes: (a) to help you understand the various types of paragraphs and (b) to allow you to see that essays, even if they have one main purpose, often incorporate different types of paragraphs.

1. What is your **subject** for this piece of writing?

_____

2. What is your **purpose**?

   To share personal experience about _____

   To explain what/how/why _____

   To change readers' opinions about _____

   To persuade readers to _____

3. Who is your **audience**?

   Are you writing for an academic audience? _____

   A non-academic audience? _____

4. What does your **reader profile** suggest about your audience's needs and expectations?

_____

5. a. Which method(s) of **gathering material** have you used?

_____

   b. Do you have **enough material** to achieve your purpose?

_____

6. What **focus** have you chosen for your subject?

_____

7. Have you written a **draft** to clarify your thoughts?

_____

8. Have you used an **outline** to organize your material?

_____

9. Have you **revised** your draft for content and organization?

_____

10. Have you **proofread** your writing to improve your style?

_____

11. Have you **proofread** your writing for careless errors?

_____

12. Have you presented your writing in an appropriate **format**?

_____

CHAPTER 1

Identifying Your Purpose and Audience

For most writing tasks, you know the subject you are to write about, such as recycling or workplace injuries. You may also know the form your writing should take—a persuasive essay on recycling or a report on injuries. However, you may be less aware of the specific kinds of writing possible within these forms and the strategies for using them effectively. One of this book's goals is to introduce you to some forms and strategies.

Every piece of writing, whatever its subject and form, is shaped by its purpose and audience. The first question to ask yourself is about your purpose: What do I want this piece of writing to do? The second is about your audience: Who will read it?

1a DEFINING YOUR PURPOSE

This book will focus on three broad writing purposes: to share ideas and experiences, to explain, and to persuade. The first purpose leads to **personal writing,** the second to **expository writing,** and the third to **persuasive writing.** Your understanding of your purpose and audience will influence your choice of form and methods of development, your relationship to your readers, and your language and style.

In some writing situations, you may be free to choose your own purpose. If you wanted to write an article on grizzly bears for a general interest magazine, for instance, you could choose to share your own adventures in grizzly country, explain the grizzly's habits, or argue for better protection for this endangered species.

Writing to Share Personal Experience

Personal writing gives you the chance to explore what you think and how you feel about ideas and experiences and to share these discoveries with others. However, you may also write about your reactions to and perceptions of the world. Nor does personal writing always have to be the serious business of revealing your innermost thoughts and feelings. You, the writer, are on centre stage, and you may therefore choose to present yourself as comic or tragic, satiric or romantic, serious or slightly mad. In personal writing, the emphasis is on the writer's experience rather than the subject.

I was thirteen at the time, in a new school, and desperate to make friends. For the first few weeks, everyone ignored me. Not that all my classmates were friends with each other. At lunch hour and after school they divided into groups and alternately ignored and insulted each other. I was afraid that if I didn't make friends soon, they would stop ignoring and start insulting me. So one day, I followed a gang of five or six into the mall at lunch. As they straggled through The Bay, I kept several feet behind, stopping every now and then to gaze intently at leather briefcases or umbrellas so they wouldn't think I was being pushy. When they clustered around the jewellery counter, I ducked down the next row. And there in front of me were bags and bags of candy, ready for Hallowe'en. Without thinking, I grabbed one and stuffed it under my jacket.

In this excerpt, the writer recounts a brief narrative that contextualizes the events, inviting us into the isolation, fear, and desire to belong that led to her shoplifting. We may disapprove of the theft, but we are drawn into the "I" and her subjective experience.

Writing to Explain

Your writing is expository whenever your main purpose is to provide information, to explain how something works or how something is done, or to explain the meaning of concepts, historical events, works of art, literary texts, etc. As the following example suggests, in expository writing, your emphasis is on your subject, rather than on your audience or on you. You and your readers have the same perspective—you are both peering through a microscope and trying to see the specimen on the glass slide.

The most basic question about shoplifting is this one: Why do people steal? According to a security guard for Sears, the reason is not need: "In all the time I've worked here, and of all the arrests I've made, and I've made over 400 arrests, not once, not once was it out of need." Most shoplifters who are caught have more than enough money with them to pay for the item; many have credit cards as well. So why do they steal? According to Bill Cheung at The Bay, the peak seasons for shoplifting are September and January–February, when new school terms begin. Presumably, at the beginning of the term, students look at the clothes or toys their peers have and want them. Children and adolescents, it seems, shoplift to fit in.

—*Amanda Thompson*

This paragraph illustrates the principal features of much expository writing. The writer explains why some people shoplift without stating her opinion about the behaviour. She presents her information and analysis objectively, avoiding slanted language; she refers to shoplifters as *people* and *students,* not as *thieves* and *juvenile delinquents.* Thus, she keeps the focus on her subject, not on her opinions or on her own personality.

Writing to Persuade

There are many questions central to persuasive writing. *What is good?*—good for one person, a group, a nation, humanity, or the planet. What is right? What should be done? What should be not done? In persuasive writing, you want to convince others to share your attitudes and beliefs, and, perhaps, to act on those beliefs. To accomplish your goal, you have to consider how to appeal to your audience. In the interplay among writer, subject, and audience, the emphasis in persuasive writing shifts toward the audience.

Sample Persuasive Writing
Purpose: To Change Opinion or Behaviour

Contrary to the popular view, most shoplifters do not steal because they are poor. A long-time security guard for Sears, who has arrested more than 400 shoplifters, points out that "not once" had the person stolen out of need. In fact, he stated that shoplifters usually have more than enough money with them to pay for the stolen goods, and they often have credit cards as well. They may tell themselves that the stores are so rich they will not miss this little eraser/tube of lipstick/makeup case/Mp3player/jacket. But it is not the stores that pay; honest customers pay through higher prices. Therefore, there is no reason to be lenient with shoplifters. Because they are as guilty of theft as the person who steals a wallet from a locker room or a CD player from a car, they should be similarly penalized. If we turn a blind eye to shoplifting, we are not only condoning a crime, but also sentencing ourselves and other consumers to pay the penalty.

Here the writer's purpose is not to explain some possible reasons for shoplifting, but to persuade readers to change their attitude, and possibly their behaviour, toward shoplifters. In contrast to the neutral language of the expository paragraph, the language here is emotionally charged: *honest, guilty, lenient, condoning, sentencing, penalized*. The writer also presents a cause-effect relationship that includes the readers: condoning shoplifting affects you. This language and approach focuses attention on the attitude and action that the writer wants readers to adopt. Perhaps the reader who is persuaded by this argument might report a shoplifter the next time he/she sees one.

1b DEFINING YOUR AUDIENCE

In many school and work situations, however, your purpose will be given or implied. An assignment asking you to write a persuasive essay on capital punishment defines your purpose. A manager who asks you to write a report on the success of the last marketing campaign assumes that you will explain such things as sales and profit, not air your frustrations about the workplace.

Thus, defining your purpose is the first step in writing; the second is defining your audience. Just as your style of speaking should change as you move from the chatroom to the classroom, your style of writing should change with your audience. You will decide, for instance, how much background information to give and whether to use a formal or an informal style. To communicate your message and purpose effectively, you need to tailor both to the needs and expectations of your audience.

But what is audience? The audience is the person or people who is/are reading your piece of writing.

In your writing and speaking, you probably address a number of audiences every day—those of your friends, your family, and your instructor. Even these can be further divided. If you were writing a letter to your six-year-old brother, you would address simpler topics and use uncomplicated language; if you were writing a letter to your mother, you would use higher language, discuss more difficult subject matter. Your purposes might also be different. Whereas you might be writing to *explain* college life to your fascinated younger brother—where and when you go to class, where you eat—you might be writing to communicate personal experience to your mother, such as your difficulties with the new college environment.

The writers most concerned about audience are those in the advertising business, who devote much time to analyzing their target audience—those who will be watching or reading the ad—in order to successfully persuade this audience to buy this product or service.

Although you don't need to so intently research your audience, you should still consider it. Your audience might be your instructor, classmates, potential employer, or newspaper reader. Furthermore, your audience might be neutral, friendly, or hostile.

The two main audiences you will have are academic audiences and non-academic audiences. Your academic audience will be your instructor, who is grading your paper not according to his/her own tastes, but according to the standards and formats of writing in his/her profession and discipline. For instance, a sociology instructor might want you to write in the first person, including your personal experiences and how they relate to your field of study, whereas a philosophy instructor might want you to adopt an objective tone, presenting a clearcut argument. An English instructor might want your thesis and main argument at the end of your introduction; however, your biology instructor might want a long summation of research before you state your main point. Although the advice offered in this book is useful across disciplines, pay attention to the expectations of your instructor, who represents a specific academic audience.

To determine the needs of your specific academic audience, study the assignment's instructions and the instructor's expectations. Is the instructor looking for a carefully balanced deductive argument? Is the writer allowed to include personal experience? How formal must the writing be? To determine the demands of your academic audience, ask questions, study the models and student examples, and read around in that discipline.

Non-Academic Audiences

Technically, these are the audiences you imagine communicating to; they do not grade you. However, your instructor might ask you to imagine writing a paper for such an audience to test your adaptation of tone, style, and purpose. Your assignment would be graded according to how it met the needs of its audience. Here are some examples of assignments for non-academic audience.

Write a letter to the editor stating your opinion about the "problem of graffiti" in cities. Here, your purpose is to persuade newspaper readers of your opinion of graffiti. To accommodate the varied education of your audience, you need to state your points using unpretentious language. To accommodate the form and purpose—a short persuasive letter—you need to state your opinion and your reasons for it right away.

Write a humorous expository essay for Chatelaine. Here you are being asked to explain a subject to an audience of women. If you were a male student given this assignment, you might want to pick up this magazine, analyzing its content, article length, and level of language. What subject do you choose? Do you write as a man or a woman? How would you go about making this article funny?

Write a review of a video game for Wired. To determine the audience for *Wired,* you would have to study the magazine to figure out the gender, level of education, and so on of its readers; you might also read one of its reviews, noting the length and language.

Whatever audience you are writing for, whether it be academic or non-academic, there are general questions to determine your audience and construct a reader profile.

Making Reader Profiles

You can develop a clearer sense of your audience by asking these questions.

1. **Who** will read this piece? A specific person, such as a supervisor? A group of people with similar interests, such as *Matrix* fans? A group of people of varying ages and backgrounds, such as newspaper readers?

2. **Why** are they reading this piece? Are they looking for explanations? Are they looking for problems, solutions? Is my reader going to make a decision based on this piece? Or does my reader want another side or more information?

3. What **attitude** will my reader(s) probably bring to this piece of writing? Interest and enthusiasm? Hostility and defensiveness? Critical detachment?

4. How much **knowledge** will my reader(s) already have about my subject? What information do I need to provide? How much background information do I need to give? What terms, if any, do I need to define? What level of language or specialized terminology is appropriate to use? (You really want to determine what your readers know so you can save your words to present new points and arguments.)

5. What **expectations** will my reader(s) have about the way this piece is written? Is there a specific format I should follow? (If unsure, look for *examples* of the piece in other publications, textbooks, or from your instructor.)

Answering these questions will give you a **reader profile**: a general sense of your audience's needs and expectations. Remembering this reader profile as you write or revise will help you communicate more effectively. If you consider what a potential employer looks for in a letter of application, for example, you can tailor your letter to match those expectations. Similarly, you can tailor any piece of writing to your audience.

1b

Defining
Your
Audience

Exercise 1.1

Choose two of the following subjects. Using the example of writing articles on grizzly bears as a guide (see p. 3), show how each subject could be the basis for three pieces of writing with different purposes: one expository, one persuasive, and one personal.

Example: Subject—Bicycles

Expository: to explain how to choose a bike
Persuasive: to persuade newspaper readers to wear helmets
Personal: to share my experience cycling from Jasper to Banff

- budgeting for vacation
- access to postsecondary education
- belly dancing
- needs of people with disabilities
- extreme sports
- *The Lord of the Rings* (the books or the movies)

Exercise 1.2

Choose one piece of writing from your response to Exercise 1.1 and make a reader profile for one of the audiences below. If you have difficulty filling in some of the profile, ask a classmate for his/her opinion.

Example: Letter to the editor in which you are arguing that adults should wear helmets when riding with children. I want to argue that adults should wear helmets so that their children wear helmets.

1. **Who** will read this piece?
   - A group of people of varying ages and backgrounds
   - Probably mostly adults

2. **Why** are they reading this piece?
   - A person who reads the letters to the editor is probably interested in opinions, arguments, and local issues

3. What **attitude** will my reader(s) probably bring to this piece of writing?

   - Adults opposed to wearing helmets might be hostile. I might have to appease this audience by acknowledging their objections, by comparing helmets to seatbelts, and so on.
   - Parents with children might have a mixed attitude or be receptive.

4. How much **knowledge** will my reader(s) already have about my subject?

   - I might have to describe helmet laws for adults versus those for children, as well as the outcome of accidents for cyclists with and without helmets. I might have to stress the stats for children.
   - I might also have to iterate the commonly known but overlooked fact that children learn by example.

5. What **expectations** will my reader(s) have about the way this piece is written?

   - A letter to the editor must be short, persuasive, and in clear language. I might look at letter format as well as examine the letters that get published in that particular paper, looking at their length, tone, and so on.

- a magazine for elementary schoolchildren
- a newspaper
- an ezine devoted to that subject
- a television newscast
- an instructor
- an employer

Exercise 1.3

Using the same piece of writing you chose for Exercise 1.2, make a reader profile for a different audience from the list above.

Exercise 1.4

Based on your reader profiles, briefly explain the major similarities and differences in the way you would write the piece for the two audiences you have chosen.

CHAPTER 2

Gathering Material

Good writing, whether it's a job application letter or a term paper, begins with strong content focused on a central point. This chapter presents techniques to help you generate ideas, collect information, and find a focus. Feel free to change the order of these steps; you might prefer to narrow your topic before brainstorming or to outline before drafting.

2a BRAINSTORMING

When you brainstorm, you capture your spontaneous responses to your subject. Put a key word from your writing task in the centre of a blank page. Free associate by writing down ideas, examples, questions, memories, and feelings. Surround your key word with notes; do not reject or edit your thoughts, regardless of how strange or off-topic they seem. If you were preparing a report on the need for life skills courses in high school, for instance, you might end up with a brainstorming diagram like this:

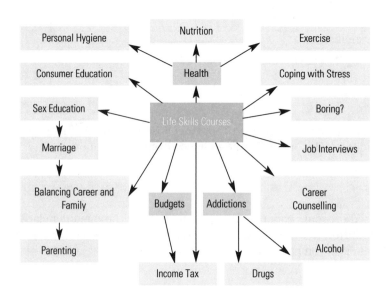

Because brainstorming gives you so many ideas to consider, you can find a fresh angle on your subject or choose material of special interest to your readers.

2b FREEWRITING

Many people disregard their most creative ideas, intuitions, and memories before they start. To avoid this internal censor, try **freewriting,** which is writing spontaneously and continuously about your subject for five or ten minutes. If you run out of material, jot down, "I can't think of anything to say" but still keep writing. Do not hesitate or worry about your words. After ten minutes, look over what you've written and sum it up in one sentence. If your summary suggests new ideas, freewrite for another ten minutes. Repeat this process until you have some worthwhile ideas.

2c KEEPING A JOURNAL

Keeping a **journal** can help you keep up with your class reading as well as gather ideas and information for a long-term writing project. Use your journal entries to reflect on issues, respond to your reading, collect relevant newspaper or magazine items, note questions to pursue, and record your progress. When you sit down to write your essay, you will have plenty of material. Journalling will also help you develop original thinking that goes beyond class discussion—what your instructor really wants to read.

2d ASKING DISCOVERY QUESTIONS

Asking discovery questions is probably the most focused way to gather information for your topic. Discovery questions can help you narrow your topic and mode of development. There are three ways to use this technique.

1. *Start with the journalist's five Ws and an H: Who, What, When, Where, Why, and How.*

   Answering these questions will provide all the information that your reader might need. If you were writing a problem-solving report on theft from gym locker rooms, for instance, you might ask questions like these: Who reported the thefts? Who investigated? What was stolen? When? Where—men's or women's locker room or both? How did the thieves gain access to the articles? What changes would reduce the incidence of theft?

   If you are writing about an unfamiliar or complicated topic, such as global warming, you may need to do research to answer even these basic questions.

2. *Ask questions based on methods of developing your ideas (see Chapters 4, 5, and 6). For an essay on alcoholism, for instance, you might ask questions such as these:*
   - How is alcoholism defined?
   - What are the types of alcoholism?

- What other problems are associated with alcoholism?
- What are the causes? the effects?
- How does alcoholism compare with other kinds of addictions?
- Is there a difference between alcoholism and alcohol abuse?
- Is there a story I could tell about alcoholism?
- What are the typical behaviours of alcoholics?
- How do social factors contribute to alcoholism?
- What are the strengths and weaknesses of current treatment programs?
- What analogy would help to explain the difficulties in overcoming alcoholism?
- What examples would support my points?

2e

Finding
a Focus

3. ***Ask questions specific to the appropriate academic discipline or area of inquiry*** (for examples, see the questions for analyzing imaginative literature, pp. 112–114, and the questions for evaluating an argument, pp. 124–125).

Exercise 2.1

Make a brainstorming diagram for one of the following subjects.
- current trends in hip-hop music
- public figures you admire (or dislike)
- benefits of dog ownership
- use of ethanol fuel
- the popularity of YouTube
- your favourite/least favourite type of movie

Exercise 2.2

Choose a different subject from the list above and generate material for an essay by freewriting or by asking discovery questions.

2e FINDING A FOCUS

After you have defined your purpose and audience and gathered ideas and information about your subject, you might be bewildered by the amount of information you have collected. To decide what to include and omit, you need a **focus.**

To find a focus, link your purpose and audience with one or more aspects of your subject. For a short piece, you might discuss one aspect in detail. For a longer piece, you may include several. Suppose, for example, that your subject is coyotes and that your purpose is to explain some aspect of this subject to newspaper readers. For a short piece, you might narrate an encounter with a coyote. For a longer piece, you might explain coyotes in urban areas.

Exercise 2.3

Using the material you have generated in Exercise 2.1 or 2.2, show how you could focus your material for five different purposes and audiences.

Example: Subject—Life skills courses

(see brainstorming diagram, p. 10)

Purpose: to persuade teachers that preparing for job interviews by role-playing should be a part of every life skills course.

Audience: teachers

2f FORMULATING A ROUGH THESIS STATEMENT

Thesis statements, which are discussed in more detail in Chapter 7, are only briefly introduced here.

Some students discover their main point after drafting and outlining whereas others prefer to begin with a main point. Although it is not advisable to begin an essay with a refined thesis (for you will distort your subject), you might want to begin with a draft thesis or a rough idea of the main point that you intend to make about your subject.

After narrowing your focus, begin working on your thesis statement. If your focused subject is coyotes in urban areas, for instance, your thesis needs to make a point about these coyotes. Are they desirable? Problematic? A nuisance? A symptom of urban development? You also need to consider your audience and the length of your composition. If this assignment is a research essay for an environmentalism course, for instance, you might decide to *explain* the reasons that coyotes are invading urban areas. Your rough thesis for this paper might be the following: "Coyotes are invading urban areas because of the destruction of traditional coyote habitat and reduced food sources." Because this is a rough thesis, you might discover, when writing your draft, that there are other reasons coyotes are appearing in cities.

If you are writing a proposal for city council, on the other hand, you might briefly explain the effects of urban coyotes and try to *persuade your audience* to adopt a solution. Your thesis might be the following: "The city should have a plan to control the coyote population because coyotes are causing property damage, preying on domestic pets, destroying livestock, and attacking people." You might discover, when writing this essay, that coyote attacks on people are rare and choose to omit this point.

In general, then, a thesis has a subject, a main point (or opinion) about that subject (a *what*), and at least one reason for supporting this main point or for holding or stating that opinion (a *why*). The *why* could be how you arrived at the opinion or why you think that point is relevant, depending on your essay type and purpose. In the example above, the subject is coyotes, the main point is that they need to be controlled, and the *why* consists of their effects. Before you write your essay, please read the detailed information on the thesis presented in Chapter 7.

Once you determine your rough thesis, you can move onto the fast-drafting and outlining phases.

2f

Formulating a Rough Thesis Statement

Exercise 2.4

To understand how thesis statements are structured, examine the sentences below, separating the subject, the main point (or opinion) about the subject, and reasons for holding or stating that main point (or opinion). Remember that thesis statements can be structured in different ways.

Example: Eastern Canada is alienated from Western Canada because of geographical, political, and economic differences.

Subject = Eastern Canada
Main point about subject = is alienated from Western Canada
Why or Reasons for this alienation = geographical, political, and economic differences

Example: "The Cask of Amontillado" uses irony and symbolism to express its main theme that revenge is not always sweet.

Subject = "The Cask of Amontillado"
Main point = has a main theme that revenge is not always sweet
Reasons for this main point = uses irony and symbolism to express
(In this literary analysis essay, why you believe that "revenge is not sweet" is the main theme of the story and is synonymous with *how* you arrived at your interpretation.)

- Parents should wear helmets to prevent their children from getting injured.
- Because shoplifting has become so widespread, methods of identifying and apprehending shoplifters have changed.
- By giving users access to cheap and free music, music-share services like Napster threaten the music industry.
- Proper training for a marathon requires long runs, tempo workouts, and easy jogs.
- Training a puppy is like training a child; both require a sense of humour, patience, and discipline.
- To reduce taxes for the average Canadian, the Government of Canada should eliminate wasteful spending.

2g DRAFTING, OUTLINING, AND REVISING

An outline shows you, at a glance, the main divisions of your paper and the relationships among major points, minor points, and details. Making an outline thus helps you to classify your material and detect gaps in it. We will discuss various ways of using fast-drafting and outlining so that you can choose the method most suitable to your writing task and your work process. Although we discuss making a preliminary outline first, you might draft before outlining.

Making a Preliminary Outline

Some writers are very organized from the beginning; they carefully plan what they want to say, either in their minds or in an outline, so that their first draft develops their rough thesis and a clear pattern of organization. If you are one of these writers, you might prefer to make a *preliminary outline* before fast-drafting. Using your focused subject or your rough thesis as a guide, jot down your main points and supporting details for each main point. After completing your preliminary outline, write a fast-draft.

Fast-Drafting

If you decide to write a fast draft to flesh out your outline or help clarify your thinking, allot a fixed period—usually an hour or two. Using the material you have gathered through the previous stages—2a to 2e, and, if applicable, 2f and 2g, write a complete draft. Don't let yourself get bogged down. If you have trouble with the introduction, for example, either leave some space and come back to it later, or write your statement of focus and go on from there. If you didn't begin with a thesis, and you discovered your main point in the process of writing, go back and revise the introduction.

Making a Revision Outline

If you find that your fast-draft is unbalanced and disorganized, you might want to make a revision outline. For each paragraph, write down the main points and supporting details. The outline will reveal problems in content and organization: paragraphs that need to be combined or divided, points that need further explanation, or topic sentences that could be improved. This step allows you to critically analyze your own work and take your reader's perspective.

To see which process works best for you, practise outlining and fast-drafting an essay.

Exercise 2.5

Using material from Exercise 2.3, make a draft outline. Put your statement of focus at the top of the page as a guide to your main points. Under each main point, jot down necessary details. Then write a paragraph on the process. How well did making a draft outline work for you? Could you more easily see how to organize your material? Did the outline reveal areas where you needed more ideas or information? Or did the process seem mechanical and boring?

Exercise 2.6

Using your material from Exercises 2.1 or 2.2, fast-draft an essay. Then write a paragraph on the process. How well did fast-drafting work for you? Were you able to continue writing or did you get stuck? Did you begin with a thesis statement or did a main point emerge as you wrote? Did you come up with new ideas or examples?

2h MAKING A FORMAL OUTLINE

You can also make a **formal outline** of your final version to accompany a lengthy report or research paper. Some instructors, in fact, might ask for a detailed formal outline before submitting a long essay, such as a research paper. Put your thesis—the main point of your piece—at the top of the page. List your major points with Roman numerals, your subpoints with capital letters, and details with Arabic numerals. The format of your outline should resemble the one below.

Sample Formal Outline

Thesis Childhood obesity is a widespread but complicated problem, which has several causes and numerous short- and long-term physical effects.

I. Extent of the problem

    A. Definition of obesity

    B. Percentage of obese children in Canada

    C. Comparing Canadian children to other children

II. Causes of childhood obesity

    A. Poor nutrition

        1. At home

        2. In schools

    B. Lack of exercise

        1. Statistics on lack of exercise

        2. Causes of lack of exercise

            a. More sedentary living than physical activity

            b. Physical education absent or reduced in schools

III. Effects of childhood obesity

    A. Associated physical problems (immediate effects)

        1. Early maturation

        2. High blood pressure

        3. Diabetes mellitus type 2

    B. Long-term effects

        1. Obese adults

        2. Physical problems of obese adults

IV. Solutions

    A. Educate parents

    B. Restore physical education in schools

    C. Early intervention

As you can see, each level of the outline (Roman numerals, capital letters, Arabic numerals) represents a division of the level above. For this reason, you should have at least two items at each level. (If you have an A, you must have a B; if you have a 1, you must have a 2.) Each item at a particular level must be an equivalent subdivision of the level above. For example, *Early maturation, High blood pressure,* and *Diabetes* are equivalent items under *Effects of childhood obesity.* This equivalence will be more obvious if you make items at each level grammatically parallel; for instance, these effects are all nouns. An outline will disclose whether you have adequately developed your ideas and sufficiently covered your subject.

Exercise 2.7

Make a formal outline to accompany either the provided Sample Non-Literary Research Paper (13i) or the Sample Literary Research Paper (13j).

2i REVISING AND PROOFREADING

Because some of the terminology of revising has not yet been discussed, this section is just an overview of these processes. For more detailed advice on revising and proofreading, go to Chapters 14 and 15 of this text.

Revising and proofreading are two important, but separate, time-consuming steps of the composition process. Keep in mind, however, that strategies for revising and proofreading vary from form to form. For a brief letter, you may simply type out your request, proofread for mistakes, and seal it in the envelope. A letter of application, a report, or an essay will require a more careful consideration of content, organization, and style. Essays, of course, will require more time to both revise and proofread.

When you revise, you are looking at the big picture, gauging your piece of writing for appropriate content, organization, and tone. To revise, evaluate the content and organization of your draft according to the appropriate checklist(s): for paragraphs, p. 22, and for essays, p. 72. As well, go through the steps detailed in Chapter 14 and check the requirements of your composition or assignment. Make any necessary alterations.

If you are working on a computer and moving text around, you should make separate documents for your drafts. You might even want to work on your document in "markup," a view that is available under *Tools.* This view, among other things, allows you to insert commentary and see material you deleted; this view allows you to have an interactive conversation with your draft and to anticipate the questions of your reader.

Next, read your work aloud to get a sense of its tone and how it sounds to another reader. If some sections seem wordy, monotonous, or stilted, consult the relevant sections of Chapter 15. This section will help you decide on the level of formality of your writing.

After you have viewed your essay from this broad perspective, you need to examine it more closely. This is the proofreading stage. Read every sentence to seek out typos and errors in grammar and punctuation. For more information on these aspects of writing, see the checklist for Proofreading (p. 182) and the relevant sections of Part 5 (Chapters 16–21).

Finally, make sure that you have presented your work in the appropriate format. You will find examples in Appendix A, Format Conventions; Appendix B, Documentation: MLA System; and Appendix C, Documentation: APA System. Taking the time to perfect all aspects of format shows that you are serious about presenting a professional-looking assignment.

Weblinks

- York University Pre-writing Strategies Online Tutorial—an excellent resource that provides techniques and strategies for writing essays.

   www.yorku.ca/tutorial/prewriting

- Writers on the Net—classes, tutoring, mentoring, and writers' groups. Subscribe to the free newsletter.

   www.writers.com

- Canadian-Based Publications Online—articles and abstracts from newspapers, magazines, and trade journals. If you want to study formal and professional writing, this is a good source.

   www-2.cs.cmu.edu/Unofficial/Canadiana/CA-zines.html

- Drew University Writing Program Web Resources—good material on peer critiques as well as links to search engines, writing centres, and other resources.

  www.users.drew.edu/~sjamieso/Webresources.html

- Kent State Mini-Portal for First Year Writing—a portal that responds to FAQ with a series of useful weblinks.

  dept.kent.edu/english/WritingCent/Portal/MiniPortal/

- The Owl at Purdue University—one of the oldest, best, and most reliable sites for all kinds of information on composition.

  owl.english.purdue.edu/owl/

- University College Writing Workshop from the University of Toronto—this site offers useful advice and printable pdf handouts.

  www.utoronto.ca/ucwriting/organizing.html

- The University of Victoria Writer's Guide—one of the best sites for systematic coverage of the writing process.

  web.uvic.ca/wguide/Pages/MasterToc.html

2i

Revising
and
Proofreading

PART 2

DEVELOPING YOUR WRITING STRATEGIES

	OK	NEEDS WORK

1. Is your purpose clear?

2. Have you chosen an appropriate method of development for your purpose and audience?

3. Does the topic sentence state the main point?

4. Are the details adequate?

5. Are the details relevant?

6. Is the paragraph a readable length (neither too long nor too short)?

7. Have you used effective transitions?

8. Have you chosen language appropriate to your purpose and audience?

9. Is your writing varied, concise, and stylistically interesting?

CHAPTER 3

Writing Better Paragraphs

Topic
Sentences

Paragraphs are the building blocks of writing. Introductory paragraphs lay the foundation; concluding paragraphs provide the capstone, or finishing touch. In between are the middle paragraphs, each one discussing one aspect of your subject (one point in an analysis, one step in a process, one event in a narrative, and so on). Each middle paragraph is thus both a self-contained piece of writing and a part of a larger structure.

In this chapter, we focus on general strategies for writing paragraphs. You will find more detailed guidelines for developing paragraphs for particular purposes in the following chapters: Chapter 4, Methods of Sharing Personal Experience; Chapter 5, Methods of Explaining; and Chapter 6, Methods of Persuading.

3a TOPIC SENTENCES

The purpose of a topic sentence is to state the paragraph's main point. You will therefore need to figure out exactly what idea you want to develop in each paragraph and clearly state that idea in a sentence. This topic sentence, then, controls the content of your paragraph, helping you decide which details to include and which to omit.

The paragraph below reveals what can go wrong if you don't have a topic sentence:

> Some people regard physical fitness as a means to physical health and well-being. They believe that vigorous exercise strengthens the heart and lengthens life. Unfortunately, these exercise enthusiasts tend to monopolize all the equipment in a fitness centre. Other people exercise to make themselves more physically attractive. They want to reshape their bodies to fit the model that society presently holds as representative of physical perfection. I see both young and middle-aged women struggling to create a body that is genetically impossible for them. Still others are more interested in exercise clothes than in exercise itself. They wear the latest fashions in running shoes and yoga wear, but they would never work out for fear that sweat might ruin such expensive gear.

The writer's main point seems to be that people have various reasons for wanting to be part of the fitness scene, but the paragraph drifts into comments on the use of exercise equipment and unrealistic goals for physical appearance. Beginning with a good topic sentence not only helps the writer stay on track but also transforms a jumbled paragraph into a stronger one describing the groups of people who exercise:

> For various reasons, people want to be, or want to appear to be, part of the fitness scene. Some people regard physical fitness as a means to physical health and well-being. They believe that vigorous exercise strengthens the heart and lengthens life. Other people exercise to make themselves more physically attractive. They want to reshape their bodies to fit society's present model of physical perfection. Still others are more interested in exercise clothes than in exercise itself. They are attracted to the latest fashions in running shoes and yoga wear, but they would never work out for fear that sweat might ruin such expensive gear.

Knowing your main idea will help you to determine which details are relevant.

However, not all writers are going to know their topic sentences immediately. In actual writing situations, you may need to begin with the details you have collected before determining your main point. Suppose, for example, that you were writing an essay on the popularity of online communities. One paragraph of this essay could focus on a particular one, such as Facebook. Your notes for such a paragraph might look like this:

- Facebook refers to itself as a "social utility" that brings people together.
- All you need to join Facebook is an existing email address and access to a computer.
- You set up an account with an email address and a profile, which can be as limited or as detailed as you want.
- With this account, you get a webpage, inbox, message board, and access to other friends.
- You can prevent strangers from seeing your profile.
- You can decide which information to share.
- You can join existing groups on Facebook or create your own.
- Facebook allows you to choose your friends and maintain the privacy of your information.
- You can communicate with individual people or with groups.
- You can upload and share photographs.
- You can create graffiti walls and movie lists.
- You invite friends to join, but they can refuse.

By reading through this list of details, you can see that it is somewhat disorganized and that it actually develops two points: one about the general process of joining and using Facebook and another about the security of this online community. After you refined these main points into topic sentences, you might have paragraphs like those below.

Facebook, a popular online community that is easy to join, is stocked with tools for connecting to people. Using your email address and some select personal details, you follow the prompts and set up an account, which gives you a webpage, inbox, wall, and other amenities. Along with other activities, you can post messages, upload and share photographs, create albums, join existing groups, and create your own. You can build graffiti walls and favourites lists. Using the email addresses of your friends, you can invite them to join Facebook, assembling a group of friends.

This popular online community also has several secure features. When asking friends to join, you can confirm how you know them. You also decide what information to share and who to share it with, deciding who is allowed to be your friend. Furthermore, you can block your profile from strangers and remove people from your friends list if they fail to act appropriately.

3b TYPES OF TOPIC SENTENCES

Although all topic sentences control the content of the paragraph and state the main idea, they differ according to the purpose of the paragraph: to communicate personal experience or describe, to explain, or to persuade. These topic sentences, then, will differ in both tone and structure. Below are a few examples of topic sentences:

PERSONAL EXPERIENCE	Although I was initially reluctant to join an online community, doing so made me feel more connected to other people.
EXPOSITORY (CLASSIFICATION)	There are three basic types of online communities: local communities online, virtual communities of interest, and organizational communities.
EXPOSITORY (PROCESS)	If you follow these four steps, you can choose an online community that suits your interests and lifestyle.
PERSUASION	Although people are hesitant about joining online communities because of privacy issues, the benefits of joining these communities far outweigh the risks.

Exercise 3.1

Read the following paragraph in which the writer attempts to pin down how his father influenced his life. Figure out the writer's main point and state it as clearly as you can in a topic sentence. Then rewrite the paragraph, eliminating any irrelevant details.

I must have gone out with Father many times: to the movies, to the pub (where I sat on the bench outside drinking pop), to football and hockey games. Always I had a sense of extreme pleasure and pride. Our dog Whiskers would sometimes tag along, and I enjoyed throwing sticks for him to retrieve. My father and I also had lots of personal fun and games. He would toss a football and I would pretend that I was the heroic receiver speeding away from fierce Argonaut defencemen. Or I would stand between two horse chestnut trees in the Crown Inn Gardens pretending that I was the Canadiens goalie waiting for Father's speeding puck, exulting in every spectacular save, every reckless plunge between flashing blades. "Great save, Lorenzo!" my father would shout. These trees have now been cut down to enlarge the parking lot. My fun was intensified by my father's own leaps of mind. He was never flamboyant in any of this; instead, he maintained a simple, involved plausibility.

3c THE BODY OF THE PARAGRAPH

As we have seen, topic sentences make a point that you then develop with more specific details. If your paragraph lacks these, you will have trouble explaining your ideas and convincing your readers of their validity. Consider the following example.

> **Cyclists who ignore the rules of the road are a danger to themselves and others.** Most motorists hate and fear cyclists just as most cyclists hate and fear motorists. When I see how cyclists ride anywhere and any way they want on the road, I wonder what they are protecting inside their helmets.

This paragraph consists of three generalizations making similar points, when it needs one topic sentence with a general statement followed by specific supporting details.

The topic sentence about cyclists, for example, suggests two subpoints to be explained further. Which rules of the road do cyclists ignore? How do they endanger themselves and others by ignoring these rules? You would develop the body of the paragraph by using details to explain these subpoints: not wearing helmets, not signalling, riding on the wrong side of the road, and ignoring lights and signs. These details show the rules cyclists ignore as well as how they endanger both themselves and motorists.

If you have trouble developing your ideas, you may need to clarify your purpose: Is your aim to explain something? to persuade? to share your experiences? You can then choose an appropriate method (or methods) of development discussed in the next three chapters. These guidelines will help you improve your paragraph content.

Whichever method(s) of development you choose, you will need examples illustrating your main points.

In the examples below, two paragraphs are broken down into their components: the first is an example paragraph whereas the second is a causal analysis paragraph from a persuasive essay on the effects of our fast-paced lifestyle.

Cockroaches, members of the order Blattodea who have been around for some 300 million years, are one of the hardiest of insects.[1] They are able, with the exception of the polar regions,[2] to live in a wide range of environments around the world. Mostly nocturnal, they know how to avoid their most dangerous predators—humans—living in households for an annoyingly long time. Cockroaches are **also** capable of surviving a month without food, and, as scavengers and omnivores, can eat anything. **For instance,** some have survived on the glue from postage stamps. **In addition,** these pests can hold their breath for forty-five minutes, lower their resting heart rate, and can withstand, per their body weight, six to fifteen times the radiation of humans.[3] Some science fiction writers **even** believe that after a nuclear blast, cockroaches will out-survive humans. The resilience of cockroaches, though amazing, makes them one of the most maligned group of insects.[4]

3c

The Body
of the
Paragraph

Sample Causal Analysis Paragraph

Finally, speeding up life causes health problems.[5] First, going too fast, combined with poor management skills, has made us reliant on fast food not only for its convenience, but also for its comfort. This fast-food addiction has helped to create an obese Canadian population. **In fact,** Statistics Canada (2004)[6] in its bulletin *The Daily,* reported that "5.5 million individuals were obese, and this statistic has increased substantially during the last twenty-five years" (¶2). Obesity, which technically is defined as having a BMI of 30 or higher can cause additional health problems, such as "high blood pressure, breathing problems, stroke, heart disease, diabetes, hyper-lipidemia, gall bladder disease, gout, and cancer" (*The Daily,* ¶5). Because people who don't eat properly often don't exercise regularly, the effects of poor eating are compounded. As these examples show, living too fast is bad for your physical health.[7]

Exercise 3.2

List several subpoints and examples to develop each of the following topic sentences.

1. Fast-food chains could help combat the rising levels of obesity.

2. Cell phone use is contributing to the rudeness of people.

---

[1] This is the topic sentence, which will focus on the hardiness of the cockroach.
[2] Following this topic sentence are examples about the hardiness of cockroaches. The transitional words linking sentences are bolded.
[3] Parallel structures here stress the amazing physical qualities of this insect.
[4] This is the concluding sentence that brings the paragraph to a temporary close. This sentence stresses the hardiness of cockroaches by repeating the word.
[5] This is the topic sentence for the third paragraph in a causal analysis paragraph on obesity. In this paragraph, the writer works on this chain of events: speeding up causes poor time management skills and anxiety. Rushed and anxious people avoid exercise and rely on fast food. This lifestyle leads to a host of other physical problems.
[6] In his examples, which are effects, the writer combines his own analysis with secondary sources. Here he is using APA parenthetical citation format. For more on integrating primary analysis and secondary sources, see Appendices B and C.
[7] This final sentence brings the paragraph to a temporary close.

3. *Pirates of the Caribbean: Dead Man's Chest* had too many plotlines.

4. There are many ways that Canadians can recycle.

5. Owning a dog can benefit the health of a senior citizen.

3d PARAGRAPH STRUCTURE

There are two main ways of organizing information in a paragraph. You can begin, as in the above paragraphs, with your topic sentence and then fill in the reasons, examples, and other supporting details, or you can begin with these details and examples and gradually lead your reader to your main point. The first, which emphasizes your main point, is a deductive paragraph. The second, which emphasizes the process of thinking and leads to the main point, is an inductive paragraph.

Note: If you begin with a deductive paragraph, do not end this paragraph with the topic sentence for the next paragraph. Although your intention may be to provide a transition, you will actually confuse your readers about your main point and paragraph structure.

The examples below reveal the differences between these paragraph structures.

Sample Paragraph: Topic-Sentence-First Arrangement (Deductive)

Working nights in a convenience store introduced me to a side of my neighbourhood I hadn't known before. One surprise was the discovery of neighbours who emerged from their homes only after midnight, but the night lives of people I had met before were also surprising. I discovered that old Mr. Moses, with whom I had exchanged perhaps twenty sentences in the past ten years, was a talkative insomniac, addicted to corned beef sandwiches at 3 a.m. He had been an intelligence agent with an amazing career, which he unfolded in successive nightly installments. And then there was Mrs. Anderson. I had always imagined her to be one half of a happily married older couple, but twice in the first month I worked at the store, Mrs. Anderson met a man (who was definitely not her husband) and disappeared into the night. I was beginning to see new meaning in the term "convenience store."

Sample Paragraph: Details-First Arrangement (Inductive)

Before I started working in one, a convenience store was just a place to go when you ran out of milk late at night. I hadn't realized that I had many nocturnal neighbours who emerged from their homes only after midnight. More surprising, however, were the night lives of people I knew. Old Mr. Moses, with whom I had exchanged perhaps twenty sentences in the past ten years, turned out to be a talkative insomniac, addicted to corned beef sandwiches at 3 a.m. In nightly installments, he unfolded his amazing career as an intelligence agent. And then there was Mrs. Anderson. I had always thought of her as one half of a happily married older couple, but twice in the first month I worked at the store she met a man (who was definitely not her husband) and disappeared into the night. Working nights in a convenience store introduced me to a side of my neighbourhood I hadn't known before.

Paragraph
Structure

Although the above paragraph is from a personal essay, inductive paragraphs are also effective in expository and persuasive writing. If you are trying to convince a resistant or uninformed reader, or attempting to make an unpleasant proposal or a controversial point, consider presenting the details first, such as in the paragraph below:

Recently, our overall profits have decreased by 10 percent. Additionally, our rate of sales per hour is down from $88 per employee to $74. We are also, because of increasing gas prices, produce scares, and crop shortages, experiencing a time when our costs are inordinately high. For every $1000 loss in each department, the store has had to cut twelve hours; for every $3000 loss, the store has cut the equivalent of one part-time employee. **Thus, in order to manage our losses, to prevent any future cuts in hours, and to avoid firing staff, management are urging part-time employees to take a temporary pay cut.**

Exercise 3.3

Write a paragraph on any subject that interests you. Begin with your topic sentence. Then rewrite the paragraph, putting the details first and ending with your topic sentence. Underline your topic sentences in each paragraph.

3e PARAGRAPH UNITY AND COHERENCE

Whether you are writing a descriptive, expository, or persuasive paragraph, it is essential that your paragraph be both **unified** and coherent. In a unified paragraph, every sentence develops the main idea of the topic sentence, by explaining, exemplifying, or expanding on this idea. A unified paragraph, then, contains no extraneous details.

To check paragraph unity, test every sentence against the topic sentence. Sentences that don't develop the main idea should be removed or relocated. That is, move rather than delete particularly effective examples, for they may belong in another paragraph.

The best way to explain this concept is to examine a paragraph that is not unified. In the paragraph below on "blackouts," which sentences do not develop the main point?

To understand the dangers of blackouts, we need to first define them. A blackout is an alcohol-induced memory loss caused by a blockage of neurotransmitters that send memories from short-term memory to long-term memory. A blackout typically occurs when the blood alcohol level is over .15, far over the legal limit. It is commonly believed that only alcoholics get blackouts. People in blackouts appear to be functioning as a normal intoxicated person, having conversations, and so on. The actual blackout, or memory loss, which can last a few minutes to a few hours or more, does not appear until the next day. Blackouts should be distinguished from passing out or from drinking to the point of unconsciousness. Several college students have reported blackouts. At this point, the person usually fails to remember what happened after he or she left the bar.

The sentences that don't belong, and which could be incorporated into another paragraph discussing the common misconceptions of blackouts are these: "It is commonly believed . . ." and "Several college students . . ." As well, unless the person is going to give more information distinguishing blackouts from other alcohol-related episodes, the sentence "Blackouts . . . unconsconsciousness" should also be removed.

The revised paragraph would be as follows:

To understand the dangers of blackouts, we need to define them. A blackout is an alcohol-induced memory loss caused by the blockage of neurotransmitters that send memories from short-term memory to long-term memory. A blackout typically occurs when the blood alcohol level is over .15, far over the legal limit. However, a person experiencing a blackout appears to be functioning as a normal intoxicated person, having conversations, and so on. The actual blackout, or memory loss, which can last a few minutes to a few hours or more, does not appear until the next day. At this point, the person usually fails to remember what happened after he or she left the bar.

Paragraph Coherence

Whereas unity is the development of one idea, **coherence** comprises those qualities of the paragraph that make that idea understandable. Coherent paragraphs, then, develop their one main idea by presenting their information in the most effective and logical order, and by having smooth connections between their sentences. In other words, coherent paragraphs flow. If your instructor comments that your paragraphs are unified but not coherent, he or she is saying that though your paragraphs develop one idea, they lack flow. You probably need to reorder your sentences and add transitions.

Because the ordering of details depends on paragraph type, which is discussed in detail in Chapters 4–6, we will focus on using transitions here.

As you move from sentence to sentence and paragraph to paragraph, you constantly present your readers with a mixture of known information (terms and ideas you have already introduced) and new information. You can emphasize the continuity between known and new information and reinforce paragraph coherence (and flow) by using these stylistic devices. Transitional words not only order ideas and indicate relationships between them but also establish tone.

3f TRANSITIONS

1. *Use transitional words and phrases.*

The transitions in the list on the next page can clarify how you have organized your material, making it easier for your readers to move from one point to the next. (The terms before each semicolon are less formal; those after the semicolon are more formal.)

Transitions

	Informal	Formal
NARRATION	first, next, then, last, as soon as, early the following morning, later that day	in the beginning, in the end
DESCRIPTION	nearer, farther, on the right, on the left, at the top, at the bottom, to the east, beside, between, above	adjacent to
CLASSIFICATION	one group, another kind, a third type	one subcategory, moreover, furthermore
EXAMPLE	for example, for instance	to illustrate, a case in point
PROCESS ANALYSIS	first step, second step, next stage, final stage	
SYSTEMS ANALYSIS	one component, another part	the most important element
CAUSAL ANALYSIS	one reason, a final reason, the most important effect, although, because, despite, however	therefore, nevertheless, consequently, as a result, thus, if/then, provided that
DEFINITION	one meaning, another meaning, the most relevant meaning	primary meaning, secondary meaning
COMPARISON	and/also, but/too, in comparison, in contrast, similarly	just as/so too, not only/but also, neither/nor
EVALUATION		a practical advantage, a logical inconsistency, another legal aspect, from a moral perspective, an aesthetic weakness

A comparison of the following paragraphs reveals how transitions can dramatically increase the clarity of your ideas and the smoothness of your writing.

Sample Draft Paragraph without Transitions

I had been working as a carpenter for five years. I injured my back. I needed to find a different sort of job. I had always been interested in starting my own business. I decided to take business courses at a community college. I was uneasy about taking college courses. My writing skills needed work. I got a D on my first essay. I was discouraged and considered dropping the course. My instructor asked me to speak with her. She explained how I could improve my essay and gave me a chance to revise it. I decided to stay in the course and pursue my dream of a new life.

Sample Revised Paragraph with Transitions

After working as a carpenter for five years, I injured my back. **As a result of this injury**, I needed a different kind of job. I had always wanted to start my own business, **so** I decided to take some business courses at a community college. I was, **however**, uneasy about taking college courses. English, **for example**, scared me **because** I knew my writing skills were weak. **When** I got a D on my first essay, I was discouraged and considered dropping the course. **Then** my instructor asked me to come in and speak with her. **During this interview**, she explained how I could improve my essay and gave me a chance to revise it. **Because of this encouragement**, I decided to stay in the course and pursue my dream of a new life.

2. *Repeat key words or phrases.*

Don't be afraid of some repetition; recapping a key word lets your readers know you are still talking about the same subject. If you introduce too many synonyms, readers may think you are offering new information. In the short paragraph below, the many synonyms for *bear* and *hunting partner* distract attention from the main subject, the father and the act of surprising the wounded bear.

Dad was fearless. Once when he and a hunting partner were tracking deer in the foothills, they surprised a wounded bear in a thicket. When the maimed animal knocked his friend down, Dad struck the brute with an empty rifle, distracting the angry monster long enough for his companion to get up and shoot the beast.

The paragraph reads much more smoothly when fewer terms are introduced:

Dad was fearless. Once when he and a hunting partner were tracking deer in the foothills, they surprised a wounded bear in a thicket. When the bear knocked George down, Dad struck it with an empty rifle, distracting it long enough for George to get up and shoot it.

3. *Use personal pronouns to refer to subjects previously named.*

Pronouns (*he, she, it, they*), like repeated terms, signal known information; in the example above, the pronoun *it,* which refers to the bear, is much clearer than *the brute* or *the beast.*

Below is an excerpt from Winston Churchill's speech on the evacuation at Dunkirk ("Wars Are Not Won by Evacuations"). Note the key words, phrases, and pronouns Churchill repeats. How do these repeated words and phrases affect the tone?

Even though large tracts of Europe and many old and famous states **have fallen** or **may fall** into the grip **of the Gestapo** and all the odious apparatus **of Nazi rule**, we shall not **flag** or **fail**. We shall go on to the end, we shall fight **in France**, we shall fight **on the seas and oceans**, we shall fight **with growing confidence and strength in the air**, we shall defend our island, whatever the cost may be, we shall fight **on the**

beaches, we shall fight **in the landing grounds**, we shall fight **in the fields** and **in the streets**, we shall fight **in the hills**; we shall never surrender, and even if, which I do not for a moment believe, this island or a large part of it were **subjugated** and **starving**, then our Empire beyond the seas, **armed** and **guarded** by the British fleet, would carry on the struggle, until, in God's good time, the New World, with all its power and might, steps forth to the rescue and liberation of the old.

4. *Put the idea you plan to discuss next at the end of the sentence.*

   Link sentences by repeating the last word(s) of one sentence at the beginning of the next or by using a synonym and a demonstrative pronoun (*this, that, these, those*). Notice how the second paragraph is an improvement.

   British suffragettes challenged the existing system first through marches on Parliament, then through civil disobedience. When civil disobedience failed, they turned to property damage.

   British suffragettes challenged the existing system first through marches on Parliament, then through civil disobedience. When these measures failed, they turned to property damage.

5. *Use sentence structure to indicate logical relationships.*

   To show that two or more sentences contain equivalent points (as when you are giving a list of reasons, examples, or actions), use **parallel sentence structure** (see Faulty Parallelism, 17h).

FIRST SENTENCE	Slander may involve . . .
SECOND SENTENCE	It can also be . . .
THIRD SENTENCE	It is quite often . . .

When you move from a general point to a specific detail, or vice versa, signal the shift by changing your sentence structure.

GENERAL POINT	To be blunt, slander is an ugly, malicious lie about someone. [The sentence begins with an introductory modifier.]
SPECIFIC EXAMPLE	It may involve . . . [The sentence begins with a subject and verb—change in sentence structure.]

If you compare the following paragraphs, you will see how these devices achieve continuity and dramatically increase the flow of your writing. The material is from a personal essay on the writer's experiences with judo. The added transitional words indicate the process of bullying.

Sample Draft Paragraph

Bullies always have their little rituals. They go through a talking phase with a new kid who might be tough. If they aren't sure, they leave subtle threats and go away. After this little talk, they hammer an opponent who reveals a weakness. They try to make friends with the "mark" who appears too formidable. I was skinny and scared, and so bullies always beat me up.

When bullies encounter a "mark" who might be tough, they go through little rituals. First they talk to him. If this talk reveals a weakness in their opponent, they hammer him. If they still aren't sure, they leave subtle threats and go away. If he appears too formidable, they make friendship gestures. But when the new kid is skinny and scared, like me, there is no ritual. It's all fists.

—*Dan Martin*

Exercise 3.4

Write a descriptive paragraph on one of the items below. Use appropriate transitional devices that allow your reader to visualize spatial relationships among the things you describe.

- your bedroom
- a painting
- the view from your window
- your favourite restaurant
- your dog or pet

3f

Transitions

Exercise 3.5

Improve the following paragraph, which is somewhat choppy, by adding transitions and revising sentences to show the steps in the process and the details of these steps. You may need to combine or rewrite some sentences.

If you have a compact car, packing for a camping vacation, either for the weekend or for an entire week, requires a strategy. There are several procedures to take that will limit the stress of fitting all of the camping gear into a smaller vehicle. Pack one small bag of clothing for each family member. Take what is needed, not wanted "just in case." Bring only one bathing suit, one sleep toy for the children, and one pair of long pants. Arrange everything outside the car prior to loading. See how much is selected so that you can make a further re-evaluation. Place everything according to size and weight. The larger, heavier things should be at the bottom. Set them closest to the trunk. Meticulously pack everything into the car. Maximize the space you have and utilize every available nook and cranny, especially that area between the two (often fighting) children. Following these three easy steps will result in a happy start to your family camping vacation.

Exercise 3.6

Improve the following paragraph by adding transitions and combining and revising sentences.

My dog, Memphis, a rescued racing greyhound, is the laziest dog I have ever seen. He is one of the most slothful creatures on the planet. Like a teenager or a rock star, he can sleep until at least 10 a.m. He sleeps about eighteen to twenty hours a day. He usually sleeps on the couch, which he has claimed, or on my bed. Place a treat in front of him, and he will try to avoid getting up. He will stretch out his neck to get it. He will stare you down until you retrieve the treat. He can eat lying down. Sometimes he doesn't feel like exercising. He walks in slow motion and often spreads out in the middle of the field.

You will find reminders about using transitional words and phrases with specific methods of development in Chapters 4, 5, and 6. For more information on choosing appropriate language, see Part 4: Revising Your Essay.

3g PARAGRAPH DIVISIONS

By dividing your material into paragraphs, you signal that all the information in a particular paragraph relates to one aspect of your subject. But paragraph division is also visual; you need to consider what your reader sees on the page. Paragraph length also affects the tempo of the piece as well as the engagement of the reader. Longer paragraphs, such as those in a persuasive paper, take a while to read and invite the reader to slow down and concentrate, whereas short paragraphs, such as those often found in newspaper and magazine articles, quicken the pace of reading and are appropriate for less weighty subjects.

Although the length of your paragraph depends on your subject matter and mode of development, in most college writing, your paragraphs should be neither too long nor too short.

Normally, you should be able to discuss one aspect of your subject adequately in about half a page. If you need more room to develop your ideas, or if your explanation is quite complicated, subdivide your paragraph. Instead of trying to discuss, in one paragraph, several effects of global warming, focus each paragraph on one effect, such as icecap melting or climate change.

If you are double-spacing and using a 10- to 12- point font, the ideal paragraph length is about $1/2$ to $2/3$ of a page long. Avoid paragraphs that are a page long.

Although long paragraphs bog the reader down, a series of too-short paragraphs not adequately developing points creates a fractured piece of writing. If several short paragraphs discuss only one aspect of your subject, such as how you get more exercise when you have a dog, combine them. If the paragraphs are too short but cannot be combined because they discuss different aspects of your subject, you may have to develop them with more examples and details or remove them altogether.

Similarly, random paragraph divisions—paragraphs that span for pages accompanied by ones that are only a few lines long—are visually unappealing and confusing. If you want to vary your paragraph lengths, make sure there is a logical reason for doing so. Save your short paragraphs for emphasis, summaries, and transitions.

In the example below, notice how the writer uses a combination of short and long paragraphs.

> Although in my two years of employment as a bartender at Hazelmere Golf and Country Club I have come across a number of drinks including "The Harvey Wallbanger" and the infamous "Rocky Mountain Bear," I was recently introduced to one of the finest shots this side of the border: **The Flaming Lamborghini**.
>
> **This drink, which gets it name from the way that it is prepared and the elements that it incorporates**, is worth trying at home. **To make it**, you will need to acquire the following items: four 1 oz. shots of Kahlua, Sambuca, Blue Curaçao, and Baileys Irish Cream. Along with these you require a chilled cocktail glass, matches, and one straw (colour is up to you). After gathering all the ingredients, **begin** by taking the 1 oz. shots of Kahlua and Sambuca and pouring them into the cocktail glass. **After** you have the two shots in the glass, set the mixture on fire and begin to "knock it back." As you reach the bottom of the glass, pour the two remaining shots into the glass to douse the flames. Faster than you can say the name of this drink, it should already be gone.
>
> This flaming drink has its obvious advantages and disadvantages. Some appreciate being able to go from "0-inebriated in under 5 seconds." Others scoff at the price. For $15.95, you can get you local bartender to whip up a "Flaming Lamborghini," or you can invest your money on the ingredients and make one yourself.
>
> *—Adapted from a composition by Cody Heath*

In the next three chapters, the paragraph types are discussed individually, so that you can understand how they differ.

Do realize, however, that when writing essays, you will probably combine more than one writing strategy or more than one paragraph type per composition. For instance, in a persuasive essay, you might begin with a descriptive paragraph or incorporate an expository paragraph into a personal essay.

The next three chapters, then, give you the tools to compose effective paragraphs and powerful writing.

3g

Paragraph Divisions

CHAPTER 4

Methods of Sharing Personal Experience

As newspapers, magazines, and television networks have discovered, readers and viewers have a seemingly insatiable interest in the personal lives of others. You too can enliven your writing by incorporating paragraphs about your own or someone else's experience. In this chapter you will learn how to tell stories that illustrate your point; how to describe people, places, and things so that they come alive; and how to use analogies that convey your feelings and attitudes. Keep in mind that all of these methods of sharing personal experience can be developed into longer pieces or incorporated into other essays.

4a TELLING A STORY

Telling stories is one of the main ways we make sense of our lives for ourselves and share our world with others. Funny, heroic, and romantic stories—they all have something to say about who we are. The stories we keep hidden—stories about our fears, our failures, our struggles— are often the ones that, when told, connect us to others. To see how you can develop these stories into personal essays, see Chapter 9.

Short personal narratives, composed of a paragraph or two, are often used to enliven other kinds of writing. An article criticizing cuts to health care, for instance, may begin with a story about a patient who died while waiting in the emergency room. These personal narratives will be our focus. You will find narration combined with analysis in the samples illustrating causal analysis (5d) and plot summaries (11a).

Here are some suggestions for writing personal narratives.

■ *Choose a single meaningful event with a definite beginning and end.*

The event may be part of a larger story that you could write about in a personal essay. For instance, you might write a narrative paragraph about the last few miles of your first marathon, when the real pain begins for many.

■ *Decide what point you want to make about this event.*

Did your adventure, for example, teach you something about taking risks or about taking precautions? About trust or about self-reliance? About patience? Pain? You could state this point explicitly in a topic sentence, or you could allow it to emerge implicitly from the way you tell the story.

■ *Decide how to organize your paragraph.*

To heighten suspense, place the events in chronological order, with your main point emerging at the end. Or, if you want to emphasize your reflections on the incident, you could begin with your point and then tell the story.

■ *Use transitions to help your reader follow the sequence of events.*

Show how events are related in time by using terms such as *first, next, then, last, in the beginning, in the end, soon, later, as soon as, meanwhile,* and by referring to specific times, days, months, seasons, and dates.

■ *Select details that will create in readers a response similar to your own.*

Recording small details is one way to individualize your stories. In writing about a familiar situation, such as training your dog to sit, for example, you might make the experience fresh and humorous by describing in exaggerated detail the circumstances under which Rufus first learned this command.

■ *Choose words that make the experience vivid for your reader and convey your attitude toward the event.*

Use concrete language and imagery. For more on word choice, see Checking for Appropriate Language (15a).

■ *Include your thoughts, feelings, and judgments about the event.*

Direct statements about thoughts, feelings, and judgments help readers understand the significance of details. For example, you might begin or end a series of seemingly random and contradictory ideas with the statement *I was confused.*

Sample Personal Narrative

This narrative paragraph creates suspense through its precise details, expressions of feeling, and chronological arrangement of events. The image in the last two sentences implicitly makes the writer's point about overcoming fear. These two sentences therefore serve as the topic sentence for the paragraph. A paragraph such as this would make a good introduction to a personal essay.

Others have ascended the incredibly high platform, seemingly thousands of metres above the pool. More than one has returned by the wet ladder, a sensible choice in my mind. Why then is my foot on the first rung? It is colder and slicker than would appear. My feet leave the safe ground and propel me toward the high roof of the pool. Partway up I consider turning back. Yes. But another below has decided to follow, and I must reach the top before turning around. Halfway up, I guess, but I dare not look down lest my arms and legs freeze in terror. I keep my eyes focused on the ladder, only centimetres from my nose. The last step comes into view. With dangerously stiff muscles and complete lack of grace or courage, I plant my feet on the concrete slab. I see my wet footprints and decide to look at nothing else. With the slap of feet an older boy makes his entrance onto this platform in the sky. He passes, grinning at me, and in one quick fluid motion he disappears over the edge. I hear nothing, nothing, then a faint splash. Something deep inside me snaps and I follow suit. Crazy. Stupid. Stop! I'm in the air, hand clasped tight over my nose as I shut my eyes. Dear God, I'm drowning. I must be at the bottom of the pool. Frantically kicking, I break the surface. It's hard to wipe this maniac smile off my face. Perhaps once more.

—*Ken Miller*

Exercise 4.1

Identify a quality you particularly like or dislike in yourself or someone else. Then write a narrative paragraph about an incident that reveals this quality.

Example: a roommate's stinginess—refusing to share nachos and pizza while we watched the Grey Cup.

Exercise 4.2

Choose a significant experience in your life (such as a birth, death, marriage, divorce, move, accident, achievement, or failure). Use brainstorming to help you recall the small but meaningful incidents you associate with the experience (such as riding in an ambulance). Choose one of these incidents with a definite beginning and end, and write a narrative paragraph that shows its significance.

Example: Experience—the death of the family cat. Event—seeing the cat get run over and trying to hide its body from my sister. Significance—the need to protect loved ones from pain or loss.

4b DESCRIBING A PERSON, PLACE, OR THING

When you describe people, places, or things, you attempt to translate into words how they look, sound, feel, smell, move, or taste. In description, then, your goal is *not to tell but to show*. Saying that Aunt Minnie's living room is horribly decorated is *telling*. Writing that Aunt Minnie's living room features greasy wood panelling left over from the seventies, a coffee-stained and cigarette-burned moss-green loveseat, a selection of glaring neon-colored macramé cushions, and a velvet Elvis overlooking a bedraggled wicker chair is *showing*. These details allow the reader to visualize Aunt Minnie's room, and, hopefully, agree with your opinion about her questionable decorating.

Although your goal is to connect to your reader's senses, there are, in fact, two kinds of description: objective and subjective. In objective description, such as in a scientific report, you are more concerned with stating facts; in subjective description, you choose details to create a snapshot that captures a certain mood, image, or dominant impression of your subject. Subjective description, then, is more personal.

For instance, a geographer writing a scientific article about the Canadian Shield would probably use a lot of objective description, such as geographical coordinates, number of species, size of area, and so on. However, a real estate agent selling holiday properties would no doubt use a combination of objective and subjective description.

In personal writing, in which you share experiences—such as your father's delight in reading bedtime stories, your fear as you walk down a deserted street at night, your love-hate relationship with an unreliable car— you will rely on subjective description. You must decide which details to include and omit; if you try to describe everything, your reader will be confused and overwhelmed. If you wanted to show your father's delight in bedtime reading, for example, you would ignore the note of exasperation that crept into his voice if you interrupted too often, and instead describe his excitement as he "became" different characters in *Peter Pan*.

Although vivid descriptions of people, places, and things are central to most personal essays, they also make good introductions for expository and persuasive essays. For example, you might begin a persuasive essay on rescuing greyhounds by detailing how racing greyhounds live in cramped kennels for most of the day. A descriptive paragraph like this adds human interest to discussions of general issues.

Follow these guidelines for writing descriptive paragraphs:

■ *Choose a familiar subject or one you can observe while you write.*

It is surprisingly hard to remember the kinds of detail to bring your paragraph to life—the colour of a friend's eyes, the sound of wind through trees, the smell of a schoolroom. If you choose to describe something from memory, try closing your eyes and putting yourself into the scene before you write about it.

■ *Focus your paragraph.*

To help you *describe* rather than give examples, focus on the details of your subject at a particular time or performing a particular action. For instance, you could vividly *describe* a kitten's playfulness—how it looks, moves, sounds—by taking one detail, such as how it acts in the mirror, and zeroing in on it. Without this focal point, you might give many examples of a kitten's playful behaviour without describing any of them sufficiently.

■ *Decide what dominant impression you want to convey about your subject.*

A good description is not merely a catalogue of features: "Her house is a stucco bungalow from the fifties." Decide what *dominant impression* you want to create: a kitten's playfulness, an aunt's stubbornness, the peacefulness of a landscape.

■ *Select details that contribute to your dominant impression.*

Include a broad range of sensory details—not just how something looks, but also how it sounds, feels, tastes, smells, moves. You don't have to use all of them, however, for you don't want to overwhelm the senses of your reader. If you were describing the atmosphere of a hockey playoff game, for example, you might want to focus on the sounds and the sights to convey the excitement.

■ *Arrange the details in a spatial order, with the most important detail last.*

Choose an arrangement that reflects how you, as an observer, would perceive your subject: in a panoramic sweep from left to right; from close up to farther away, or vice versa; or from the most obvious feature to the least obvious.

■ *Show how objects are related in space.*

Use transitional words such as *nearer, farther, on the right, on the left, at the top, at the bottom, to the east, to the west.* You want the reader to clearly see what you describe.

■ *Begin or end with a point about the person, place, or thing.*

"My cat is very playful" is a descriptive generalization, but it is not an interesting point about the kitten's behaviour. You could make a more interesting point about the transitory nature of youth and playfulness in a topic sentence: "Watching my kitten play, I remember how I used to make faces at myself in the mirror, not realizing that the scowls of childhood would settle into the lines of middle age." Or you could let it emerge implicitly through your description: "Each day the kitten tires of the game more quickly, and soon we will both pass the mirror without a glance."

In the following paragraph from a personal essay, the writer tells us almost nothing about the physical appearance of a teacher who "shocked me so much that I experienced a marked change in my attitude toward school and the subject of English." Instead, he chooses details that show how Mr. Wellington's surroundings reflect his vulnerability, and then makes this point in a topic sentence at the end.

Sample Personal Description

Mr. Wellington was neither neat nor tidy. The chaos of his room seemed to echo the sound of someone saying, "Hang on, it's in here somewhere. I just put it down yesterday. I'll find it." The walls were covered from top to bottom with posters, but not a single one was hung straight. His desk was inhabited by masses of paper that had somehow gathered there as if attracted by a "paper magnet." Surrounding his desk was a whole herd of dictionaries, including a condensed version of the *Oxford English Dictionary,* which required a magnifying glass to peer into the depths of its compiled wisdom. Mr. Wellington would frequently consult these books in efforts to stop the arguments waged against him about the meanings of words in the poems we analyzed in class. Throughout all this activity, his coffee cup was never to be seen detached from his hand. I cannot blame him for needing a cup of coffee to carry him through to the next period. It was his coffee cup that made him look human, vulnerable—not like the other teachers, who were not human but "teachers." Perhaps it was his vulnerability that inspired confidence, even though he was surrounded by what looked like ineptitude.

—Steve Marsh

Exercise 4.3

Make a list of the sensations you experience as you eat something, such as an ice cream cone or a slice of pizza. Use all of your senses. Arrange your list so that a point emerges from your description.

Exercise 4.4

Write a descriptive paragraph about one of the following: a person who has had an impact on your life, a place where you feel safe (or unsafe), or an object to which you have a strong attachment.

Exercise 4.5

Sit for half an hour in a public place—on a bus, in a mall, in church, at a hockey rink—and make notes about what you see, hear, and smell. If you have a MP3 player, you can dictate into it. Then write a descriptive paragraph about the place as a whole, one or more people in it, or a particular object. Be sure to select details that convey a dominant impression and make a point about your subject.

4c USING ANALOGIES

Attitudes and emotions are difficult to describe without falling into clichés and generalities. Analogies allow you to translate inner experiences into vivid images for your reader. They also grab your reader's attention, forcing him/her to see your subject in a new and startling light. Analogies, therefore, are effective in personal, expository, and persuasive writing. Consider, for example, the attitudes suggested by these metaphors:

Life is an exhilarating ride on a roller coaster.

Life is "a tale told by an idiot, full of sound and fury, signifying nothing" (*Macbeth*).

Each of these metaphors could be developed into an analogy by exploring the similarities it suggests. These analogies would tell us much more about the writer (or character) than would statements such as "Life is great" or "Life sucks."

To write an effective analogy, follow these steps:

■ *Make a list of metaphors or similes comparing your subject with a variety of things that are different in appearance, form, or kind but similar in behaviour.*

Overcoming an addiction is like
—salvaging a wrecked ship
—weaning a baby
—saying goodbye to an old friend

■ *Choose the metaphor or simile that best fits the attitude or experience you want to convey.*

✗—salvaging a wrecked ship [does not acknowledge the pleasurable aspects of the addiction]
✗—weaning a baby [suggests we "grow out of" addictions]
✓—saying goodbye to an old friend

■ *Develop your metaphor or simile into a paragraph by exploring the similarities it suggests.*

What is it like to say goodbye to an old friend? There's the memory of good times and bad, the desire to hold on, and the need to let go. By emphasizing the positive aspects, this analogy may help readers who do not share the addiction to understand why it is hard to give up.

In the following example, the writer helps readers understand the debilitating effects of an unfamiliar health problem by comparing it to a more familiar condition.

Sample Analogy

Think back to the most persistent flu or cold you have ever had. Remember that day when the virus was at its worst, you know, around day two, three, or four. You wished you could remove your head from your body, and you were too exhausted to remove it even if you could have, and it was all you could do to get up and drink some juice and maybe take a cold tablet before you collapsed back into bed. Add to it: sides so tender and sore that when someone touches you, you yelp in pain; kidney infections so extreme you are doubled over as you walk and cannot right yourself. Add food allergies to most of the foods you used to eat with no problem, including a complete intolerance for sugar. Add chemical sensitivities so extreme that walking past a running vehicle, passing through a smoky room, or standing near an acquaintance wearing hairspray or perfume can result in muscle convulsions or an unexpected mood swing, severe headaches or more fatigue. Add seizures or blackouts. These are some of the physical symptoms experienced by the more than 250,000 people in Canada who suffer from Myalgic Encephalomyelitis, otherwise known as Chronic Fatigue Syndrome.

—Patti Skocdopole

Exercise 4.6

Complete each of the following similes.

1. Looking for a job is like _____.
2. Finding your way around an unfamiliar city is like _____.
3. Visiting the dentist is like _____.
4. Going on a blind date is like _____.

Exercise 4.7

Make a list of the similarities suggested by two of the similes in Exercise 4.6.

Review Exercise 4.8

Write a paragraph about a hard-to-communicate experience or feeling, using at least two of the methods discussed in this chapter: narration, description, and analogy. For example, you might convey the intensity of your feelings about your first car by both describing the car and developing an analogy with Aladdin's magic carpet.

CHAPTER 5

Methods of Explaining

When your purpose is to explain, your focus is on your subject and what your readers need to know to understand your subject. In this chapter, we will discuss four ways of explaining: **classifying,** which groups your material into manageable chunks; **comparing,** which highlights similarities and differences; **defining terms and concepts,** which lets your reader know what you are talking about; and **analyzing,** which shows how parts of your subject relate to the whole.

This chapter will give you practice in using these methods to explain a subject within a single paragraph. However, expository paragraphs often appear within pieces of writing that persuade or share personal experience. If you were writing a persuasive essay about allowing gay marriage, you might devote a few paragraphs to explaining the definition of marriage in various cultures. To see how to write a longer piece of expository writing, see Chapters 10 and 11.

5a CLASSIFYING

Classifying and dividing are similar processes that organize facts. When you classify, you begin with many items and group them into categories. For instance, if you were writing an essay on the effects of unemployment, and your brainstorming gave you a long list of effects, you might decide to classify these effects into economic, social, and psychological. When you divide, you start with a general category, such as *effects of unemployment,* and break this category into specific types or kinds of effects. In classification, you move from details to generalizations whereas in division, you move from generalizations to details. You will move between both of these processes when writing, but, for the purpose of clarity, we will refer to these as classification paragraphs.

Both of the examples above could be expanded into essays, in which you would dedicate a paragraph or more to developing each of your subcategories.

For this reason, classification/division paragraphs make good overviews of material you will then explain further, and good summaries of material you have already covered. And, as the example below shows, they are also ideal for making humorous points.

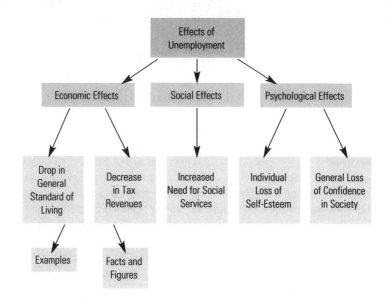

Homo Camperus, an abundant and diverse species of nomadic wanderers, can be divided into three sub-species according to their differing modes of shelter: Homo Camperus Motorhomeous, Homo Camperus Fanaticus, and Homo Camperus Miscellaneous. The Motorhomeous sub-species is easily recognizable by the giant, house-like structures its members inhabit, variously known as "motorhomes," "Winnebagos," "camper-trailers," and last but not least, "highway menaces." While members of this sub-species enjoy the campground's version of nature as much as the other Camperus groups, they also need the security of sturdy walls, real beds, and their own porta-potties. Fanaticus, in contrast, does not believe in sleeping under anything but a nylon roof. While Motorhomeous lurks within the relative safety of the forest, Fanaticus braves the windy, treeless beachfront, relishing the challenge of having to extra-stake a tent. For Fanaticus, the tent is the ultimate sign of high status and economic/social well-being, and so the more tents one has, the better. Usually, there are two colossal ones: one tent for sleeping and the other for meals and for planning the daily outings to climb mountains or kayak raging rivers. The third and most abundant sub-species, Miscellaneous, is made up of members of the abnormal and unconventional Camperus who wander into the campground for the first time. Miscellaneous groups never have more than one tent, a small, inferior one that they don't know how to erect. They always forget some key piece of equipment, such as tent pegs, which they end up borrowing from the smug Fanaticus. In windy, rainy, or otherwise inclement weather, they abandon their flimsy shelter and retreat to their cars, to the delight of the cozy Motorhomeous and intrepid Fanaticus.

—*James Stevenson*

Here are suggestions for writing classification paragraphs:

* **Choose a general category that you know enough about to divide into two to four subcategories** (for example: customers, country music, Stephen King novels).

- **Decide on a principle of classification, and state this principle at the beginning of your paragraph.** A principle of classification tells you how to divide things into groups. In the above example, campers are divided according to their preferred mode of shelter. Likewise, you could divide running-shoe store customers according to attitudes toward staff, dedication to running, or spending habits. Each of these is a principle of classification.

- **Make a list of the types represented by your principle of classification.** If you chose "dedication to running" as your principle of classification, you might come up with types such as these: the recreational runner, the weekend warrior, the beginning runner, the fitness runner, and the amateur athlete.

- **Describe two to four types, depending upon how much you need to say to explain each type.** Use actual examples (the man who runs three times a day) or hypothetical examples (the kinds of running shoes the weekend warrior buys).

- **To signal your shift from one subcategory to another, use parallel sentence structure and/or transitions that indicate enumeration** (*first, second, next, finally*).

- **Begin or end your paragraph with the point you want to make.** For example, "As you snicker at recreational runners, remember you were once one of them."

Exercise 5.1

Complete the following diagrams with appropriate categories and examples. Notice that movies can be classified in different ways. Can you figure out two other principles of classification for this subject?

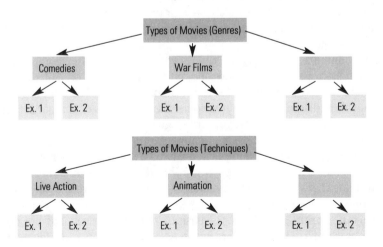

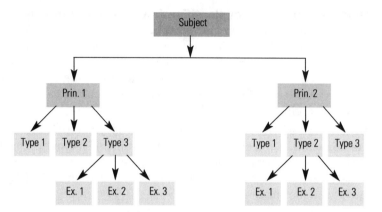

Exercise 5.2

Choose one of the listed subjects and make a four-level diagram showing how you could divide your subject according to two different principles of classification. Use this model:

- hip-hop music
- dog owners
- employers
- superstitions
- vehicles
- fast-food restaurants

Exercise 5.3

Write a classification paragraph based on *one* of the principles of classification you developed for the diagram above.

5b COMPARING

When you compare, you match similarities and differences in two or more subjects. **Comparison** may be your primary method of development in a piece of writing, or you may combine comparison with other methods of development.

To compare subjects effectively, you need a basis of comparison, which tells you which similarities and differences to focus on. For example, if you are asked on a biology exam to compare the fertilization process in mammals and amphibians, you have been given a basis of comparison: the fertilization process. When you aren't given a topic, your purpose and audience may suggest a basis of comparison. If you are comparing two computers, your basis of comparison will be determined by whether your reader is a college instructor, a graphic designer, or a gamer. If you determine that your reader is a gamer, you might compare the multimedia options of two computers.

In other writing situations, the basis of your comparison may not be so obvious. Suppose you were writing an essay comparing attitudes toward immigrants in Canada and the US. You would need to consider many facts and opinions before deciding on a general similarity or difference to use as a basis of comparison.

When your basis of comparison is not obvious, follow these steps.

List Similarities and Differences

Although making lists seems time-consuming, it serves three purposes: it ensures that you have lots of material, that you compare equivalent aspects of your subjects, and that you provide the same information about both. Let's take an example.

In writing about the differences between First Nations' storytelling and Western storytelling, for instance, one student wanted to reinforce her point by comparing similar folk tales, "The Ghost Owl" and "The Three Bears." She compiled these lists:

"The Ghost Owl"	**"The Three Bears"**
—The main character is a small girl who brings trouble on herself by crying when she doesn't get what she wants.	—The main character is Goldilocks, who brings trouble on herself by following her impulses (sampling the bears' food, chairs, and beds) instead of completing her errand.
—She is put outside the lodge, carried away by an owl, rescued by a hawk, and restored to her home when she has killed the owl and has "grown up" enough to follow grandfather hawk's instructions.	—She is frightened and jumps out of the window when the bears discover her wrongdoing, but her fate is uncertain.
—Animal figures are distinct from humans but equal to humans and part of the same world.	—Animal figures are symbols of human society (the bears live and act like "civilized" humans, not bears).

These lists provide more than enough material for a paragraph, so the student would need to select the most appropriate material for her purpose.

Choose a Basis of Comparison

The next step is to decide on a *basis of comparison,* that is, the general characteristic that will be the focus of your discussion of similarities and/or differences. The lists above suggest two main possibilities: the fate of the main character and the role of animal figures. The student chose the fate of the main character as her basis of comparison because that difference would best support her thesis (see below).

Formulate a Main Idea

Then you must decide what point to make about your basis of comparison and put it in a topic sentence. Do not merely say something like *The main characters come to different ends in "The Ghost Owl" and "The Three Bears"* or *Differences between First Nations storytelling and Western storytelling are evident in folk tales such as "The Ghost Owl" and "The Three Bears."* If you are writing a self-contained comparison paragraph, think about the general meaning you can draw from the specific details.

Suppose, for instance, that you were comparing the endings of the two folk tales in response to a short-answer exam question. You know that in "The Ghost Owl," the main character, now a young woman, passes a final test of obedience and returns to her village, where no one recognizes her because grandfather hawk has dressed her as a warrior. After she admits she is the girl whose mother put her out for the owls for being naughty, her mother cries and pleads for forgiveness. The young men ask if they can wear warrior clothes like hers, thus giving her a role in creating the Cheyenne soldier societies. You might conclude that this story's ending emphasizes the reintegration of the girl into the community and the valuable contributions of her personal experience. In "The Three Bears," in contrast, the bears never see Goldilocks again and her fate is uncertain: she might have broken her neck in jumping from the window; she might have become lost in the woods; or she might have gone home to be reprimanded. The ending thus focuses on Goldilocks' punishment and banishment from the "civilized" society of the bears. You could combine these ideas about the fates of the two characters in this topic sentence:

> The fate of the main character in "The Ghost Owl" emphasizes the benefits of reintegrating troublesome individuals within the community, whereas the fate of Goldilocks in "The Three Bears" emphasizes the dangers of defying authority.

If you are writing a comparison paragraph as part of an essay, you must figure out a main idea that both explains the specific details relevant to your basis of comparison and shows how those details support your thesis. The student's thesis is that First Nations' storytelling reflects the cultural belief in a universe in which all life is equal and in balance, whereas Western storytelling reflects the cultural belief in a hierarchical order in which humankind is separate from and superior to the natural world. To connect her paragraph on the two stories with this thesis, she might write this topic sentence:

> The fate of the main character in the folk tale "The Ghost Owl" reflects Native beliefs about equality and balance in the universe,

whereas the fate of Goldilocks in "The Three Bears" reflects Western society's emphasis on hierarchy and separation from nature.

To clarify the connection between her topic sentence and the details about the stories, she would explain that in Native culture, reintegrating troublesome individuals is necessary to restore equality and balance, whereas in Western culture, punishing transgressors or exiling them to a threatening natural world is necessary to maintain hierarchical authority. (See The Comparative Thesis in 7c for more information.)

Organize Your Comparison

Block Method

The block method is the simplest way of organizing a brief comparison. In this method, you mention both subjects in your topic sentence, saying everything about one subject before moving on to the other. When you are ready to discuss the second subject, you signal the shift by a transitional word or phrase. Organizing the comparison of the two folk tales by the block method might give you the following paragraph:

Sample Block Method

The fate of the main character in "The Ghost Owl" emphasizes the benefits of reintegrating troublesome individuals within the community, whereas the fate of Goldilocks in "The Three Bears" emphasizes the dangers of defying authority. In "The Ghost Owl," the main character is reunited with her community only when she has "grown up" enough to want to do so and has successfully passed a final test of obedience. Because grandfather hawk has dressed her as a warrior, no one in the village recognizes her until she humbly admits she is the naughty girl whose mother put her out for the owls. The responses of her mother and the young warriors signal her reintegration into the community. Her mother cries and pleads for forgiveness, and the young men ask if they can wear warrior clothes like hers. The warrior clothes represent the strength, courage, and cunning she has learned through following the teachings of grandfather hawk. The ending thus emphasizes not only her reintegration into the community but also the valuable contribution she can make: her instructions to the young men lead to the creation of the Cheyenne soldier societies. In "The Three Bears," in contrast, Goldilocks' fate is uncertain: she might have broken her neck in jumping from the window; she might have become lost in the woods; or she might have found her way home and been whipped for being naughty. The ending thus focuses on Goldilocks' banishment from the "civilized" society the bears represent and her possible punishments for disobeying her mother and flouting social conventions. Unlike the girl of "The Ghost Owl," she is not given the chance to learn valuable lessons from her experience or to contribute to the good of her community.

If the material is too long for one paragraph, you can easily start a new paragraph when you shift to your second subject.

Point-by-Point Method

The **point-by-point method,** in which you shift back and forth between subjects, is sometimes more effective than the block method when you are organizing a longer piece of writing, such as a comparison essay.

If you have several points you want to make in a paragraph, however, shifting between subjects can produce an annoying or confusing ping-pong effect, as in this revised version of the previous example:

Sample Point-by-Point Method

The fate of the main character in "The Ghost Owl" emphasizes the benefits of reintegrating trouble-some individuals within the community, whereas the fate of Goldilocks in "The Three Bears" emphasizes the dangers of defying authority. In "The Ghost Owl," the main character is reunited with her community only when she has "grown up" enough to want to do so and has successfully passed a final test of obedience. In "The Three Bears," in contrast, Goldilocks' fate is uncertain: she might have broken her neck in jumping from the window; she might have become lost in the woods; or she might have found her way home and been whipped for being naughty. When the girl in "The Ghost Owl" returns to her village, she is dressed as a warrior, and so no one recognizes her until she humbly admits she is the naughty girl whose mother put her out for the owls. Her mother cries and pleads for forgiveness, and the young men ask if they can wear warrior clothes like hers. In contrast, the bears never see Goldilocks again; if she has made her way back to her home, her mother would have been angry and whipped her. The responses of the mother and the young men in. . . .

Exercise 5.4

Choose two topics from the following and list the similarities and differences between the subjects being compared.

- golf and hockey (or two other sports)
- listening to music and playing music
- love and infatuation
- assertiveness and aggressiveness
- the cleaning habits of you and your roommate
- the climates in two places you have lived
- two funerals or burial rites you have attended

Exercise 5.5

Find a basis of comparison for each of the two topics that you chose in Exercise 5.4 above. Then decide what point you would make about each topic.

Exercise 5.6

Select a method of organization (block or point-by-point) and write a comparison paragraph based on one topic that you selected in Exercise 5.4. Keep in mind that your purpose is to explain, not to persuade or to share personal experience (though of course you may draw on your experience).

5c DEFINING TERMS AND CONCEPTS

"There's glory for you!"

"I don't know what you mean by 'glory,'" Alice said.

Humpty Dumpty smiled contemptuously. "Of course you don't—till I tell you. I meant 'there's a nice knock-down argument for you!'"

"But 'glory' doesn't mean 'a nice knock-down argument,'" Alice objected.

"When I use a word," Humpty Dumpty said in a rather scornful tone, "it means just what I choose it to mean—neither more nor less."

—From *Through the Looking Glass* by Lewis Carroll

Humpty Dumpty may get away with arbitrarily deciding what words mean, but most of us cannot. If we want to communicate, we have to use words in ways that others will understand. Thus, when you use words unfamiliar to your readers, or use familiar words in an unfamiliar way, you need to provide **definitions.**

In exams and other kinds of academic writing, you may be asked to define terms to show that you know what they mean. In most writing, however, you provide definitions not to demonstrate your own knowledge but to help your reader understand what you are talking about. Depending on what kind of information your reader needs, you may use a synonym, a class definition, an extended definition, or a restrictive definition.

Synonyms

A **synonym** is a word that means the same, or nearly the same, as another word. Use synonyms, set off by commas or enclosed in parentheses, to define slang expressions, specialized terms of trades and professions, regional and dialect usages, and foreign words and phrases. This example illustrates how to integrate synonyms smoothly:

> As we entered the Air India 747, the steward clasped his hands and said, "Namaste" ("Greetings to you").
>
> —*Vijaya Rao*

Class Definitions

A **class definition** explains a term by saying what kind of thing it is (its class) and how it is different from other members of its class. CD's, for instance, are in the class of recorded music, but so are vinyl albums, cassettes, and music files.

This is the standard form of the class definition:

An *X* is a member of the class *Y* with the characteristics *A, B, C.* . . .

A bailiff [term to be defined] is a person [class] who performs limited functions within a judicial system, such as having custody of prisoners in court, serving warrants, or serving as magistrate for minor offences [distinguishing characteristics].

Extended Definitions

When a synonym or class definition does not offer enough explanation, you will need an **extended definition.** Some writers take a paragraph, even a whole essay, to define a term. In a persuasive essay, for example, you might give an extended definition of the word *violence* to show that the term also applies to the destruction of the environment. Don't insult your readers by defining words they know, but never assume your subject is as familiar to them as it is to you. Try to read through their eyes. You might, for instance, need to define "online community," but probably not "internet."

Here are three ways to expand definitions:

1. Add examples.

2. Give negative examples—that is, refine your term by giving words or things that might seem to be included in the class but actually are not.

3. Use an analogy to compare your term with something familiar. For instance, if you wanted to explain random sampling to readers who were not social scientists, you might use the analogy of pulling a handful of assorted candies from a jar.

Restrictive Definitions

Our understanding of words, especially of abstract terms such as *violence, loyalty, pornography,* and *censorship,* is shaped by our own experiences, and we bring these personal connotations to our reading. You can make sure that you and your readers are talking the same language by using a **restrictive definition.**

Because restrictive definition specifies which meaning, from a range of possible meanings, you are using, it allows you to limit your treatment of your subject. For instance, you might first consider various meanings of the word *censorship* before specifying that you will use the word formally to mean the passage of laws designed to prevent the publication of certain material. Accordingly, your readers cannot expect you to discuss other actions that they might consider censorship, such as withdrawing books from libraries or banning T-shirt slogans. As this example suggests, restrictive definitions are particularly necessary when the meaning of a term is controversial.

Because they establish common ground with readers and mark out the territory you will discuss, restrictive definitions also make good introductions. If you were writing a research paper on the debate over family values, you might begin by defining the term so that your readers understand your main purpose: to replace the current restrictive definition with a more inclusive one.

Sample Restrictive Definition

Conservative thinkers often attack social policies they perceive to be harmful to "family values," and yet they seldom define what they mean by "family" or "values." Before the Industrial Revolution, most of Europe's population lived in extended families consisting of assorted grandparents, parents, children, and other adults, related or unrelated, for this extended family was the most efficient economic unit. With the expansion of the middle classes in the early nineteenth century, more couples could afford to establish their own households, which usually consisted of parents and children (and perhaps a servant or two). This family unit evolved into the North American ideal nuclear family, in which the father provided the income, the mother stayed home and looked after the children, and the children obeyed their parents. It is this ideal that conservative thinkers generally have in mind when they defend "family values." However, economic pressures created by divorce, unemployment, and the changing role of women are again forcing us to redefine what we mean by family and to recognize the diversity in family values.

Sources of Definitions

When you need to define a word, begin with a standard dictionary such as those published by Gage, Random House, and Oxford. For more detailed information about specialized meanings, changes in meaning over time, and current usage, consult works such as the following, found in the reference section of your library.

- **Unabridged dictionaries.** The *Oxford English Dictionary* provides a history of each word's use and changes in meaning. Schools often have the OED online; the OED is also available as a CD-ROM that you can download onto your desktop.

- **Specialized dictionaries.** Available for many professions and academic disciplines. Some examples are the *Dictionary of Business and Economics, Dictionary of Philosophy,* and the *Oxford Dictionary of Twentieth-Century World History.*

Exercise 5.7

Give a synonym or class definition that would explain each of these terms to readers unfamiliar with your subject.

1. rave (or other term from popular culture)

2. quasar (or other scientific term)

3. the 'hood (or other slang expression)

4. slapshot (or other sports term)

5. *joie de vivre* (or other non-English expression)

6. profit margin (or other business term)

Analyzing:
Dividing
Your
Subject
into
Parts

Exercise 5.8

Write an extended definition of one of the following terms.

- sweat lodge
- bodybuilding (or other physical pursuit)
- Tai Chi (or other martial art)
- pysanka (or other cultural artifact)
- reiki (or other alternative health technique)

Exercise 5.9

Write a paragraph of restrictive definition for one of the following terms.

- patriotism
- equal opportunity
- intelligence
- justice
- euthanasia
- living will

5d ANALYZING: DIVIDING YOUR SUBJECT INTO PARTS

Analysis is a way of explaining a subject by dividing it into its parts and showing how the parts relate to the whole. We will discuss three types of analysis. **Systems analysis** shows the relation of parts in space; **process analysis** shows the sequence of parts in time; and **causal analysis** shows the relationship between causes and effects.

By dividing up a complex or unfamiliar task, situation, or idea into smaller units, you can often make it easier for readers to understand your subject. For particular writing assignments, you may use these three types of analysis alone or in combination. In writing a how-to article on gardening, for example, you would use process analysis to develop your material. But in writing an expository essay on gardening, you might include sections on the various processes, on the types of plants suitable for Canadian climates, and on the effects of too much or too little watering. For examples of essays and other types of writing developed through analysis, see Chapters 10 and 11.

Explaining Systems

We tend to think of a system as a physical object with working parts, such as a computer or the body's digestive system. You can also explain how abstract systems, such as governments or ideologies, "work" by showing how the parts are related to the whole. Aesthetic objects—such as music, dance, drama, film, video games, and literary works—can likewise be considered as systems in which parts work together to create a whole. For instance, you might find that a certain movie communicates the theme of despair. To explain how the movie creates this theme, you would consider elements such as lighting, pacing, dialogue, characters, costume, setting, shots, etc. Additional guidelines for analyzing specific texts are in Essays Analyzing Literature (11c), Summaries (10g and 11a), Position Papers (12d), and Appendix A.

A systems analysis is like a blueprint providing an objective general description of your subject rather than a subjective particular description. If you were analyzing the functions of the federal Cabinet, for instance, you would discuss the role of the minister of the environment, not his personality or his height.

Usually you begin with a topic sentence that identifies the system and explains its purpose. Next you describe the most obvious or most important part of the system, such as the prime minister, and show how other parts function in relation to it. Then, using appropriate transitions, you explain the function of each part in relation to the whole.

5d

Analyzing:
Dividing
Your
Subject
into
Parts

Sample Systems Analysis: Abstract System

In this example, the writer shows how the parts of an abstract system— the Hollywood movie studios of the early twentieth century—worked together to create a film industry that continues to dominate world markets.

The Hollywood studio system, which dominated the production of American movies from the 1920s to the 1950s, was essentially a system for efficiently mass-producing movies. At the head of the major studios (such as Columbia, MGM, Paramount, RKO, and Warners) were the movie producers. Like the heads of factories, movie producers controlled the financing of their products and exercised considerable control over how the products were made. The producers hired actors and approved script choices and script writers. They also hired the director for each film, and thus influenced how the action was staged and photographed. Movies were shot under tightly controlled conditions in the huge holdings of land, buildings, and sound stages that constituted the studio lot. The staples of the Hollywood system—westerns, thrillers, science fiction, and horror movies—could thus be shot quickly on ready-made sets. In addition, each studio had all the departments necessary to make a movie, including publicity, costuming, set design, story production, and makeup. Like the personnel of these departments, actors were constantly available on low-salary, long-term contract, such as Humphrey Bogart, Joan Crawford, Bette Davis, Clark Gable, and John Wayne. These low-cost production methods enabled the studios to produce hundreds of films a year and thus laid the groundwork for Hollywood's continuing dominance of the world film industry.

Exercise 5.10

Write a paragraph explaining the parts of a physical object with which you are familiar and showing how these parts function as a whole. Here are some possible subjects.

- weight-training equipment
- an iPod, BlackBerry, or iPhone
- a home entertainment system
- a full-suspension mountain bike
- a cell phone

5d

**Analyzing:
Dividing
Your
Subject
into
Parts**

Exercise 5.11

Write a paragraph explaining the parts of an abstract system with which you are familiar and showing how the system functions as a whole. Here are some possible subjects.

- an organization you belong to
- a band, choir, or similar musical group
- a particular ecosystem, such as your backyard
- a video game
- an ad or a commercial

Explaining Processes

Process analysis is of two types: informational, which explains how something happens ("How Airplanes Fly"); and instructional, which explains how to do something ("How to Fly an Airplane"). In each case, you emphasize what happens (or should happen) every time the process is repeated ("How to Sew from a Pattern"), rather than what happened during one particular instance ("How My Bad Sewing Ruined My Prom Dress").

The amount of detail you include depends on your purpose and audience. When you are writing informational analysis or explaining how a process unfolds, focus on the major stages so that your readers get a sense of the whole process. On the other hand, when you are writing instructional process analysis or giving readers directions to follow, discuss each step in detail, allowing your reader to imagine the process and drawing your readers' attention to potential problems. In informational process analysis, you want the reader to understand the process, whereas in instructional analysis, you want the reader to understand and replicate the process.

For both types of process analysis, begin with a topic sentence identifying the process and its major stages. Then discuss the stages, and the steps within each stage, in the order they occur. Use transitions indicating time relationships (*next, after, then*) or enumeration (*first, second, third*) to signal movement from one stage or step to the next.

Below is an instructional process paragraph on the process of painting a wall. For an example of more detailed instructions, see the Sample How-To Article (10d).

Sample Process Analysis

The five major stages in painting a wall are testing the paint, painting the trim, taping, doing the edging, and filling in the wall. First, test the paint on the wall to make sure you have the correct colour. Put a few coats of paint on a small section and wait a few days for the colour to settle. If the colour is off or too bright, you might want to return to the store to darken the paint or select a new colour. If your room has doors or window ledges, you should paint these first, usually in a white or off-white colour with an eggshell to semigloss finish. After the trim is dry, tape it, along with the ceiling, making sure you use the medium green painter's tape. Next, do the edging, which means using a fine brush or trim roller to paint a 3–4 inch swath around the room, taking special care around doors and windows. Make sure you have at least two coats of edging; you may need more with watery or red-tinted paints. When the edging is complete, you are ready to paint the interior of the wall. Start rolling in a V formation, using large clean strokes. Keep in mind that if you are using a paint in the red family, you may need many coats, whereas you will need fewer coats with paints containing a lot of brown or black. When you are done, get an artist's brush, filling in minor mistakes before removing the tape. Following these steps will ensure a neat and thorough painting job.

Exercise 5.12

Write a paragraph explaining a process. Choose your own topic or one of the following:

- how to operate a piece of equipment
- how to teach a child a particular skill, such as tying shoelaces
- how to settle disputes with a partner or roommate
- how to take blood pressure
- how to train a dog to heel

Explaining Causes and Effects: Causal Analysis

Whereas process analysis explains *how something happens* or *how to do something,* causal analysis explains *why something happens.* Thus, analyzing causes and effects is central to much of the writing you will do in school or at work. You may write a research paper for a history course on the causes of the War of 1812; a report on how the threat of terrorism has affected the travel industry; or a letter to your insurance agent on the causes of a traffic accident. Keep in mind that most interesting subjects have multiple causes and effects. Brainstorming, asking discovery questions, and researching will help you avoid oversimplifying your analysis.

For a research paper on the effects of cutbacks in government spending on education, for instance, your first response might be to focus on the financial strain students are under because of higher tuition fees. You would gain a broader perspective, however, by brainstorming about other effects on students and reading about the effects on schools and postsecondary institutions. Your final essay might examine the effects of funding cuts on students, teachers, and institutions.

If you are explaining independent causes or effects, arrange your material in an order that suits your audience. You might discover, for example, that the three main causes of traffic accidents are poor road conditions, impaired driving, and mechanical failure. There is no causal connection among these three factors. (Drinking too much doesn't cause icy roads or malfunctioning cars.) If you were writing an essay, you would decide which cause to emphasize, and discuss it last. However, if you were writing a report for the city transportation department, you would discuss the main factor first.

When discussing a chain of causes and effects (A causes B, B causes C, C causes D), make sure that your topic sentence focuses on the most significant cause(s) and effect(s). Arrange your material in chronological order, but, to clarify that you are writing a causal analysis rather than a narrative, choose words and expressions that emphasize causal connections (*a major effect, a second cause, one consequence; caused, resulted, affected; as a result, because, consequently, therefore, thus*). An essay on the effects of the Riel Rebellion on federal politics might have these notes:

1. Riel's execution **caused** a renewed demand for rights by the French Québécois.

2. These demands alarmed the federal government, which consequently abolished French language rights in Manitoba.

3. This action **resulted** in loss of support for the Conservative Party in Quebec.

4. This decline in support **caused** the party to lose the next federal election.

5. Quebec's pivotal role in federal politics is a continuing **effect** of its position as the sole defender of the rights of French-speaking Canadians.

In writing your paragraph, you would add a topic sentence emphasizing the most significant effect (Quebec's increased power). You would also fill in additional details while keeping the focus on the chain of causes and effects, as in the paragraph below.

Sample Analysis of Causes and Effects

Although the failure of the Riel Rebellion weakened the position of French-speaking Canadians in Manitoba, it had the enormously significant effect of strengthening the power of French-speaking Canadians in Quebec. Before Riel was executed in 1885, Quebec had ignored the

5d

Analyzing:
Dividing
Your
Subject
into
Parts

struggle of the French-speaking Manitobans to maintain their cultural identity. As a result of his execution, Riel became a martyr to the cause of rights for all French Canadians and the focus for a renewed demand for French rights in Quebec. Alarmed, the federal government abolished French education rights in Manitoba in 1890; Quebec thus became the only province where provincial rights guaranteed the survival of French culture in Canada. The consequence of this action, it soon became obvious, was that no federal government could remain in power if it lacked Quebec's support. The Conservative Party, weakened by MacDonald's death in 1891, lost the election of 1896 mostly because it had offended Quebec by abolishing French rights in Manitoba; the Liberals, led by Wilfrid Laurier, gained power by securing a large majority in Quebec. Since that time, no federal government has been able to ignore the province.

Exercise 5.13

Write two separate lists of causes explaining why you were (or were not) successful in your last job (or job search). Make one a list of independent causes; present the second list as a chain of causes and effects.

5d

Analyzing:
Dividing
Your
Subject
into
Parts

CHAPTER 6

Methods of Persuading

Persuasion takes a wide variety of forms, from the snappy jingles of television commercials to the carefully reasoned arguments of social critics. As these examples suggest, persuasive writing may appeal primarily to our emotions (television commercials), to our ethics (charity campaigns), or primarily to our minds (logical arguments). Most persuasive writing—reviews, editorials, opinion pieces, political speeches—appeals to all three.

Because the purpose of persuasive writing is to change readers' opinions or behaviour, and/or to motivate readers to act, the nature of your audience greatly influences the extent to which you appeal to your readers' intellect or emotions. Your audience for most writing in college and university will prioritize logic, expecting you to present carefully considered opinions and to support those opinions with evidence—such as facts, examples, and references to authorities on the subject. Thus, in this chapter, we will focus on two strategies for making persuasive arguments: giving reasons and examples, and evaluating strengths and weaknesses. We will also demonstrate how you can give a persuasive edge to methods used for explaining and sharing personal experience. In Chapter 12, persuasive writing, the three appeals of persuasion, and logical fallacies are discussed in greater detail.

6a GIVING REASONS AND EXAMPLES

Whenever you state an opinion, your readers' first response is likely to be "Why do you think so?" Giving one or more reasons is the first step toward convincing your readers. The next step is giving examples—specific instances that show your reason(s) to be valid. For your argument to be convincing and strong, you must give reasons and examples that readers can verify independently. Consider these examples:

> This street is dangerous at night [opinion] because it is badly lit [verifiable reason]. In one four-block stretch, there is only one street lamp [verifiable example].

> This street is dangerous at night [opinion] because vampires hang out here [reason not verifiable]. Drops of blood on the corner show where there was a vampire attack [example not verifiable].

As you can see, both reasons and examples must have some basis in reality. Even if they do, not all readers will agree with you. They may not find your particular reasons convincing, or they may point to counter-examples. Nevertheless, by using sound reasons and good examples, you demonstrate how you arrived at your opinion and persuade them that your view is at least worth considering. Don't assume that your point is so obvious that you don't need to prove it, for you will both annoy your reader and weaken your logic. For guidelines on writing essays based on reasons and examples, see Opinion Pieces (12b).

These guidelines will help you use examples effectively.

Guidelines for Effective Use of Examples

■ *Include an example to support any important general point.*

Consider these two versions of a paragraph on the Marxist definition of violence. The first is a series of general statements.

> The Marxists maintain that an act of violence is quite different from a violent act. An act of violence is an act that causes harm and suffering whether or not it is done violently. This distinction between an act of violence and a violent act allows the Marxists to point out that acts of violence do not necessarily involve physical force.

In the improved revised paragraph, sufficient examples illustrate the main points.

> The Marxists maintain that an act of violence is quite different from a violent act. Stirring a cup of tea, for example, can be done violently and therefore could be described as a violent act. An act of violence, on the other hand, is an act that causes harm and suffering whether or not it is done violently. Such acts do not necessarily involve physical force. To illustrate this point, one need only envision a situation in which urban terrorists poisoned the air, with the result that citizens died quietly in their sleep. Although there was no physical contact, there was obviously an act of violence.

Without the **examples**—the specific instances used to explain the general statements—it is difficult to grasp the distinction between an act of violence and a violent act.

■ *Make sure your examples are typical.*

Suppose, for instance, you were arguing that mandatory retirement is unfair. You might want to support your position by giving the example of your mother, who was not eligible for a full pension when she was forced to retire at sixty-five because she did not begin to work full-time until she was forty. If you used only this example to support your argument, readers might object, saying that your mother's case is atypical and therefore is poor evidence. This example would be effective, however, if you could show that many women are in the same situation. You would also want to use examples of people in different circumstances who also suffer because of mandatory retirement, such as those who change employers or careers.

■ *Explain the meaning of your examples.*

Don't expect an example to speak for itself; you must show its connection to the generality or point. Don't skip steps in your explanation.

> Advertisements make life easier in some very basic ways. A good example is the commercials that play a few bars of many songs included on a tape.

How can playing snippets of songs "make life easier"? A sentence or two of explanation would make this connection clear.

Explain your point first with a reason and then give your example:

> Advertisements make life easier in some very basic ways. One way is by offering the consumer an opportunity to sample products before buying. A good example is the commercials for musical compilation CDs that play a few bars of many songs.

Where there are several steps in the argument, as here, add another sentence, like the one below, after the example to remind your reader of your main point. The paragraph on advertising ends with this sentence showing how commercials make life easier:

> These snippets give the consumer a fairly good idea of whether or not the CD suits his or her taste in music and is thus worth buying.

■ *Integrate your examples smoothly.*

If you haven't had much practice using examples, you may be tempted to introduce them with awkward phrases such as *An example of this is when . . .* (see Mixed Constructions, 17j). You can integrate your examples more smoothly by using constructions such as these: *for example, a further example, is exemplified by, for instance, an instance is, such as, this point is illustrated in, an illustration of this point is.*

> This government's indifference to the needs of ordinary people is revealed in its plan to tax basic foods and children's clothing.

> The adolescent's desire to conform is best exemplified by the popularity of the X-box.

> The half-hour line-ups in the cafeteria are further evidence of the need for more staff.

Exercise 6.1

Choose one of the following opinions and give two or three reasons you agree or disagree. List at least two examples to support each of your reasons.

1. *Maclean's* rankings of universities are useful (not useful).

2. Assisted suicide should (should not) be a criminal offence.

3. Young offenders should (should not) be given jail terms.

4. The federal government should (should not) require labelling of all genetically modified foods.

5. High schools should (should not) offer training programs for specific jobs.

6b EVALUATING STRENGTHS AND WEAKNESSES

To evaluate means to make judgments about the quality, worth, or importance of something according to specific criteria. Others may arrive at different judgments about the same thing. If you were judging a figure-skating competition, for instance, your scores would likely differ from those of other judges using the same criteria. If you were allowed to discuss the performances, you would likely try to persuade the other judges that your evaluations were more accurate. From this point of view, every evaluation, no matter how seemingly objective, includes an element of persuasion.

When persuasion is your main purpose, your evaluations are likely to have both an emotional and a logical dimension. To ensure that your judgments are nevertheless fair, you must thoroughly understand the thing you are evaluating. The basis for evaluation is therefore analysis: dividing things into parts to determine how the parts contribute to the whole (see Analyzing, 5d). For instance, if you were trying to persuade someone not to see *Norbit,* arguing that it has a demeaning attitude to obese people, you would show how various parts of the film reveal this attitude: its plot, characters, and humour.

In evaluating, however, you take analysis one step further: You ask not only "What is the function of this part?" but also "How well does this part fulfill its function?"

Asking Evaluative Questions

There are many perspectives from which to make judgments. Some perspectives depend upon the specialized knowledge of a profession (such as law or medicine) or an academic discipline (such as economics). Others are more broadly applicable. You can make the basis of your own judgments clearer to your readers by identifying your own perspective(s). Are your objections to a film, for instance, aesthetic (the acting is bad) or moral (it glorifies violence), or both?

Here are questions to ask about your subject from four general perspectives.

Aesthetic

Is it aesthetically pleasing? What are its strengths and weaknesses? Do the parts make a satisfying whole? Is the form suited to the content or function? Is it well-made? Is it appealing to its intended audience or users? For an example of evaluation from the aesthetic perspective, see the Sample Review (12i).

Moral

Is it morally right or wrong? Why? Who does it help or harm? Is it ethical? Does it promote values I accept or reject? What are they? Why do I accept or reject them? For an example, see the sample opinion piece "Why I Won't Buy a New Car" (12c).

Logical

Is it true? What are the arguments for and against it? Is the reasoning logical? Is the information accurate and complete? Does the evidence justify the conclusions or recommendations? Are there logical fallacies? For a detailed example of how to evaluate the logic of an argument, see Evaluating Logical, Ethical, and Emotional Appeals (12d).

Practical

Is it practical? What are its advantages and disadvantages? Will it work? Is it cost-effective? Is it useful?

You can clarify your thinking about your subject by considering each set of evaluative questions. You might use columns to make parallel lists of good and bad points.

Suppose, for example, that you were writing a persuasive essay on whether pornography should be banned. You might begin with these points.

	Against Banning	For Banning
AESTHETIC	Some "pornographic" works have literary and artistic merit	Most pornography is crude and boring
MORAL	Right to freedom of expression	Contributes to violence against women and children
LOGICAL	Difficulty of defining "pornography"	Research studies suggest social harm
PRACTICAL	Difficult to enforce	Protect children from sexual exploitation

Deciding Which Questions to Answer

Often your subject or form will limit the range of evaluative questions you answer. If you are writing a short essay, consider one set of questions thoroughly instead of skimming through them all. For a longer essay, you may appeal to more readers and do more justice to your subject by considering two or three aspects, such as the moral and practical issues facing the reform of Canadian health care.

Whether you consider both sides of a question or only one depends on your purpose and audience. You may emphasize either the good or the bad, but if your judgments are too one-sided, you are likely to bore or alienate your readers or make them suspicious of your argument. Suppose, for instance, you were writing about renovating your house. You could emphasize either the pleasures or the pains of this activity, but if the picture you paint is too rosy or too gloomy, readers may reject it as unrealistic and slanted. Your best bet is to briefly acknowledge the other side.

Writing Evaluative Paragraphs

When you evaluate, you support your opinion with reasons, examples, and other evidence. This paragraph from a beginner's guide to opera discusses the reasons for starting opera-going with *Madama Butterfly* in order to persuade the reader.

Sample Evaluative Paragraph

The best piece for opera novices is that perennial favourite, Puccini's *Madama Butterfly*. Why has this suicidal geisha made such an impact? The answer is found in the stylistic term that describes this genre of opera—*verismo*, or truth. Operas in this tradition deal with real people handling their real situations with real emotion. The heroines are typically vulnerable, abused, forgotten. Puccini capitalized on this idea more or less successfully in *Manon Lescaut, Suor Angelica, Turandot, Tosca,* and *La Bohème.* But the most sorrowful, most charming, most naïve, is Cio-Cio-San, the teenage heroine of *Madama Butterfly,* who falls in love with the philandering Captain Pinkerton of the U.S. Navy and commits hara-kiri when he deserts her. The music is exquisite, beautiful yet coloured with sadness, and the drama disturbingly realistic. If nothing else, it's worth the price of admission to see an opera that is set in Japan, involves American characters, and is sung in Italian.

—*Peter Phoa*

Exercise 6.2

On what grounds (aesthetic, moral, logical, practical) would you evaluate each of the following? Several of the topics can be approached from various perspectives.

1. A provincial government's decision to reject rent control.

2. A musical version of the book *Frankenstein.*

3. A school board decision to reduce services for special-needs children.

4. The yoga classes at a local health club.

5. A proposal to designate a building as an historic site.

6. A rapper's latest recording.

7. A proposal to raise the legal drinking age to twenty-one.

8. An educational institution's decision to raise admission standards.

Exercise 6.3

State your position on one of the subjects in Exercise 6.2. List the arguments you would use to support your position.

Exercise 6.4

Write a paragraph based on your list of arguments in Exercise 6.3.

6c USING OTHER METHODS TO PERSUADE

As the three paragraphs on shoplifting in Chapter 1 demonstrate, you signal your purpose in a piece of writing partly through the language you use. You can give a persuasive edge to any of the strategies discussed in Chapters 4 and 5 by using evaluative language in your topic sentences and throughout your paragraphs. Methods of explaining (classifying, comparing, defining terms and concepts, and analyzing) allow you to present a more logical, more carefully reasoned argument. Using evidence responsibly appeals to the ethics of your reader, whereas telling stories, describing people, places, and things, and using analogies appeal to your reader's emotions.

The following analogy between the behaviour of a rich family and the behaviour of rich nations, for example, makes a strong appeal to readers' emotions.

Sample Analogy: Persuasive Writing

Picture a rich family living on a hill in splendid luxury. Look down on the plains around the hill and see the people in shacks, starving; hear the children cry. The rich family sends down a bit of food and clothing once a year, but otherwise they live as always. "We have the right to enjoy our wealth," they say. "We cannot feed and clothe and care for all those people," they explain as they add another foot of barbed wire to the fence around their property. Meanwhile the anger and frustration of the poor grow against them. The rich Western nations are very much like this family. A recent estimate numbered over 1.2 billion people living in poverty on the plains of the world spread at our feet. Like the rich family, we send bits of food and clothing. Like the rich family, we make it harder and harder for the poor to get in. Meanwhile the anger and frustration of the poor grow against us.

—Ken Ainsworth

Here are two cautions about using analogies in persuasive writing:

1. Do not use analogies to make unfair emotional appeals—ones that arouse prejudice. For example, smearing an opponent's reputation

by charging that "Voting for X would be like voting for the Devil" might appeal to some voters, but would likely alienate many more.

2. Analogies do not provide strong logical support for an argument. Because you are comparing things that are basically different, your analogy may break down if it is pushed too far. For example, if you compared marriage to prison, your readers might spot weaknesses in your analogy and reject your argument. See Position Papers (12d).

6c

Using
Other
Methods to
Persuade

Exercise 6.5

Write a persuasive analogy to illustrate one of the following subjects.
* the plight of the homeless
* the disadvantages of a particular occupation
* the advantages (or disadvantages) of decriminalizing marijuana
* the advantages of using a BlackBerry or Sidekick

Weblinks

* Information on Argument and Logic from the OWL.
  owl.english.purdue.edu/handouts/general/gl_argpers.html

* This Persuasion Map helps you plan out a persuasive argument.
  www.readwritethink.org/materials/persuasion_map/

* This interesting site gives you practice in analyzing persuasive techniques.
  webserve.govst.edu/pa/

* The University of Victoria Writer's Guide.
  web.uvic.ca/wguide

* Indiana University Writing Resources—short entries on a number of topics, including paragraphs and topic sentences.
  www.indiana.edu/~wts/pamphlets.html

PART 3

WRITING ESSAYS

Checklist ESSAYS

	OK	NEEDS WORK

Purpose and Audience

1. Does the essay have a clearly defined purpose (to explain, to persuade, to describe, or to share your personal experience)? ☐ ☐

2. Does the essay meet the needs of your intended audience? Is your intended reader your instructor or another non-academic reader? Have you defined, by using reader profiles, who your audience is and what your audience needs to know? (See Chapter 1 for more information on audience.) ☐ ☐

Thesis

3. Does your thesis state a specific idea that the rest of the essay develops or proves? ☐ ☐

Development

4. Is all the material in the essay relevant to your thesis? ☐ ☐

5. Are you satisfied that you have adequately supported your thesis? ☐ ☐

6. Are the connections among your ideas stated as clearly as possible? ☐ ☐

Essays That Begin with the Thesis (Deductive Essays)

7. Does the introduction identify your subject and the range of material you will cover? ☐ ☐

8. Does the introduction end with the thesis? ☐ ☐

9. Do your paragraph divisions indicate the major sections of your essay? ☐ ☐

10. Does each topic sentence clearly state the main point of the paragraph and show how the paragraph relates to or develops the thesis? ☐ ☐

11. Do transitions help your reader to follow the connections among your ideas? ❏ ❏

12. Does the conclusion return to the thesis, sum up the main points, and suggest a broader context or the implications of your subject? ❏ ❏

Essays that Lead Up to the Thesis (Inductive Essays)

13. Does the introduction identify your subject, get the reader's interest, and suggest the structure of your essay? ❏ ❏

14. Does the essay seem divided into the appropriate number of paragraphs? ❏ ❏

15. Do transitions help your reader to follow the sequence of ideas, events, or details? ❏ ❏

16. Does the conclusion sum up the ideas, events, or details by stating or clearly implying your thesis? ❏ ❏

Comparison Essays

17. Have you effectively used either the block or the point-by-point method of organization? ❏ ❏

Research Essays

18. In a research essay, have you included appropriate and correctly documented secondary sources? ❏ ❏

19. Is all the secondary material relevant to your thesis? ❏ ❏

20. Have you explained why you agree or disagree with this material? ❏ ❏

CHAPTER 7

7a WHAT IS AN ESSAY?

"Write an essay on euthanasia," one instructor says. Others ask you to write an essay about your first job interview or about the life cycle of the dragonfly. These instructions might make you ponder what, exactly, an essay is. The term *essay,* in fact, can be applied to a wide variety of nonfiction writing: light newspaper columns and impassioned letters to the editor; thoughtful magazine articles and scathing movie reviews; academic articles and research papers. Regardless of their different purposes and audiences, all these types of writing share a thesis, a main point about their subject.

7b WHAT IS A THESIS?

An opinion, which comes from the Latin stem *opinari* (to think or believe), is a view or judgment not necessarily supported by facts or knowledge. If you say, for instance, that the movie *Mr. and Mrs. Smith* is not worth seeing, you are giving an opinion. But if you say that the movie is not worth seeing because of its incomplete script, its questionable acting, and its gratuitous special effects, then you are stating a thesis.

As the above example suggests, clearly stating your reasons controls the content of the essay and limits your discussion. You are not going to discuss all the reasons the movie is not worth seeing, but only those mentioned. Your thesis, then, is a sort of contract with your reader, telling him or her the material you will cover.

A thesis, then, states an opinion that is supported by one or more valid reasons. There are three main types of thesis statements:

In a **personal essay,** the thesis is a generalization based on your personal experience: "What this means to me is . . ."

EXAMPLE OF PERSONAL THESIS   Sleeping on the streets taught me about the humiliation and hopelessness that the homeless experience.

In an **expository essay,** the thesis is the overall point you want to explain: "What I am trying to explain is . . .

EXAMPLE OF EXPOSITORY THESIS   The three main causes of homelessness are the following: . . .

In a **persuasive essay,** the thesis presents the argument you want to convince your readers to accept: "What you should think (or do) is . . ." You can keep your persuasive thesis on track by including the word "should" in it.

EXAMPLE OF PERSUASIVE THESIS   Canadian cities should budget more time and money to eradicating homelessness.

Here, you are writing a causal analysis essay, a type of expository essay, in which you are describing the main causes of homelessness.

Use these guidelines to formulate a better thesis, whatever the type:

■ *State an opinion or a main point about your subject rather than merely restating your subject or essay topic.*

Suppose, for example, that your subject is *group homes for the mentally disabled* and you have narrowed this subject to the topic of *licensing regulations.* You will not have a thesis if you merely restate your subject: *This essay is about group homes for the mentally disabled.* Merely repeating your topic is no more useful: *This essay will discuss the licensing of group homes for the mentally disabled.* The phrasing of your thesis will depend on what type of essay you are writing: personal, expository, or persuasive.

A thesis stating an opinion provides a much clearer focus for your essay:

PERSONAL THESIS   My experience working at a group home taught me the need for stricter licensing regulations. (Here, your opinion about your subject is the need for stricter licensing regulations.)

EXPOSITORY THESIS   Mandating the licensing of group homes is a difficult process because it involves the input of several organizations and governmental bodies.

PERSUASIVE THESIS   To prevent the exploitation of clients, social services should tighten regulations governing the licensing of group homes for the mentally disabled.

■ *State an opinion rather than a fact.*

Factual statements don't suggest a topic for discussion. The thesis has to be a point that you are going to prove in your entire essay, so facts are too specific; they are best for grabbing your reader's attention or proving your thesis. Let's say that in writing a letter to your local paper about encouraging greyhound rescue, you want to state that in the US, thousands of ex-racing greyhounds are killed each year. Although this fact is shocking, it is too specific for a thesis, and could, instead, lead up to one. Your thesis might say, "To stop the killing of so many racing greyhounds, we should work to limit excessive breeding, ban greyhound racing, and encourage adoption."

■ *Make sure your thesis states your opinion, not the writer's.*

When you are analyzing a piece of writing, you will include the writer's main point somewhere in your analysis, but it will not be your thesis.

Your thesis will explain *your* interpretation of the piece or your evaluation of its strengths and weaknesses. In the above example, for instance, your thesis might be the following: *In the newspaper article, the writer presents a solid case for rescuing greyhounds by using a strong causal analysis argument, startling facts, and moving descriptions.*

■ *Avoid generalizations and make the thesis as precise as possible.*

7c

Discovering
Your
Thesis

If you state a well-defined opinion with one or more reasons to support it, as in the above example, you will know exactly what points to develop in your essay. Avoid generalizations: *These stories have a lot in common* or *The Second World War had a big impact on Canada.* Instead, state the most important similarities in the stories or the most important social, political, or economic effect(s) of the war: *The diversification of manufacturing caused by the Second World War transformed the Canadian economy.*

Because a thesis is your opinion with reasons, there is no one correct thesis on a subject. Your thesis will reflect your unique perspective of the material. It will also, as the above examples suggest, be shaped by your purpose, audience, essay structure, and methods of development.

Exercise 7.1

Consider the following sentences as thesis statements for an essay. If you think the sentence makes a clear point that would control the content of the essay, write **C**. If it doesn't, explain how it could be improved and/or rewrite it.

1. There is at least one television set in 97 percent of Canadian homes.

2. Rehabilitation practitioners don't get paid enough.

3. Certain cancer treatments are available in the United States but not in Canada.

4. This essay will analyze postpartum depression in "The Yellow Wallpaper."

5. In the last twenty years, the internet has changed the world.

6. We should not allow our genetic information to be collected, for this information could be used against us.

7. The sequel *Spider-Man 3* is worse than the original movie.

7c DISCOVERING YOUR THESIS

Although we have been talking about formulating your thesis, it is customary, as discussed in Chapter 2, to gather some material or even write a first draft before determining your thesis. In fact, if you formulate a thesis first and then look for information to support it, you might limit your thinking and distort your subject.

To figure out your thesis, follow these steps:

1. ***Gather information about your subject. Use one or more of these methods—brainstorming, freewriting, asking discovery questions, keeping a journal, conducting interviews, or doing research.*** See Part 1: The Writing Process for more information on the first four of these.

2. ***Group this material into three or four categories.*** These categories could be effects, causes, steps, types, parts, descriptions, events, and so on, depending on your essay. That is, if you were writing a personal essay on your experience in group homes, this material might be details of a few experiences; if you were writing an expository essay on the difficulty of regulating licensing, these categories might be the bodies responsible for this regulation (systems analysis/classification), the steps involved in regulating licensing (process analysis), or the reasons this regulation is so difficult (causal analysis).

3. ***Formulate a thesis that focuses on the meaning of these broader categories.*** Suppose, for example, that you have been asked to write an essay on your first job. If you have returned to school after a career as a nurse, you might write a personal essay on the satisfactions and frustrations of nursing when you began work twenty years ago; an expository essay comparing working conditions then and now; or a persuasive essay arguing that working conditions for nurses have hardly improved over the twenty years. Whatever your focus, begin by jotting down information about various aspects of your job.

Nursing Twenty Years Ago

1. Earned $275/month with reasonable rates for room, board, and laundry in nurses' residence.

2. Advancement by seniority.

3. Good job security.

4. Not many chances to develop new skills.

5. Performed menial and routine tasks, no clinical specialization.

6. Worked 40-hour/five-day week; split shifts and short changes (e.g., worked 3:30 p.m.–midnight, then 7:30 a.m.–4 p.m.); understaffed.

7. Nurses supervised or administered; did little nurturing or ministering to patients.

8. Nurses expected to follow doctor's orders, not to make independent decisions.

9. Basic level of technology.

10. Doctors viewed nurses as subordinate.

11. Little interaction with management.

12. Education required: basic three-year diploma; training based on practice.

You would then group these aspects of nursing into more general categories:

7c

- financial dimensions of employment (1, 2, 3, 6)
- professional responsibilities (4, 5, 8, 9, 12)
- possibilities for emotional satisfaction (7, 10, 11)

Discovering Your Thesis

To work out a thesis, you would need to decide what point you could make about each of these dimensions of the job. You might choose the following points:

- Twenty years ago, nurses worked long hours with strenuous shift changes for low wages, but their jobs were relatively secure.
- Opportunities for nurses to show initiative and develop new skills were quite limited.
- The emotional satisfactions of nursing were also limited by lack of direct contact with patients and their subordinate position to doctors and hospital administration.

The main idea emerging is that twenty years ago nursing was a secure job, but one with limited opportunities for intellectual growth and emotional satisfaction.

The Personal Thesis

Whether a personal essay is narrative, descriptive, or reflective, your thesis should make a point about what your experience taught you about yourself, about others, or about life itself. The thesis, then, should still be relevant to your reader.

> As a young woman seeking independence, I saw only the job security that nursing promised, not its limited opportunities for intellectual growth and personal satisfaction.

The Expository Thesis

The thesis for an expository essay is the generalization that grows out of your analysis of your material. The thesis explains the significance of your subject by telling your readers *what* its parts are, *how* it got that way, *why* it has the nature it has, or all three. This thesis explains *why* nursing twenty years ago was as it was.

> The relative abundance of health-care dollars meant that nursing jobs were secure; however, the hierarchical nature of the system meant that nursing provided limited opportunities for intellectual growth or emotional satisfaction.

The Persuasive Thesis

A persuasive thesis tells readers *what* they should think or do and *why*. You reach your thesis by evaluating the strengths and weaknesses of your subject (see Evaluating Strengths and Weaknesses, 6b). Your thesis may focus on strengths (*Nursing was a good career choice twenty years ago because of the job security it offered*) or weaknesses (*Nursing was a bad career choice because of the limited opportunities for intellectual growth and emotional satisfaction*). On most issues, however, readers are more likely to be convinced by a thesis that gives a balanced perspective—one that acknowledges the other point of view, as in the example below.

7c

Discovering
Your
Thesis

> Nursing twenty years ago bore little relation to the idealized notions invoked by critics of today's practitioners. Although jobs were secure, the profession offered few opportunities for intellectual growth or emotional satisfaction.

The Comparative Thesis

When you are comparing, whether in a personal, expository, or persuasive essay, your thesis should do more than state the most important similarities or differences in your subjects. It should also explain how or why they are similar or different. If you were comparing working conditions in nursing twenty years ago and today, for instance, you might discover that opportunities for intellectual growth and personal satisfaction have increased, but job security has decreased. Your thesis might explain the reasons for these differences in this way:

> Changes in medical technology and in the structure of the health-care system make nursing more intellectually and emotionally satisfying than it was twenty years ago, but current cuts in health-care spending make jobs less secure.

Exercise 7.2

Choose one of the following subjects. Using the nursing example above as a guide, gather material and develop a rough thesis for personal, expository, persuasive, and comparative essays.

- being a student
- working part-time
- the controversy over Frankenfoods
- going back to school as a mature student
- fighting in hockey
- racism/sexism in rap music
- your favourite book, film, or television program

CHAPTER 8

Essay Structure

Although essays, like houses, come in a variety of shapes, they all have a structure—a principle of organization binding the parts together. The structure generally has two functions: to show your readers how parts of your essay relate to each other and to create interest. Your choice of structure for a particular piece of writing depends on your overall purpose and audience.

The overall structure of your essay is determined by where you put your thesis—near the beginning or near the end. Beginning with the thesis is effective for academic and persuasive essays, whereas ending with the thesis is most effective for some kinds of personal and persuasive essays. That is, if you were writing a persuasive letter to your newspaper about supporting the local SPCA, you might open with a thesis stating the positive effects of such support; however, if you were writing a personal essay on owning a dog, you might end with what pet ownership taught you about dogs and yourself.

Comparison essays, which present special problems of organization, have two main structures: the block method and the point-by-point method. For suggestions about how to organize other kinds of essays, see the appropriate section.

8a BEGINNING WITH YOUR THESIS

Putting the thesis in your introduction provides a framework for the rest of the essay and emphasizes the results of your thinking.

Advantages and Disadvantages

This method's main advantage is clarity. By stating your main point first and then supporting it with evidence, you show your reader the relevance of your material. This method is particularly effective when discussing a complex or technical subject. Most readers will have trouble following several pages of specific detail if they don't know your main point. Thus, for most of the essays you write for academic courses, you will probably state your thesis first.

Beginning with your thesis may not be the best strategy, however, if you are writing on a controversial subject or an unfamiliar topic. You may alienate readers who feel forced to agree or disagree with your conclusions before they have had time to consider the controversy or understand the topic.

The Basic Components

Thesis and Topic Sentences

Your thesis, you will recall, gives your opinion about your subject and your reason(s) for holding that opinion. Giving your reasons in the order you plan to discuss them provides a map for your readers. To show them where they are along the way, you use topic sentences that elaborate on your reasons, which you develop in your body paragraphs.

In the following example, you can see how the thesis and topic sentences create a structure that focuses the reader's attention and controls the content of the essay.

8a

Beginning with Your Thesis

> **Essay Topic** What are the effects of stress? Is any stress good? Incorporating research, write a 1,500-word causal analysis essay on this topic.
>
> **Thesis** Although stress plays a crucial role in the survival of species, and some stress is beneficial, an overload of stress causes a wide variety of psychological and physical ailments.

The thesis answers *both* questions by saying that stress, though it once served a useful purpose, now has a number of harmful effects. Putting the benefits of stress in a subordinate clause tells the reader that though this minor point will be discussed, probably near the beginning of this essay, the bulk of the essay will elaborate on the negative psychological and physical effects of stress. The causal analysis essay, then, moves toward the most important effect.

Topic Sentences

— In the early history of humankind, stress was beneficial, for it ensured survival.

— Furthermore, some stress is actually beneficial.

— Constant stress, nonetheless, has been linked to several mental ailments.

— Constant stress also wreaks havoc on our bodies.

Giving an essay such a clearly defined structure is not easy; don't expect a perfectly worded thesis and matching topic sentences on your first attempt. Although you may discover a tentative thesis and major categories (such as physical and psychological effects), these categories— or the thesis—may change when you write an outline or a draft. When you revise, you can rewrite your thesis and topic sentences so that they provide a clear, logical framework.

The Introduction

In this type of essay structure, the opening sentences define the range of material you will cover and provide a context for the thesis, which ends the introduction. Keep in mind, however, that some instructors might prefer that you begin your introduction with the thesis. Ask your instructor about his or her preference and check the assignment format.

Your introduction can be based on any of the methods of developing ideas discussed in Chapters 4, 5, and 6. In academic essays, for example, you may classify the material you plan to discuss (such as types of stress), define a key term from your thesis (such as *autism*), or sketch the development of a current situation (such as previous attempts to decriminalize marijuana). For a more personal essay or an essay for a more general audience, you may want to create interest by providing a vivid example, telling a relevant anecdote, or describing a detailed scene. You might begin this essay on stress, for instance, with a description of the typically harried, stressed individual.

Whatever method you choose, give your readers all the background information they need, including authors and titles of works, and dates and places of events.

Remember the following points when you are writing your introduction:

- **Avoid making large claims that the rest of your essay does not support.** Do not, for example, begin by saying *Since the beginning of time . . .* or *Everyone is under stress* unless you can (and will) provide hard evidence to support the generalization. Because you weren't there at time's beginning and because there are some people who don't suffer from stress, these claims will get a thumbs-down from your instructor.

- **State your thesis, not your topic.** Don't include a sentence that merely repeats the assigned topic, such as *In this essay I will discuss the dangerous effects of stress*. The title of your essay should clarify your topic.

- **Focus on the big picture, not the details.** You may choose to open with an example or incident that captures the essence of your argument. For instance, you might zoom in on the morning of a rushed businessman who is frantically commuting to work while checking his BlackBerry and eating his McBreakfast. Be wary, though, of including detailed information that belongs in the body of the essay.

Sample Introduction for an Expository Essay on Stress

Cell phones, BlackBerrys, drive-through takeouts, 24-hour grocery stores, all-night gyms, and microwaveable foods—these amenities feed our busy-ness and speed habits. Electricity, the internet, and caffeine permit us to cram even more into every moment and to extend our waking hours into the wee hours of the night. We are an underslept and overworked society. And the price we pay is stress—lots of it. Although stress once played a crucial role for survival, and some stress is indeed beneficial, an overload of stress causes a wide variety of psychological and physical ailments.

Sample Introduction (Literary Example)

Customs can be traditions we adore, rules we blindly follow, and rituals we grudgingly adhere to. We may understand tradition without following it or follow tradition without understanding it. **These contradictory attitudes toward tradition and custom are illustrated in Shirley Jackson's**

"The Lottery," which, through its symbolism, setting, and characterization, illustrates this unsettling theme: traditions, even when violent and senseless, are difficult to change and harder to relinquish.

Middle Paragraphs

Sometimes, such as when you are tracing the development of a concept or analyzing a chain of causes and effects, your material will determine the order of your middle paragraphs. Usually, however, you will have to decide how to arrange your points and how to keep the reader interested. You might begin with the point that your readers will find easiest to understand and end with the most difficult. Alternatively, you might build interest by beginning with your least important point and ending with the most important.

To see how you would determine the most important point, consider the structure of the essay on the effects of stress. The thesis and topic sentences suggest three blocks of material: the positive benefits of stress, the negative psychological effects, and the negative physical effects. The writer moves toward the more insidious but least obvious effects of stress, such as obesity, also her most significant point.

Remember that you can't always cover a block of material in a single paragraph. To support the point about *the negative psychological effects of stress*, for instance, you might need several paragraphs.

Whenever your discussion of a point takes up more than half a page (typed, double spaced), you need to use umbrella topic sentences and topic sentences.

Sample Umbrella Topic Sentence That Could Control Three Paragraphs

Constant stress has been linked to minor psychological problems, several anxiety disorders, and depression.

Topic Sentence 1	Constant stress has been linked to minor psychological problems such as temporary insomnia and lack of libido. [Examples]
Topic Sentence 2	In addition, there is a connection between several anxiety disorders and high stress levels. [Examples]
Topic Sentence 3	Probably the least obvious but most common effect of stress is depression. [Examples]

Conclusion

Your conclusion should draw together the evidence and reinforce the main idea of the essay. Your conclusion should have three basic components: a rephrasing of your thesis, a brief explanation of the significance of the major points, and a suggestion of the broader implications of the subject. Although you don't want to raise new issues or ask questions, do show how your essay fits into a wider context. Here are the three main ways to do so:

- Move from the specific to the general to suggest that the material you have covered is part of a larger issue.

    If we don't slow down now, we will pass down our fast-paced, super-stressed, unhealthy lifestyles to our children.

- Compare your subject with another subject with which your reader is likely to be familiar.

    Although medical professionals are worried about cancer, perhaps they should also be concerned about the effects of stress, which are also killing Canadians daily.

- Reinforce the significance of your subject by emphasizing its causes or effects.

    Because of the side effects of our fast-paced, super-stressed lives, we might want to consider a healthier option: slowing down.

Sample Conclusion

Although we still have the "fight-or-flight reaction," a primitive response left over from our cave-dwelling past, we must not let this reaction take over our lives. If we do, we risk developing a plethora of psychological and physical disorders and adding to the stress of our society. Carl Honoré, founder of the *Slow Movement*, urges us to grasp "that middle point between fast and slow: going fast when it makes sense to be fast; going slow when it makes sense to be slow; and choosing the right speed, the right time for things" (359). The solution, for all of us, lies in minor lifestyle changes, knowing when to stress and when to relax, and living a balanced, healthy life between fast and slow.

For other examples of essays beginning with the thesis, see Sample Essay Analyzing Literature (11d) and Sample Literary Research Paper (13j).

8b LEADING UP TO THE THESIS

If you choose this method, your thesis may appear later on in your essay or at the end, or it may be implied rather than stated directly. This pattern emphasizes the process of your thinking rather than your conclusions. Before choosing this pattern, make sure that it is appropriate for your topic and that your instructor approves of it.

Advantages and Disadvantages

By delaying the presentation of your thesis, you can create suspense and interest. This approach is particularly effective in personal essays, in which you invite readers to share the process of coming to understand an experience. Leading up to your thesis is also useful in persuasive essays in which you want readers to consider a potentially controversial point of view or to think in new ways about an old problem.

The danger with this method is that you may end up with many details but no main point. You can prevent this problem by structuring your essay according to one of the patterns discussed below.

Questions and Answers

In this pattern, your introduction poses a question that the essay answers. You may consider and reject possible answers before concluding with a satisfactory one, or you may give a series of partial answers that add up to a comprehensive one.

Introduction The introduction sets out the problem or issue and asks the question to be answered. For instance, you might ask: "Why does Johnny, a six-year-old, have high blood pressure?" You would then rule out the typical answers before arriving at the real one.

Middle Paragraphs The body of your essay presents possible answers in detail. Each answer forms a major section of the essay, composed of one or more paragraphs. You can help your readers follow the structure of your essay by repeating key terms and using parallel sentence structures. Arrange your paragraphs in a sequence such as simplest to most complex, or weakest answer to strongest answer. For instance, you might begin with the answer Johnny is stressed, which is unlikely for most six-year-olds, and move to the answer that Johnny is overweight and under-exercised.

Conclusion The conclusion presents the best or most comprehensive answer as your thesis. Signal that you've reached your thesis by repeating the question from the introduction or by summarizing previous answers. Why does Johnny have high blood pressure? He has high blood pressure because at six years old, he is morbidly obese and severely unfit; Johnny is representative of the growing problem of childhood obesity in Canada.

The example below again demonstrates how the question-and-partial-answers pattern works.

Introduction [Question]	How can teachers help reduce violence in school?
Middle Paragraphs [Topic Sentences]	We can watch for signs . . .
	We can discuss the issue with students . . .
	We can also teach students ways of resolving arguments . . .
	Most important, we must model good problem-solving behaviour in our conflicts with students . . .
Conclusion [Thesis]	To reduce violence in schools, we must educate both ourselves and our students about the uses and misuses of power.

The sample opinion piece "Why I Won't Buy a New Car" (12c) displays elements of this pattern. Note that the question is raised in the title.

Specific Details to General Meaning

In this pattern, you begin with particular details and end with a thesis, either stated or implied, about the meaning of the experience as a whole.

Introduction By using narrative or descriptive detail, you plunge your reader into the subject of your essay and arouse interest. You give a sense of structure by suggesting the final event of the narrative (*We wouldn't rest until we found the lost treasure of the Incas*) or the scope of the description (*The old neighbourhood was unrecognizable*).

Middle Paragraphs In the body of the essay, fill in the specific details. As units of thought, your paragraphs will correspond to units of your narrative (*first week, next day, that afternoon, the moment had come*) or description (*the streets, the houses, our house*). Arrange your paragraphs in a chronological or spatial sequence that will lead naturally to your conclusion's generalization. Foreshadow this generalization by references to thoughts and feelings (*I wondered whether we were on a fool's errand*), or by choice of diction (*narrow streets, cracked sidewalks, shabby houses, our house shrunken and decayed*).

Conclusion In the conclusion, sum up the meaning of the experience, either through explicit commentary (*The real treasures were those we had left behind: family, friends, and country*), or through an image that makes the point (*Staring back at me was the image of a white-haired old man, his face deeply creased by sorrow and worry. Several moments passed before I recognized my own reflection in the glass*).

For an example of this pattern, see the sample descriptive essay "Smokey Mountain" (9d).

8c PATTERNS FOR COMPARISON ESSAYS

Just as you can use either the block or the point-by-point method to develop comparison paragraphs, you can use these methods to develop comparison essays. Both methods have their advantages and disadvantages.

Block Method

When you use the block method, you cover all the aspects of one subject before you discuss the other.

Advantages: Clarity and Simplicity

The block method allows you to develop the points about one subject before you turn to the other. That is, you might discuss setting, structure, and characterization in story A before comparing or contrasting these three elements in story B. It is, therefore, simple to work with when you don't have much time to organize an essay, such as in an exam. The block method can work well for short essays on familiar subjects. It is also effective when you are using a brief treatment of one subject as a basis for a more lengthy treatment of another. Finally, if you are comparing more than two subjects, you will probably need to use the block method to avoid fragmenting your material.

In the block method, you are less likely to distort your material by trying too hard to find similarities or by exaggerating the importance of one aspect of a subject. The drawbacks of one cancer treatment, for instance, may outweigh those of another.

Disadvantages: Repetition and Loss of Focus

One disadvantage of the block method is that readers may forget what you have said about your first subject by the time they read about your second subject. For this reason, you may have to repeat certain points. Another danger is that you may dilute or lose the basis of your comparison: the common element you are discussing (such as the training of child-care workers versus babysitters or the economic effects of two policies). As a result, your reader may decide that you have discussed both subjects but not compared them. To avoid this problem, make tight comparisons and contrasts.

Sample Outline: Block Method

If you were using the block method to organize an essay comparing your experiences of city life and small-town life, your outline might look like this.

I. Small-town life
    A. Lack of amenities and poor infrastructure
    B. Absence of culture/entertainment
    C. Lack of crime
    D. Quiet, friendly atmosphere

II. City life
    A. Wealth of amenities and solid infrastructure
    B. Plenty of entertainment, nightlife, and cultural activities
    C. More crime
    D. Noisy, impersonal atmosphere

Notice that this structure leads naturally to putting your thesis at the end, where you draw together your comparisons. In this case, you might argue that although the advantages of city life are access to amenities and entertainment, the disadvantages are its higher crime rate and its atmosphere. You conclude that you prefer small-town life.

Point-by-Point Method

When you use the point-by-point method, you consider one aspect of both subjects before moving on to another aspect of both subjects.

Advantages: Focus and Conciseness

An important advantage of the point-by-point method is that, by bringing specific points about your subjects closer together, you help your reader to grasp the most important similarities and differences. This method, then, avoids one of the main disadvantages of the block method: repetition. This emphasis on points of similarity and difference also keeps you focused on the task of comparing. For these reasons, this method is often better for organizing a lengthy and complex comparison.

Disadvantages: Complexity and Fragmentation

Because you have to identify all the points of similarity and difference you plan to discuss before you begin writing, this method is time-consuming and difficult to use for in-class essays. Another disadvantage is that if you don't have much to say about each point, your essay may ping-pong rapidly from one subject to the other. You can correct this problem by brainstorming to gather a lot of material, by refining your points, or by combining subpoints so that you write separate paragraphs on each aspect of each subject, as illustrated in the outline below.

Sample Outline: Point-by-Point Method

Chemotherapy vs. Radiotherapy:

    I. Introduction

    II. Definition of both treatments
        A. Definition of chemotherapy
          1. Main kinds of drugs
        B. Definition of radiotherapy
          1. Internal radiotherapy
          2. External radiotherapy

    III. Treatment plan
        A. When and why chemotherapy is used
        B. When and why radiotherapy is used

    IV. Side effects
        A. Side effects of chemotherapy drugs
        B. Side effects of radiotherapy

V. Effectiveness of both treatments
    A. Effectiveness of chemotherapy alone
    B. Effectiveness of radiotherapy alone
    C. Effectiveness of these treatments combined

VI. Conclusion

**Patterns for
Comparison
Essays**

CHAPTER 9

Personal Essays

Although your main purpose when writing personal essays is to share your thoughts, feelings, and experiences, you must also explain what your experience means or why it is relevant. As we consider two kinds of personal essays (narrative and descriptive), we will discuss how to fulfill your readers' expectations. Most of your personal essays are likely to be based on events in your life, so we will examine narrative essays most closely.

9a NARRATIVE ESSAYS

Like other essays, **narrative essays** must have a point, a main idea. To see why a main idea is important, let's consider an example.

Suppose you decide to write about "My MS Bike Tour." The title, as you can see, doesn't suggest any point about the tour. It offers no principle to help you select which events to include and which to omit, or how to arrange them effectively. So you might begin at the beginning, go on to the end, ramble on, and stop. However, if you present the events in this manner, you will limit your audience; that is, a disorganized description might interest your mother or your best friend but probably not your instructor or your desired reader—someone considering doing the MS Bike Tour.

Imagine, then, that you decide to focus on one incident and write about "Pain, Suffering, and Friendship on My MS Bike Tour." You would now have a way of deciding what to include in your essay, and you might even think about how to present your material—such as describing your throbbing muscles as you pedalled up that long hill, battered by gusts of wind and driving rain.

Think about your physical struggle. What did you learn from it? There are many possible lessons that you might have learned—your ability to push against personal limits, for instance, or the power of nature, or empathy for those who encounter daily physical challenges. Most of us learn these lessons at some time. The deeper significance of your narrative will engage your readers. They not only will find out what happened, but also will discover the meaning of the experience, both for you and for their own lives. This meaning will be the thesis that you state or imply through the telling of your story.

What you have learned should not be a moral tacked on to the end— *From this incident I learned to appreciate my* . . . The meaning should emerge from how you present the concrete details of the experience as well as your specific points. Instead of telling, show. Telling that this experience has changed your outlook is less effective than saying the following: *Whenever I feel not up to the challenge, I think of pedalling up that endless hill in the driving rain, my bodily aches reminding me of the joy of being alive.*

Writing Narrative Essays: The Process

Follow these guidelines when writing a narrative essay:

1. Focus on a single experience so that you can include a wealth of detail about it.
2. Make a central point about the meaning of this experience.
3. Put this central point (your thesis) at the beginning, at the end, or at the place in the narrative where the meaning of events becomes clear to you.
4. Include only events and details relevant to the central point.
5. Provide enough specific details about *who, what, when, where, why,* and *how* so the reader understands how events and actions relate to the central point.
6. Within this overall structure, arrange your material to create a specific effect, such as suspense, humour, or sorrow.
7. Make the sequence of events clear to readers by using transitional words and phrases to indicate time relationships (*the next morning, now that I look back*).
8. Create interest through diction, figurative language, and a good writing style.

9b SAMPLE NARRATIVE ESSAY

Unwelcome Guest: The Case of the Snake
by Sydney Singh

In the backwater village in Guyana where I grew up, snakes were not uncommon. But they were rarely seen. They hid from humans, and for a very good reason: we killed them as routinely as we killed rats, mice, and other rodents. In my childhood, I may have killed a dozen snakes or so, but I do not recall the circumstances and details of any of the killings, except the last one. So fresh and vivid is my memory of this particular death that it would appear as if the event occurred only yesterday, and not forty years ago.

It was a very hot day in July, and I was home alone. I came out into the front yard, and there it was: a snake of unusual size, at the edge of the vegetable patch. For a moment I stood still, petrified with fear. The snake was unlike any I had seen before. It was brown as the earth, and larger than the common garden variety: about five feet long and two inches thick. Its head was held erect, a foot from the ground. There was dignity in its posture. Yet, my first impulse was to kill it. And I did.

Armed with a long, heavy piece of firewood, I struck. A sudden blow: a broken back. The snake immediately doubled up in a paroxysm of pain. As it writhed and thrashed in agony, I struck again and again, savagely and unerringly. With each blow, its convulsive struggle grew less and less. Eventually it lay still. I poked its limp body with the end of the stick; it made no movement. The intruder was dead.

Gradually, the thumping of my heart subsided, and my initial fear vanished. I felt quite elated at my daring feat, and could hardly wait for my father to come home so I could proudly show him the victim of my fearless courage. In the interim, I went inside to do some chores. A few minutes later, I came outside to glory in my act of bravery. Much to my horror, I saw another snake near the body of the dead one. I froze in my tracks. The newcomer was identical to the snake I had killed earlier, only slightly smaller. Even in my limited understanding, I recognized it was the female of the species, the mate of the dead snake.

My first thought was to kill her too. But I was arrested by her strange behaviour. She sniffed at the dead snake. Then she nudged him indifferently. When there was no response, she became more aggressive. She nudged him fiercely and frantically, urging him to move. Then realization seemed to dawn on her: her mate was dead. What followed was as incredible as it was fascinating. She threw herself on her mate; then she jumped high in the air and fell upon the body of her lifeless husband. She did this several times, wild with grief. Finally, wearied of her exertions, she gently rested her head on the dead body. After a little while, she slowly slithered into the thick grass and disappeared.

The spectacle of grief was not new to me. I had seen it in the exaggerated wailing of our women at funerals, and in the mournful cries of animals which had lost their young to sickness or starvation. But I had never seen such a display of genuine grief as that shown by the dead snake's companion. Child though I was, I was not without a moral sensibility. I realized, even then, what I had done, and my heart grew sick. It grew even sicker when my father musingly observed that the snakes were merely passing through our yard, on their way to some unknown destination. Later in life, I would refer to them as sojourners.

My father neither commended nor scolded me for my action. But in my guilty conscience I interpreted his words, "Dey was just passin' through," as a tacit expression of disapproval. That night I hardly slept at all. The dead snake and his disconsolate companion tormented my consciousness. I wondered where they came from, where they were going, and what would become of the widow. And then, for the first time, the enormity of my crime sank home: through my wanton act of cruelty, I had killed the husband, leaving the wife to continue, alone and lonely, on a journey they had begun together. There was no thrill in my victory, only a remorse sharper than a serpent's fang.

Many years passed before I realized that my aversion to snakes was associated with a myth that was part of my education. Snakes, we were taught both in school and in church, were our mortal enemies; it was the snake that was responsible for humanity's loss of paradise. According to the Bible, Satan, disguised as a snake, successfully tempted Eve to eat the forbidden fruit, and for his role in her disobedience God pronounced a curse upon the serpent: "And I will put enmity between thee and the woman, and between thy seed and her seed; it shall bruise thy head, and thou shalt bruise his heel" (Genesis 3:15).

This curse has informed our relationship with the snake. Through the ages humans have systematically hunted the snake, and in many parts of the world decimated snake populations, to the detriment of our own survival. Yet there is no record that snakes have hunted men; few people in the world have died from snake bites. But perhaps more important, ever since that episode in the Garden of Eden, the snake has been the archetypal symbol of evil. We associate it with deceit, cunning, and treachery. A person who betrays us, for example, is referred to as "a snake in the grass." A sly person has "beady snake's eyes." It is no exaggeration to say that the snake is perhaps the most maligned creature in the animal kingdom.

Many years ago, in an introductory literature course, I read a poem by D. H. Lawrence entitled "Snake." This poem did not lessen my loathing for snakes, but it gave me a whole new perspective and respect for these creatures, which inhabited the earth eighty million years before the appearance of humans. In the poem, the speaker tells of his encounter with a snake that has come to drink from his water-trough. His first instinct, like mine, is to kill the snake: "The voice of my education said to me, `He must be killed.'" But the speaker, much to his credit, resists the temptation; instead, he feels "honoured" that the snake should seek his hospitality. However, after the snake has drunk its fill and is about to return to the "horrid black hole" from whence it came, the speaker, overcome by "a sort of horror," picks up a log and throws it at the water-trough. He misses the snake, but is still racked with guilt:

I thought how paltry, how vulgar, what a mean act!
I despised myself and the voices of my accursed human education.

The poem concludes with the speaker's regret at the departure of the snake; a wish for its return; and a realization that he has missed a rare opportunity:

And so, I missed my chance with one of the lords
Of life.
And I have something to expiate;
A pettiness.

So do I.

9c DESCRIPTIVE ESSAYS

If the unifying principle of narrative essays is *what happened to me*, the unifying principle of **descriptive essays** is *what I experienced*. Keep this distinction in mind because narrative essays may include descriptions of people, places, and objects, and descriptive essays may include accounts of things happening. In description, however, your main focus is rendering your impressions of the world or of an experience.

Subjects

You can write descriptive essays about places, people, or other animate and inanimate things. You might write, for example, a brief essay about the habits of your next-door neighbour, a character sketch of a coach who taught you the importance of dedication, or a personal piece about a family heirloom to explain its meaning in your life.

Image and Meaning

As in narrative essays, concrete images create meaning more effectively than do direct statements. Specific images of people, places, and objects allow your reader to see through your eyes and thus to empathize with your thoughts, feelings, and judgments. In the following excerpt from the sample descriptive essay "Smokey Mountain" (9d), the writer uses repeated images of water to convey his complex attitude toward the scene.

> As I looked down from the safety of my perch high above the swarming crowd, the garbage appeared as faint streams spread across the valley. Bits of tin foil and splintered glass sparkled like breaking waves in the sunlight. The smear of black smoke rising out of spontaneous combustion appeared like thick steam from the water's surface. From where I stood, the whole scene had a certain beauty about it . . . but then, from the right distance, so does a raging hurricane.

This passage emphasizes how a Canadian observer might feel safely distant from this scene of poverty and squalor; it also conveys, in the image of the hurricane, the writer's recognition of the potential for violence and upheaval. These images, which encourage us to see the meaning, are more effective than a direct statement.

Organization

For short descriptive essays, such as "Smokey Mountain" (9d), you might allow the meaning of the whole to emerge gradually from the accumulation of details. However, in longer descriptive essays, you may need to state your main point near the beginning and bring in other methods of development—such as a comparison of one person with another or an analysis of the effects of a shifting population on a town.

Whatever overall structure you choose, you should arrange the parts of the essay by an appropriate principle of organization, usually spatial. This spatial organization may be literal (moving from one part of the town to the next) or figurative (moving from what is "easy to see" about a person to what is "hard to see"). Most important, your method of organization should culminate in an image conveying your dominant impression.

Smokey Mountain
by Bill Howe

The young boy struggled up the side of the hill. His legs were straining under the weight of the sack he had slung over his shoulders, and his one arm was flailing to catch his balance as he teetered over the narrow path. His shirt and trousers were soiled with sweat and dirt, and his legs were buried deep inside his oversized rubber boots. A floppy cap sagged over the side of his blackened face, hiding the scowl of dignified scorn he directed at the intruders. He quickly turned away and made off towards a sculpture of bed springs, tires, and scrap metal.

The hill I was standing on is known to the Filipinos as Smokey Mountain. It has been built up over many years from garbage deposits delivered from the streets of Metro Manila. Over eight million people contribute every day to this towering masterpiece, but its dismal appearance has not discouraged the poor who find their home within its refuge of waste. A population of some 15,000 squatters has developed into a thriving community, complete with a division of labour natural to such territory. There are people who sort through the garbage for cherished bits of plastic and metal, people who work in the distribution centres selling salvaged goods to local recycling plants, and people who go out into the streets at night to collect the garbage from the richer districts before it is diluted by the rest of the collection.

Most of the people migrated here to escape the hopeless life in the remote provinces, only to find the economic depression of their new surroundings worse than what they had left behind. The putrid smell of rotting debris wafting through the air continually reminds them of their own decay. The villagers are plagued with diseases contracted in their own backyard. On a good day, their labour might earn them only two or three dollars, but still they consider themselves fortunate to be able to earn money at all. The people appear proud and content with their life, and the children play in the garbage pile as if it were a giant sandbox filled with buried toys.

From where I stood, I had a panoramic view of the flow of garbage below. The convoy of tawny yellow dump trucks formed a brilliant streak which faded into the distant skyline of Manila. As the trucks dropped off their loads, people eagerly surrounded the untouched deposits, in hopes of discovering some carelessly discarded treasure to take home to their families. Tin cans, tires, wooden crates, plastic bottles, discarded clothing—nothing was overlooked for its value on the salvage market.

Attacking the hill from below was a huge bulldozer burrowing into the debris like a mechanical mole. As it lurched forward, it uncovered a trail of pristine spoil, its rutted tracks quickly filling with pools of mud freshly squeezed from the rubble below. The people followed the beast as though it was their master. As their bent frames waded slowly through the soggy mess, they seemed enslaved to the garbage beneath their feet, imprisoned by their own poverty.

These were the fringe dwellers of Manila, people who survive in an industry brutally isolated from the rest of the population. As I looked down from the safety of my perch high above the swarming crowd, the garbage appeared as faint streams spread across the valley. Bits of tin foil and splintered glass sparkled like breaking waves in the sunlight. The smear of black smoke rising out of spontaneous combustion appeared like thick steam from the water's surface. From where I stood, the whole scene had a certain beauty about it . . . but then, from the right distance, so does a raging hurricane.

One of the dump trucks passed me as I was leaving the smouldering mountain. I grinned to myself as I read the words inscribed across its side boards—"Manila on the Go!"

CHAPTER 10

Expository Writing: Essays and Other Types

In expository writing, you explain something to a particular audience. Your subject might be a short story, a problem, an historical event, a current situation, a theory. To move beyond saying what your subject is to saying what it means, you need to use methods of development such as analysis, comparison, and definition. The meaning you see in your subject—your interpretation of it—serves as the thesis for your essay.

10a WRITING EXPOSITORY ESSAYS: THE PROCESS

Regardless of the subject of your expository essay, you use the same steps in formulating your thesis and organizing your material.

Choosing a Primary Method of Development and a Focus

Some essay assignments state or imply a primary method of development and a focus (*Compare theories of fetal development*). Others simply give a list of possible subjects (*Native land claims*), leaving you to choose your focus. If a primary method of development is not given or implied, make notes on what each method of exposition could contribute to your essay.

You might begin work on an expository essay on child poverty by making this list:

Method of Development	Possible Material
PROCESS ANALYSIS	Not applicable?
SYSTEMS ANALYSIS	How agencies dealing with the needs of poor children fit into the system of social services
Method of Development	**Possible Material**
CAUSAL ANALYSIS	What causes poverty among children
	How poverty affects children's short-term and long-term development
	How poverty among children affects society as a whole

(continued)

97

(continued)

CLASSIFICATION	Child poverty by region
	Child poverty by types of households
COMPARISON	Differences in the development of impoverished children and middle-class children
	Child poverty in Mexico and Canada
DEFINITION	Meaning of poverty

From a list of possibilities, you choose a focus and a method of development, keeping in mind your audience. If you are writing for a newspaper or a magazine, your interests and your assumptions about the interests of your readers will guide you. If you are writing on child poverty for *Chatelaine,* most of your readers will be middle-class women with children. To appeal to them and make them consider underprivileged children, you might focus on differences in the development of middle-class children and impoverished children. Your primary method of development, then, would be comparison.

However, if you are writing for *Frank,* a satirical magazine that often criticizes the excesses and biases of the media, you might want to write an exposé comparing the coverage of child poverty in Third World countries to the coverage of child poverty in Canada. You might argue that although child poverty in undeveloped nations is considered a serious problem, child poverty in Canada is often ignored. Along with statistics and facts comparing the coverage of both issues, you might interview Canadians about their awareness of child poverty. You then decide that you are going to write a persuasive essay that primarily uses examples and compare/contrast.

When you are writing an essay for a course, you will probably choose a focus reflecting the concerns, objectives, or methodology of that discipline. Sociologists, for example, study the relationships between groups and society. For a sociology course, you might focus on what causes elder abuse or how this problem is dealt with by social services. For these topics, you would use causal or systems analysis to develop your essay.

Gathering Material

There are many sources of material for expository essays. For subjects you are familiar with, brainstorming about your personal knowledge and experience will often provide enough information. From your own dining, for example, you could write an essay comparing different Vietnamese restaurants in your city.

Sometimes, however, you may have to gather information from other sources. You can conduct interviews (10e), do field research, or consult other print materials.

However you gather material, keep your focus and method of development in mind. They will help you decide what information is relevant to your essay.

Formulating a Thesis

After gathering various bits of information, ask yourself what they add up to. This process of synthesizing your material will lead you to a main idea, a thesis. A good thesis for an expository essay should state an opinion about your subject and give reasons that set the limits of your discussion: why one definition of a controversial term is better than another; how the setting in a short story contributes to the theme; what causes abusive relationships among family members. A statement such as *Obesity has many causes* does neither. In contrast, the following thesis states an opinion and clearly defines the scope of the essay. *Although obesity is a complicated problem, it has three identifiable causes that can be amended: lack of physical activity; an overabundance of cheap, unhealthy food; and inadequate education about nutrition and poverty. Understanding these causes is the first step to a solution.*

10b

Sample
Expository
Essay

Including Other Methods of Development

Write your first draft using only your primary method of development (process, causal analysis, and so on). When you revise, however, you may discover that to explain the meaning of your subject clearly, you need to add definitions of terms (*nutrition*), comparisons (*money budgeted to food in middle-class families and in poor families*). You might create interest by using the methods for sharing personal experience.

Organizing Your Essay

Expository essays written for college and university courses are usually organized with the thesis in the introduction, topic sentences showing how each middle paragraph relates to the thesis, and a restatement and extension of the thesis in the conclusion. This method of organization offers your instructor a well-defined framework and emphasizes what he or she is most interested in—your interpretation.

If you are writing in a different situation or for a different reader, such as a resistant or uninformed one, you may want to consider leading readers through your explanation before stating your thesis in the conclusion, as explained in Chapter 8: Essay Structure.

10b SAMPLE EXPOSITORY ESSAY

Let's consider the choices facing the writer of the sample expository essay "The Effects of Child Poverty." This piece, based on interviews and first-hand observation, was intended for readers of a local newspaper. Since many readers would not have any direct experience of poverty and thus might not understand its grim realities, the writer begins with facts and details that lead gradually to the thesis.

Jimmy is a two-year-old living with his mother and baby sister in government-subsidized housing. The complex is reasonably well maintained if you ignore the rusting shopping carts abandoned here and there, and the mattresses soaking up rain in the disposal bins. Today is a good day at Jimmy's place because there is food in the fridge. A week from now the fridge will be empty and it will be ten days before the child tax credit comes through. It is now about two o'clock and Jimmy has been staring at the soaps for three hours. His mother feels she should turn off the television and take him to the playground, but he outgrew his rain boots a couple of months ago. Not that the playground offers much for him to do: two of the three swings are broken, the slide is gritty, and the sand around it is pebbled with shards of broken beer bottles. The local library has plenty of books for children, but it's five kilometres away and his mother has no money for bus fare. The relief daycare centre is closer and it has other children for him to play with, but his mother is reluctant to take his sister there because she has run out of baby food and does not want anyone to know.

Jimmy's situation helps to define child poverty in Canada. The problem is not just that Jimmy is missing out on the extras. His family fits the federal government's definition of poverty: more than half his mother's monthly income is spent on food, shelter, and clothing. Even so, the children are poorly clothed and fed. Because most poor children in Canada live in single-parent families headed by women, Jimmy's situation is fairly typical. In 1989, the International Year of the Child, the House of Commons unanimously passed a resolution to end child poverty in Canada by the year 2000. Ten years later, according to a report on the progress of Campaign 2000, the number of poor children in Canada had increased by 60 percent (Deanna Shorten, "Children and Poverty," *Our Voice*, May 1999, p. 7). The year 2000 has passed; child poverty remains.

How does poverty affect Jimmy? How does poverty affect all children? How does poverty affect our society?

Let's begin with the basic physical needs for shelter, clothing, and food. Jimmy's need for shelter has been met by the subsidized housing his mother was lucky to get. The reduction in rent does not, however, give her more money to spend on food and clothing. The amount of the subsidy is just subtracted from her welfare cheque. At two, Jimmy doesn't worry about designer labels, but his mother worries about replacing the rain boots and snowsuit he's outgrown. Without appropriate clothing, Jimmy won't be able to attend a play group when he turns three. Jimmy's opportunities are thus limited.

Meanwhile, what happens if Jimmy doesn't get enough to eat? Children between one and three, according to nutritionists, need 4-5 servings of grain products, 4-5 servings of vegetables and fruits, 2 servings of meat or meat alternatives, and 3 servings of milk products every day. Of course, these servings are quite small (half an apple, one third of a cup of dry cereal), but a child needs food from all the food groups every day. Unlike adults, who can cope reasonably well with periodic food shortages, a child deprived of food will be stunted both physically and intellectually. After a week of crackers and bargain macaroni dinners, Jimmy is lethargic, uninterested in his toys, and only too willing to park himself in front of the television. He falls asleep when his mother tries to read to him. He is among the one in three children in Edmonton who, according to the Edmonton Social Planning Council, are malnourished (Shorten, p. 7). At two, going on three, most children can understand complex sentences and repeat simple ones. If they've been read to, they can identify a picture of an elephant or a farm. The effects of Jimmy's nutritional deficiencies show up in his inability to talk in sentences and the limitations in his vocabulary. He can't identify a picture of a horse or pick out a red crayon.

The widening gap between what Jimmy knows and what other children his age know means that he's likely to do poorly in Grade One. Children who are tired, cold, and hungry can't learn much. Schools are increasingly called upon to provide children with a place to sleep, warm clothing, and food. In some schools, teachers spend much of their time trying to meet children's physical needs. Moreover, many children like Jimmy succeed in school only if they get extra instruction. But as schools try to do more with less money, helping some children often means depriving others. In Jimmy's neighbourhood school, funding for a teacher's aide was taken from money originally earmarked for library materials. As a result of the poverty of some children, educational opportunities for all children decline.

The broader effects of poverty are also visible in the current strains on the health care system. For example, inadequate nutrition for expectant mothers often results in low birth-weight babies. Research studies indicate that such babies not only need more hospital care at birth, but may also need more hospital care as adults. In a low birth-weight baby, organs such as the liver may not be fully functioning. The baby with the underdeveloped liver is more likely to need a coronary bypass as a middle-aged adult. Expensive, high-tech procedures that drive up health care costs are thus, in part, the effect of a diet of crackers and macaroni.

The costs of poverty extend far beyond welfare cheques and rent subsidies. Poverty creates a cycle of deprivation, failure, and despair. Children raised in poverty are more likely to become part of a permanent underclass of people who no longer believe they can break out of the poverty cycle. The effects of poverty, however, are not confined to the poor. Limitations in education and health care decrease the quality of life available to all citizens.

10c SPECIAL TYPE OF EXPOSITORY ESSAY: PROCESS ANALYSIS

Probably the most prevalent form of expository writing is the how-to-article. If you browse your local bookstore or your favorite magazine, you will find instructional books and articles on several topics: managing your money or your children, choosing a doctor or a spouse, dealing with anger or the plumbing. Because you probably have skills to teach other people, you too can write how-to articles.

Although how-to articles cover a wide range of subjects, the method of development is basically the same: instructional **process analysis.** In instructional process analysis, you are explaining the steps in a procedure so that the reader can understand and replicate them.

Writing How-To Articles: The Process

Follow these steps:

1. Choose a procedure that you know well and that you can explain in five to ten steps. Making a sandwich is too simple; building a spacecraft is too complex.

2. Decide how much explanation and what level of language is appropriate for your intended audience. If you were telling children how to make cookies, for instance, you might say, "Put the mixing bowl in the refrigerator for an hour. Then take small pieces of dough and form them into balls about half the size of your fist." For experienced cooks, you would say, "Chill the dough and form into balls."

3. Write a short introduction pointing out the benefits of learning the procedure. Include a list of tools or materials required and where to obtain them, if appropriate.

4. Describe the steps for your procedure in the order in which your reader should follow them. Number the steps or use transitional phrases that clearly identify them (*the first step, the next step, the third step*). Explain the purpose or reason for each step. Don't be vague; provide enough detail for the reader to visualize and carry out the process.

5. Anticipate any problems that your reader might have and suggest solutions.

6. Write a short conclusion emphasizing the desirable qualities of the finished product or the benefits of learning the procedure.

10d SAMPLE HOW-TO ARTICLE

Fast Relief for You and Your Dog

Dogs live for the moment; they play roughly, eat anything, and will roll in things that would bring a tear to a skunk's eye. These beloved members of our families will even bring home new-found friends, such as lice. Have no fear: the canine louse is one of the most easily managed parasites that you can encounter. With a proper diagnosis, the careful and repeated use of topical treatments, and a thorough cleaning of your home and dog, you can easily expel these pests from your home.

The first sign that something is wrong with Rover is intense itching and a general feeling of doggie discomfort. Call the veterinarian and make an appointment to get the appropriate diagnosis of your mutt's malaise. The vet will probably inform you that your dog is providing a warm and hairy home to hundreds, perhaps thousands, of little lice. He will tell you not to be so upset, for lice cannot move as fast as mites and they certainly cannot jump like fleas; he will also inform you that lice will not cause any serious ailments and they can only live on their canine host, preferring to remain where they are, sucking, biting, and laying eggs throughout their short lifespan. Then he will tell you to find them. Lice are tiny brownish-red specks attached to the skin, and their eggs are tiny white bits attached to the hair shaft, close to the scalp. If you see them, you must begin dealing with the situation immediately.

Your first step in eliminating the lice is purchasing some commonly used delousing items and getting your tub ready. You will need a three-month topical flea and tick treatment, a flea comb, and a good quality hypoallergenic shampoo. Next, in the bathtub, you should start the delousing process; make sure you have a rubber mat in the tub and several towels around the tub. Then, try to remove as many of the lice as possible, using the flea comb to loosen the lice and eggs from the skin and fur. To wash them off, wet the dog down and then apply shampoo liberally. It is important to get your fingers down to the scalp and rub the skin, for you are trying to detach the lice so that they will be washed down the drain. Do not worry if you cannot get all of the eggs or lice as this process will be ongoing.

Once the dog is bathed and thoroughly dried, carefully apply the topical treatment. It is extremely important to follow the instructions included in the package. You will apply this treatment to five different locations from the base of the tail to the bottom of the neck, making sure to part the fur and apply it to the skin. Don't apply too much in one spot because you do not want it running off the dog. This product will kill almost all of the lice and eggs that did not get washed off in the bath. Do not bathe the dog for at least a week afterward because you do not want to wash the product off the dog. The topical treatment should be applied once a month for three months to ensure complete annihilation of the unwanted guests.

During the next few months, you must clean your house and maintain your dog so that neither is infested again. You must regularly vacuum all floors, carpets, and furniture, paying special attention to the dog's sleeping quarters. It is important to routinely inspect and clean your dog as well to make sure that any remaining eggs have not hatched. From one week after the first application until the second application, you can bathe your dog as much as is necessary. The more you comb and bathe Rover, the more pests you will wash off him. Bathing must be done at home and not at the groomer's unless you would like to share your problem with his other canine friends.

Discovering lice on your dog, then, need not be a stressful experience. Once diagnosed, this problem can be eliminated without too much disruption of your daily routine. Of all the external parasites a dog can pick up, lice are the easiest to get rid of. If lice ever infest your dog, have faith that if you follow the process outlined above, you can turn your walking louse house back into the faithful companion you know and love.

—Erin Zier

10e INTERVIEWS

When you are writing essays, interviews can provide additional information and create interest. Conducting an interview, or a series of interviews, is useful for obtaining information about local people, issues, and events. If you were writing an essay on fetal alcohol syndrome, for instance, you might supplement your reading by speaking to teachers working with children who have FAS. Interviews are also interesting and self-contained pieces of writing that allow readers to enter into another person's world.

Here are some guidelines for conducting a good interview.

Preparing for the Interview

1. ***Choose your informant carefully.*** The most obvious choice is not always the best one. The drummer in a band, for instance, may

have shrewder insights into the band's strengths and weaknesses than the lead singer.

2. **Make a limited list of questions to gather the information you need.** Start the interview with straightforward questions. Alternate key questions with less relevant ones, so that you can finish your notes on important points while your informant answers the next question. Don't ask questions that can be answered with yes or no; ask open-ended questions that invite full responses.

3. **Decide whether to take notes or to record the interview.** Your choice depends on how comfortable you and your informant feel with each method and how you will use the material. If you plan to use only a few direct quotes, taking notes should be sufficient. Tape the session if you want a lengthy first-hand account of the informant's experiences, if you plan to present your material in a question-and-answer format, or if misquoting your informant could cause problems.

4. **When you request an interview, identify yourself and your project.** Explain why the interview is important and how you will use the information. Give the person a sense of what you already know about the subject so that he or she will know how technical to be in response to your questions.

5. **Arrange a convenient time and place for the interview and suggest how long you think the interview will take.**

10e

Interviews

Conducting the Interview

1. Express appreciation for the interview. Then, tell the person again how you will use the information, assuring him or her of the confidentiality of his/her information.

2. Refer to, but don't be confined by, your list of questions.

3. Ask your informant to clarify, expand upon, or give examples of points. Specific details bring interviews to life.

4. If you are taking notes, don't write down everything; jot down facts and opinions, using key words to remember the context. Take down a few direct quotes to capture the informant's personality and view. Review your notes with your informant before leaving.

5. If appropriate, jot down details of the person's appearance, actions, manner of speaking, and the place so that you can include them in your piece.

Writing Up the Interview

You can present interview material in a variety of ways. The question-and-answer format, which works like a dialogue, is effective when you want to probe some questions in detail. The edited transcript, in contrast, allows your informant to tell a story without interruption. Or, you can integrate your interview into an essay combining quotations, paraphrased material, background information, and a character description.

Here are some guidelines for writing up your interview:

1. Use only the material that best suits the purpose of your piece.
2. Combine material from different parts of the interview to fully explain a point. Just make sure that you indicate that you are doing so.
3. Edit direct quotations to eliminate repetition, correct obvious mistakes, and so forth, but do not distort the meaning or tone of the original.
4. If you discover that you need to check facts or fill in missing information, make a list of questions and call your informant. Try to call only once.

After the interview, write a brief letter to the person you interviewed, expressing your thanks. If possible, send the person a courtesy copy of the piece.

10f SAMPLE INTERVIEW

Short excerpts from the interview below were integrated into a research essay on "The Yellow Wallpaper." Before the interview, the student asked the informant to read the story, comment on it, and think about her own experience with postpartum depression.

Q: What did you think of the story?

A: I thought it was terrifying, yet realistic and believable, but mostly I was mad at John for not listening to his wife. I had to put the story down twice because I felt so frustrated for poor Jane. No one would take her seriously, listen to her.

Q: In what ways was your experience similar to Jane's?

A: I remember that after my second baby, I was so down, like the bottom had fallen out of me; I didn't want to do anything. I didn't even want to eat or brush my hair; all the little things were such a task, yet I was supposed to be taking care of this helpless baby. I wasn't up to it. Like Jane, I had mixed feelings about my baby. I wanted to see him, but he also made me nervous, and, I hate to say it, I was worried about hurting him; I could see myself . . . drowning him . . . smothering him . . . I was really, really scared. Jane never says it out loud, but the images of strangled heads must be her wish to strangle her baby. I didn't hallucinate, of course, but I was a little paranoid. I remember thinking that the Atco guy reading the meter was watching me, evaluating me as a mother.

Q: Did you talk to anyone about your feelings?

A: Not immediately . . . I had so much shame and uncertainty. I mean, how can you tell your husband that you can't look at your baby, that you are thinking about killing your own child, your own flesh and blood? And Philip, like John, was hardly home, so busy, and he has always been so rational—he only saw what he wanted to see.

Q: Then, how did you get help?

A: Believe it or not, I saw this special on PPD on TV, and there was this lady, this well-dressed professional, talking about the same feelings and how drugs helped her. She said she was thinking of committing suicide with her baby. Driving off a bridge one Sunday. Can you imagine? She was a CEO! But she looked so together right now—like a different lady. I didn't call my doctor right away, but soon afterwards.

Q: What did the doctor prescribe and how long did it take the drug to work?

A: I took antidepressants, for the first time in my life. It's hard to say how long it took me to feel better, but I remember that a week or so later . . . a cloud was lifted from me; I could think a lot more clearly and those dangerous thoughts went away. It's too bad the narrator of the story didn't get the proper help.

10g SUMMARIES OF NONFICTION BOOKS AND ARTICLES

10g

Summaries of Nonfiction Books and Articles

Summarizing a nonfiction book or an article from a newspaper, magazine, or scholarly journal means briefly explaining the work's content, not analyzing its meaning. Self-contained summaries appear in annotated bibliographies, abstracts accompanying research papers, formal reports, and proposals. You will most likely integrate your summary into a review (12i), position paper (12d), or research paper (13). Follow the steps below when summarizing nonfiction works.

Steps for Summarizing Nonfiction Works

1. Write down complete bibliographical information for the article, chapter, or book, using the appropriate format (MLA, APA, or other) for your audience.

2. Identify the thesis, which is most likely in the introduction or conclusion, and restate it in your own words. If no thesis is stated, formulate one in your own words.

3. Identify the main sections. Look for guideposts: Does the thesis outline the structure of the piece? Do topic sentences or transitions indicate stages in development? Do headings or other typographical devices suggest the main divisions?

4. State the main idea of each section in your own words.

5. Locate and record subpoints and examples for the main idea of each section. Using point form will remind you not to merely paraphrase

every sentence. Include brief quotations when the author's own words seem particularly important. Put quotation marks around any three or more consecutive words and include the page reference.

6. Define all important key terms in your own words and include them in your summary. Pay special attention to words in italics or boldface. Look up unfamiliar words.

Writing the Summary

1. Give complete bibliographical information (author, title, place of publication, publisher, date), either as a heading or in the first sentence of your summary.

2. First, state your summing up and the writer's thesis in a sentence or two. Then, in a few paragraphs, explain the main idea of each section, using enough subpoints and examples to clarify it. Show how these points are connected by emphasizing the writer's purpose or method of development, such as comparison or classification.

3. Keep the material in the same order and proportion as in the original. Do not exaggerate the importance of an interesting point or ignore a confusing one.

4. Use denotative (emotionally neutral) language, and focus on the article or chapter itself rather than your responses to it. Mention the writer frequently to make it clear that you are presenting his or her opinions on the subject, not your own. Remember to use quotation marks and to give page references for all quotations.

5. If you have been asked to include an evaluation of either the content or the style of the original, put your evaluation, clearly indicated as such, in a separate paragraph.

10h SAMPLE SUMMARY OF EXPOSITORY ESSAY

Note: John Intini's essay is in Part 6: Readings.

John Intini's article "Look at Us: Suddenly We're All Celebrities," published in *Maclean's* magazine in November 2006, uses causal analysis and examples to support its thesis: that the "Me Media" generation, which is both a product of technology and an instigator of technological innovations, is both narcissistic and solipsistic.

Intini begins his article with a typical example of what Allison Hearn terms the "Barney generation" (¶3): Michael Tyas, who creates a blog of his daily existence. In subsequent paragraphs, Intini explains how technology allows people to immortalize themselves or transform into celebrities. He mentions a company that makes personal home movies (eDv), websites allowing "users to create their own soap operas by posting messages, pictures and video from their own lives" (¶5), and a video camera that places gamers in the game. Even your genetic code, Intini says, can be transformed into a unique piece of art.

Intini blames technology and media trends for causing and perpetuating this narcissism. Firstly, the digital camera made it easy to take pictures and post them on the web. Secondly, the media, first through reality TV and now through YouTube, has glorified the hyper-personalized and elevated the ordinary.

In the end, Intini points out the effects, some ironic, of people expressing their individuality. Because people are modelling their behaviour after celebrity culture and other bloggers, they end up being more similar than unique. Also, according to cultural studies professor Marc Ouellette, openly sharing actually creates an adolescent solipsism for a whole culture continually preoccupied with "What's in it for me?" (¶11).

Sample
Summary
of Expository
Essay

CHAPTER 11

Expository Writing: Writing about Literature

11a PLOT SUMMARIES

Plot summaries, which condense what happens in novels, films, and similar narratives, are useful when you write reviews (12i) or essays and research papers analyzing narrative works. Most plot summaries are a paragraph or two long, depending on the amount of detail appropriate for your purpose and audience. Follow these steps when writing a plot summary:

1. Analyze the work to determine its main issue: Is it the conflict between good and evil? Or the horrors of war? State this issue in your topic sentence, along with the author or director and title of the work.

2. In the body of the paragraph, describe the plot's main events. Clarify the causal connections among these events by emphasizing why an event occurred and by explaining its effects. If you are summarizing a long or complex work, you might need to classify the events in the main plot and those in the subplot. Present events in the same order as in the original unless you need to modify this order to fit your classification. Include other elements, such as characterization and setting, if necessary to explain the plot.

3. End your summary with the last major event. Your concluding sentence should return to the main point about the work stated in your topic sentence.

11b SAMPLE PLOT SUMMARY OF A NOVEL

We will illustrate these principles with a plot summary of Margaret Atwood's *Oryx and Crake.*

In *Oryx and Crake,* Margaret Atwood creates a disturbing but accurate dystopian world of unethical science, climate change, and environmental devastation. In the beginning of the book, the reader is introduced to Snowman, a vermin-infested sheet-wearing creature huddling in a tree. Through a series of flashbacks, the reader learns the story of Snowman and the world he once inhabited. Snowman, a.k.a. Jimmy, and his academic elite parents once lived in one of the compounds, a gated community run by a biotech corporation. His father worked in eugenics, but his mother, disgusted by her world, left the family to become an environmental terrorist. As an adolescent, Jimmie meets Glenn, a.k.a. Crake, a genius haunted by his father's mysterious death. The two spend their adolescence playing violent video games and exploring their eroded world. After graduating, they go their separate ways—one to a high-end science university and the other to a decaying arts academy—until Crake hires Jimmy to work on the BlyssPluss pill, and Paradice, a project creating model humans. At Paradice, Jimmy meets Oryx, whom he believes is a young girl from a porn site he once viewed. After working at Paradice for some time, Crake disperses the BlyssPluss pill, enacting his plan and leaving Jimmie as guardian of these strange green-eyed beings called the Crakers. At the end of the novel, Snowman is about to encounter some strangers; the reader is left wondering whether he will make human contact, whether the Crakers will continue to evolve, and whether Crake's "utopia" will devolve.

11c ESSAYS ANALYZING LITERATURE

Purpose and Audience

Some students confuse writing a summary with writing a literary analysis when these are definitely separate tasks with different goals. In a summary of a literary text, your main goal is to **synthesize,** or put together, the events of the text in order to describe what happened. In a literary analysis, on the other hand, your purpose is to **analyze,** or take the text apart, in order to describe some aspect of the text's meaning. In a summary, you state the facts; in an analysis essay, you study the significance of textual details to arrive at its possible theme(s).

By reading the text carefully, you develop a sense of its ideas, such as the idea that "choices have consequences" running through the novels of David Adams Richards. Then you analyze the work, or a portion of it, such as a play's scene or a novel's setting, by asking discovery questions. After this analysis, you refine your sense of theme, showing how you arrived at your interpretation.

Because you are writing primarily for an instructor familiar with the work, you may be unsure of how much to say. You don't need to provide all the details you would for someone who has never read the text—you don't need to summarize the plot, but you do need to use quotations and examples as evidence of your claims. These quotations and examples show how you developed your interpretation and allow your reader to engage with your discussion.

Writing about Literature: The Process

When you analyze works of nonfiction, such as essays, research articles, and proposals, you focus more on the validity of their arguments. Contrarily, when you analyze works of imaginative literature—novels, stories, plays, and poems— you concentrate on their aesthetic qualities and moral implications.

You can write a more effective essay on literature by following these steps:

1. ***Decide on a focus and a method of development.***

    Most assignments in introductory literature courses give you a focus, such as explaining how one or more elements—the setting, characterization, or style—relate to the theme of the work as a whole.

The method of development for this type of exposition is **analysis,** the division of something into its parts (your chosen elements) in order to explain the whole (the theme) more clearly. Some instructors might ask you to focus on certain elements, whereas others will let you choose the elements that best contribute to the theme.

In addition to analysis, some topics require **comparison:** *Compare the theme of initiation in stories X and Y.* Other topics will ask you to assess the strengths and weaknesses of a work: *Which film version of* Hamlet *better interprets Hamlet's difficulties in avenging his father's death?* For this topic, in addition to analysis and comparison, you would also use **persuasion** (see Chapter 12).

If your topic is more general, such as *Discuss three poems by Margaret Atwood,* you will have to brainstorm first to narrow your topic. By doing so, you will decide which poems to discuss based on what elements they have in common.

2. *Analyze the relevant element(s) or section(s) of the work.*

Using the discovery questions for imaginative literature in the next section, take notes on each of the literary elements to determine which ones you will use in your analysis. If you are writing a compare/contrast essay on two literary works, divide your page into two columns, systematically taking notes on each element as you proceed. By doing so, you can easily see which elements can best be compared/contrasted in your essay.

3. *Formulate a thesis.*

The thesis should make a point about the theme of the work and how each element contributes to that theme. Be sure that you have not merely restated the essay topic (*This essay will analyze the use of landscape in a poem by Margaret Atwood*) or made a vague generalization (*Many poets use landscape to express their moods*). To direct your reader to the relevance of the use of landscape, you would need a thesis such as this one: *In Margaret Atwood's poem "Journey to the Interior," landscape mirrors the struggle against depression.*

4. *Organize your essay.*

In your introduction, give the authors and titles of the works you plan to discuss and establish your essay's **focus.** *Put your thesis at the end of your introduction.* In the body of your essay, keep your reader's attention on your subject by beginning each paragraph with a topic sentence identifying one aspect of your subject. If you were writing an essay on the symbolism in William Faulkner's "A Rose for Emily," each sentence might state the significance of one symbol.

The Grierson mansion symbolizes how Miss Emily is caught between the past and the present.

Miss Emily's parlour represents her mental decay and her continued subservience to her father.

Being trapped in time is revealed by Miss Emily's physical description.

Miss Emily attempts to preserve Homer while satisfying her father.

These topic sentences all address symbols, but their different structures give the essay variety. In these paragraphs, you would give reasons, details, examples, and quotations to support each interpretative point, making sure to clearly link the point to the supporting evidence. For instance, you would discuss how certain features of the house reveal how Emily is caught between the two time periods.

Sample Literary Analysis Paragraph

Dramatic irony is used in Kate Chopin's "A Story of an Hour" to demonstrate the secret longings behind the façade of the content nineteenth century wife.[1] After she is told of her husband's death, Mrs. Mallard retires to her bedroom. Although her friends believe she is mourning her husband's death, the reader sees her sitting in her room feeling the first hints of joy.[2] The reader spies on Louise as she sees[3] "in the open square before her house the tops of trees that were all aquiver with the new spring life. The delicious breath of rain was in the air" (66). The irony in this moment is obvious. Instead of feeling the despair and loss that society expects, Louise feels hope and bliss because she is now not a widow who has lost her husband but a woman who, like the reawakening trees, is reborn and "aquiver" with passion, life, and freedom.[4] Though she acts, just as she has always acted, like the dutiful mourning wife, newly widowed Louise reveals her passion, relief, and joy to both herself and to the readers.[5]

In your conclusion, restate your thesis and summarize your important points. If appropriate, suggest a broader context into which your interpretation fits.

DISCOVERY QUESTIONS: IMAGINATIVE LITERATURE

Subject What is this work about?

Genre What kind of work is this (detective story, revenge tragedy, dramatic monologue)? What are the characteristics of this genre?

Setting What is the time, place, and social environment in which the work is set? (Alice Munro's *Lives of Girls and Women* is set among the working poor in rural Ontario in the late 1940s and 1950s.) What effect does the setting have on characters' lives?

---

[1] This is the topic sentence.
[2] This sentence summarizes an event from the text and contextualizes a quote.
[3] Notice how the quote is grammatically integrated into the sentence and how the parenthetical citation, in MLA format, follows the quote but precedes the period.
[4] These two sentences elaborate on the significance of the quote and connect the quote to the main idea in the topic sentence.
[5] This sentence brings the paragraph to a temporary close.

What values are associated with different times, places, or social environments? In drama and film, what do costumes, lighting, sets, and music contribute to the setting?

Structure How is the work put together?

Narrative/Dramatic Structure: What sets the plot in motion? What are the main events? Does the plot reach a crisis? How are the events arranged (chronologically, from present to past, from main plot to subplots)? What is the underlying issue or purpose that connects the events (a spiritual quest, a critique of society, a revelation of the main character's true nature)?

Poetic Structure: How are the thoughts and feelings organized? Why does the poem begin and end as it does? Does the structure follow the conventions of a particular kind of poem (an Italian sonnet, for example)?

Characterization What are the characters like? Is there a broad range of characters? How would you classify them? Are the characters given depth and complexity (are they developed?) or are they stereotypes? Are the characters symbolic? What techniques are used to portray them (appearance, characteristic actions, speech, opinions of others, self-revelation)? Do characters change? What do we learn about the workings of race, class, gender, or other factors from the way characters live their lives? What do their names reveal about them?

Point of View Whose eyes do we see through? Whose voice do we hear? In stories and novels, this voice is referred to as the narrator. Because you cannot be sure that the voice you hear in a poem is the poet's, it is customary to use the term *speaker* when you refer to the point of view in a poem.

Is the narrator (stories, novels) or the speaker (poetry) a participant, referring to himself or herself as "I"? How reliable is this narrator or speaker? Does he/she seem to be telling the whole truth?

Is the narrator or speaker a non-participant, referring to the characters as *he, she,* or *they*? Is the narrator/speaker omniscient, seeing into the minds of all the characters? Does the narrator/speaker comment directly on the characters or the action?

Style (Diction and Sentence Structure) What are the effects of language level (formal, standard, informal) and word choice? Are there any unusual or especially effective words? Is slang used? Specialized language? In poetry, what effects are achieved through the sounds of words? How does word choice contribute to the characterization, setting, and theme? What are the effects of sentence patterns? Does the writer favour long, complex sentences or short, simple ones? Are sentence fragments used to create emphasis, excitement, informality? Is parallelism used distinctively? In poetry, how are lines and stanzas used? In films and plays, what are the effects of the pacing of dialogue and action? How does language contribute to characterization, setting, and theme?

Style (Imagery and Symbolism) Does the writer use any significant figures of speech (similes, metaphors, personification)? Do images and symbols create patterns of meaning? How do imagery and symbolism contribute to the characterization, setting, and theme?

Theme What is the central idea of the work?

Sample Essay Analyzing Literature: Essay on Poetry

Integrating Secondary Sources

If you wish to integrate other critics' interpretations into your essay, you will find help in Integrating Research Material (13h) and in the sample literary research paper. For information on citing your sources, see Appendices B and C.

11d SAMPLE ESSAY ANALYZING LITERATURE: ESSAY ON POETRY

The following sample essay demonstrates how you can analyze a piece of writing to explain its theme. Here is the poem the essay analyzes:

Warren Pryor

When every pencil meant a sacrifice
his parents boarded him in town
slaving to free him from the stony fields
the meager acreage that bore them down.

They blushed with pride when, at his graduation,
they watched him picking up the slender scroll,
his passport from the years of brutal toil
and lonely patience in a barren hole.

When he went in the Bank their cups ran over.
They marvelled how he wore a milk-white shirt
work days and jeans on Sundays. He was saved
from their thistle-strewn farm and its red dirt.

And he said nothing. Hard and serious
like a young bear inside his teller's cage,
his axe-hewn hands upon the paper bills
aching with empty strength and throttled rage.

—*Alden Nowlan*

Wasted Sacrifices in "Warren Pryor"

In his poem "Warren Pryor," Alden Nowlan explores the sad consequences of good intentions. Like most parents, Warren's parents want the best for him. Their vision of a good life for their son, however, is based on what they imagine he wants, not what he really wants. For this reason, their sacrifices create a trap of duty from which Warren cannot escape. Every element in this poem—structure, sound patterns, rhythm, diction, and imagery—reinforces the central irony: children who are forced to fulfill their parents' dreams end up with lives as imprisoning as those their parents dreamed of escaping.

Nowlan develops the contrast between what Warren wants and what his parents want for him through the sequence of events and shift in point of view that create the structure of the poem. The poem begins with Warren's parents painfully scraping together the money for their son to live in town and complete high school. The second stanza is devoted to their enormous pleasure and pride when he graduates and gains "his passport from the years of brutal toil" (l. 7). In the third stanza, when Warren gets a job in a bank, his parents "marvel" that he now wears his good clothes every day but Sunday. The final lines of this stanza, which describe the parents' triumph at rescuing their son from "their thistle-strewn farm," mark the turning point of the poem.

In the fourth stanza, Nowlan abruptly shifts the point of view and at last we see Warren himself: caged, miserable, strangled by his parents' sacrifices. The rigid structure of the poem emphasizes the imprisonment Warren feels as he paces in his teller's cage. Most of the lines have ten syllables. Every stanza has four lines and the same rhyme scheme: abcb. The rhythm of the lines, especially in the first two stanzas, is mostly regular iambic pentameter:

When every pencil meant a sacrifice
his parents boarded him in town

When the point of view shifts in the fourth stanza, so does the rhythm: "And he said nothing" (l. 13). The extra stressed syllables and the dramatic pause within the line give us a vivid sense of Warren's agony.

Both the diction and imagery of "Warren Pryor" emphasize the theme of wasted sacrifices. The words describing the farm—"stony fields," "meager acreage," "barren hole," "thistle-strewn"— make it easy for us to see the hardships his parents have endured. Surely his assistance would have made their lives easier; instead, they "slaved" in "lonely patience" to "free" their son. The allusion to the Twenty-Third Psalm in the comment "their cups ran over" suggests their complete happiness when Warren secures a job in a bank. Indeed, the cup of their contentment spills over the "milk-white shirt" he wears to work.

By comparing Warren to a "young bear," Nowlan suggests that the son is by nature unsuited for the job his parents delight in. The simile stresses his youth, power, wildness. He is both literally in a cage—the barred cubicle bank tellers used to work in—and figuratively imprisoned by his parents' expectations. The idea that Warren is trapped in a bank seems especially apt, for he will spend his life paying for the sacrifices his parents have made for him. The metaphors describing Warren's hands emphasize his sacrifices. His hands are "axe-hewn" (strong and roughly made), suggesting that he is better suited to wielding an axe than handling paper bills. His hands are "aching with empty strength" because, in the irony that concludes the poem, he longs to do exactly the work his parents' sacrifices have kept him from. As he strangles his frustration, he sacrifices his own desires so that his parents can keep their illusions.

Nowlan develops the real sadness of wasted sacrifices through every element of "Warren Pryor." Through the first three stanzas, we share the parents' pleasure in their own accomplishments. The central irony of the poem, of course, is that they have gained their happiness at the expense of their son's. Throughout the poem, Nowlan's skillful diction and imagery emphasize the sad reality of what

11d

Sample Essay
Analyzing
Literature:
Essay on
Poetry

their sacrifices have actually accomplished. While they congratulate themselves on rescuing him, Warren paces within the cage his parents' sacrifices have created for him. In a few short lines, Nowlan vividly captures the all-too-common conflict between parents' expectations and their child's fulfillment.

11e SAMPLE ESSAY ANALYZING LITERATURE: COMPARATIVE ESSAY ON FICTION

The Ties That Bind
by Toni Williams

Both "The Boat" written by Alistair MacLeod and "Snow" by Frederick Philip Grove depict lives of struggle and hardship in the unforgiving and harsh Canadian landscape. In both stories, the land seems to preordain the destiny of one or more characters, both in life as well as in death. In these tales of Canadian lives, MacLeod and Grove employ different points of view, descriptions of setting, and character development to depict the struggle of human beings bound both to the land and to the emotional ties of tradition and culture.

Grove and MacLeod use point of view to demonstrate their main characters' struggle with the harsh environment and the rigid expectations of culture. In "Snow," Grove employs a limited omniscient point of view to describe the setting, characters, and action. Grove only enters the consciousness of one character very briefly when, halfway through the story, the men enter the squalor of a sparsely furnished farmhouse and discover the wife of the missing farmer. She is resolutely awaiting news of her husband's demise. The author provides a glimpse into the emotions of one of the characters, Abe, a stoic, capable neighbour whose thoughts display empathy for the woman: "He would have liked to say a word of comfort, of hope. What was to be said?" (370). This limited insight into the character's thoughts and feelings reflects the settlers' acceptance of their lot in life: Their life is to be hard and there is no use in thinking about it nor talking about it. This approach also focuses the reader on the harshness of the landscape and its menacing personality rather than on the specific identities of the characters.

In "The Boat," MacLeod uses the first person point of view to display the narrator's connection to family and to a mariner's way of life. The narrator, the son of the story, looks back into the past to recall how he displaced himself from the landscape and his father's chosen profession. The "I" reinforces the need for individuality in this world; not all characters should follow the call of the sea. But the "I" of the story also enforces the narrator's feelings of guilt about finishing his education and becoming a fisherman: "And I felt that I had been very small in a little secret place within me and that even the completion of high school was for me a silly shallow selfish dream" (460). The "I" of the narrator is contrasted with the "we" of the family and the "we" of the community of fishermen: "And so we fished through the heat of August and into the cooler days of September" (461) and "we fished on into October when it began to roughen" (461). Through the feelings and observations of the narrator, the reader is able to relate to his struggle between the emotional and cultural ties of his family and his yearning for another identity and another world entirely.

Through the descriptions of setting, the authors demonstrate the connection their respective characters have with their seemingly preordained way of life. The author of "The Boat" uses rich description and attention to detail to describe the family's home, the boat, the people, and the community. The description of the home depicts a lifestyle almost completely centred on a livelihood connected to the sea. In this house, two rooms are focused on: the kitchen, which is the locus of the family and "a buffer zone between the immaculate order of ten other rooms" and the "disruptive chaos of the single room that was my father's" (453). The books of this room are described in great detail: they "covered the bureau," "overburdened the heroic little table," "filled a baffling and unknowable cave," and "spilled from the walls and grew up from the floor" (453). The personification of these books represents how reading and a desire for a life beyond fishing make the father's life bearable. His passion for reading reflects his interior life, his yearning for something other than the role dictated by circumstance of geography. It is also in this room that the father shares with his children his interest in the world beyond the tiny fishing community. "Shortly after my sisters began to read the books, they grew restless and lost interest in darning socks and baking bread . . . " (455), wanting to leave the small fishing community. This room, then, is both the father's sanctuary and a doorway to other possible lives. Despite the mother's constant protests about reading "trash" and her arguments "against what she had discovered but could not understand" (455), the father continues to share the outside world through books and conversation, giving the children permission to break tradition and to follow their own dreams.

Whereas MacLeod develops a cultural setting by describing the family home and by focusing on the thoughts and interactions of his characters, Grove's setting is more minimalist. The narrator is more interested in describing the harsh climate and the environmental challenges of a prairie settler's lifestyle. The narrator describes a beautiful, but menacing land: "Stars without number blazed in the dark-blue sky which presented that brilliant and uncompromising appearance always characterizing, on the northern plains of America, those nights in the dead of winter when the thermometer dips to its lowest levels" (367). Through his limited description and interaction of people in the story and the stark, cold description of the land, Grove paints a picture of a matter-of-fact, unquestioning people, struggling to survive in an unrelenting battle against the elements. Although MacLeod vividly describes the home of the family in his story, Grove pays little attention to the details of the two homes in "Snow"; the houses are not seen as homes but as shelters. How they are decorated is inconsequential to people who live in this spare, limited environment and who are at the mercy of the land. Grove's detailed description of the harsh climate and the daunting landscape create a sense that the land is bigger than the people and, as such, in control of their fate.

Grove and MacLeod approach character development quite differently as they portray the struggle of human beings against the environment and the expectations of tradition and culture. Grove's sparse character descriptions reinforce the harshness of the prairie landscape and the isolation of the settlers. The characters in "Snow" also interact very little, again demonstrating their seclusion and, perhaps, stoicism. The author also uses labels such as "the newcomer" (368) and "the home owner" (367) to describe the men in the story; they are not people so much as they are types. Their

11e

Sample Essay Analyzing Literature: Comparative Essay on Fiction lives and fates have been played out before. Likewise, the narrator does not give the young woman in the story a name, nor does he describe her children. Character development in this story comes not through illustrations of the people themselves, but rather through the language used to capture the rugged and hazardous landscape they inhabit—the most important character and the most daunting antagonist. The reader gets a sense of a resolute people, determined to relinquish their selfishness and even their identities to thrive in a harsh and unforgiving land.

MacLeod, on the other hand, provides rich detail when describing the characters in "The Boat," especially the attributes of the narrator's father. Much attention is paid to describing his appearance, his interests, and his interactions with others, therein portraying his attitude towards the maritime way of life. The reader easily realizes that the man has never really accepted his lot in life and probably shouldn't be at sea. "My father did not tan—he never tanned—because of his reddish complexion, the salt water irritated his skin as it had for sixty years" (460). And in that summer, the narrator realizes that "perhaps my father had never been intended for a fisherman either physically or mentally" (460). The father's inability to tolerate the salt water and his body's unending reaction to and rejection of the elements display his resistance to the lifestyle forced upon him. In the end, the father succumbs to the ravages of the sea, as does Grove's Redcliffe, the missing man, to the prairie snowstorm.

Whereas both stories focus on human beings' indelible ties to the land and to culture, they illustrate these ties by describing very different landscapes and by employing different points of view and character development. The narrator of "The Boat" leaves his home to pursue his academic interests, forever haunted by the expectations of his mother and the undeniable pull of the mariner's lifestyle. Though many of the characters in "The Boat" leave their home community, in "Snow," they seem resolved to (perhaps foolishly) stay on and continue to struggle against the land. This sentiment is evident in the comment made by Redcliffe's mother-in-law, who, upon realizing that the death of her son-in-law means that they will lose their farm, replies, "God's will be done!" (373). Her statement exemplifies the acknowledgement of a fate ordained not by choice, but by nature, tradition, culture, and God, forces still haunting the lives of Canadian farmers and fishermen.

CHAPTER 12

Persuasive Essays

12a PERSUADING YOUR AUDIENCE

In any form of persuasive writing, your purpose is to change or reinforce your readers' opinions and, in some cases, encourage those readers to act. Persuasion rests on three principal kinds of appeals to readers: logical, ethical, and emotional.

Logical appeals are the reasons and evidence to support your position. Through logical appeals, you demonstrate your ability to think critically about an issue, to evaluate other points of view, to see connections between general principles and particular facts. **Ethical appeals** are the direct and indirect ways you connect to your reader's ethics. You build a bridge to your reader by grounding your arguments in your reader's beliefs, appearing fair, and considering counterarguments. **Emotional appeals** are the direct and indirect ways you engage readers' feelings, usually through language. You create emotional appeals by considering the denotations and connotations of words, using sharp anecdotes, images, and analogies, and using forceful language. Although it is sometimes difficult to distinguish these three appeals, they are all part of a successful persuasive argument.

Consider the passage below. What appeals are most obvious?

Our oceans are in serious crisis. It is tragic that we know more about Mars than we know about deep ocean life, yet we are destroying the ocean floor with pollution and seabed trawling. "Dead zones" of life-lessness, fishing stocks decimated, whales hunted to extinction: is this the future of our oceans? Not if we act now. They are our oceans and it is our choice. We must save our seas.

This passage, through its use of highly charged negative words ("crisis," "tragic," "destroying," "lifelessness," "dead," "decimated," "extinction") and its imagery of the devastation of our oceans, is obviously appealing to the readers' emotions. Yet it also uses the second person ("we," "our," "us") several times to build a bridge to the reader. Just as *we* have created this problem, *we* must find a solution. For this proposal to be successful, however, it would have to incorporate some concrete facts about the problem as well as solutions to it.

To choose an effective combination of appeals for a particular piece, you must decide whether you are addressing a friendly, hostile, or neutral audience.

A friendly audience shares your basic concerns but needs to be roused to action or renewed commitment. A parent speaking to community league members about building a new playground would be addressing a friendly audience, who, though receptive to the idea, needs to be convinced of its practicality. For reviews, letters to the editor, or opinion pieces on noncontroversial topics, you can usually assume a friendly audience.

At the other extreme is the hostile audience, actively opposed to your position. An employer trying to persuade workers to accept cutbacks in wages would face such an audience. For a hostile audience, you need to consider using all three appeals. Workers, for example, might be more willing to accept lower wages from an employer who argued that "we're all in this together" (ethical appeal) than from one who seemed overly logical and unconcerned about their welfare. When you write essays on controversial subjects, such as abortion and euthanasia, you will need to take special care not to alienate readers hostile to your position. Your goal is to win over a hostile audience, transforming it into a neutral or even friendly audience.

Most of the essays you write for courses are directed to neutral readers who expect a carefully reasoned argument without too many emotional appeals. These readers will pay more attention to persuasive pieces that do not take extreme positions, that consider the merits of different points of view, that present extensive evidence to support their position, and that contain few logical flaws (see 12d).

Organizing Persuasive Essays

How you arrange the parts of your essay will be determined by what your readers need to know and what you think they will find most convincing.

If you expect strong opposition, either because you are writing for a hostile audience or taking an unpopular stand on a controversial issue, you may want to anticipate your readers' objections by discussing the merits and drawbacks of the counterarguments first before presenting your thesis and the arguments supporting it. When you reach your conclusion, your opponents may be more willing to acknowledge your position than they would have been if you had abruptly stated your thesis in your introduction.

This type of organization also works well for a friendly but perhaps complacent audience. To encourage readers to think more carefully about a position they may take for granted, you might begin with arguments upon which there is widespread agreement, such as the problem with the GST, and then raise the question of whether the situation is really as simplistic or as satisfactory as it appears. You might begin by arguing that the GST is not perfect and that there are valid arguments for eliminating it, but that removing this tax could cause several negative effects.

When you are writing for a neutral audience, state your position up front. Your readers will appreciate a clearly defined thesis in your introduction, topic sentences indicating the stages of your argument, substantial paragraphs showing clear reasoning and supporting evidence, and a conclusion summarizing and extending your argument.

Here you will find some basic guidelines for four types of persuasive writing: opinion pieces, position papers, letters to the editor, and reviews.

12b OPINION PIECES

Using your own knowledge and experience, you can write opinion pieces: short persuasive essays about topical issues. Columnists such as Heather Mallick, Allan Fotheringham, and Margaret Wente write opinion pieces for newspapers and magazines.

Many opinion pieces often begin with a personal anecdote and then employ the strategy of giving reasons with examples as supporting evidence (see 6a). The opinion piece below follows this pattern. Notice that the writer gives only partial reasons for not buying a new car, leading up to a complete statement of his thesis in the final paragraph.

12c

Sample
Opinion Piece

12c SAMPLE OPINION PIECE

Why I Won't Buy a New Car
by Peter Banks

The third time my car broke down within a year, my friend Rebecca teased me, "Why don't you just buy a new one?" This advice was coming from someone whose parents gave her a Miata convertible for her sixteenth birthday. The carefree way she suggested I "just buy a new one" echoed through my mind for quite some time. I began to realize that in our throwaway society, many people are all too willing to "just buy a new one" regardless of any future consequences. However, an object that is more technologically advanced is not necessarily superior.

Many North Americans are deceived by the notion that acquiring the latest inventions will somehow bring them happiness. Although many new objects can bring enjoyment, they do not make the consumer any better as a person. The media prey on society's search for material happiness. Automobiles are often portrayed as the means to achieve power, success, inner peace, and popularity. They are often shown as the instant ticket to becoming a sex symbol. The one thing that advertisements seem to neglect is that these fancy machines are just that— fancy machines. The driver of a red Lamborghini would still be the same person if he or she were behind the wheel of a rusty brown station wagon. However, the media continue to portray the acquisition of material possessions as the avenue through which goals such as peace, good work, family stability, and personal happiness can be achieved. Mini-van commercials are loaded with images of loving families enjoying quality time together. Sports car advertisements attempt to associate driving that particular car with popularity and sexual attractiveness.

While consumers are racing to keep up with the latest in technology, many valuable resources are needlessly wasted. Thousands of auto wrecking yards across North America are filled with vehicles left to rust into an ecological nightmare. Although some are eventually crushed and recycled for future use, these instances do not occur as often as they could. Many of the mechanical components left in these automobiles are still in perfect working order.

However, because the majority of modern engines are composed of a tangled web of hoses and computer chips, any working parts from the older cars are completely incompatible. This makes re-using any of the older parts impossible, thereby putting to waste an entirely functional mechanism.

The needlessly complex mechanical designs of new vehicles make it impossible for individuals to take responsibility for even the most basic car maintenance. With consumers wholly dependent upon the dealership's mechanical services, the dealership is free to list exorbitant prices, to which customers must agree. When the alternator of my 1981 Honda Accord wore out, my dad and I simply rebuilt a part from an auto wrecker and replaced it ourselves. The design of the engine compartment left every component easily identifiable and accessible. The entire job took just over an hour and we spent less than eighty dollars on it. The alternator on Rebecca's Miata, however, is buried far beneath the engine block. This particular part, which is prone to wear out with accumulated mileage, is positioned so that when it does have to be replaced, the entire engine must be removed. However, a regular garage will probably not have the necessary equipment to work on this particular vehicle. When her alternator does go, Rebecca will thus have to take her car to the Mazda dealership and pay whatever price is asked.

If I did buy a new car, it probably would not break down as often as the one that I am currently driving. But it might destroy my relationship with my dad. The easiest, most enjoyable times my dad and I spend together are while we work as a team, desperately trying to repair my car. I know that "I love you" has always been a hard thing for him to come out and say. But as I think back, nothing says it louder than the time we spent working in the garage last summer. I was shocked to find him using the old, crooked tool box that I made for him in grade 5. I almost broke into tears when I saw that crooked, unsymmetrical Father's Day present loaded up with tools, while Dad's numerous other boxes, which are much sturdier and more convenient, sat in the basement unused. Buying a new car would end the wonderful times my father and I spend together doing repairs, times that I have grown to cherish.

No, I won't buy a new car. It would cost too much—in the destruction of the environment, the waste of precious resources, the loss of self-reliance, and the loss of human contact.

12d POSITION PAPERS

The purpose of a position paper is to present arguments showing why you agree or disagree with an argument. Writing this kind of essay will help you develop your critical thinking skills, for it requires you to analyze, evaluate, and formulate your own opinion.

Writing Position Papers: The Process

Here are the main steps:

1. *Summarize the piece you are responding to (see Summaries of Nonfiction Books and Articles, 10g).* State the article's subject, thesis, its organization of ideas, and its most important points. Summarizing the article is a useful first step

because it helps you to thoroughly understand the author's ideas. Include a brief version of your summary in your position paper to help your readers understand your response.

2. ***Analyze and evaluate the author's three appeals (see the chart on the next page).*** To analyze the logical appeal and decide your position, whether you agree or disagree with the author's argument, make a list of points you agree with and those you disagree with. Make a list of potential counterarguments and evidence. After evaluating the argument, analyze the emotional and ethical appeals.

3. ***Identify the writer's basis of evaluation (see Evaluating Strengths and Weaknesses, 6b).*** Is the writer's position based on moral, practical, logical, or aesthetic criteria, or a combination of these perspectives?

4. ***Clarify your own basis of evaluation.*** Do the points you agree with reflect your moral position on the subject? Do you doubt the practicality of the author's position?

5. ***Formulate your thesis.*** It should present both your evaluation of the writer's point of view and your own opinion.

6. ***Organize your response to include opposing arguments.*** In persuasive writing, it is wise to address counterarguments, or arguments opposing your position. Doing so demonstrates your credibility and shows you have considered both sides of the issue before arriving at an informed decision. When addressing counterarguments, be considerate yet firm; do not use rude or deprecating language or personal attacks.

One approach is to take up an opposing argument point by point, examining its strengths and weaknesses and pointing out alternatives. You might adopt this method if you wanted to argue directly against a series of proposals contained in a document.

Another way to introduce counterarguments is to briefly summarize other views about your subject and indicate why you agree or disagree before stating your thesis. You might use this method if you wanted to argue that positions X, Y, and Z were all based on self-interest whereas your position is based on the common good. These two methods are examples of an evaluative or "pro-con" structure—an organization based on arguments for (*pro*) and arguments against (*con*) your position.

Consider the way that the writer contends with counterarguments in this position paper arguing against the negative effects of TV violence:

There is no denying that television has an effect on its viewers, and that television, thanks to shows like *CSI* and *Criminal Minds,* is far more violent today than it was even twenty-five years ago, when the most violent shows on television were the relatively tame *Hill Street Blues* and *Miami Vice.* Accompanying these contemporary programs are videos, video games, and even the nightly news, which all contain smatterings of violence. The media is definitely becoming increasingly violent.

However, there is also no denying that for as long as television has been around, society has scapegoated it, blaming it for society's behaviour. And before television, other forms of media were censored, such as the radio. Blaming the media not only oversimplifies the extremely complicated problem of violent behaviour, but also misleads the public. The causal relationship between violent media and violent behaviour, as this essay will show, is very suspect.

Evaluating Logical, Ethical, and Emotional Appeals

Logical Appeals First, evaluate the evidence.

- Do all the points support the thesis?
- Are key terms defined (5c)?
- Do comparisons proceed from a common basis (5b)?
- Are examples used appropriately (6a)?
- Is there enough evidence to support the points made?
- Are facts and figures accurate, up to date, and taken from reliable and identified sources? Are they used appropriately? (That is, if you are arguing about child obesity in Canada, using American statistics is inappropriate.)

Next, look for logical fallacies.

Logical fallacies, which are flaws in reasoning leading to illogical claims, are either unintentional or intentional; that is, they are caused by either errors in the writer's reasoning process or by the writer's attempt to manipulate readers. You can test the validity of the author's reasoning and evidence by searching for these logical fallacies. (This list is by no means extensive. If you would like to learn more about logical fallacies, or know the formal Latin terms for the fallacies below, consult the web.)

- Does the author assume the truth of a point that actually needs to be argued?
- Does the author intentionally omit points that could weaken the argument?
- Does the author jump to conclusions based on too little evidence?
- Does the author make generalizations about a group of people (stereotyping)?
- Does the author make sweeping generalizations that are difficult to prove or disprove?
- Does the author oversimplify an issue by reducing it to two extreme alternatives (either/or fallacy)?
- Does the author claim that two things are alike when they are more different than similar (misplaced analogy)?
- Does the author make faulty causal connections? Watch for these problems with causal reasoning: (1) claiming that what is true in some instances is true in all instances; (2) claiming that something happening after an event was caused by it; (3) claiming a single cause or effect of something that may have multiple causes or effects; (4) claiming unlikely or exaggerated predicted effects; and (5) claiming that one event will cause a domino effect or a series of uncontrollable consequences (slippery-slope reasoning)?

- Does the author sidetrack the reader by bringing up unrelated matters that distract the audience (red herring)?
- Does the author cite authorities cited within their field of expertise? Or are the authors cited not experts (argumentum vericundiam)?
- Does the author trivialize or distort opposing points of view?
- Does the author attack the person making the argument instead of the argument (ad hominem argument)?

Ethical Appeals These questions help you define the author's values and attitudes.

- Does the author appeal to values he or she assumes readers share (such as patriotism, family values, concern for the environment)? Sometimes the author will appeal to these values if he or she assumes a friendly audience or if he or she is trying to convert a hostile audience.
- Does the author establish a relationship with the reader through direct comments, choice of personal pronouns (I, we), or emotional appeals (12a)? Is this relationship friendly? hostile? Does the author sound like an expert?
- Does the author present a balanced perspective? Address counterarguments?
- Does the author use evidence responsibly?
- Does the author make personal attacks on those who hold different opinions or appeal to readers' prejudices against certain groups?

Emotional Appeals

- What attitude toward the subject (such as anger, concern, sadness) does the writer convey through choices in diction, sentence structure, and other stylistic devices? What uses, if any, does the writer make of humour, wit, irony?
- Does the writer use appropriate emotional appeals for the audience?
- How does the author's personality, as reflected in the piece, affect your response?
- Does the writer use too much slanted or emotional language? (Keep in mind that emotional appeals, when they *substitute for* or *warp logic*, are a logical flaw.)

12e SAMPLE EVALUATION OF AN ARTICLE

Let's work through these steps for a position paper responding to Paul Sullivan's article.

A $55-Million Ride—Worth Every Cent
by Paul Sullivan

The leaders in my city are about to spend $55 million on a bobsled run.

My city, of course, is Vancouver, as of last week, host of the 2010 Winter Olympics. And by the time the last national anthem has been played, some time in February, 2010, we'll have spent $4.5 billion—never mind $55 million—to make the whole thing happen.

But, in the bewildering swirl of words and emotions stirred up in the wake of the news that the Olympics are really coming to Vancouver, I can't stop thinking about the bobsled run.

Actually, it's called the Whistler Sliding Centre and when it's finished in 2007, it will accommodate not only bobsled races, but luge and skeleton races as well. What are luge and skeleton races, you ask? As far as I can tell, in skeleton, you go downhill really fast on a sled. In luge, you go downhill really fast on a sled, on your back. It's not the sort of thing that appeals to most rational people, so it doesn't get a lot of coverage in the sports pages. You may not know, for instance, that the current world bobsled champion is a Canadian, Pierre Lueders, of Edmonton.

Canada already has one world-class sliding facility in Calgary, a legacy of the 1988 Winter Olympics. So, you ask again, we need another one for $55 million?

Right now, there's a tent city in Victory Square, in the heart of the city's Downtown Eastside, where people are asking themselves that question.

The protesters aren't exactly sure why they're protesting or who their targets are, but they're poor and inarticulate, unlike the Vancouver Olympic bid committee members, who are rich and smooth and much better at getting what they want. The tenters want more social housing, welfare, free jobs, that sort of thing, and they're going to stay there, at least until the city's leaders have slept off their Olympic champagne hangover, and figure out what to do about it. At some point, perhaps Councillor Jim Green, who was a high-profile advocate of social housing and jobs for the poor before he went to city hall, may even explain to these folks why it's a good idea to spend $55 million on a sliding centre. That money could buy a lot of social housing. I'd like to be there for that one.

So what if we're already in the red? The provincial deficit is forecast to be $3.2 billion at the end of the fiscal year in March, but that's less than the original $4.4 billion estimate. And if these guys figure spending $55 million to bring the skeleton races to Vancouver is a good idea, who are we to argue?

Of course, I suspect you could divide $4.5 billion in Olympic funds evenly among the city's drug addicts and wipe out the problem overnight. (Let's see. Divide $4.5 billion by an estimated 10,000 addicts and you get $45 million each. They could spend a couple of months getting clean at the Betty Ford Center and still have enough left over to buy a condo in Whistler to take in the 2010 sliding events.)

Such a thing will never happen, should never happen. We already have enough drug wealth in this town and, apart from the luxury car dealers and the luxury condo developers, who benefits? Whereas, if you build a $55-million track for the skeleton races, "they" will come.

"They" are the television networks, who will beam tantalizing images of Vancouver to the tourists and conventioneers of the world. "They" are the people who will bring dollars to invest in the B.C. economy and keep the 2010 benefit alive long after the Games have moved on. "They" are us, the people of Vancouver and Whistler, who will have to work together to stage the biggest sports event on earth. For the first time since Expo 86, we have a common purpose. Even if right now we don't know skeleton from slalom, by 2010, we're going to be experts.

That, after all, is the point of laying out $55 million for the Whistler Sliding Centre. Today, despite the natural splendour that sold the International Olympic Committee, Vancouver is a mess, a chaotic patchwork of two dozen municipalities and as many nationalities and cultures. We all seem to want different things. Now, we have an opportunity to come together.

Granted, that opportunity means saying yes to the skeleton races and keeping a straight face long enough to sell this marvellous nonsense to the world.

But if we can do that together, we can do anything. Even, one day, do something really marvellous and solve the intractable poverty and misery of the Downtown Eastside.

—*The Globe and Mail,*
July 7, 2003, A13

Steps in Preparing Your Position Paper

1. ***Summarize the article you are responding to.***

   For a summary of Sullivan's article, see the Sample Position Paper (12f).

2. ***Analyze and evaluate the author's logical, ethical, and emotional appeals.***

Strengths

- Sullivan indicates his awareness of logical arguments against his position.
- Sullivan's ethical appeals to civic pride and community spirit remind us of the benefits of cooperation.
- Sullivan's humour and irony support his "we're all in this together" attitude.

Weaknesses

- Sullivan trivializes the basic moral question about the use of government resources.
- He also *oversimplifies* the position of protesters by reducing the issue to two alternatives: *either* "we" spend $4.5 billion to host the Olympics *or* we divide the money among Vancouver's drug addicts.
- Sullivan predicts economic and moral benefits for the Greater Vancouver region from the Olympics, but gives no evidence to support his points (assuming a point that needs to be argued).

- Sullivan ignores other practical and moral objections to the Olympics raised by First Nations, environmentalists, and other groups (not considering other arguments).
- He characterizes the tent city protesters as ignorant, inarticulate people who want "free jobs, that sort of thing" and as drug addicts (stereotyping).

3. *Identify the writer's basis of evaluation (see Evaluating Strengths and Weaknesses, 6b).*

Sullivan's argument is based on both practical and moral grounds. He argues that television coverage of the Olympics will have the practical benefits of attracting tourists, conventioneers, and investors. He also argues that working together to host the event will have the moral benefit of encouraging cooperation among the "chaotic patchwork" of municipalities, nationalities, and cultures that make up the Greater Vancouver region.

4. *Clarify the basis of your evaluation.*

I disagree with Sullivan's position on logical, practical, and moral grounds.

5. *Formulate your thesis statement.*

Although Sullivan's piece skillfully uses emotional appeals, his argument has logical, practical, and moral weaknesses. By putting the strengths of the essay in a subordinate clause (*Although . . . appeals*), you are telling the reader that you will mention the strengths but that the main part of the essay will be dedicated to the weaknesses.

6. *Organize your essay to include opposing arguments.*

You could begin by writing a paragraph or two taking up all the arguments against your position or you can address these arguments one by one throughout your essay. You can make the main points in the body of your essay much more obvious with strong topic sentences. In each topic sentence, make a point about some aspect of the writer's logic, evidence, or use of emotional appeals.

12f SAMPLE POSITION PAPER

The 2010 Olympics: Taken for a Ride?

In "A $55-Million Ride—Worth Every Cent," columnist Paul Sullivan justifies, on practical and moral grounds, the $4.5 billion that will be spent to stage the 2010 Vancouver/Whistler Winter Olympics. Television coverage, he argues, will attract tourists, conventioneers, and investors long past the games themselves. More important, hosting the games will bring a unity of purpose to the "chaotic patchwork" of municipalities, nationalities, and cultures that make up Greater Vancouver. Learning to work together, Sullivan maintains, will ultimately allow the region to solve other common problems, including "the intractable poverty and misery of the Downtown Eastside." Although Sullivan's piece skillfully uses emotional appeals, his argument has logical, practical, and moral weaknesses.

One of Sullivan's strengths is his use of emotional appeals, particularly his ability to create a friendly relationship with the reader, a sense that "we're all in this slightly crazy thing together." He creates a strong bond by carrying on a dialogue over the need for the Whistler Sliding Centre, a facility for sports with which readers, like the writer himself, may be unfamiliar: "What are luge and skeleton races, you ask? As far as I can tell. . . ." This tactic allows Sullivan to distance himself both from the "leaders" responsible for this decision and from the protesters in the Downtown Eastside: "The tenters want more social housing, welfare, free jobs, that sort of thing, and they're going to stay there, at least until the city's leaders have slept off their Olympic champagne hangover, and figure out what to do about it." Having joined the writer in poking fun at both sides, the reader then becomes part of "us, the people of Vancouver and Whistler," with an opportunity to share a "common purpose": "Granted, that opportunity means saying yes to the skeleton races and keeping a straight face long enough to sell this marvellous nonsense to the world."

Sullivan's emotional appeal is heightened by other stylistic devices that rein-force community spirit, such as references to "my city," the playing of "the last national anthem," and "the current world bobsled champion" from Edmonton. Most tantalizing of all is Sullivan's assurance that if we learn to cooperate, "we can do anything"—even "solve the intractable poverty and misery of the Downtown Eastside." His article offers freedom from hard choices: we can have the Olympics *and* eradicate social problems.

Such a vision is attractive, but Sullivan offers no evidence to support either the practical or moral benefits of the Olympics. According to a news release by the Canadian Centre for Policy Alternatives, the Winter Olympics are likely to result in a "substantial net cost to British Columbians in the order of $1.2 billion" (par. 2). Figures compiled by the No Games Coalition suggest that this is a reasonable pro-jected loss, given the debts resulting from previous Olympics in Canada: Montreal, 1976—$1 billion over budget; Calgary, 1988—$539 million over budget. The results from Australia are even more sobering. Politicians assured taxpayers that the Games would be self-financing. According to the official report of the Auditor General of New South Wales, however, the Games incurred a $2.3 billion loss (par. 10).

Furthermore, Sullivan weakens his position by trivializing and oversimplifying opposing views. His explanation of what the protesters want is dismissive: they "want more social housing, welfare, free jobs, that sort of thing." He does not mention provincial budget cuts that have severely curtailed programs for the disadvantaged. His suggestion that "you could divide $4.5 billion in Olympic funds evenly among the city's drug addicts and wipe out the problem overnight"—a suggestion he of course rejects—sets up a false dichotomy: *either* we stage the Olympics *or* we turn the money over to drug addicts. This sugges-tion also makes an unfair emotional appeal, for readers may associate the pro-testers with the city's "10,000 addicts." In this instance as in others, Sullivan attacks not the arguments against the Olympics but those who make them. His ad homimen argument characterizes the tent city protesters as not only "poor and inarticulate" but also ignorant: they "aren't exactly sure why they're protesting or who their targets are."

If the tent city protesters are "poor and inarticulate," this is not the case with other groups that objected to Vancouver's Olympic bid. Sullivan does not address the concerns raised by First Nations, environmentalists, local businesses, provincial taxpayers. Nor does he address the basic moral question about the allocation of resources. In the face of a provincial deficit of over $3 billion, it is not enough to shrug one's shoulders and say, " . . . if these guys figure spending $55 million to bring the skeleton races to Vancouver is a good idea, who are we to argue?"

The final cost of the Olympics, as Sullivan says elsewhere, is expected to be $4.5 billion. Some of that cost will be recouped. But if the experience of other host cities is any guide—and what else do we have?—taxpayers will be left with a hefty bill. Without a massive infusion of government funds and government will, no amount of cooperation learned through hosting the games will alleviate the misery of the Downtown Eastside and similar areas. Governments should not provide circuses while people are hungry.

Works Cited

Canadian Centre for Policy Alternatives. "Olympics Cannot Be Justified on Economic Grounds." *Creative Resistance* 14 Feb. 2003. 18P. 10 Nov. 2003 <http://www.creativeresistance.ca/awareness01/2003-feb14-olympics-cannot-be-justified-on-economic-groupds-ccpa.htm>.

No Games 2010 Coalition. "Do the Olympics Generate Money for the Economy?" *Creative Resistance* 14 February 2002. 50P. 10 Nov. 2003 <http://www.creativeresistance.ca/awareness01/2002-dec02-do-the-olympics-generate-money-for-the-economy-no-games-coalition.htm>.

Sullivan, Paul. "A $55-Million Ride—Worth Every Cent." *The Globe and Mail* 7 July 2003: A13.

12g LETTERS TO THE EDITOR

Most letters to the editor are intended to persuade readers that something is good or bad: the premier is doing a good job or a lousy job, park trails should or should not be paved, nurses should or should not have the right to strike. They are generally short, about 250–500 words. Paragraphs within the letter are also short because letters are usually printed in narrow columns. The following guidelines will help you make your point quickly and effectively:

1. *Focus on a particular issue of interest to a number of readers, and, if possible, link that issue to a current situation.* A general plea for world peace, for example, is less likely to hold your readers' attention than an argument against selling arms to warring countries. Identify the issue in your first paragraph.

2. *Explain why the issue concerns you.* Are you writing as a spokesperson for a relief organization? As a pacifist? As a citizen upholding the ideal of Canada as a peacekeeping nation?

3. *Instead of condemning people who hold other views, try to establish common ground with them.* Summarize their

positions accurately, acknowledging their point of view. You might acknowledge a country's need to defend itself but point out that access to more powerful weapons increases the likelihood of bloodshed.

4. ***Briefly state your own position and your reasons for holding it.***

5. ***If possible, suggest a practical action that readers can take.*** They can't ensure world peace, but they can write a letter to an MP.

12h SAMPLE LETTER TO THE EDITOR

In this letter, the writer focuses on the uproar caused by the racist remarks of radio personality Don Imus, who, on April 4, 2007, when having an animated discussion about the Women's NCAA basketball championship, referred to the Rutgers University team as "some rough girls" and "some nappy-headed hos." Though he made public apologies, and he even went on Al Sharpton's radio show on April 9, Don Imus was fired from his CBS job shortly after, on April 12, 2007.

12h

Sample
Letter to
the Editor

Dear Editor and readers,

As a feminist, I am writing in response to the racist remarks of Don Imus and his subsequent firing. Although I was appalled by his racist and sexist remarks, and felt deeply for the Rutgers' basketball team, I was not shocked by them, and I do not think he was treated fairly.

Because Don Imus has made his living with off-colour remarks and with biting insults to celebrities and public figures, I was not surprised by his words. The members of Rutgers' Women's Basketball team ARE stars right now, and, as such stars, they are fair game to Imus. Secondly, he has previously, though much under the radar, made even worse racial slurs, once referring to Arabs as "ragheads" and media critic Howard Kurtz as a "beanie wearing Jew boy." In his career, he has insulted the Irish, Italians, Jews, and alienated the entire gay community. What is MOST shocking about this incident is not that he made racist sexist comments about black women but that he was allowed to broadcast such defamatory, hateful language for some thirty years.

Even though I, as a woman of colour, find Imus morally reprehensible and his language disgusting, I do not think he was treated fairly. Why? Because he, as a white man, used these words. Because he, unfortunately, did not invent the word "ho" and is not the one who uses it most frequently. This derogatory epithet to describe women, particularly black women, was invented and is perpetuated by rap music, which has made its reputation and its millions on denigrating and exploiting women. The word "ho" is a word of the black community, and although Imus is reprehensible for appropriating it, perhaps his off-colour comments will turn much needed attention to more powerful racist and sexist cultural forces. No one, black or white, should be able to talk about women this way.

Ellen Holmes

12i REVIEWS

You are probably most familiar with the brief reviews of books, films, television programs, and eating places printed in newspapers and general-interest magazines, such as *Maclean's* and *Time*. These reviews are intended to give casual readers some sense of whether a new movie is worth seeing or a new restaurant is worth visiting.

Longer reviews—often called **review articles** or **review essays**—are designed for readers with some knowledge of the subject. Gamers, for example, might read the reviews of all the new videogames in *Electronic Gaming Monthly*. Academic journals often carry review articles on research in specific areas, such as new treatments for diseases. Because these reviews provide substantial background information and extensive commentary, they are very useful sources for research papers.

We will focus on guidelines for writing brief reviews for a general audience. If you wish to expand your treatment of your subject into a review essay, do so by consulting appropriate sources of information: other reviews, other works by the same person or group, articles relevant to your subject, biographical dictionaries, newspaper files, and so forth.

Follow these guidelines when writing a brief review:

1. *Include identifying information somewhere in your review.* The most essential information (determined by your intended audience and type of publication) usually appears in a separate heading before your review or in your introduction. Here is what you should include:

Book review author, title, publisher, price, type, length, hardcover or paper. As applicable: name of editor, translator, or other contributors; supplementary material provided (such as maps, illustrations, appendix, index); date of publication; edition.

CD-ROM review title, publisher, price, system requirements.

Computer software review product, manufacturer, price, system requirements. As applicable: other products in category, ordering information.

Film review title, director, distributor, type, principal actors. As applicable: date of release; length; suitability rating; other contributors (music, special effects, etc.).

Live performance review as applicable: title, name of person or group, place, date(s), type, price.

Product review manufacturer, model, price, availability, warranty, service record.

Recorded music review title, person or group, type, label, price.

Restaurant review name, address, type of food, business hours, price range, credit cards accepted, availability of alcoholic beverages, decor, service. As applicable: reservation requirement, dress code.

2. *Try for a lively introduction, one that will catch your readers' interest and convey your general opinion of what you are reviewing.*

3. *Give readers a sense of the whole through a brief summary or description.* Don't include so many details that you leave readers with nothing to discover. Never give away surprise effects or the endings of films, plays, or novels. (Remember that a review of a work includes much less plot detail than a summary of a work.)

4. *Using specific examples, discuss what you liked and disliked about what you are reviewing.* Try for a balanced view: even the aspects you like the most may appeal only to certain people. For suggestions about what to consider, see Evaluating Strengths and Weaknesses (6b).

5. *End with a snappy summary of your overall judgment.*

12j SAMPLE REVIEW

Here is a sample movie review, written for a newspaper.

Stranger than Fiction: One Odd but Delightful Movie

After all the hype given to *Borat*, Bond and the summer blockbusters, it was refreshing to see a movie that quietly lived up to its expectations: *Stranger than Fiction*. Starring Will Ferrell as Harold Frick, an unassuming tax fraud investigator who discovers that he may be a fictional character, this charming movie explores the tenuous boundary between reality and fiction. After hearing someone narrating his every move, Harold decides to explore what this voice means, ending up at the office of literature professor Dr. Jules Hilbert, played by quirky Dustin Hoffman. With humorous results, Harold investigates the type of book he is in so he can figure out his ending, eventually meeting up with his nemesis and creator, chain-smoking obsessive-compulsive author Karen Eiffel (Emma Thompson). Harold's charm forces the author to question her genre of tragicomedy as well as her dismal, uneventful life. This movie also features Maggie Gyllenhaal, perfectly cast as Ana Pascal, the tax-evading baker who becomes Frick's love interest. *Stranger than Fiction*, which is indeed a movie stranger than most of the recent fare, is bursting with literary allusions, subtle ironies, and stunning moments. If nothing else, this movie will make you appreciate the written word. Go see it.

CHAPTER 13

Research Papers

A **research paper** is an expository or persuasive essay including facts and opinions from other sources to support your analysis or point of view. As you will see in the two sample research papers (13i and 13j), these sources are usually published books and articles on the subject. Research material, however, can also include interviews, primary research, and other data.

The purpose of a research essay is to examine a subject in greater depth than would be possible using only your own knowledge. In many cases, you may not have any prior knowledge to draw upon. How many of us, without using research material, could write an essay on the introduction of Buddhism into China, for example? Writing research essays, then, is one of the best ways to extend your knowledge of a subject.

13a CHOOSING A TOPIC AND NARROWING YOUR FOCUS

Your first step is to choose a topic. Because you will be working on your research paper for a while, choose a topic that fascinates and provokes a strong response in you.

Having a focused idea before starting to write and research will help you write a better essay. Although instructors can ask pointed questions, many will give you a vague topic to explore, such as the effects of violent media. In this example, you know that you are expected to write an essay that explores causes and/or effects, but you must further narrow your topic by asking pertinent questions:

- On what type of media do I want to focus?
- What effects do I want to consider?
- What particular group do I want to discuss?

Because you have adult friends who enjoy violent video games, and because you are weary of the argument about the negative effects of violent media on children, you decide that in your causal analysis essay, you will concentrate on adults, arguing that violent video games, instead of being dangerous, can actually be beneficial.

13b FORMING YOUR OWN OPINION

A research paper should not be merely a compilation of other people's ideas, however. In the research paper, you want to integrate your secondary sources with your own opinion and knowledge; therefore, you need to have some idea of your own opinion or direction before beginning your research. You can use brainstorming or discovery questions (2a and 2d) to gather some questions to answer in your paper.

For non-literary research papers, sketch out your own opinion first, however undeveloped it seems. You may not know actual facts about violent video game use, but you have some personal experience of them and understand the arguments against them. To clarify or broaden your own thinking, you might first write a short draft.

In research papers that ask you to respond to a text, you need to thoroughly understand the **primary** source(s) before choosing your research or **secondary** sources for the essay. If you are writing a literary research paper, write out a draft containing your answer to the question or your interpretation of the text so that you can easily distinguish your interpretation from those of the secondary sources.

In the world of work, research papers are written by specialists for other specialists. Citations and references allow these readers to evaluate facts and opinions and to follow up possible lines of investigation. As a student writing a research paper, you are learning to act like a specialist in a particular field. As such a specialist, you will present your material differently than you would for a general audience, using a more specialized vocabulary, adopting a slightly more formal tone, and assuming your readers' general familiarity with the subject. Still, a research paper should not sound as though it has been compiled by a committee. The best research papers are those in which the style and tone reflect something of the writer: flashes of wit, clear thinking, depth of knowledge, sudden insights, and a genuine respect for language.

13c A NOTE ON RESEARCH SOURCES

A good place to start researching is your library's reference desk, which offers general reference materials, such as encyclopedias and dictionaries, and more specialized ones, such as *The Guide to Literary Theory and Criticism, The Cambridge Dictionary of Human Biology and Evolution, The Animal Behaviour Desk Reference,* and *The Dictionary of Health Economics and Finance.* Your library probably has an impressive array of such books. Starting in the reference section is especially useful if you need ideas to narrow your search or have to define essential terms.

Using your library's online catalogue, search for **books** by author, title, or subject. Subject searches, which are quite useful, allow you to locate dozens of potentially valuable items in seconds. They can also be frustrating if you have not chosen appropriate search terms or if you fail to limit your search sufficiently.

Your instructor will probably also ask you to find articles from periodicals relevant to your subject. Periodicals are simply magazines and journals printed "periodically." Periodicals are divided into three main types: scholarly, which are written for a specialized discipline, and which usually have an extensive bibliography (*literature* or *medicine,* for example); trade journals, which are written for people in a particular industry or profession; and popular magazines, which are written for a generalized audience, contain lots of pictures, and have no bibliographies. For most academic research essays, scholarly articles are ideal; however, your instructor may also allow articles from other periodicals, particularly if you are writing on a contemporary issue, a controversial subject, or a recently published literary work.

Periodicals, whatever their type, are located by using article indexes. Articles published prior to 1980, which may not have been transferred to electronic databases, will most likely be found in the hard copies of these indexes. Consult a reference librarian for help with using these resources. Also make sure that your instructor permits older sources.

Most of your articles will be found in online periodical indexes, otherwise known as electronic databases. Databases are either general (they carry periodicals from across several disciplines) or subject-based (they focus on one or closely related disciplines). Two valuable general databases are *Expanded Academic ASAP* (book reviews and journal articles in humanities, education, science, and social science) and *MasterFILE Premier* (articles and pamphlets on numerous topics, including business, multiculturalism, and consumer health). These two databases contain the full text of more than a thousand journals and magazines published since January 1990. Other useful general databases are CPIQ (Canadian Periodicals Index Quarterly), Health Reference Center Academic, and ProQuest Science Journals. Some subject databases are Biological and Agricultural Index, CINAHL (Cumulative Index to Nursing), and Communication and Mass Media Complete. For information on searching these databases, see 13d.

Keep in mind that your learning institution chooses which databases to subscribe to based on its budget and its programs, so some of those above may be unavailable. Don't panic, for there *is* a wealth of information out there. Also, don't forget to consult with a librarian about the databases most useful to your research topic.

For topics in most fields, it is wise to use both articles and books. Articles are more specialized, more current, and often easier to find. (In the sciences, research proceeds so rapidly that you may need to rely primarily on articles.) Books, however, provide a broader scope and a fuller treatment of a topic; they may also be harder to obtain.

You may also find material on your topic on the World Wide Web. Be cautious, however, about the authenticity and credibility of information from general websites, listservs, and newsgroups. Familiarize yourself with the most popular suffixes so that you can recognize types of websites: com (businesses), ca (Canada), org (organization), edu (educational institutions in the US), and gov (American governments). For instance, www.utah.gov is the official site for Utah whereas www.canada.gc.ca is the official site for the government of Canada.

Although it is immensely popular, Wikipedia is probably not a source permitted by your instructor. Because Wikipedia employs no fact-checkers and editors, and because anyone with a web browser can contribute to it or edit it, its information can be unreliable. If you are unsure about the reliability of any other web-based sources, check with your instructor. For useful websites created by academics and librarians, see the weblinks at the end of this chapter as well as those suggested by your instructor or approved by your library.

13d THE BASICS OF SEARCHING DATABASES

Electronic databases allow you to search for articles in several ways: by subject, keyword, peer-reviewed, full text, abstract, and so on. Electronic databases can be accessed from the library computer or from the comfort of your own home. To understand how to search in these databases, let us imagine that you are writing a psychology paper in which you are looking for sources on the effects of violent media.

To come up with some viable search terms, do some brainstorming and get your thesaurus out. For media, for instance, you might come up with *movies, videos, video games, games,* and for effects, think of some of the possible ones: *aggression, desensitization, violence, violent behaviour,* for example. Use these search terms for a **keyword search,** which locates the word in many different parts of the record. Keep in mind that most electronic databases are extremely literal about spelling. If you put in *violet media,* instead of *violent media,* you will get no sources returned.

You can narrow your keyword search by looking for only peer-reviewed or full-text articles, depending on your research project. You can also further refine your keyword search by using connectors from Boolean logic, a system of formulating precise questions invented by nineteenth-century mathematician George Boole. The true/false nature of Boolean logic, compatible with the binary logic of digital computers, makes it ideal for searching indexes. Although you don't have to know *all* of Boolean logic, you should be familiar with some basic Boolean operators used to search within databases.

QUOTATION MARKS: Putting these around the phrase tells your computer to keep this phrase as is. Keywords "*violent media*" tell the computer to look for *violent media* together.

AND is the connector that *narrows* your search. Putting AND between your search terms indicates that those terms joined by AND must appear somewhere in the document, in any order and any distance apart. The more words connected by AND, the fewer documents you get. If you type in *violence* AND *media* in Academic Onefile, you will retrieve about 1,300 entries, but if you type in *violence* AND *media* AND *effects,* you will get 130 entries. And if you put in *violence* AND *media* AND *effects* AND *adults,* your list has a mere 3 entries. This connector is very useful when you are searching in or refining a heavily studied topic, such as *Hamlet* or heart disease.

OR is the connector that expands your search; it requires that just *one of the terms* appears in your document. That is, if you put in *violence* OR *media,* you will now get almost 95,000 sources! The OR connector, then, is most useful for small topics in which you want to cast a wide net. You might use the OR connector, for instance, if you are looking up sources on a recently published literary text or contemporary issue.

( ) tell the computer to search for these terms *first.* You must use OR inside the parentheses if there is any other operator being used in the search. For instance, if you put in *violent media* AND *adult* AND (*effects* OR *aggression*), you would get the two first terms somewhere in the document and either *effects* or *aggression.*

Truncation tells the computer to search for forms of word. For instance, *adapt** would bring up *adaptation, adaptations,* and *adaptive* in your entries.

Ask your librarian about other Boolean operators or useful search tools.

If possible, save your sources as pdf files to a memory key or send them to your email account. A pdf file, which looks like a photocopy of the article, preserves the original pagination and is easy to work with. If the article is only available in html format, you can send it as well, but when you cite it, you will have to count the paragraphs and cite it by paragraph number: (Adams ¶4). (In word processing programs, you find the paragraph symbol by pulling down "insert" in the top menu bar and selecting "symbol.")

13e COMPILING A WORKING BIBLIOGRAPHY

Your next step is to compile a **working bibliography** that is at least twice as long as your final list of sources: a list of twelve to sixteen books, articles, and other material on your topic. This should give you six to eight usable references, an adequate number for a research paper in an introductory course. (Students in advanced courses are generally expected to have more sources.) A longer list of references allows you to eliminate unavailable or irrelevant material and ensures that you do not depend too heavily on one or two sources. Also, if your material is too limited, you may get an inaccurate idea of the central issues or find it difficult to develop your own perspective.

There are a few key things to remember when compiling your working bibliography. Prepare it in a computer file so that you can cut and paste once you are ready to do the Works Cited or References page of your essay. For each entry in your list of possible sources, include the call number or electronic address so you can easily retrieve the book or article. Remember that the database entries for your retrieved sources will probably not be cited in APA or MLA format. To get a jump start on your References or Works Cited list, take the time to carefully format your sources at this point.

Compiling a working bibliography is a time-consuming process; don't expect to hammer out a working bibliography the night before the essay is due. You can prevent the panic that may lead to deliberate or unintentional plagiarism by allowing *at least* three weeks to brainstorm, compile a working bibliography, draft, and revise your research paper.

13f TAKING NOTES AND AVOIDING PLAGIARISM

Skim each item in your working bibliography, selecting the six to eight most relevant sources. You are now ready to read these sources and gather material from them. Making careful notes as you read will help you understand the material and figure out how to integrate it with your own ideas on the topic. Put these notes in the same computer file as your working bibliography, preferably immediately after each source.

Taking notes will also help you to avoid **plagiarism**, a serious academic offence that many students commit unintentionally. Plagiarism is the use of others' *words or ideas* without acknowledging the source. Although there is a clear moral difference between intentional and unintentional plagiarism, the consequences are the same: penalties may range from a mark of zero on your paper to expulsion from your college or university.

Intentional plagiarism usually involves

- submitting a paper done wholly or in part by another person
- pasting together passages from one or more sources and using them without quotation marks and without properly acknowledging the source(s)

  Unintentional plagiarism may include

- occasionally failing to use quotation marks to indicate quotations
- paraphrasing or summarizing in a language too close to the original source
- not carefully acknowledging where paraphrases begin or end
- omitting in-text references and/or a References or Works Cited page
- having a discrepancy between the sources used in the essay and those on the References or Works Cited page

Whether you are **quoting**, **summarizing**, or **paraphrasing**, you must acknowledge the source of information and ideas immediately *in the text of your essay* AND *in the list of sources* at the end of your essay.

Quoting

Quote sparingly in your preliminary notes so that you won't be tempted to copy long passages into your essay. Be sure to put quotation marks around any passage of three or more consecutive words taken directly from the source, and record the page (for printed texts) or paragraph number (for unpaginated electronic texts) where the passage can be found in the original, along with the author's name and the title. This information will allow you to keep track of your sources so that you can identify them appropriately in in-text citations and in your list of sources.

Summarizing

You will probably need to condense most of the material in your research sources. Read the passage(s) until you can summarize, in your own words, the essence of the material. Record the author's name, a short version of the title, and page(s) or paragraph number(s).

Paraphrasing

If you have extremely complex, technical, or dry prose, you may prefer to paraphrase it, or put it in your own words. When paraphrasing, be sure to change the original's sentence structure, phrasing, and wording. The passage must be in *your* own style. Record the page(s) or paragraph number(s), the author's name, and date (APA).

Once you have a working bibliography and a full set of notes on the most relevant sources, you can begin the first draft of your research paper. As you write, carefully include author, title, and page or paragraph number for each quotation, summary, and paraphrase. It is better to be overly careful at this stage, for when you revise, you can then check that these references are in the appropriate format.

13g DOCUMENTING SOURCES

In North America, two main styles of documentation are used: MLA style, developed by the Modern Language Association, which is used primarily in the humanities; and APA (American Psychological Association) style, which is used in the social sciences. Determine which style you should use for your research essay; then read through the explanations and samples in appendix B (MLA) or appendix C (APA).

Both styles require **in-text citations,** basic information identifying the source of your research material at the *exact* place you use it in your essay as well as a list of sources at the end of the paper that cross-references the information given in the in-text citations. Failing to include *both* of these references constitutes **plagiarism.**

You need not fear plagiarism if you do your own work and completely and accurately document your sources. Do not attempt to mislead instructors; they are trained to recognize plagiarism. Also, your instructor, who knows your writing style, will immediately suspect dishonesty if you submit someone else's words as your own.

Documenting Quoted Material

When you **quote** three or more words directly from a source, you must enclose these words in quotation marks. However, passages of more than forty words (APA) or four lines of typing (MLA) are indented but not enclosed in quotation marks. Whenever you quote, you must state the author (and, in APA style, the date of publication), and the page or paragraph number locating the quoted passage in your source. For more information on quoting, see Quotation Marks (21f) and Quoting Effectively, Appendix A3.

Imagine, for example, that you were writing a literary research paper entitled "*Tom Sawyer* and *Anne of Green Gables:* Two Models of Heroism." You discovered the following paragraph in James L. Johnson's book *Mark Twain and the Limits of Power* (Knoxville: U of Tennessee, 1982). Here, Johnson argues that because Tom's village is not portrayed realistically, Tom is not changed by his seemingly serious experiences:

> Simply put, St. Petersburg is not a world in which children are easily turned into adults, for such a change requires that the child meet a real world and adjust himself, painfully but with more or less success, to its undesirable circumstances. Much of the idyllic quality of St. Petersburg is attributable to the fact that Twain has excluded from the novel a world in which experience produces consequent changes in character. Tom's world is one in which "adventure" replaces "experience"; his encounters with the alcoholic Muff Potter, the grave-robbing Dr. Robinson, the vengeful Injun Joe—encounters which should ordinarily produce some difference in his perception of the world—leave his character essentially untouched. (51)

If you were not careful to indicate quoted material and its source in your notes, your essay might contain a sentence like the one following.

Undocumented Quotation—Plagiarism

Tom Sawyer's adventures leave his character essentially untouched.

Documented Quotation

Tom Sawyer's adventures, as James L. Johnson argues, "leave his character essentially untouched" (51).

The revised sentence demonstrates one way to show the necessary information. For other examples, see the sample research papers at the end of this chapter.

Documenting Summarized or Paraphrased Material

Because integrating summarized and paraphrased ideas from your research sources is somewhat more complex than quoting directly, you may be tempted to not document. Let's suppose, for example, that you transferred your paraphrase of Johnson's passage from your notes to your essay without acknowledging the source.

> Tom's village, St. Petersburg, is not presented as a real world. A real world turns children into adults by forcing them to adjust to aspects of life they find undesirable. Twain presents St. Petersburg as idyllic (simple and charming) partly by excluding the kinds of experiences that would produce changes in character. In this idyllic world, Tom has adventures, such as his encounters with Muff Potter, Dr. Robinson, and Injun Joe, rather than experiences that would change his character or his perspective of the world.

How would you indicate that these are Johnson's ideas? If you merely added a citation at the end (Johnson 51), it would be unclear whether *all* the ideas in the paragraph were Johnson's, or merely the last point. Some instructors might even consider this faulty documentation to be plagiarism. To avoid this error, you can clearly distinguish your own thinking from the work of others by using a signal phrase to introduce the author's ideas and putting the appropriate citation at the end, as in this example.

Documented Paraphrase

13g

Documenting Sources

> **James L. Johnson argues that** Tom's village, St. Petersburg, is not presented as a real world. A real world turns children into adults by forcing them to adjust to aspects of life they find undesirable. Twain presents St. Petersburg as idyllic (simple and charming) partly by excluding the kinds of experiences that would produce changes in character. In this idyllic world, Tom has adventures, such as his encounters with Muff Potter, Dr. Robinson, and Injun Joe, rather than experiences that would change his character or his way of looking at the world (51).

In most cases, you should not rely so heavily on a single critic; you should rely on your own interpretation and examples from your primary source(s). Even so, this paragraph is an improvement because the reader knows whose ideas are being presented and exactly where the paraphrase begins and ends. If you carefully identify others' facts and opinions, your reader has more confidence that what remains is your own.

For other ways of acknowledging your sources, see Appendices B and C, as well as the examples in the research papers at the end of this chapter.

Creating a List of Sources

As stated earlier, for each source you have cited within the body of your essay, you must provide further information so that a reader can locate the source. This information is compiled in a list of bibliographical entries on a separate page, which follows the end of your paper and which has a page number. There should be an exact match between the sources in the paper and the sources stated in your references list. If there isn't, your instructor might suspect an undocumented source (plagiarism) in the paper.

13h INTEGRATING RESEARCH MATERIAL

In your previous education, you may have written research papers in which you merely collected information on a subject and presented it in an orderly fashion. In postsecondary courses, however, research papers, like other kinds of essays, must have a thesis, a main point that the research material addresses. Your research material should relate to your thesis and your specific points. We will illustrate this process with two examples, one non-literary and one literary.

Non-Literary Example

Sample First Draft

Marleen C. Pugach of the University of Illinois has recommended these selection criteria for prospective Education students: (1) basic skills testing, consisting of entry-level tests in reading, mathematics, and written and oral communication; (2) a minimum grade point average; and (3) a structured interview to assess the applicant's personal qualities (161-63). At universities such as Oregon State and Northern Kentucky, students must successfully complete a two- to five-day full-responsibility teaching experience prior to being accepted into a teacher training program. The number of dropouts increased from approximately 5% to 25% (Edgar 96).

This draft paragraph serves the writer's need to gather information from a variety of sources. However, it does not serve the reader's need to state the significance of this information because the point of the paragraph gets lost among the examples.

Here is the material as it appeared in the student's final draft. With the added topic sentence, sentences explaining the relevance of each example, and a summarizing sentence to connect this material to the thesis, the original paragraph has become two.

Sample Final Draft

If teaching is to be regarded as the important job that it is, pride must first be generated within the profession itself.[1] One way to do this would be to have a more rigorous and effective set of criteria that applicants must meet before they are allowed into the profession.[2] Marleen C. Pugach of the University of Illinois has recommended a set of criteria that would function together to provide "entry-level hurdles to encourage self-selection, to serve as initial points in the process of continuous judgment of student progress, and to assist faculty members in making discriminations between applicants based on multifaceted data" (161). Pugach recommends these selection criteria: (1) basic skills testing, consisting of entry-level tests in reading, mathematics, and written and oral communication; (2) a minimum grade point average; and (3) a structured interview to assess the applicant's personal qualities (161-63).[3]

---

[1] This is the topic sentence.
[2] This is a statement supporting the topic sentence.
[3] These are examples of the criteria.

Another criterion used in universities such as Oregon State and Northern Kentucky is also helpful in selecting suitable candidates.[4] Students must successfully complete a two- to five-day full-responsibility teaching experience prior to being accepted into a teacher training program. The number of dropouts increased from approximately 5% to 25% (Edgar 96).[5] Clearly, such intensive selection policies would attract applicants who seriously wish to pursue teaching, while deterring those who casually drift into teacher education. The sense of personal achievement that would come from gaining entrance to a faculty with such high entrance standards would contribute to a feeling of professionalism among candidates.[6]

—*Carol Murray*

Literary Example

Showing how your own interpretation of a literary text relates to other critics' opinions takes practice. We will look first at a draft paragraph on *The Adventures of Tom Sawyer* written before consulting the critics. Then we will discuss two ways of integrating other interpretations.

Sample Draft Paragraph: Student's Analysis

In *The Adventures of Tom Sawyer,* the adults are not presented as models of behaviour. They are often shown to be acting like children. When Tom tricks Aunt Polly at the beginning of the book, for instance, Aunt Polly has been attempting to trick him. Similarly, Tom shows off at Sunday School when Judge Thatcher visits, but the superintendent and the teachers are also described as "showing off." Even serious events in the adult world seem to parallel Tom's actions. The fight that ends with Injun Joe murdering Dr. Robinson has many of the same elements as Tom's fight with the new boy in town. It is no wonder then that even after his harrowing escape from the cave and his recovery of the treasure, Tom returns to playing at robbers. The adult world is not portrayed as different from the world of childhood, and so there is no reason for Tom to grow up.

Sample Draft Paragraph: Adding Support from Research Material

In this revised paragraph, the material from Johnson that we noted earlier is added to summarize and expand the point of the topic sentence.

The adults in *The Adventures of Tom Sawyer* are not presented as models of behaviour, but simply as older versions of Tom himself . . . [continue with examples from the original draft]. It is no wonder then that even after his harrowing escape from the cave and his recovery of the treasure, Tom returns to the boyhood world of playing at robbers, for the adult world offers no incentives for growing up. James L. Johnson argues that Tom's adventures "leave his character essentially untouched" because "such a change requires that the child meet a real world and adjust himself, painfully but with more or less success, to its undesirable circumstances" (51). But St. Petersburg, as Johnson points out, is an idyllic world, not a real world that would bring about change.

---

[4] Transitional statement that introduces another criterion.
[5] Another example.
[6] Commentary on the relevance of the examples, which connects the examples to the topic sentence.

In outstanding research papers, the writer does more than cite authorities for support: he or she synthesizes material from various sources by showing basic similarities and differences. This synthesis then provides a context for the writer's own interpretation. Note how the writer demonstrates her grasp of the debate about Tom Sawyer's relationship to the adult world in the following paragraph.

What, then, is the relation between Tom and his world? Robert Regan supports the view, originally put forward by Walter Blair, that the narrative strands of the novel "trace Tom's progress from childishness to maturity" (Regan 116). Several critics disagree. They argue that because the adults of St. Petersburg are essentially childish, there is no impetus for Tom to change (Fetterley 300; Johnson 51; Miller 73; Whitley 60). Numerous incidents in the book support this contention . . . [continue with examples from the original draft].

As you can see, crediting your sources, integrating research material, and synthesizing different points of view are not easy tasks, so do not leave them until the last minute.

13i SAMPLE NON-LITERARY RESEARCH PAPER

You will likely write research papers on non-literary topics in biology, psychology, sociology, and associated courses. For such assignments, you may be given a detailed topic specifying a method of development or focus for your essay, or you may simply be given a subject, for which you must find your own focus. If so, review Chapter 2, Gathering Material, for methods of exploring your subject and defining a focus.

When you write on a non-literary topic, your research includes finding facts as well as opinions about your subject. You must clearly indicate the source of these facts as well as the source of opinions from experts in the field, whether you use direct quotations or paraphrases. The following research paper shows how to give in-text citations and bibliographical references using the American Psychological Association (APA) format. For guidelines on APA format, see Appendix C.

13i

Sample
Non-Literary
Research
Paper

Male Involvement in Social Services and
Healthcare Volunteer Programs

by Sharon Cornelius

Volunteerism is the backbone of most communities, and involvement of volunteers of all ages and both genders is critical to the success of many programs. According to social services and healthcare agencies in the Parkland area, however, the number of male volunteers is dwindling and consequently compromising the scope of many volunteer programs. Understanding the trends affecting volunteerism in general, such as personal motivation, demographics, and economic issues, will help such agencies to devise strategies for increasing the potential number of male volunteers.

The local decline in male volunteers reflects a national trend. An analysis of Ontario hospital volunteers conducted by an International Year of the Volunteer Research team determined that women comprise 74% of the hospital volunteer base while men make up 26% (Handy & Srinivasan, 2002, ¶3). The report *Caregiving Volunteers: A Coming Crisis?* further substantiates the imbalance of women (78%) to men (22%) in caregiver volunteering. Male volunteers also start later in life—in their 50s and 60s—and 70% are retired (Phillips, Little, & Goodine, 2002, pp. 2–3). At WestView Health Centre in my own community of Stony Plain, men account for only 13% of the volunteers.

Why do so few men volunteer? In *Recruiting Male Volunteers: A Guide Based on Exploratory Research*, Stephanie T. Blackman discusses social perceptions of male roles as an impediment to volunteering, especially in healthcare programs. Blackman (1998–1999) indicates that one challenge for men is "overcoming the breadwinner syndrome." Although research participants noted that attitudes are changing, they still perceived that men are considered the breadwinners of the family and therefore would not have time to volunteer (1998–1999, Part 1, ¶2). Another challenge, according to Blackman, is that society does not think of men as "nurturers." She reports that research respondents felt women were better "nurturers," and men were more "aggressive," "independent," and "strong" (Part 1, ¶4).

These attitudes are reflected in the types of job assignments volunteers prefer. During an initial interview at the WestView Health Centre, for example, the volunteer coordinator outlines the various jobs new volunteers may choose. Interestingly, 45% of new volunteers prefer to drive clients to and from appointments or to assist with activities or outings in continuing care. These assignments are single events and the volunteer does not need to make a long-term commitment. This fits the lifestyle of the senior volunteers as they can pick and choose the extent of their involvement. The coordinator of volunteers also revealed that visiting clients in their home, playing cards, or going for a walk with a male client is not as appealing as driving clients. Volunteers, especially those under the age of 35, have mentioned feeling uncomfortable in the client's home. They often have difficulty starting and sustaining a conversation with the client. The younger volunteers prefer hands-on activities such as planting flower boxes, cutting wood for crafts, or cleaning out the client's storage areas.

These preferences reflect the ways in which social perceptions of male roles influence potential volunteers. Yet these perceptions may prevent men from volunteering in programs where they have a unique contribution to make. Hospice & Health Services, Inc. vigorously recruits male volunteers, for example, because they can share common life experiences and allow terminally ill men to face their fears without embarrassment (¶6). Luckily for patients in the Parkland area, male hospice volunteers are available at WestView Health Centre to provide this valuable support.

Social service agencies face similar challenges in attracting male volunteers. The Big Brother program across the country recruits men to work one-on-one with young males called Little Brothers, boys between the ages of 6 and 16 who are in need of a friend and a male influence in their life. Big Brothers are in great demand, and often all the requests cannot be met. *The Big Brothers Focus Groups: Final Report*, prepared for Big Brothers of Ontario in 1995, determined two main barriers to volunteering: lack of time and a fear of a close one-on-one relationship (Sage Research, 1995, p. 17). Interviewees worried, for example, that because they live busy lives, they might need to cancel meetings and disappoint the assigned Little Brothers. Others felt they could not make the required one-year commitment. One Big Brother in his 20s suggested that the time commitment be relaxed to five or six months, especially for university students (Sage Research, 1995, p. 20). In a finding consistent with Blackman's research, some men did not think of themselves as "nurturers." Prospective Big Brothers indicated they didn't want to be responsible for the way the Little Brother turns out (Sage Research, 1995, p. 21). Others worried that they might be paired with a "problem kid" (Sage Research, 1995, p. 25). *The Big Brothers Focus Groups: Final Report* noted that "Men with kids are more prone to choose a volunteer role that allows them to be with their own kids—such as Scouts, or sports teams" (Sage Research, 1995, p. 27). These men have a limited amount of time they can give, and if the choice is between helping with their own child's team and being a Big Brother, the former usually wins. All these factors contribute to the continuing dearth of male volunteers.

The perception that men are less nurturing than women, which was reported in both Blackman's study and *The Big Brothers Focus Groups: Final Report*, affects other social services programs. The Parkland Adult Literacy program, for example, does not actively recruit male volunteers. The goal of the program is to increase the literacy skills of students, to a level they have determined, by matching them with a volunteer tutor. Students come from many different walks of life, ethnic backgrounds, and, of course, from both genders. For the past three years, the fifteen volunteer tutors have included only three men. The program coordinator, who matches students with tutors, has discovered that students of both genders prefer a female tutor. This preference suggests that male students, particularly those from male-dominated ethnic groups, do not want to show their reading weakness to another man. The nurturing quality of the female tutors enhances the learning and completion rate of the students.

To increase men's involvement as volunteers in healthcare and social service programs, administrators must review and revamp their message, their methods of advertising, and the recruitment process to appeal to men. Recruiters should be knowledgeable about the current need for additional male volunteers. They should also be able to name the benefits and positive experiences that volunteering brings. Among the reasons people give for volunteering are developing new skills, adding their experience to a résumé, believing in the "cause," meeting new people, filling spare time, and feeling a sense of duty. Many people also want to give back to the community. John, an elderly male healthcare volunteer at the WestView Health Centre, made the following comment: "I volunteer because it will help with the total care of the patients. A member of my family was a patient in the Health Centre, and she received such great care. I want to give back to this facility" (personal communication, April 30, 2003). To attract more male volunteers, recruiters must ensure that their message appeals to men's personal motives for being involved.

Recruiters must also be aware of general trends in volunteering. The *2000 National Survey of Giving, Volunteering and Participating*, conducted by Volunteer

Sample
Non-Literary
Research
Paper

Canada, discovered a number of changes since the 1997 survey. One significant change is that seniors as a group have less time available for volunteering because they travel or have multiple activities. Two groups are replacing seniors as new volunteers: young people who want to gain work-related skills, and new Canadians who want to develop work experience and to practise language skills (Volunteer Canada, 2002, ¶4).

These trends definitely apply to male volunteers in social service and health-care programs. At WestView Health Centre, for example, a man in his early 20s volunteers in Diagnostic Imagery to prepare for his postsecondary education. Volunteering is one of the entrance requirements for the program he will be taking, and his volunteer experience has cemented his desire to pursue this field of work. Another man, also in his early 20s, continues to volunteer in the emergency department while he trains for the police department. The knowledge he gains of its inner workings will assist him when he is on active duty.

Focus groups can also help to ensure that the agency's recruitment message appeals to the men being targeted and addresses their concerns. For example, Big Brothers used research participants of all age groups, current and potential Big Brothers, to create the message. The group agreed unanimously that the message must show the Big Brother's role as "fun" (Sage Research, 1995, pp. 30–31) and include sub-messages about friendship, time commitment, and lack of expense (Sage Research, 1995, pp. 31–33). Other organizations could use the same technique by simply pulling together a focus group to discuss the message.

Advertising is a powerful tool for volunteer agencies to convey their message to the community. Depending on the financial resources of the program, advertising could include television, radio, newspapers, and websites. Each of these outlets has pitfalls to be aware of. Television shows the "faces" of the organization but is very costly. In order to reach the target audience, television and radio spots should be aired during the times that men typically tune in: for example, during a sports game or the news. Free publicity from the local newspaper may depend upon the whims of the editor. To ensure that the complete and correct message gets printed, paid advertising is the best option. The World Wide Web increasingly connects communities; the challenge is to keep all the information current and relevant. In my experience, the best form of advertising is word of mouth. Coordinators could talk to current male volunteers and ask them to encourage a friend to become part of the team.

The interview process should also be reviewed. Because many potential volunteers work full-time, interviews may need to be held in the evenings or on weekends. Recruiters should explain the organization's mission, vision, and beliefs to enable potential volunteers to determine if their beliefs and values match those of the organization. Recruiters should also discuss time commitment, scope, and responsibilities of the various job assignments, keeping in mind the factors that affect male volunteerism.

Finally, if they want to increase the number of male volunteers, healthcare and social service agencies must stress the unique contribution men can make: as stated by Blackman (1998–1999), "One volunteer can create a ripple effect that may influence an organization, a client population, public opinion, and other volunteers" (¶3). Many healthcare and social service volunteer programs, not to mention the patient/client and the community, can benefit from an increased male volunteer base. It is now time for action.

References

Blackman, S. T. (1998–1999). *Recruiting male volunteers: A guide based on exploratory research*. Washington, DC: Corporation for National Service.

Handy, F., & Srinivasan, H. (2002). *IYV Research Program, Ontario hospital volunteers: Who they are and what they do*. Toronto, ON: Canadian Centre for Philanthropy.

Hospice & Health Services, Inc. *Hospice volunteers . . . making each day count . . . bringing light—and love—into people's lives*. Lancaster, Ohio. Retrieved April 27, 2003, from http://www.hhsfc.org/hhsfc.org/ volunteer.htm

Phillips, S., Little, B. R., & Goodine, L. (2002). *Caregiving volunteers: A coming crisis?* Toronto, ON: Canadian Centre for Philanthropy.

Sage Research. (1995). *Big Brother focus groups: Final report*. Mississauga, ON: Sage Research Corporation.

Volunteer Canada. (2002). *Trends in volunteerism*. Retrieved May 6, 2003, from http://www.volunteer.ca/volcan/eng/volincan/ trendsinvol.php

13j SAMPLE LITERARY RESEARCH PAPER

You will notice that this research paper presents a comparative analysis of two novels. Pay close attention to the thesis and to the way each major point announced in the thesis is worked out in the middle paragraphs.

Tom Sawyer and *Anne of Green Gables:* Two Models of Heroism
by Lanette Thornton

13j

Sample
Literary
Research
Paper

When we think of heroic quests, we usually envision a pattern very much like that of Mark Twain's *The Adventures of Tom Sawyer:* the hero engages in a series of adventures through which he proves his worth and is rewarded with riches and the love of a beautiful maiden. In this version of the heroic quest, as is obvious from the way I've described it, the hero is male. L. M. Montgomery's *Anne of Green Gables,* I will argue, presents a female version of the making of the hero. In the mythic pattern of separation, initiation, and reintegration into society, Tom's tests of courage and his rewards are largely external, and neither he nor his world is transformed by them. Anne's tests, on the other hand, are largely internal, and her rewards depend upon her ability to transform both herself and her world.

Tom's separation from his community lies in his flouting of convention. Although one critic has argued that finally "Tom sacrifices freedom to gain community" (Towers 520), the first episode of the book seems to bear out John Whitley's contention that Tom "is never in any danger of expulsion from the community" (64). In this episode, which sets up our expectations for the rest of the novel, Tom escapes punishment for sneaking jam by outwitting his Aunt Polly. Her response—"a gentle laugh" (8)—immediately establishes her as an indulgent parental figure who likes Tom's mischievousness:

> He 'pears to know just how long he can torment me before I get my dander up, and he knows if he can make out to put me off for a minute, or make me laugh, it's all down again, and I can't hit him a lick. I ain't doing my duty by that boy, and that's the Lord's truth, goodness knows. . . . Every time I let him off my conscience does hurt me so; and every time I hit him my old heart 'most breaks. (8)

Furthermore, the "model boy" of the village—Tom's half brother Sid—is presented as dull and self-righteous, always willing to get Tom into trouble by tattling. Whenever we as readers, like Aunt Polly, are ready to condemn Tom's lying, his thoughtlessness, his prankish behaviour, Twain reminds us, usually through Aunt Polly, that Tom is good at heart. And we, like his aunt and the community gathered for his mock funeral (Miller 71–72), forgive him.

Although Leslie Willis dismisses *Anne of Green Gables* as sentimental because Anne "suffers no real hardships" except over her initial reception and Matthew's death at the end of the novel (250), Anne does not have the security in her world that Tom has in his. Tom is at home in St. Petersburg, under the care of a doting, if at times punitive, aunt. But the orphaned Anne has already lost a series of homes. When she reaches Green Gables, she learns that Matthew and Marilla had wanted a boy to help with the farm, not a girl at all. Furthermore, although Marilla soon discovers that Anne is "smart and obedient, willing to work and quick to learn" (57), the girl is also a talkative, imaginative, hot-tempered redhead. Anne, like Tom, is presented as essentially good. But unlike Tom, if Anne is to have the home she so desperately wants, she must learn to control her behaviour.

This control, moreover, must come from her desire to please others rather than from a fear of punishment. When Anne's temper flares up over Mrs. Rachel Lynde's disparaging comments about her looks, for example, Marilla admits that her neighbour "is too outspoken. But," she adds, "that is no excuse for such behaviour on your part. She was a stranger and an elderly person and my visitor—all three very good reasons why you should have been respectful to her" (72). Although at first Anne refuses to apologize to Mrs. Lynde—the punishment Marilla lights upon—Anne eventually does so to please Matthew. As Matthew had immediately recognized, Anne is "one of the sort you can do anything with if you only get her to love you" (52). The threat of expulsion is always present, however, for as Muriel Whitaker points out, Marilla's favourite punishment when Anne has misbehaved is isolation, banishment, ostracism (53).

To secure a place in the community, Anne must learn "the importance of keeping fantasy and reality segregated," as Julie Fenwick points out (61). Tom, on the other hand, learns to translate his imaginary heroism into real heroism. If Tom were a "model boy" like his half brother Sid, he would not fight, play truant from school, sneak out at night, "hook" provisions, and so on. But without these boyish pranks, he would not have the courage and resourcefulness he needs to become a hero. Thus, the ingenuity, self-sufficiency, and leadership Tom demonstrates when he, Joe, and Huck run away to Jackson's Island to become pirates are the same qualities he needs to find a way out when he and Becky become lost in the cave. Similarly, Tom's desire to act on his book-knowledge of buried treasure and the ways of robbers leads him and Huck to discover the whereabouts of Injun Joe and his treasure. As a result of these exploits, Tom becomes rich, by his standards, and wins the approval of Becky's father, the imposing Judge Thatcher. As Lyall Powers puts it, "the heroic game becomes impressively the Heroic reality" (321).

Anne's quest, on the other hand, leads her to heroic sacrifice: she gives up her hard-won scholarship to university to stay on the farm and care for Marilla. She is able to make this loving choice because she has learned to consider the rights and welfare of others without sacrificing her own individuality. As she tells Marilla on several occasions, Anne never does "the same naughty thing twice" (102). When her scrapes are her own fault—as in losing her temper with Mrs. Lynde, meddling with Marilla's brooch, and hitting Gilbert Blythe with her slate—Anne takes her punishment and mends her ways. But when her scrapes are not entirely her own fault—as when Diana gets drunk on mulberry wine or Anne puts liniment in the cake instead of vanilla—Anne also learns valuable lessons, for the willingness of Marilla and other adults to admit their own failings makes possible the sense of love and security that turn this initially hostile world into the home Anne so intensely desires. When her romantic views are "sabotaged by `life' in incident after incident," Anne learns to distinguish romance from reality (Ross 46–48).

In the process of learning from her experiences, Anne is both transformed and transforms others (Whitaker 55). She overcomes Matthew's fear of females; awakens Marilla's undeveloped sense of humour; humbles the judgmental Mrs. Barry; sweetens the temper of Diana's crochety Aunt Josephine. By the end of the novel, even Mrs. Rachel Lynde, who is initially presented as the norm of the village, has become less rigid (Rubio 29). Anne is thus presented as a child who can exert some control over her environment by furnishing the "psychological, emotional, and imaginative dimensions which are lacking" in the adults' own lives (Rubio 35). In the process, as Whitaker points out, Anne has come to conform "pretty closely to the adult view of propriety" (52). By the time she reaches seventeen, Anne has become what Marilla wanted: "All I want is that you should behave like other little girls and not make yourself ridiculous" (89). But she has done so because this is what she too wants. Her essential nature, like her imagination, has been tempered by her trials, but not destroyed. This match between desire and fulfillment is possible because the world of Green Gables, like Anne herself, is essentially good. Integration into the community is thus itself the goal of Anne's heroic quest and her reward, earned through experience.

In contrast, neither Tom nor his world is transformed by his adventures. Although Robert Regan supports the view, originally put forward by Walter Blair, that the novel "trace(s) Tom's progress from childishness to maturity" (Regan 116), several critics disagree. They argue that because the adults of St. Petersburg are essentially childish, there is no impetus for Tom to change (Fetterley 300; Johnson 51; Miller 73; Whitley 60). Numerous incidents in the book support this contention. Thus, Tom's trickery is echoed by Aunt Polly's attempt to catch him out, and Tom's showing off when Judge Thatcher visits the Sunday School by the antics of the staff:

> Mr. Walters [the Sunday School superintendent] fell to *showing off* with all sorts of official bustlings and activities. . . . The librarian *showed off*, running hither and thither with his arms full of books. . . . The young lady teachers *showed*

off—bending sweetly over pupils that were lately being boxed. . . . The young gentleman teachers *showed off* with small scoldings and other little displays of authority. . . . (33) [emphasis mine]

Similarly, the fight that ends in the murder of Dr. Robinson is an adult version of Tom's fight, at the beginning of the book, with the new boy in town.

It is no wonder then that even after his harrowing escape from the cave and his recovery of the treasure, Tom returns to playing at robbers. The adult world is not portrayed as different from the world of childhood, and so there is no reason for Tom to grow up. Indeed, as Harold Aspiz remarks, "The town exists largely as a setting for Tom's adventures . . ." (147). In this respect, the worlds of Tom Sawyer and Anne of Green Gables are not similar, as Mary Rubio suggests (30), but radically different. If, as one critic suggests, Tom is not required "to sacrifice his boy's freedom in return for his success" (Regan 121), the reason may be that Twain "protects Tom from any experience that might seriously impair his 'unrestricted domination': boredom, humiliation, the serious threat of death, lasting or serious disappointment, growing up . . ." (Johnson 59). Tom's initiation thus consists of a series of adventures, not experiences that would lead to maturity (Johnson 51), and his rewards are correspondingly external.

I suggested earlier that these novels can be seen as presenting male and female models of heroism, Twain's novel celebrating individual exploits that lead to external rewards and Montgomery's celebrating a reciprocal process of internal change that leads to transformation of self and society. Robert Keith Miller points out that Twain saw himself as rebelling against the stereotype of the Model Boy portrayed in nineteenth-century children's books and creating instead a portrait of (in Walter Blair's words) "what a normal boy should be" (67). Montgomery's goal seems somewhat different. As we have seen, Anne's first task is to convince Matthew and Marilla that she is worth keeping even though she is not a boy. Anne's rivalry with Gilbert throughout the novel establishes their equality, in keeping with Montgomery's view of there being little difference between men and women (Burns 44–45). If we are tempted to read Anne's story as stereotypically that of the female who triumphs through self-sacrifice, we must remember that Gilbert is also forced to relinquish his chance for a university education because of his responsibility for his family.

This observation leads us to the possibility that the difference between the models of heroism portrayed in the two novels is not merely one of gender but also one of nationality. Tom's story, Lyall Powers argues, reflects the American dream and the American paradox: "The ideal hero is the stout individualist, the non-conforming natural man, American Rousseau, who yet lives snugly in suburbia as a regular fellow" (323). Does Anne then reflect the Canadian dream of social harmony with the recognition of the price we pay in individual sacrifice?

Works Cited

Aspiz, Harold. "Tom Sawyer's Games of Death." *Studies in the Novel* 27.2 (1995): 141, 13p. Online. AcademicSearch. 04 June 1999.

Burns, Jane. "Anne and Emily: L. M. Montgomery's Children." *Room of One's Own* 3.3: 37–47.

13j

Sample
Literary
Research
Paper

Fenwick, Julie. "'The Silence of the Mermaid: *Lady Oracle* and *Anne of Green Gables*." *Essays on Canadian Writing* 47 (1992): 51, 14p. MasterFILE. 7 June 1999.

Fetterley, Judith. "The Sanctioned Rebel." *Studies in the Novel* 3.3 (1971): 293–304.

Johnson, James L. *Mark Twain and the Limits of Power: Emerson's God in Ruins.* Knoxville: U of Tennessee P, 1982.

Miller, Robert Keith. *Mark Twain.* New York: Ungar, 1983.

Montgomery, L. M. *Anne of Green Gables.* Toronto: McGraw, 1968.

Powers, Lyall. "The Sweet Success of Twain's Tom." *Dalhousie Review* 53.2 (1973): 310–24.

Regan, Robert. *Unpromising Heroes: Mark Twain and His Characters.* Berkeley: U of California P, 1966.

Ross, Catherine S. "Calling Back the Ghost of the Old-Time Heroine: Duncan, Montgomery, Atwood, Laurence, and Munro." *Studies in Canadian Literature* 4.1 (1979): 43–58.

Rubio, Mary. "Satire, Realism, and Imagination in *Anne of Green Gables*." *L. M. Montgomery: An Assessment.* Ed. John R. Sorfleet. Guelph: Canadian Children's P, 1976. 27–36.

Towers, Tom H. "'I Never Thought We Might Want to Come Back: Strategies of Transcendence in *Tom Sawyer*." *Modern Fiction Studies* 21.4 (1975–76): 509–20.

Twain, Mark. *The Adventures of Tom Sawyer.* London: Penguin, 1986.

Whitaker, Muriel. "'Queer Children': L. M. Montgomery's Heroines." *L. M. Montgomery: An Assessment.* Ed. John R. Sorfleet. Guelph: Canadian Children's P, 1976. 50–59.

Whitley, John S. "Kids' Stuff: Mark Twain's Boys." *Mark Twain: A Sumptuous Variety.* Ed. Robert Giddings. London: Vision, 1985. 57–76.

Willis, Leslie. "The Bogus Ugly Duckling: Anne Shirley Unmasked." *Dalhousie Review* 56.2 (1976): 247–51.

Weblinks

- UBC Writing Centre's Writers' Toolbox—tips on various aspects of writing an essay, with sections on argument and writing a rhetorical analysis.

  www.writingcentre.ubc.ca/workshop/toolbox.htm

- Advice on Academic Writing, University of Toronto—links to planning and organizing, reading and researching, using sources, and specific types of writing.

  www.utoronto.ca/writing/advise.html

- The University of Victoria Writer's Guide—especially useful for essays on literature with a link to literary terms; also summaries, logic.

  web.uvic.ca/wguide/

13j

Sample
Literary
Research
Paper

- The Purdue Online Writing Laboratory Research and Documenting Sources—includes research paper guidelines.

  owl.English.purdue.edu/handouts/research/index.html

- A Guide for Writing Research Papers based on MLA documentation

  webster.commnet.edu/mla/index.shtml

13j

Sample Literary Research Paper

PART 4

REVISING YOUR ESSAY

Checklist REVISION

	OK	NEEDS WORK
1. Is your purpose clear?	☐	☐
2. Have you analyzed your audience?	☐	☐
3. Is the essay's organization/overall structure effective?	☐	☐
4. Is the thesis clearly stated at the essay's beginning or end?	☐	☐
5. Is the essay divided into the appropriate number of paragraphs?	☐	☐
6. Are the paragraphs effectively ordered?	☐	☐
7. Does each paragraph have a clear topic sentence or linking sentence?	☐	☐
8. Does each paragraph have enough details to support it?	☐	☐
9. Is each paragraph unified and coherent?	☐	☐
10. Does each paragraph use appropriate transitional words and expressions?	☐	☐
11. Does the essay have a powerful introduction?	☐	☐
12. Does the essay have a strong conclusion?	☐	☐
13. Are the style and language appropriate?	☐	☐
14. Is the format of the document correct?	☐	☐

CHAPTER 14

Revising Your Essay: Structure

14a CHECKING YOUR PURPOSE AND YOUR AUDIENCE

Although you may have combined various rhetorical modes, and used various paragraph types within your essay, your essay will still probably have one main purpose: to narrate/describe/reflect on personal experience, to explain a subject or event, or to argue a main point. When revising, consider this main purpose as well as your audience. For instance, if you were writing an essay to a friend or a narrative for a blog, your audience is your peers, so you might include more personal details and use more casual language than you would for a personal essay for an English course. For more on evaluating audience, see Chapter 1.

14b CHECKING OVERALL ESSAY STRUCTURE

When revising your essay, check to see that your structure suits your purpose.

Expository and persuasive essays, as already mentioned, usually have deductive structures, with thesis statements in the introduction and topic sentences at the beginning of each paragraph. If you have chosen this structure, ensure that your thesis is at the end of your introduction and that each paragraph has a clearly stated and refined topic sentence *at or near* the beginning of each paragraph. Deductive essays, especially persuasive ones, often build to their strongest point; if your most important point is buried in the middle of your essay, you might need to reorganize your paragraphs.

Alternatively, if you have decided that your audience is unknowledgeable or hostile/resistant—you are explaining a very difficult process or arguing a controversial point, such as violent video games actually benefiting adults—you might have chosen an inductive structure. To check the structure of your essay, get a friend to read it without the conclusion and get him or her to guess the thesis. If your reader grasps your main point, he or she has induced the thesis, and your content and organization are probably sound. If your reader is surprised or shocked by your thesis, you have not achieved your desired effect, and you may have to further develop or reorganize your argument.

In inductively structured personal essays, in which you are trying to create an effect or communicate an experience, remember that you still need a main point. You can similarly "test" the effectiveness of your essay by getting someone to read the essay, *sans* conclusion, and asking him or her about the main point.

14c CHECKING AND REVISING YOUR THESIS STATEMENT

In the process of writing your essay, you may have come up with new arguments or directions; thus, you may have to refine your thesis. Remember that your thesis, which predicts and controls your argument, is a very important sentence in your paper. Your thesis should match the structure and content of your finalized essay.

Recall that your thesis statement should contain an opinion with at least one reason to support it and that it should be neither too vague nor too detailed.

Below are some weak and revised thesis statements for various essay types:

WEAK	There are steps to bathing your dog. (This thesis for an expository essay sounds too general and irrelevant.)
REVISED	*If you follow these three main steps to bathing your dog, both you and your dog will have a more pleasant experience.*
WEAK	Choosing a cancer treatment can be difficult. (This thesis for a persuasive essay contains an opinion, but a vague opinion, and no reasons to support it; additionally, this thesis does not indicate a clear basis of argument or structure.)
REVISED	*Because cancer treatments have various side effects, you should thoroughly consult with your doctor about which treatment option is best for managing your disease.*

Here are some additional pointers for refining the structure of your thesis:

- If your instructor has asked you to blueprint your thesis or indicate the main divisions of your essay, use tight parallel structures. In the example below, which is from a literary analysis essay, the three poetic elements are clearly listed as nouns.

  In "To His Importunate Mistress," the inability of modern man to seize the day is revealed in the poem's speaker, structure, and prosody.

- If you are writing a persuasive essay, and you have to acknowledge a counterargument, you might consider structuring your thesis as a *complex sentence.* Put the minor point or counterargument in the dependent clause and your main point in the independent clause.

  Although some stress is indeed beneficial, an overload of stress causes numerous psychological and physical ailments.

- If you are writing a personal essay, avoid the temptation to make your thesis too vague or oblique; make your thesis specific and meaningful to the reader.

Training for a marathon taught me about pain, patience, and perseverance.

14d CHECKING PARAGRAPH LENGTH AND PARAGRAPH DIVISION

Although paragraphs can vary in length, make sure that your paragraph length suits your essay's purpose. For instance, an expository essay on the steps to paint a room might require one long paragraph on choosing the colour, two short paragraphs on buying materials and prepping the room, two medium-length paragraphs on the processes and techniques of painting, and one short paragraph on cleaning up. Alternatively, a comparison/contrast essay on two health plans might require longer equally developed paragraphs. A persuasive essay on the dangers of violent media might place its most important point in TWO final longer paragraphs.

Some instructors may approve of short transitional paragraphs; most approve of equally developed paragraphs. Check to see how your paragraphs look on the page; if you have really lengthy paragraphs—those over a page long—look for a natural break to divide them. If you have several really short paragraphs, consider how to combine them under a single topic sentence.

If you see a weakness in your essay, your instructor will no doubt see it too.

14e CHECKING TOPIC SENTENCES

Now is also the time to go back and revise your topic sentences, making sure that they are neither too vague nor too specific. Because topic sentences function as mini-thesis statements for the paragraph, they must "match" the content of the paragraph.

Examine the two topic sentences below for an essay on the dangers of blackouts.

EXAMPLE 1   A blackout is an alcohol-induced memory loss.

Because this topic sentence simply defines blackouts, it is too specific for an expository essay on the causes and effects of blackouts.

EXAMPLE 2   To understand the dangers of blackouts, we need to understand what they are and distinguish them from passing out and from drinking to the point of unconsciousness.

This topic sentence limits the discussion to defining blackouts and distinguishing them from other alcohol-related episodes.

14f CHECKING PARAGRAPH UNITY AND COHERENCE

Now that you are sure that your paragraphs are properly ordered and your topic sentences are sound, it's time to examine the internal structure of each paragraph. You need to check that your paragraphs are unified (they contain only information that develops the topic sentence) and coherent (their details are placed in the most effective order).

To check for unity, test every sentence against the topic sentence. Does each sentence support or develop the topic sentence's main point? If not, highlight, rather than delete these extraneous sentences, for they may belong in other paragraphs. If you are crossing out a lot of unnecessary sentences, you might have to go back and rethink the paragraph, either fleshing it out with more details or removing it entirely. If you don't have enough details to support your point, you might be accused of "jumping to conclusions," a serious logical flaw.

Next, verify the order of your details; a coherent paragraph is one in which the sentences are in the most effective order. This order, for instance, could be chronological, spatial, from least to most important, and so on, depending on what type of paragraph you are writing. See whether you need to reorder or remove sentences. Check to see that you are using ample and appropriate transitional words and sentences to enforce the existing relationships between ideas and to make your paragraph flow. For more information on appropriate transitional words for paragraph types, see Chapter 3: Writing Better Paragraphs.

14g REVISING YOUR INTRODUCTION

14g

**Revising
Your
Introduction**

Students often write their introductions and conclusions last, so these often get the least revision. However, because these parts of your essay leave the first and the last impressions on your reader, they really merit your careful attention.

Your main point gets clarified as you write, so your best statement of your thesis might actually be in your conclusion. If it is, move it to your introduction.

- Check the length of your introduction; it should neither be too terse nor too rambling. Your individual instructors may have specific guidelines about introductions; check with them if you are unsure.

- Check that you have not opened with a vague statement, such as "Since the beginning of time" or a truism, such as "Humans have always struggled with death." These are surefire ways to annoy your reader.

- Check that you have grabbed the reader's attention in a way that is appropriate to your purpose and audience. A persuasive essay on the need for handwashing might begin with a statistic about how many bacteria regularly reside on your hands, whereas a narrative essay on training for a marathon might open with a detail about hitting the notorious wall. Consider using description and narration in your introduction.

- Check that you have chosen *one* way to begin and that there is a clear bridge or segue between your opening material and your thesis statement.
- Below is an example of a strong introduction from a classification essay about television crime dramas. In the example, the segue has been <u>underlined</u> and the thesis **bolded.**

CSI, Law and Order, NYPD Blue, and *DaVinci's Inquest.* Bikinis, exotic locales, gritty interrogation rooms, political controversies, gory autopsies, fast cars, amoral characters, and straight shooters. Above are just of the few examples of North American police/crime dramas and a partial list of their ingredients. Cop shows comprise a bewildering buffet indeed. <u>In order for the viewer to choose the most satisfying bite of crime drama, he or she needs to become familiar with the cop show menu</u>. **Crime dramas can be divided into three major groups: location-driven shows, plot-driven shows, and character-driven shows,** each offering a different but satisfying entertainment experience.

This introduction, which actually uses a series of effective fragments, gives examples of the "ingredients" of crime shows before stating its thesis. Below is an example of an introduction from a literary analysis essay. Why is it weak? How would you go about revising it?

Depression is a confusing, scary state, how can a person recover or at least be kept as comfortable as possible? Secluded from family and friends confined to an eerie, smouldering room covered in pale, smelly old wallpaper? Charlotte Perkins Gilman wrote this story in the nineteenth century, it was forgotten until feminists claimed it in the 60s. The story has an autobiographical connection, but the narrator is not Gilman, her name is Jane. Jane is a new mother struggling with postpartum depression. Although her husband is a well-known doctor, his techniques for helping his sick wife heal are somewhat questionable. He chooses a secluded house standing alone about three miles from the nearest village. "It makes me think English . . . there are hedges and wall and gates that lock, and lots of separate little houses for the gardeners and people" (p. 83). Jane is placed in a nursery at the top of the house with bars on the windows. The walls are covered in old, smelly, faded paper. Mary is an author, although she is forced to hide her writing from her husband. I will talk about how the wallpaper symbolizes three different interpretations: how she felt suicidal, her confusion, and finally how she went completely insane.

14h REVISING YOUR CONCLUSION

Just as your introduction leaves a first impression on your reader, your conclusion leaves a final impression. Your conclusion, then, should not be an afterthought but a powerful end to your essay.

Although you should summarize your main points, check that you have not restated your thesis verbatim and that your wording is substantially different in your introduction and conclusion. Don't simply cut your introductory material and paste it into your introduction. After all, you have already explained a subject, narrated a personal experience, or argued a point—travelled from point A to point B, so to speak—so returning to point A doesn't make sense. After summarizing the main points, suggest the wider implications of your thesis or subject. In theory, then, a conclusion, which moves from the specific (your thesis) to the more general, has the opposite structure of an introduction.

Below is an example of a conclusion from an essay on how technology has affected literacy; the summary of the writer's thesis is in bold font. Because this is a persuasive essay, she pushes her argument outwards by making suggestions for educators.

Andrea di Sessa optimistically suggests that "computers can be the technical foundation of a new and dramatically enhanced literacy" (4). **However, as this essay has shown, in the relatively short time that computer technology has been widely available to the public, literacy levels have not, in fact, increased but actually plummeted.** Therefore, as technology continues to be integrated into and even take over the classroom, educators must be mindful of the absolute necessity of cultivating the basics: grammar and reading skills. This is a daunting undertaking for the education system; however, it cannot fail, for the readers the education system produces will be the ones carrying the torch of literacy into the future.

Below is an example of a conclusion from a literary analysis on Gilman's "The Yellow Wallpaper."

In Gilman's story "The Yellow Wallpaper," John symbolizes the patriarchal medical idea that women had to be protected from work and stimulation and the patriarchal male idea that women should be "seen and not heard," ideas that Mitchell also revisited and later refined. That is, after he read "The Yellow Wallpaper," Dr. S. Weir Mitchell changed both his Rest Cure treatment (Berman 237) and his thinking about appropriate treatments for women's ailments. Thus, Charlotte Perkins Gilman's "queer story" about one woman's depression not only changed the fate of women in her time but also changed the fate of women for all time.

14i

Checking Your
Presentation
and
Assignment
Format

14i CHECKING YOUR PRESENTATION AND ASSIGNMENT FORMAT

After you have checked the overall structure of your essay, you need to examine how your essay looks. It is good to format your essay in the early stages so that you are not obsessing over these details at the end.

First, examine the presentation of your essay, specifically your margins, spacing, font, and paragraph indentations. See Appendix A for useful formatting guidelines.

Next, ensure that you have followed the requirements of your chosen format, specifically the format for title page, headers, parenthetical citations, and References/Works Cited page. Information on MLA and APA format is located in Appendices B and C.

Instructors, especially in later assignments, often expect you to make few formatting mistakes.

After going over essay structure and format, it is time to check the language and style of your paper, topics explored in Chapter 15.

14i

Checking Your Presentation and Assignment Format

15b

Revising
Language:
Guidelines
for Formal
Writing

Revising Your Essay: Appropriate Language and Style

15a CHECKING FOR APPROPRIATE LANGUAGE

Some writers use informal language in writing requiring more formal diction. Others adopt an overly formal vocabulary so that their writing becomes stilted. Still others coast along, using words that are safe but dull. Paying attention to the words you use will help you remedy these problems and develop a more lively and effective prose.

Understanding **levels of language** will help you choose words appropriate for your purpose and audience. Consider these words meaning *poor:*

Formal	Standard	Informal
impecunious, destitute, poverty-stricken, poor, hard up, broke, busted		

These words illustrate what we mean by levels of language, with "big words" such as *impecunious* and *destitute* at the formal end of the scale; colloquial and slang terms such as *hard up* and *busted* at the informal end; and the standard vocabulary of public writing and speaking in the middle (*poverty-stricken, poor*). Although you might use colloquial diction among friends, the words you use in writing for college or university should come from a standard vocabulary.

15b REVISING LANGUAGE: GUIDELINES FOR FORMAL WRITING

When you are writing academic essays, keep these suggestions about word choice in mind. Because students often are confused about writing that is not formal enough or that is too formal, the first suggestions aim to help keep your writing appropriately formal enough, whereas the latter suggestions aim to keep your writing lively and prevent it from becoming too wordy or stuffy.

1. *Avoid slang and colloquial expressions.*

   an acquaintance rather than *a guy I know*

2. *Avoid clichés.*

   Clichés serve a useful purpose in spoken language, but in formal writing, they may suggest that the writer is treating the subject superficially or vaguely.

   He was a straight shooter who always hit the nail on the head.

164

3. **Use contractions sparingly.**

Some readers object to contractions in formal writing; others don't. If you use an occasional contraction, make sure you use the apostrophe correctly.

4. **Use I and you sparingly.**

Don't distract your readers from your subject by constant references to yourself: *I think, I feel, it seems to me.* The reader knows you are expressing your opinion. However, when it is appropriate to use *I*, use it rather than *one* or *this writer.*

NOT   It seems to me that this anthology is unsuitable for the high school curriculum.

BUT   This anthology is unsuitable for the high school curriculum.

OR   Although other reviewers consider this anthology suitable for the high school curriculum, I disagree.

Similarly, avoid using *you* in formal writing to mean *people in general.*

NOT   The university's marking system can be frustrating when all of your professors have their own scale within the scale.

BUT   The university's marking system can be frustrating when professors have their own scale within the scale.

5. **Aim for a serious, knowledgeable, and businesslike tone, but avoid sounding stuffy or pompous.**

In general, choose standard words rather than more formal terms (*need* rather than *necessity*). However, emphasize key points by selecting words from the slightly formal range (*poverty-stricken* or *destitute,* but not *impecunious*).

6. **Use specialized terms only when necessary.**

Part of what you learn when you study psychology, sociology, and other academic disciplines is the language that specialists in the field use when communicating to other specialists. In an essay discussing Freud's theory of the unconscious, for example, you would use Freud's terms *id, ego,* and *superego,* for there are no adequate synonyms for these concepts.

But when a specialized vocabulary is used inappropriately or out of context, it is called *jargon.* Jargon obscures meaning rather than making meaning more precise. When jargon is combined with wordiness and an unnecessarily formal vocabulary, writing can become almost unintelligible, as in the examples below.

NOT   As the precepts of individual psychology are ultimately reflected in social psychology, the psychic impairment experienced by the student as part of the educational process will be augmented within the context of the social environment.

15b

Revising
Language:
Guidelines
for Formal
Writing

15b

Revising
Language:
Guidelines
for Formal
Writing

BUT	Because students carry their self-perceptions into the larger social world, any damage to their self-esteem becomes more severe when they leave school.
NOT	Management will access the input of all interested parties, prioritize their responses, and introduce modifications to the terms of the proposal accordingly.
BUT	The manager will ask all interested parties for their reactions to the proposal, review their responses, and make changes accordingly.

Exercise 15.1

Comment briefly on the effect of jargon and big words in the following paragraph, taken from a research paper on the back-to-basics movement in education. Then rewrite the paragraph in simpler, more concrete language.

The teacher I interviewed perceived her role as a socializing agent with a humanistic approach. She added that although students lacked skills to handle Grade Five curriculum, her priority was to allow student-directed activities in a safe environment free of negative labelling. Correcting exams and clerical tasks presented a strain on her role. She felt psychology was the most beneficial course she had taken at university: she taught many children experiencing stress from broken families or families who did not share time.

Exercise 15.2

Underline inappropriate word choices in the following paragraph, adapted from a research paper on impaired driving. Then rewrite the paragraph so that the diction is more appropriate for the subject and audience.

Kathy Stechert's research on drunk driving (1984) has suggested some prevention techniques that you should consider when entertaining guests in your home: serve lots of food; provide non-alcoholic beverages; don't pressure guests to drink; water down drinks when guys are consuming too much alcohol. Don't let guests leave the house if they're tanked; ask them to wait until they've sobered up or to stay overnight. If they make a fuss and insist on leaving, drive them home. It is really amazing that many people don't think about what could happen after guests leave the party. It doesn't take a genius to see that these measures would help reduce drunk driving.

15c REVISING LANGUAGE: GUIDELINES FOR INFORMAL WRITING

For personal and persuasive writing intended for a general audience and for a non-academic audience, follow these guidelines:

1. ***Try for the friendly, engaged tone of one person talking to another.***

   To create this tone, choose most of your words from the standard to slightly informal range (*poor, hard up*). Choose short, common words (those on the right) over longer synonyms.

   possess = own, have   automobile = car

   retain = keep   residence = house

   purchase = buy   difficulties = troubles

2. ***Use more formal words to create suggestive images, humour or satire, and subtle shades of meaning.***

   the undulations of the wheat

   the writer was lionized in London, lampooned in L.A.

   serpentine streets

3. ***Use concrete over abstract nouns and specific over general nouns.***

   Abstract nouns name qualities (*friendship, heroism*) or concepts (*the state, conservatism*). **Concrete nouns** name things we perceive through our senses (*your friend, the brain*). **General nouns** apply to classes of things (*adolescents, buildings*) rather than to a single, specific thing (*the teenager who works at The Bay, the CN Tower*). Abstract and general nouns distance your reader.

4. ***Use first- and second-person pronouns (I, you), where appropriate, to establish a personal relationship with your reader.***

5. ***Use occasional contractions, colloquial expressions, or slang terms, if appropriate to your subject and audience.***

6. ***Choose* active verbs *over* state-of-being verbs *and* verbs in the passive voice.**

   By changing **state-of-being,** or **linking,** verbs (*is, seems, exists, has, contains, feels*) to active verbs, you can often transform a vague general statement into a precise, vivid image.

   NOT   She *has* short brown hair. Her face *is* round.

   BUT   Her short brown hair *cups* her round face.

   NOT   I *felt* angry.

15c

Revising
Language:
Guidelines
for Informal
Writing

BUT I *throbbed* with anger.

OR I *stalked* out of the room.

Note that verbs in the **passive voice** can take the energy out of your writing:

NOT The winning goal was scored by me.

BUT In the last few seconds of the game, I nailed the winning goal.

15c

Revising
Language:
Guidelines
for Informal
Writing

To see how changing the diction can improve a piece of writing, compare the following versions of a paragraph on the perils of sailing. In the first, the formal language makes the danger seem remote, even unreal.

Sample Draft Paragraph

Of course there are those who endure the elements as necessitated to earn a living. Traditionally they are the men of the sea. Sailors maintain many fears in terms of the elements. For instance, atmospheric electricity playing around the mast might cause a fire. To the sailor's peril, ice can cover the rigging, leaving the ship top-heavy and in danger of "turtling." Thrashing waves and Titanic swells can consume both craft and crew.

In the revised paragraph, the simpler language, active verbs, and concrete nouns create a vivid image of a ship in danger.

Sample Revised Paragraph

Sailors have traditionally earned their living by enduring the dangers of the elements. Sailors fear the blue haze of St. Elmo's fire encircling the mast, and its acrid smell of burning. They fear the surge that rises twelve metres above the mizzen and the waves that slam the hull from every direction. The wind, as it sings through the stays, charts a new course without aid of a compass, without earthly reason. But at no time is a sailor's job so perilous as when the wind chill plunges the mercury to minus thirty-five and droplets of mist condense on the supercooled rigging. Then layer upon layer of ice forms. When an ice-laden ship gets top-heavy, no amount of praying will keep it afloat. The captain's call goes out: "The gyros are toppling."

—Chris Paterson

Exercise 15.3

Underline word choices in the following paragraph that you find ineffective for a personal essay. Then rewrite the paragraph using more vivid language.

Chuck is, simply put, a mean person. One would not say that he is a sadist, exactly. He is not of the character to pull the wings off flies, albeit he does on occasion step on anthills. He merely loves practical jokes—mean-spirited practical jokes. One time a small, plastic-wrapped packet of cloves was left by Chuck on the desk of a fellow student named Ramona. Attached to the packet with tape was a note that read, "Cloves make an effective breath freshener." Ramona was, with justification, mortified and offended. On other occasions, sample bottles of deodorant and acne medication have been left on classmates' desks. One could say that these tactics work to undermine a person's self-confidence. Chuck also has an inconsiderate mouth. In the recent past, on the day we were being photographed for the yearbook, Jerry Johnson wore a new suit. Hiding behind his most sincere smile, Chuck told Jerry, "Jer, my man, that suit really suits you, ha, ha. I donated one just like it to the Sally Ann last week." I used to laugh at Chuck's peccadilloes, until this morning. As we were walking out of math class, the teacher directly behind us, that insensitive Chuck enunciated clearly, "Ken, I wish you would not say those things about Mr. Mueller. I think he is a fine teacher." I am planning how to asphyxiate Chuck in his sleep. The deed will definitely be done with malice aforethought.

15d BEING CONCISE AND AVOIDING WORDINESS

Whether your prose is formal, informal, or between the two, it is crucial that you avoid unnecessary wordiness.

There are several reasons that students often submit wordy writing, but these are the most common: they need to meet the word count; they have written only one draft; they haven't clarified what they want to say; and they think that inflated diction makes them sound more intelligent. The first three reasons can be remedied by brainstorming and draft-writing; the latter can be fixed by thinking about writing in a new way.

Don't worry about sounding intelligent or authoritative; worry about sounding clear. Understand that in good, clear writing, every word counts. Pruning the deadwood—unessential words, phrases, and sentences— clarifies your meaning and makes your writing easier to read. You want your reader immediately grasping your meaning, rather than figuring out what you are *trying to say.*

To make sure that every word counts, many writers set a goal of cutting their writing by 10 percent. If you tend to be wordy, you may need to set your goal even higher, perhaps 20 percent. Here are some practical suggestions for avoiding wordiness:

1. *Eliminate unnecessary repetition of words and ideas.*

REPETITIOUS PHRASE	Formerly, women's clothes were much more restrictive in the past.
REVISED	Women's clothes were much more restrictive in the past.

REPETITIOUS SENTENCES	Macbeth seems shaken by the witches' announcement that he will become king. He is uneasy when they tell him he is destined to gain the throne.
REVISED	Macbeth seems shaken by the witches' announcement that he will become king.

2. ***Reduce or eliminate unnecessary phrases, clauses, and sentences.***

Reduce phrases to single words (*in a short time* = *shortly*; *a lot of* = *many* or *much*; *at this point in time* = *now*).

Reduce clauses beginning with *that, which,* or *who* to words or phrases.

NOT	all employees who are interested
BUT	all interested employees
NOT	at the position that I was assigned
BUT	at my position
NOT	*The current focus of the dental profession is reducing gingivitis.*
BUT	*Dentistry currently focuses on reducing gingivitis.*

3. ***Remove any adjective or adverb that adds no new meaning to the sentence.***

Kind of, sort of, actually, basically, really, type of, generally, for all intents and purposes

WORDY	The small, sporty-looking red car just left us in the dust.
BETTER	The red sportscar left us in the dust.

4. ***Eliminate unnecessary expletive constructions (those beginning with*** it is, there are, ***and so on).***

NOT	It is a fact that the car has been stolen.
BUT	The car has been stolen.
NOT	It is obvious to everyone here that profits are down.
BUT	Profits are down.

5. ***Omit redundant word pairs.***

When you use redundant word pairs, you are repeating yourself, revealing that you have either not edited or that you are not familiar with the meanings of the words you are using. Some annoying redundant word pairs are listed below:

Achieve success, true facts, free gift, end result, past history, future plans, unexpected surprise, horrible tragedy, final outcome, important essentials

6. Replace roundabout expressions (circumlocutions) with shorter, direct expressions.

INSTEAD OF	USE
The reason for, due to the fact that	BECAUSE
On the occasion that, in a situation in which	WHEN
As regards, in reference to, with regard to	ABOUT
It is crucial that, it is necessary that	MUST, SHOULD
Is able to, has the opportunity to	CAN
It is possible that, there is a chance that	MAY, MIGHT, COULD

7. Be careful with that most dangerous of beasts: the thesaurus.

When you are revising, you may be tempted to go to your thesaurus to jazz up your vocabulary; if you do, make sure that you use the word nearest the top of the list, which is closest to the original's meaning. Normally, the words further down the list are more emotionally slanted and quite different in meaning from the original. For instance, one of the first synonyms for *like* is "feel partial to," but one of the last synonyms is "feel attraction for." You can see how misusing these synonyms might be risky. Read your sentence out loud to make sure that you are not calling up a ridiculous image or using a word out of context.

ORIGINAL   I really like Martha Stewart.

NOT   I am really attracted to Martha Stewart.

BUT   I really think highly of Martha Stewart.

To see how being concise can clarify your meaning, consider these versions of a paragraph from an essay on the importance of options in the school curriculum.

Sample Draft Paragraph

There are a lot of other courses that are very important to children growing up today. Courses such as home economics, industrial education, accounting, and computer courses help children function better in the outside world—whether in the job market or in the home. These courses enable the children to be able to learn about a wide variety of things. Students today learn about health and nutrition, they learn about first aid, how to look after a home (boys as well as girls), they learn how to look after a vehicle, and even how to budget themselves and to do their own taxes. [103 words]

Many other courses are also important to today's adolescents, such as home economics, industrial education, accounting, and computer science. These courses help them function better in both the home and the job market. They also enable students to learn about health and nutrition, first aid, home maintenance, vehicle repair, budget balancing, and completing taxes. [60 words]

Exercise 15.4

In the following paragraph, underline all unnecessary words, phrases, and sentences. Then rewrite the paragraph in 200 words or fewer without omitting any necessary ideas.

At the base of the argument for an education based on facts lies a dangerous assumption: that a person with a good grasp of general knowledge has the will and the means to examine information critically to determine whether it is true and valid. Realistically, most people who get through school by memorizing information lack either the ability to think critically or the desire to think critically. A simple science fair project conducted by a junior high school student exposes people's failure to think critically and make reasoned judgments. At the Greater Idaho Falls Science Fair in April 1997, the student presented a presentation about the dangers of dihydrogen monoxide. The student asked people to sign a petition to have the chemical banned because of its harmful effects. The harmful effects included the statements that "accidental inhalation can cause death" and that dihydrogen monoxide "is a major component of acid rain." Of fifty people asked, forty-three supported elimination of the chemical, six people were undecided, and one person recognized that dihydrogen monoxide is the chemical term for H_2O. That is, dihydrogen monoxide is water. Clearly, these people did not analyze the situation effectively. The mental habits that enable people to make sound judgments are not inherent. Educators cannot expect that an individual will use his mind to reason, analyze, and make sound judgments simply because that person has a solid base of facts and knowledge. [235 words]

15e AVOIDING COMMONLY MISUSED WORDS

When you are checking your style, be on the lookout for words and expressions that many writers confuse or misuse. Here is a partial list. You will find others in the exercise below. For problems with *its/it's*, *their/there/they're*, and *your/you're*, see Possessive Pronouns (19c).

A Lot

A lot is an informal expression meaning *many, much,* or *a great deal of.* Although you should avoid *a lot* in most writing, when you use it, spell it as two words.

I have **a lot** of chores to do tonight.

All Right

All right should be spelled as two words. *Alright* is incorrect and should not be used.

"**All right,**" the coach agreed reluctantly, "you can miss the practice Thursday afternoon."

Allude/Elude

Use *allude* when you mean *refer to,* as in an allusion to the Bible or to Shakespeare. Use *elude* when you mean *to avoid* or *escape.*

In his opening comments, the guest speaker **alluded** to Hamlet's indecision.

The wary old wolf managed to **elude** the hunter.

Among/Between

Use *between* when you are referring to two things. Use *among* when you are referring to more than two.

Divide the bill **between** Susan and Stacy.

Share the birthday cake **among** all the employees.

Amount/Number

Use *amount* to refer to things considered as a mass (*a large amount of work, a small amount of money*). Use *number* to refer to things that can be counted (*a large number of people, a small number* of desks).

A large **amount** of money is missing.

A large **number** of bills were stolen.

Bored with

Use *bored with* (never *bored of*) to mean *wearied with dullness.*

She is **bored with** her courses this year.

Hanged/Hung

Use *hanged* as the past tense of the verb *to hang* when you are referring to a person. Use *hung* when you are referring to objects.

The convict **was hanged** at dawn.

Her latest painting **was hung** in the city gallery.

15e

Avoiding
Commonly
Misused
Words

Hopefully

Hopefully is an adverb meaning *full of hope.* It is used correctly in this sentence: *The sales representative knocked **hopefully** at the door.*

Do not use *hopefully* to mean *I hope* or *perhaps.*

NOT   Hopefully, we'll be able to meet next week.

BUT   Perhaps [*or* I hope] we'll be able to meet next week.

Lead/Led

The past tense of the verb *to lead* is *led.*

Yesterday he **led** the band in the Earth Day parade.

Less/Fewer

Use *less* with mass nouns (*less unemployment, less hunger*) and *fewer* with countable nouns (*fewer courses, fewer assignments*).

I'm having **fewer problems** this year.

I'm having **less difficulty** this year.

Lie/Lay

The principal parts of the verb *to lie* (to recline) are *lie, lay, lying,* and *lain.*
The principal parts of the verb *to lay* (to place) are *lay, laid, laying,* and *laid.*
Be careful not to confuse these verbs.

NOT   She **lays** on the deck all afternoon.

BUT   She **lies** on the deck all afternoon.

NOT   He **laid** in the sun for half an hour.

BUT   He **lay** in the sun for half an hour.

Like/As

Use *like* as a preposition. Use *as* to introduce a clause.

He danced **like** a maniac.

He danced, **as** he always danced, with gusto.

Loose/Lose

Loose is usually an adjective or adverb (*loose change, loose clothing, let loose*).

Occasionally *loose* is used as a verb meaning *to set free* (*He loosed the dog on the intruder*). Don't confuse *loose* with *lose* (to misplace).

He often **loses** his way when he is in a strange city.

I can only give you a **loose** translation of that phrase.

Take Part in/Partake of

To take part in something is *to join* or *to participate*. *To partake of* is *to have a share of something* (usually a meal).

Hamlet refused to **take part in** the wedding festivities.

Would you be willing to **partake of** our simple meal?

Exercise 15.5

For each word in the nine sets below, give a brief definition and then use the word in a sentence to distinguish it from the word(s) with which it is often confused. Use the entry for *take part in/partake of* (above) as a guide.

15e

Avoiding
Commonly
Misused
Words

- affect/effect
- allusion/illusion
- cite/sight/site
- disinterested/ uninterested
- elusive/illusory
- flaunt/flout
- principal/principle
- than/then
- thereby/therefore

Exercise 15.6

Correct all the usage errors in the following sentences. Some sentences have more than one error.

1. Although you have put on a few kilos, you still weigh considerably less then your father.

2. During a chinook some people suffer from headaches or depression; others are not effected at all.

3. Louis Riel was hung at Regina on November 16, 1885.

4. My dog is laying on the porch.

5. Like I said before, I usually trust my own judgment, but this time I'll differ to your greater experience.

6. Mother divided the candy equally between all the children.

7. Hopefully, we will be able to catch David Copperfield's special on television. He is a master of allusion.

15f VARYING SENTENCE LENGTH

If you have proofed your writing for tone, wordiness, and word use, but your style still seems flat, you might want to vary your sentence length. If you want to create rhythm and emphasize important points, use a combination of short sentences (ten words or fewer), long sentences (thirty words or more), and medium-length sentences.

Short sentences are effective for rendering abrupt actions, giving directions, stating main points, making transitions, and creating emphasis.

15f

Varying
Sentence
Length

ABRUPT ACTIONS	She stopped.
DIRECTIONS	First, stop the bleeding.
MAIN POINTS	One cause of high unemployment is government policy. [Essay topic sentence]
	Safety violations have increased 10 percent over last year. [Report topic sentence]
EMPHASIS	He loved no one.
	The war was over.

Long sentences are effective for expressing continuous action, giving a series of details or examples, and creating a sense of closure.

CONTINUOUS ACTION	After discovering Jack's country address, Algernon assumes his friend's secret identity and poses as wicked Ernest Worthing for his meeting with Cecily, Jack's sheltered young ward; but when they meet for the first time, the worldly, cynical Algernon is momentarily confounded by the sophisticated wit of "little" Cecily.
DETAILS	According to the criteria for student loans, students are considered to be financially independent only if they have no parent, guardian, or sponsor; are married or a single parent; have been out of secondary school for four years; or have been in the labour force for twenty-four months.
CLOSURE	In the final analysis, the losers are not merely those who have been jailed for insider trading, nor the firms whose reputations have been sullied, nor the stockholders who have lost money; the losers are all those who have lost confidence in the integrity of the stock market.

Medium-length sentences, which will probably form the majority of your prose, are especially ideal for thesis statements and topic sentences.

THESIS STATEMENT	Although differing in their use of speaker, structure, and language, both Marge Piercy's "Barbie Doll" and Linda Pastan's "Marks" reveal the theme of the expectations that stifle women.

15g ADDING INTEREST

If your instructor has told you that your writing is grammatical but that your writing lacks interest or panache, you might consider enlivening your prose by using quotations and other kinds of allusions, dialogue, and figurative language.

Quotations

Use familiar quotations—proverbs, lines from songs, advertising slogans, sayings of famous people, well-known bits of poetry and prose—to create an emotional appeal and a sense of shared experience. You don't need to give complete bibliographical information for quotations used in passing, but do put them in quotation marks and identify the source.

> When you are backpacking through Europe, your money will start to dwindle and you will feel moments of fear and desperation. As *The Hitchhiker's Guide to the Galaxy* so wisely advises, "Don't panic."
>
> —*Lori Yanish*

Allusions

An allusion is a casual reference to a figure, event, or document from history, literature, mythology, popular culture, or religion. Allusions not only help to establish your authority as a writer by indicating the breadth of your knowledge or experience but also establish tone; allusions can be used straight or ironically.

> Like Caesar, he came, he saw, he restored order where confusion reigned.
>
> —*Chris Carleton*

> Her hopes, like Miss Havisham's wedding cake, had been eaten away.
>
> —*Chris Carleton*

> I suspected life at Stephanie's house might be just like life at Dick and Jane's.
>
> —*Suzanne Cook*

Dialogue

Use dialogue for dramatic effect. Direct speech allows you to show what happened rather than merely telling. It also gives variety to your writing by introducing other voices.

My parents were glued to a small black and white television in room #107. I wandered into the room and tugged on my mother's skirt until she lifted me into her lap. "Look, it's Neil Armstrong," she said as she directed my gaze to the small screen. "He's about to walk on the moon."

—Mario Trono

Figurative Language

Figures of speech create vivid mental images for your readers. Use them to sharpen your descriptions and to convey your attitude toward your subject. Try your hand at the five types illustrated below: simile, metaphor, personification, hyperbole, and irony. As stated before, avoid clichés (*dead as a doornail*) and mixed metaphors (*flooded with an iron resolve*), which weaken your writing.

The snow covered the ground like a thick comforting blanket. [simile]

The sea dragged its heavy claws against the shore and roared. [personification]

We are nothing but a jar full of flour beetles, continually eating and reproducing. [metaphor]

—Cheryl Lewis

Those demonic savages, those cruel, sadistic, verminous beings, those bus drivers, have persisted in their heinous acts. [hyperbole]

—Amanda Thompson

Mr. Simpson would pretend to drive into Miss Merril's little BMW just to terrify her in a neighbourly way. [irony]

—Alex Cheung

Parallelism

There are two ways to use parallelism in sentences.

- Join two or more closely related clauses with a coordinating conjunction or semicolon. (This pattern is also called a **balanced construction.**)

You can allow your anxieties to rob you of sleep and satisfaction, or you can plan your time wisely and then enjoy your free time thoroughly.

—Wendy Amy

- Arrange a series of words, phrases, or clauses in increasing importance.

Friends listen to you babble, tell you honest opinions when you prefer lies to the truth, tell you *I told you so* at annoying times, defend your reputation from others, and generally mother, father, grandparent, and sibling (brother or sister) you.

—Amanda Thompson

Rhetorical Questions

How many times have you waited in the rain or snow for a bus that is ten minutes late? How many times has a surly bus driver snapped an answer to your innocent question? How many times have you stood for half an hour in a bus crammed with people?

—*Cheryl Lewis*

Uncommon Constructions

- Use paired conjunctions (*both/and, neither/nor, not only/but also*) to link ideas.

  Neither fear of failure nor desire for glory drove her to practise that trumpet hour after hour.

Exercise 15.7

Rewrite a paragraph from one of your personal essays so that it includes two or more of the devices discussed in this section.

Exercise 15.8

Using the specific suggestions in Improving Your Style as a guide, evaluate the stylistic strengths and weaknesses of the following paragraph.

As I returned home from interviewing my new client, I could not stop thinking about Jane. She had done nothing unusual during the interview. In fact, if I had not read her chart she would have appeared like the babysitter next door, except smarter. I felt that, for my own peace of mind and the safety of society, Jane should be wearing a tattoo on her forehead that said "psychopath." Inside I felt entirely unclean. The only emotion that came through clearly was fear. She was not someone who made me feel afraid for my personal safety, but she made me feel afraid for the world. She challenged the way I had categorized the world up until then. Jane was a woman with no mental illness, no deficits of intelligence or social skills, and apparently no conscience. She tortured and killed toddlers. She terrified me.

After proofreading for style, you need to examine your sentences for correct grammar and punctuation, topics which are covered in Part 5. The chapters are in a certain order, but refer to them in the order that you need. For instance, if your instructor suggests you focus on commas, skip ahead to that chapter.

PART 5

PROOFREADING: THE FINAL TOUCHES

	OK	NEEDS WORK

1. Have you corrected errors in **sentence structure**?
   a. fragments, comma splices, fused sentences (17d, e, f, g)
   b. faulty parallelism, faulty subordination, mixed constructions (17h, i, j)

2. Have you corrected errors in the use of **verbs**?
   a. verb forms (18a, b, c, d)
   b. subject-verb agreement (18e)

3. Have you corrected errors in the use of **pronouns**?
   a. pronoun agreement (19d)
   b. pronoun form (19a, b, c)
   c. pronoun reference (19e)

4. Have you corrected errors in the use of **modifiers**?
   a. misused adjectives and adverbs (20a, b, c)
   b. misplaced and dangling modifiers, split infinitives (20d, e, f)

5. Have you corrected errors in **punctuation**?
   a. commas and semicolons (21a, b)
   b. quotation marks (21f)
   c. apostrophes (21c)
   d. other punctuation (21d, e, g, h)

6. Have you corrected errors in the use **abbreviations**, **capitalization**, and **numbers**? (21i, j, k)

7. Have you corrected errors in **format**
   a. in MLA-style writing assignments (Appendices A, B)
   b. in APA-style writing assignments (Appendices A, C)

8. Have you corrected errors in **spelling**?
   a. names, places, titles, other proper nouns
   b. homonyms, frequently misspelled words, typos

CHAPTER 16

Proofreading Strategies

After you have checked the structure, language, and style of your essay, you need to proofread. Proofreading involves looking for and correcting particular errors in sentence structure, grammar, punctuation, spelling, and format. Don't skip this last step, even if you are pressed for time or simply bored with a piece of writing. Poorly constructed sentences and slips in grammar can bring an A paper down to a B or lower, or a D paper down to an F. Spelling errors in a résumé or cover letter make your documents look unprofessional and might prevent you from being asked for an interview. Assure your reader of your competence by giving your writing a final polish.

To locate the rough spots in your writing, try these strategies:

- Leave your paper for at least a day so you can see what you wrote more clearly.

- Use the Proofreading Checklist to remind yourself of potential problems.

- Prepare a checklist of your common errors, which will focus your proofreading.

- Read your paper aloud either to yourself or to a friend. Revise awkward or unclear sentences.

- Read your paper backwards, sentence by sentence. This strategy is especially good for highlighting sentence fragments and spelling errors.

- Use the spell checker and other correction features provided by your word-processing software, but remember to customize the built-in dictionary to reflect Canadian spelling and usage.

Proofreading: Sentence Structure

Among other things, good writing is writing that "flows." Readers are quickly irritated by writing that doesn't flow because sentences are unvaried, punctuated incorrectly, or badly constructed. To help you create writing that flows, this section will go over some of the basics of sentence structure along with some of the most common sentence errors: comma splices, fused sentences, fragments, faulty parallelism, faulty subordination, and mixed constructions.

If you would like more information on essential terminology, consult Appendix F.

17a PHRASES

The foundations of sentences are phrases and clauses. A **phrase** is a group of grammatically linked words *without either* a subject or a verb; a clause is a group of grammatically linked words containing a subject and a verb. Phrases typically function as parts of speech in a sentence, acting as nouns, adjectives, and adverbs.

Types of Phrases

Verbal phrases consist of a verbal and any other objects and/or modifiers. The three main types of verbal phrases are **infinitive, participle,** and **gerund.**

Infinitive phrases include the infinitive form of the verb (*to* + verb) and the object of the infinitive and/or other related words. When participle phrases begin sentences, they must be logically connected to the main clause, or you will create a mistake called the dangling modifier, which is discussed in 20f.

> **To buy the music magazine** *Uncut,* you will need at least twelve dollars.

> If you want **to own a CD of rare music,** this magazine is worth your money.

Participle phrases include the present or past particle of the verb (formed by adding *ing* or *ed* to the present tense of the verb) along with the object of the participle and/or any other related words. Participle phrases function as **adjectives** within the sentence.

> **Jumping up and down,** Greg shouted that he had won the Lotto 6/49. [*Jumping up and down* describes Greg.]

> The astronaut **chosen to ride the space shuttle** is from Canada. [Which astronaut is from Canada? The one chosen to ride the space shuttle.]

> **Boxed in by other runners,** Rami was unable to make a break for the finish line.

When participle phrases begin the sentence, they must be followed by the subject they are describing; if they aren't, you create the dangling modifier mistake, discussed in 20f.

Gerund phrases resemble participle phrases, but they function as nouns, acting as a subject, object, or subject complement.

Riding a bike without a light is very dangerous. [subject]

A behaviour parents often frown upon is **jumping on the furniture.** [subject complement]

Adam avoided **working on his paper** while watching the soccer game. [object]

Absolute phrases resemble participle phrases that are preceded by a noun or a pronoun. However, absolute phrases have subjects; they can also modify a whole sentence.

Tom looked full, **his second dessert creeping up on him.**

Her arms and legs flailing madly, Sarah skated clumsily over the ice.

Prepositional phrases include a preposition, an object of the preposition and/or any related words. Prepositional phrases can act as adjectives and adverbs. (Don't confuse prepositional phrases beginning with *to* with infinitive phrases.)

When we were camping, we awoke to a large noise **outside our tent;** it was a flying saucer hovering **above the lake.** Terrified, we ran **to the car** as quickly as possible.

Our newly elected mayor, known for attending strip clubs, was a man **of questionable morals.**

Appositives, which rename the subject, are usually placed after it.

We waited in the pub, **our favorite meeting place.**

Memphis, **my first dog,** is immensely spoiled.

Exercise 17.1

In the sentences below, identify the phrases corresponding to the bolded words.

1. Although the practice is banned **in some countries,** cropping dogs' ears is still permissible **in the United States.**

2. However, several individual states oppose **performing the procedure.**

3. **Cropping ears, an unnecessary practice,** is controversial because some experts claim that dogs **with cropped ears** experience medical complications, such as infections, phantom pain, and even seizures.

4. Several dogs with this procedure have been known **to have behavioural problems.**

5. **Responding to the controversy,** the national clubs of some breeds have amended their standards **to include breeds with both cropped and non-cropped ears.**

6. Ear-cropping is hopefully going out of fashion, **the practice not being taught in most respectable veterinary colleges.**

17b CLAUSES

A clause is a group of words containing at least a subject and a verb. **An independent (main) clause** expresses a complete idea and can stand on its own; a **dependent (subordinate) clause** does not express a complete idea.

Adam [subject] cycles to work. [verb + prepositional phrase]

This subject-verb combination expresses a complete idea and is therefore an independent or main clause.

After Adam and Darren [subject] run in Hawrelak park. [verb plus prepositional phrase]

Although we have a subject and a verb here, the sentence does not express a complete idea. What happens after these two run in Hawrelak Park? Do they collapse? Stretch? This clause is therefore *dependent;* it needs a main clause to complete it.

After Adam and Darren run in Hawrelak park, they like to go to Tim Horton's.

Types of Dependent Clauses

Dependent clauses can be identified according to their role in the sentence.

Noun clauses, which are the most difficult to recognize, do anything a noun can do; they can act as subject, object, or object of the preposition. (See Appendix F for a more thorough definition of *object.*)

What Professor Stevenson knows about the comma could fill an entire book. [subject]

Mr. Boudreau finally revealed **what he had in mind for his staff.** [object]

Adverb clauses, which are the easiest to recognize, tell us something about the sentence's main verb: when, why, under what conditions. They begin with easily recognizable subordinate conjunctions, such as *as, because, before, since,* and *while.*

Before Sarah goes to bed tonight, she has to do four sets of crunches.

Although the price of gas keeps increasing, Albertans still drive large vehicles.

Whenever we go to Costco, we always spend at least three hundred dollars.

Adjective clauses, just like adjectives, give more information about nouns and pronouns in the sentence. They begin with *who, which,* or *that.*

Tim Berners-Lee, **who developed the World Wide Web,** could not have known the impact of his little invention.

Adjective clauses are either **restrictive,** providing necessary information or **nonrestrictive,** giving extra but nonessential meaning.

Bob's Bird World, **which is around the corner,** sells the healthiest parrots. [Because the pet store has already been identified by its name, the information about its location is nonessential. This is a *nonrestrictive* clause.]

The pet store **that is around the corner** sells the healthiest parrots. [Because we do not know which pet store is being referred to, this clause is *restrictive.*]

In formal writing, nonrestrictive clauses are introduced with *which* and set off with commas whereas restrictive clauses are introduced with *that* and have no commas.

Exercise 17.2

Underline the main or independent clause(s) in each of the following sentences.

1. To prove your hypothesis, you must not falsify data or ignore contradictory evidence.

2. Clarence cut the questioning short with a caustic remark and a withering glance.

3. Furrowing her brow in concentration, Karen wound up for the pitch.

4. When he finished his project, Gavin admired his handiwork: a two-storey birdhouse with a railed porch and cedar roof.

5. Hans scrubbed at the large blue stain on his shirt front, but he couldn't get it out.

Exercise 17.3

Underline the subordinate (dependent) clauses in the sentences below. Above each subordinate clause, identify the type.

1. African dwarf frogs, or ADF's for short, are aquatic frogs that live submerged.

2. These frogs, which get up to only two inches long from snout to tail, are small enough for medium-sized aquariums.

3. Even though these frogs are tiny, you still need to provide at least 2.5 gallons of aquarium space per frog.

4. You also need to keep the water really clean by making frequent water changes and by using dechlorinators that remove heavy metals.

5. That they need variety in their diet is well known: bloodworms, beef heart, and tadpole pellets, which are all relatively cheap, are acceptable foods for ADF"s.

6. Although they spend most of their time swimming, they also are known for their Zenlike behaviour, such as hanging upside down, standing on one leg, or floating.

7. Aquatic frogs, because they are easy to maintain and entertaining to watch, are ideal for people new to aquariums.

17c COMBINING CLAUSES INTO SENTENCES

Being able to distinguish phrases from clauses and understanding how clauses are connected within the larger structure of your sentence will help you to understand the basic types of sentences and help you to punctuate these sentences properly.

A sentence composed of only one independent clause is a **simple sentence.** Simple refers to the grammatical structure, not the content or length of the sentence.

A dragonfly is an insect. [This is a short simple sentence.]

Belonging to the order Odonata, the dragonfly has an elongated body, wide wings, and multifaceted eyes. [This sentence, though long and complicated, is still simple.]

A sentence consisting of two or more independent clauses is a **compound sentence.** Ideal for connecting related ideas, this sentence can be punctuated in three ways.

■ *Independent clause + comma + coordinate conjunction (for, and, nor, but, or, yet, so) + independent clause*

Dragonflies may appear quite frightening, but they are harmless to humans.

■ *Independent clause + semicolon + conjunctive adverb + independent clause (or clauses)*

Dragonflies may appear quite frightening; however, they are quite harmless to humans, and they are only harmful to mosquitoes, midges, and small insects.

■ *Independent clause + semicolon + independent clause*

Be careful with using a semicolon by itself. Make sure that your two sentences are either closely related and/or similar in structure.

Mosquitoes prey on humans; dragonflies prey on mosquitoes.

A sentence consisting of one independent clause and at least one dependent clause is a **complex sentence.** Complex sentences are ideal for establishing more intricate relationships between ideas. We will go over four ways to punctuate them.

■ *Dependent clause + comma + independent clause*

Although the wing span and size of dragonflies make them look formidable, they are harmless to humans.

■ *Independent clause + dependent clause*

Resting damselflies hold their wings slightly above their bodies whereas resting dragonflies hold their wings slightly level to or below their bodies.

■ *First part of independent clause + dependent clause + second part of independent clause*

The eyes of dragonflies, which are composed of at least 30,000 facets, give them 360-degree vision.

■ *Dependent clause + independent clause + dependent clause*

Although they look formidable, dragonflies are mostly harmful to mosquitoes, which they prey on mercilessly.

A special type of compound sentence is the **compound-complex sentence,** which is composed of two independent clauses and at least one dependent clause.

When I am running, I love to stop and watch the dragonflies manoeuvring like so many little helicopters, for they remind of me of nature's ingenuity.

I would love for them to follow me home, so they could clean up my backyard, which is infested with voracious mosquitoes.

Exercise 17.4

Identify whether the sentences below are simple, compound, complex, or compound-complex. Underline the dependent clauses.

1. According to a study published in *Neurology,* stressed people are more prone to age-related memory loss.

2. This study began with 1,265 people who had no cognitive impairment.

3. Over the course of twelve years, 482 people developed mild cognitive impairment.

4. When these 482 people were questioned about their stress levels, some interesting results were discovered, and they were subsequently analyzed.

5. The researchers found that 40 percent of the people with MCI complained of being frequently stressed, anxious, or angry at someone close to them.

6. This study supported the idea that chronic stressful experiences affect the part of the brain handling stress response, which is also the part regulating memory.

7. Stress plays an important role in the development of Alzheimer's; therefore, we should manage stress to avoid memory loss and to maintain brain health.

Combining Clauses into Sentences

Exercise 17.5

The following paragraph sounds choppy because it is written almost entirely in short, simple sentences. Rewrite the paragraph to improve its sentence variety.

Being your own boss has its downside. I learned the hard way. One summer I decided to go into business for myself. I was tired of my usual part-time jobs. I was tired of the long hours and low pay at the fast-food restaurants and laundries I'd worked at in the past. I decided to strike out on my own. I started up the Domestic Bliss Home and Pet Care Service. It was a house-sitting service for clients away on vacation. I contracted to water plants, take in mail and newspapers, and feed pets. This last responsibility soon proved the most challenging. One of my charges was Baby. Baby was lonely. She was affectionate. She was untrained. She was a twenty-five-kilogram Golden Retriever who leapt into my arms with joy every time I stepped into her house. Another of my charges was the Queen of Sheba. She was an overstuffed Persian cat with surgical steel claws capable of slicing through even the thickest denim. Another of my charges was Jabberwocky, the parrot, who had apparently committed to memory *A Complete Dictionary of the Vulgar Tongue*. I spent a month cleaning up accidents and cleaning up litter boxes. I longed to be back in uniform behind a counter serving up chicken and fries. I completed the contracts with my current customers. I said farewell to all my furry and feathered friends. I closed the door on Domestic Bliss.

Exercise 17.6

If you are still having difficulty distinguishing the types of sentences, choose two subjects from this list: your favorite sport, your favorite musical artist, you favourite movie, your pet, or a room in your home. On two of the subjects, write a simple, compound, complex, and compound-complex sentence.

17d FRAGMENTS

Now that you have a basic understanding of the components and the punctuation of sentences, you are ready to recognize the sentence error called the fragment. A **fragment** is an incomplete idea punctuated as a sentence. In some contexts, such as informal letters, press releases, and ads, a fragment can catch your reader's attention.

A wonderful occasion for all of us.

The best buy ever!

A small step, but an important one.

If the rest of your sentences are grammatically complete, a fragment will stand out effectively for emphasis. On the other hand, if you mix several unintentional fragments with intentional fragments, you'll confuse your reader and lose your intended emphasis.

Remember, too, that fragments will make your writing seem less formal. Unless you wish your work to appear somewhat casual, avoid fragments in reports, business letters, and essays. Also, ask your instructor how he or she feels about fragments.

17d

Fragments

Recognizing Sentence Fragments

■ *Phrases or subordinate clauses punctuated as complete sentences*

Sometimes the fragment belongs with the complete sentence that comes before or after it in the passage.

FRAGMENT	Bill could balance a glass of water on his head. Without spilling a drop. [The second construction is a prepositional phrase and, like all phrases, lacks a subject and a verb.]
COMPLETE SENTENCE	Bill could balance a glass of water on his head without spilling a drop. [The phrase has been joined to the sentence before it.]
FRAGMENT	Because there had been two major rent increases in the last two years. Maureen decided to look for a new apartment. [The first construction is a subordinate clause, not a complete sentence.]
COMPLETE SENTENCE	Because there had been two major rent increases in the last two years, Maureen decided to look for a new apartment. [The subordinate clause has been joined to the following sentence to create a complex sentence.]

■ *Sentences with missing verbs*

If you remember that verbs ending with *ing* must have an auxiliary or helping verb (such as *be, do,* or *have*) to be a complete verb, you'll be less likely to write this kind of fragment.

FRAGMENT	The child frantically searching for her mother.

COMPLETE SENTENCE The child **was** frantically searching for her mother.

Be especially careful with *being,* which is a participle, not a verb. Avoid the phrase *the reason being.* Use *because* instead.

FRAGMENT The reason for her sore back being that she had fallen.

COMPLETE SENTENCE Her back was sore because she had fallen.

Exercise 17.7

Revise the following constructions to make them complete sentences.

1. Wendell driving around in circles, unable to find his date's house in the maze-like neighbourhood.

2. According to *The Hitchhiker's Guide to the Galaxy,* forty-two being the answer to the meaning of life, the universe, and everything.

3. After getting up to change channels himself because the remote control battery was dead. Brad sank back exhausted onto the couch.

4. Lydia, the last person I expected to quit school.

5. Angry at the parking attendant for writing up a ticket because the meter had expired.

Exercise 17.8

Revise the following constructions to make them complete sentences. If the sentence is correct, write **C.**

1. Always quick to judge others, but he bridled at even the mildest criticism.

2. Open your booklets and begin the exam.

3. The fans cheering wildly as the defenceman raced down the ice.

4. Turning his head for an instant to look at his program, Brendan missed the winning goal.

5. A woman with fierce pride and a determined spirit.

6. The reason for the fire being a pot of hot oil left burning on the stove.

7. Last year Donald was the grand prize winner in the Bulwer-Lytton bad writing contest.

8. Tearing open the envelope and nervously removing the transcript of her final grades.

9. Although I could detect movement inside, no one answering my knock.

10. Because he didn't phone in or show up for work.

Exercise 17.9

Restore the following paragraph to its original form by eliminating all inappropriate sentence fragments.

In life and in literature, people create alternate versions of reality. To avoid facing the unpleasant aspects of the lives they actually live. Or just to make their lives more exciting. In "Spy Story" by Filipino writer Jose Y. Dalisay, for example, Fred has convinced himself that he is a secret agent for the US Embassy. Thinking that everyone around him is a spy and up to no good. Fred creates some excitement in his otherwise boring job as a chauffeur. It's clear to most readers that Mr. Sparks, Fred's boss, is running a prostitution ring. Forcing Fred into the role of a pimp. But Fred imagines that Mr. Sparks is entertaining high-ranking American contacts to foil dangerous espionage activities. As well as commenting on our capacity for self-deception as individuals, "Spy Story," which has a significant political dimension. By setting his story in a seedy bar in the Philippines during the Cold War of the 1950s, Dalisay comments on the distortions of reality widely shared during this time of propaganda, spies, and secrets.

17e COMMA SPLICES

After you have checked your writing for variety in the length of sentences (Chapter 16) and in the type of sentences, you now have to make sure that you have punctuated these sentences correctly. A common error is the comma splice, which occurs when two **main (independent) clauses** are joined by only a comma (when compound sentences are not punctuated properly) or when **two complete sentences** are joined by only a comma.

COMMA SPLICE	She waved at the helicopter, she did not see the pilot wave back. [two independent clauses separated by only a comma]
COMMA SPLICE	The wind whipped up dead leaves in the yard, violent drops of rain beat against the ground, which looked pulverized. [an independent clause attached to a complex sentence by only a comma]

Comma splices, which indicate a lack of understanding of sentence structure, should be eliminated from your writing. You can do so by asking the following questions, which are derived from your previous reading about clauses:

Recognizing Comma Splices

1. Does my sentence consist of two or more clauses? (If *no,* you have a clause and a phrase; if *yes,* go to 2.)

   Looking grateful, she waved at the departing helicopter. [This is a participle phrase and clause separated by a comma. This is not a comma splice, but a well-constructed sentence.]

   She waved at the departing helicopter, she was glad to see him leave. [There are two clauses here, so this could be a comma splice.]

2. Are both of the clauses in my sentence main clauses; that is, does each clause express a complete idea? (If *no,* you have a complex sentence; if *yes,* go to 3.)

   She waved at the departing helicopter, she was glad to see him leave. [These are definitely main clauses; each can stand on its own as a sentence.]

3. Have I separated these two main clauses with only a comma? (If *yes,* you have a comma splice. Now that you have recognized it, you need to fix it!)

   She waved at the departing helicopter. She was glad to see him leave.

Exercise 17.10

Mark the following sentences **SPL** if they contain comma splices or **C** if they are correct.

1. When I worked as a cashier in a local supermarket, I dreaded the monthly special on quarter chicken legs.

2. The packages were poorly sealed, the three legs oozed raw chicken juices and blood.

3. The juices leaked all over the conveyor belt and all over my hands as I scanned and packed the chicken.

4. I was concerned about contamination, I sanitized the belt and my hands with antibacterial cleanser after each order.

5. Despite my best efforts to rid myself of the smell of chicken, my dog would practically knock me to the ground when I returned home.

17f FUSED SENTENCES

A **fused sentence,** sometimes called a *run-on sentence,* occurs when two main clauses or two complete sentences are joined with no punctuation between them. Like the term *simple,* the term *run-on* refers to the grammatical structure of the sentence and not the length or content; that is, a sentence can be quite long without being run-on.

CORRECT — Wendy stopped and glared angrily at the mischievous children as another snowball flew by, narrowly missing her head and crashing into the side of her house.

On the other hand, some fused sentences are quite short.

FUSED — Open the window I need some fresh air.

If you correct a fused sentence by adding only a comma, you will, unfortunately, turn this error into the dreaded comma splice. However, the good news is that the same techniques can be used for fixing both comma splices and fused sentences.

17g CORRECTING COMMA SPLICES AND FUSED SENTENCES

There are five ways to correct comma splices and fused sentences.

1. *Use a period to separate the two clauses.*

COMMA SPLICE — An enormous wave hit the boat, all those on deck were swept overboard.

REVISED — An enormous wave hit the boat. All those on deck were swept overboard.

2. *Use a comma and coordinating conjunction (and, but, or, nor, yet, so, for) to join the two clauses. When you do so, you create a COMPOUND sentence.*

FUSED SENTENCE — Peering through the darkness, they could see the lights of the settlement they struggled onward.

REVISED — Peering through the darkness, they could see the lights of the settlement, so they struggled onward. [compound sentence introduced by the phrase "Peering . . . darkness"]

3. *Use a semicolon and a conjunctive adverb, such as however, therefore, thus, or then to join the two clauses, creating another compound sentence.*

COMMA SPLICE — Sean drifted out of high school without a diploma, he now has the job of his dreams.

REVISED — Sean drifted out of high school without a diploma; however, he now has the job of his dreams.

4. *Use a semicolon to join the two clauses if they contain closely related ideas.*

FUSED SENTENCE — Fish stocks have declined in the last ten years fishing licences are now difficult to obtain.

REVISED	Fish stocks have declined in the last ten years; fishing licences are now difficult to obtain.

5. ***Change one of the main clauses into a subordinate clause. When you do so, you create a complex sentence.*** Put a comma after the subordinate clause if it comes first in the sentence.

COMMA SPLICE	You need to get more rest, you will get sick.
REVISED	If you don't get more rest, you will get sick.

Exercise 17.11

First, identify whether the sentence contains a fused sentence or a comma splice; then, using a number of revision methods, revise the sentences to eliminate the errors. To get practice, try to revise the sentences in a variety of ways.

1. A loud crackling sound alerted Gerta to the fact that she had left the foil cover on the dish, both the meal and the microwave oven were ruined.
2. Alicia offered to replace my shift when I called to confirm the arrangement, however, she had changed her mind.
3. As we waited in line, we heard Jason's unmistakable braying laugh, we hoped he wouldn't see us before we could disappear into the darkened theatre.
4. Tina groaned in dismay at the error message she pulled out the massive user guide and started her search for help.
5. Neither team chose Maria, she took her ball and went home.

Exercise 17.12

Revise the following passage to eliminate all comma splices.

These days many people use their computers as stereo systems that not only play music but also go out and get the music they want to hear. In response, the major labels are experimenting with anti-piracy technology such as non-recordable CDs, they want to stop consumers from trading tunes on the internet or burning recordable CDs. It's not clear how many non-recordable CDs have actually been released, however, the prospect has aroused considerable commentary. Some people say they have a right to burn their own CDs, the record companies are charging too much. Other people justify CD piracy by arguing that most of the money from sales goes to the companies, not the artists. In any case, it may not be possible to create a copy-proof CD that will still play in a computer. Trying to make one may annoy many consumers, the labels may decide it's not worth the risk.

Exercise 17.13

Revise the following paragraph to eliminate all fused sentences.

My final recommendation for becoming and staying a non-smoker is to eat Popsicles. Because you are taking on such a big commitment, you deserve a sweet treat now and then. Popsicles are low-calorie treats you will not gain weight. A Popsicle also gives you something to hold and put in your mouth just like a cigarette, but it is not a cigarette. You can choose any flavour you like when you have a really strong craving, you should not tear off the wrapper and plunge the Popsicle into your mouth because it will stick to your tongue and lips. If this happens to you, as it did to me, don't attempt to pull the Popsicle out it hurts. Have one of your support team come to your aid with warm water.

—*Athena Greba*

17h FAULTY PARALLELISM

The principle of **parallelism** is that similar ideas should be expressed in grammatically similar ways. Whenever you use a coordinating conjunction (*and, but, or, nor, yet, so, for*), be sure to join grammatically equal words, phrases, or clauses. Parallel structures enhance your ideas and logic and reveal that you care about your writing style.

Her New Year's resolutions were to **quit smoking, lose weight,** and **exercise regularly.**

Faulty parallelism occurs when ideas of equal value are not expressed in the same grammatical form.

Her New Year's resolutions were to quit smoking, lose weight, and she wanted to exercise regularly. [Two phrases and a clause make a faulty-parallelism error.]

Avoiding Faulty Parallelism

■ *Use the same part of speech for each item in a series of words.*

NOT   The family has wealth, reputation, and **is powerful.** [noun, noun, adjective]

BUT   The family has wealth, reputation, and **power.** [three nouns]

■ *Use the same construction for each phrase or clause in a series.*

Do not mix phrases and clauses, or even different kinds of phrases.

NOT   Maurice decided to complete his second year at college, look for a job, and **then he and Eva would get married.**

BUT   Maurice decided to complete his second year at college, look for a job, and **then marry Eva.**

■ *Make sure that items in a bulleted or numbered list have the same grammatical form, especially when taking notes or when writing resumes.*

NOT   1. Open the packet.
       2. The contents should be poured into a bowl.
       3. Add one cup of water.

BUT   1. Open the packet.
       2. Pour the contents into a bowl.
       3. Add one cup of water.

[Note that each item in this list begins with a verb.]

■ *Make sure that you include both elements in a comparison. (This mistake is also known as faulty comparison.)*

NOT   My paper is as long as **Bill.**

BUT   My paper is as long as **Bill's** [paper].

NOT   Sally wants to get married more than him.

BUT   Sally wants to get married more than he [does].

■ *Complete balanced constructions with grammatically similar sentence elements.*

NOT   The more I work on this assignment, **I don't seem to accomplish much.**

BUT   The more I work on this assignment, **the less I seem to accomplish.**

17h

Faulty Parallelism

■ *Read your sentences closely to make sure that correlative conjunctions (either/or, neither/nor, not only/but also, whether/or, both/and) join grammatically similar sentence elements.*

NOT   Not only the curtains but the drapes were also on sale.

BUT   Not only the curtains but also the drapes were on sale.

Exercise 17.14

Make elements in the following sentences parallel. If the sentence is correct, write **C.**

1. Robert can either work and save money for college, or he can take out a student loan.
2. The more I try to convince him otherwise, he is more determined to dye his hair green.
3. The Bennetts' house is smaller than their neighbour.
4. My car needs new paint, new tires, and the transmission is shot.

5. Not only did Marvin borrow my book without asking, but he also bent the cover and wrote in the margins.

6. The store went out of business because of inferior merchandise, their prices were high, and poor customer service.

7. Gina is both a skilled pianist and she is a talented baseball player.

8. Before becoming actors, some famous stars worked in other fields. For example, Harrison Ford was a master carpenter, and there is Michelle Pfeiffer, who was a cashier.

9. Some people keep repeating their mistakes; others keep making new ones.

10. • Graduated from Bishop Stratford High, 1998
    • Diploma in Automotive Repair, Mount Royal College, 1999
    • I took off to travel in Central and South America in 1999–2000
    • Completed my BS in Computing Science in 2004

Exercise 17.15

The errors in parallel sentence structure introduced into this passage make it wordy and confusing. Revise where necessary to make sentence elements parallel.

In an essay titled "The Pain of Animals," David Suzuki's subject is the pain humans inflict on animals by using them in scientific experiments, we hunt them, and some animals are kept in zoos. Suzuki's thesis is that we use animals for these purposes because their nervous systems are like ours and humans and animals have similar emotional responses. This similarity between humans and animals means, however, that animals feel fear and have pain feelings just as we do. Suzuki develops his essay by giving a series of examples of pain inflicted on animals in zoos and scientists perform experiments on them. He ends his essay with an account of his experience watching a film about the suffering endured by chimpanzees used for medical research. Their agony provides the strongest evidence for his argument that the similarities between chimpanzees and humans ought to make us more compassionate and we shouldn't be as exploitive in our treatment of animals.

17i FAULTY SUBORDINATION

Faulty subordination is both a logical and grammatical error that occurs when you fail to differentiate less important ideas from more important ideas.

■ *When you are writing a complex sentence, check that you have attached the subordinate conjunction to the appropriate clause.*

Some common subordinate conjunctions are *before, after, since, while, when, if, unless, until, because, although.* You can signal the connections among your ideas more accurately by putting the less important idea in the subordinate clause and by beginning the subordinate clause with the appropriate conjunction.

NOT   Because he could not go to the gym, he forgot his running shoes.

The subordinate conjunction *because* is in front of the wrong clause, thus making an illogical sentence. If he knew he could not go to the gym, he would not have brought his running shoes.

BUT   **Because** he forgot his running shoes, he could not go to the gym.

■ *Avoid using subordinate conjunctions colloquially; use the most precise subordinating conjunction.*

Pay particular attention to your use of *since* and *as. Since* can mean *because,* but it can also mean *from the time that.* In some sentences, *since* is confusing. In such cases, it is best to rephrase the sentence.

CONFUSING   Since Sandy broke her leg, she hasn't been playing basketball.

CLEAR   Sandy hasn't played basketball since she broke her leg.

CLEAR   Because Sandy broke her leg, she hasn't been playing basketball.

As is another troublesome conjunction. In colloquial and informal writing, *as* is often used as *because,* but it's clearer to use *as* to mean *during the time that.*

CLEAR   As the rain poured down, we made our way to the deserted cabin.

CONFUSING   **As** she cycles to work, she never gets stuck in traffic.

CLEAR   **Because** she cycles to work, she never gets stuck in traffic.

Note: You may have been told not to begin a sentence with *because.* You can do so; just make sure to include a main clause in the sentence.

■ *Limit the number of subordinate clauses in a single sentence.*

By piling subordinate clauses on top of each other, you can make it difficult for the reader to judge how your ideas are related. Your reader has to work to sort out the clauses to understand your logic and meaning.

17i

**Faulty
Subordination**

Revise these troublesome sentences by rephrasing the sentence or by reducing some of the clauses to phrases or single words.

NOT   **Because the committee could not reach a decision,** the project was stalled **because no one knew what to do next.**

BUT   The **committee's failure to reach a decision** stalled the project because no one knew what to do next.

NOT   The party **that wins the election, which will be held on November 10,** will set economic policies **that will affect the country** for the next ten years.

BUT   The party **that wins the November 10 election** will set the **country's** economic policies for the next ten years.

Exercise 17.16

Revise the following sentences to correct faulty or excessive subordination.

1. Since their home was badly damaged by fire, the Wongs have been living in a rented house.
2. Although Gina used the proper amount of bromine, the pool sides were still covered with algae although she also shocked the pool regularly with chlorine.
3. The fireplace that is in the basement has a pilot light that frequently goes out when snow blocks the outside vent.
4. Todd forgot to include his charitable receipts in his income tax return because his refund was delayed.
5. If you want to buy a computer, the person whom you should call is Roman, who is an expert on what are the best buys.
6. Craig isn't doing well in physics although he doesn't seem particularly concerned.
7. When I entered the building, I knew I was late for class when I heard the final bell.
8. Marina hates the taste of ketchup even though she likes ketchup-flavoured potato chips.
9. As I couldn't hear what he was saying, I asked him to speak up.
10. Since the air conditioner broke down, everyone has been complaining about the heat.

17j MIXED CONSTRUCTIONS

Mixed constructions get their name because they mix incompatible grammatical units and thus produce sentences that seem awkward and illogical. In a mixed construction, the sentence's subject and verb don't go together, or the sentence begins with one grammatical structure and then switches to another. This mistake is often the result of last-minute sentence-combining. You can avoid this error by proofreading carefully and by understanding basic sentence construction and punctuation.

For example, let's say you have these two sentences in mind:

June is exhausted because she has three small children.

The reason June is exhausted is that she has three small children.

If you are not paying attention, you might lose track of what you are writing and combine these sentences to produce a mixed construction:

MIXED   The reason June is exhausted is because she has three small children.

You can recognize awkward constructions by reading your work aloud to yourself or a classmate. Here are ways to avoid four common types of mixed constructions:

1. ***Think of definitions and explanations as equations joined by the linking verb is.***

When you use *is* in these equations, it must join two nouns. That is, avoid writing definitions and introducing examples with *is when, is where,* and *is because.*

MIXED   True love is when you lose your mind.

REVISED True love is the state of losing one's mind.

MIXED   A comma splice is where one joins two independent clauses with a comma and no coordinating conjunction.

REVISED A comma splice occurs when one joins two independent clauses with a comma and no coordinating conjunction.

MIXED   **The reason** the brakes failed **is because** the brake fluid was removed.

REVISED The reason the brakes failed is **that the brake fluid was removed.**

REVISED The brakes **failed** because the brake fluid was removed.

2. ***Make sure that when combining sentences, you don't have an adverbial subordinate clause acting as the subject.***

MIXED   **Because he was always late** [subordinate clause] **was the reason** he was fired.

REVISED **His habitual lateness** was the reason he was fired.

REVISED Because he was always late, he **was fired.**

3. **Make sure you have a subject in the main clause.**

Remember that a prepositional phrase is never the subject of a sentence.

MIXED   In the article "Anorexia and the Adolescent" [prepositional phrase] explains Lilian Donaldson's views on the connection between self-starvation and the adolescent's need for control.

REVISED   In the article "Anorexia and the Adolescent," Lilian Donaldson [subject] explains the connection between self-starvation and the adolescent's need for control.

REVISED   The article "Anorexia and the Adolescent" [subject] explains Lilian Donaldson's views on the connection between self-starvation and the adolescent's need for control.

4. **Don't confusingly combine questions and statements.**

MIXED   She wondered how long will it be until I see him again?

REVISED   She wondered how long it would be until she saw him again.

REVISED   She wondered, "How long will it be until I see him again?"

Exercise 17.17

Revise the following sentences to eliminate mixed constructions.

1. Geraldine asked her brother Ben how much longer will he be in the shower?
2. Because my dog ate my computer disk is the reason my paper is late.
3. Portaging is when you carry a boat overland between navigable lakes or rivers.
4. In Darrin's letter explained why he resigned his position.
5. The reason we cut our vacation short is because it rained for a solid week.
6. Without more donations means that the shelter will have to close.
7. Looking at his bank statement, Dominic wondered how did he spend so much money in only a month?
8. An example of Mary's thoughtfulness is when she cuts the lawn for her elderly neighbours.
9. In the theatre program lists all the actors in the play.
10. The next day is when Frank finally thought of a snappy come-back to Vincent's insulting remark.

17j

Mixed Constructions

Weblinks

- Jack Lynch's Guide to Grammar and Style
  andromeda.rutgers.edu/~jlynch/Writing/

- A Ten Minute Tour of Complex Sentences, Phrases, and Clauses
  http://writing-program.uchicago.edu/resources/complex-sentences.htm?

- Grammar Bytes' Interactive Exercise on Comma Splices and Fused Sentences
  www.chompchomp.com/exercises.htm#Comma_Splices_and_Fused_Sentences

17j

Mixed Constructions

CHAPTER 18

Proofreading: Verbs

Because the most important components of sentences are subjects and verbs, it is important that we use the right tense and form of verbs and that we make our subjects and verbs agree. It is also crucial to use the right verb voice. These are not easy tasks, however. Because the English verb system is quite complex, it's easy to make errors involving both verb tenses and verb forms.

18a THE PRINCIPAL PARTS OF VERBS

Each verb has four principal parts, from which all its other forms can be derived.

- The **infinitive** form (*to* + a verb) names the verb: *to walk, to run, to think.* The present tense is derived from the infinitive: *I **walk,** you **walk,** she **walks.***
- The **past tense**: *Yesterday I **walked** to school.*
- The **present participle**: I ***am walking** to school right now.*
- The **past participle**: I ***have walked** to school every day this week.*

Regular verbs form the past tense and the past participle by adding *ed* to the infinitive: *walked, have walked; visited, have visited.*

Irregular verbs form the past tense and the past participle in a variety of ways: *drank, have drunk; brought, have brought.* If you are not sure of the principal parts of an irregular verb, check your dictionary.

18b AUXILIARY VERBS

A number of verb tenses are formed by combining a participle with one or more **auxiliary verbs**:

am, is, was, were	*can, could, may, might*
be, being, been	*shall, should, will, would*
have, has, had	*ought to, have to, used to*
do, does, did	*supposed to*

18c COMMON ERRORS WITH VERBS

■ *Using the past participle instead of the past tense*

NOT   I **seen** [past participle] him yesterday.

BUT   I **saw** [past tense] him yesterday.

■ *Using an auxiliary verb with the past tense*

NOT   Ahmed **had went** to visit his parents in Manitoba.

BUT   Ahmed **went** to visit his parents in Manitoba.

OR   Ahmed **had gone** to visit his parents in Manitoba.

■ *Using* being *as a main verb instead of* is *or* was

NOT   The reason **being** that I was already late.

BUT   The reason **is** that I was already late.

■ *Using* of *to mean* have

NOT   He should **of** known better.

BUT   He should **have** known better.

■ *Using too many* coulds *or* woulds *in* if/then *statements*

NOT   If you **would have asked** me, I would have helped.

BUT   If you **had asked** me, I would have helped.

■ *Omitting verb endings*

Be sure the verb ending agrees with the subject of the sentence and that the tenses are consistent.

NOT   She **walk** to the video store.

BUT   She **walks** to the video store. [simple present tense]

NOT   After they **watched** the movie, they **walk** home.

BUT   After they **watched** the movie, they **walked** home.
     [simple past tense]

■ *Misplacing prepositions that are part of phrasal verbs*

If English is not your first language, you may find phrasal verbs (verb + preposition that functions as part of the verb, such as *figure out, look up, take care of*) confusing. Keep the preposition with the verb.

NOT   He **looked** his brother **after.**

BUT   He **looked after** his brother.

Exercise 18.1

Revise the following sentences so that auxiliaries and principal parts are used correctly. If the sentence is correct, write **C.**

1. You should of did the dishes instead of playing computer games.
2. How could you have wore a hole in your new running shoes already?
3. Whenever Martin gets the urge to work, he lies until down he feels better.
4. If I would have known you were in town, I would have invited you to the party.
5. The reason being that they couldn't find a babysitter.
6. Yvette rung the doorbell and waited to be admitted.
7. Susan has not wrote to her parents in over two months.
8. If Tom had submitted the essay on time, he would not have lost marks.
9. I am positive that I seen Jocelyn at the concert, but she insists that she wasn't there.
10. Rosa has swum in that lake every summer since she was a child.

18d KEEPING VERB TENSES CONSISTENT

Once you have decided on the tense—present, past, or future—of a particular piece of writing, be consistent. You may have to shift tenses to clarify time relationships, but don't do so unnecessarily. Use the present tense when you are writing about literature.

Note the use of the present tense in the following paragraph analyzing Stacey MacAindra, who is the central character in Margaret Laurence's novel *The Fire Dwellers.*

> Stacey's inability to communicate with her husband and children is a manifestation of the "tomb silences" of her own parents. Again we see Laurence's concern with the past as a source of isolation, for Stacey's background does not give her the means to be fully open with others. Moreover, she is a victim not only of her own past but also of the past influences that shape her husband, Mac, who inherits his reticence and his tendency to misinterpret Stacey's remarks from a father who is himself often restrained and imperceptive. Because of their childhoods, both Stacey and Mac believe that "nice" people do not talk about fear or pain. Stacey understands the limitations of this belief, but her inability to free herself from its influence leads her to remark that everyone in her family is one-dimensional. This image conveys Stacey's feelings of dissociation from her husband and children.

Exercise 18.2

Revise the following paragraph to eliminate unnecessary tense shifts. Use the present tense. The paragraph deals with Thomas Hardy's novel *The Mayor of Casterbridge.*

It's important to see that Michael Henchard in Thomas Hardy's novel *The Mayor of Casterbridge* is a kind of Everyman figure. Like most of us, he is motivated by psychological forces that he did not recognize or understand. For example, he never seems to understand why he sells his wife and then remarried her. Henchard was also affected by external forces over which he, like the rest of us, has no control. During the 1840s when the novel was set, long-established agricultural practices were being modernized by machines, and business practices are now much more complex. In addition to the forces of industrialization, Henchard, as a wheat trader, is especially vulnerable to natural forces such as the weather. After all, he made his living by predicting the harvest yields. Finally, Henchard is affected by chance and coincidence. It just happens that Farfrae, the man with exactly the skills Henchard needed, showed up when he is looking for an assistant manager.

18e MAKING SUBJECTS AND VERBS AGREE

Along with keeping your verb tense consistent, you also need to make sure that your subjects and verbs agree.

The principle of **subject-verb agreement** is that singular subjects take singular verbs and plural subjects take plural verbs.

This **ornament goes** on the top of the tree. [singular]

The **lights go** on first. [plural]

Here are the most common causes of errors in subject-verb agreement:

■ *The indefinite pronouns* everyone, no one, *or* each *as the subject*

Remember that the indefinite pronouns *everyone, no one,* and *each* as subjects are *always* singular.

Everyone is going to be at the party tonight.

No one leaves until I say so.

■ *Pronouns* either *or* neither *as the subject*

When *either* and *neither* appear alone (without their sidekicks *or* and *nor*), they are singular.

Neither of these menus appears to be satisfactory.

Either movie is fine with me.

- *Subjects linked by paired conjunctions:* either/or, neither/nor, not only/but also

However, in sentences with the paired conjunctions above, the subject closer to the verb makes the verb singular or plural.

Neither Reuben nor **his cousins were prepared** to kiss the bride.

Not only the students but also the **teacher was delighted** by the unexpected holiday.

- *A prepositional phrase separating subject and verb*

The subject and verb may be separated by a prepositional phrase (*of the workers, between the houses, across the field, including all team members, along with all his supporters*). Disregard these words and concentrate on matching the verb to the actual subject.

One of the workers **has filed** a complaint with the grievance committee.

Mrs. Murphy, along with her five noisy children, **attends** mass regularly.

- *Sentences beginning with* there *or* here

There or *here* may be the first word of the sentence, but neither will be the subject of the sentence. Look for the real subject after the verb.

There **are** only five **bananas,** not enough for everyone.

Here **come** the **Jackson twins,** just in time for dinner.

- *Subjects that may be singular or plural*

The verb accompanying pronouns such as *all, none,* or *some* as well as fractional expressions will be determined by whether what follows is countable or not.

None of the cake **is** left.

None of the cookies **are** left.

Some of the students **are** going.

Some of the student body **is** here.

Half of the grain **has** been damaged. (cannot really count the grain)

Two-fifths of the students **were** convinced that there would be no final exams.

Collective nouns, such as *team, group,* and *committee,* are considered singular when they refer to people or things acting as a unit.

Our **team is** on a five-day road trip.

The **herd has settled down** for the night.

They are considered plural when they refer to people or things in that group acting individually.

The **team do** not **agree** about the need for a new manager.

The **herd have scattered** in every direction.

Collective nouns of quantity (*number, majority, percentage*) are singular when preceded by *the,* plural when preceded by *a.*

The number of unemployed people **is increasing.**

A number of unemployed people **are** still **looking** for jobs.

Words joined by *and* are considered singular when they refer to a single unit or to the same person.

Bread and butter makes a fine basis for a sandwich.

My **neighbour and best friend has moved** to another city.

Exercise 18.3

Make subjects and verbs agree in the sentences below. If the sentence is correct, write **C.**

1. Neither Stephanie nor her sisters is available to help at the bazaar on Saturday.
2. The team have won the championship fours years in a row.
3. Neither of the applicants are willing to relocate to a branch office.
4. There goes the Pied Piper, along with all the children of Hamelin.
5. Fear of falling and of loud noises are instinctive.
6. Either the love birds or the goldfish make a suitable pet for an apartment resident.
7. The number of hamburgers sold has increased significantly this quarter.
8. The jury have been sequestered for three days.
9. Each of the committee members have made a different selection for Citizen of the Year.
10. Nothing I've seen in the last three clothing stores seem suitable for graduation.

18f UNDERSTANDING AND USING THE ACTIVE AND PASSIVE VOICE

English verbs have two voices: the **active** and the **passive.** In an active construction, the subject performs the action of the verb and the sentence is set up as subject + verb in the active voice + object. In a passive construction, the subject is acted upon and the sentence is set up as object + verb in passive voice + subject. In the passive voice, the subject may be present, preceded by the preposition *by,* or the subject may be absent.

> Edward made the announcement. [active]
>
> The announcement was made by Edward. [passive]
>
> The announcement was made. [passive]

When to Use the Active Voice

In most writing situations, it's best to use the active voice. Active constructions are usually clearer, more concise, and more forceful than passive constructions.

PASSIVE   The homeowners were informed by the city that the weeds would have to be cleared from their lots immediately.

ACTIVE   The city informed the homeowners that they would have to clear the weeds from their lots immediately.

When to Use the Passive Voice

However, there are certain circumstances in which you should use the passive voice.

- When you don't know the person or agent that performed the action

  My bike was stolen last night.

  The streets of prairie cities are typically laid out on a grid.

- When you want to emphasize the person, place, or object acted upon rather than the agent performing the action

  Her sister was run over by a drunk driver.

- When you want to avoid blaming, giving credit, or accepting responsibility

  Jeremy's two front teeth were knocked out by Paul's slapshot.

  The lowest bid was submitted by Megaproject Developments.

  "My ring was lost."

- When you want to sound objective, as in scientific, technical, and legal writing

  The experiment was repeated with four groups of subjects.

  All construction work must be completed by November 15.

  The defendant was found guilty and sentenced to five years in prison.

Note: Passive constructions distance you and your reader from your material. Don't use them merely to sound more formal; use them in the previous situations only. Your writing will be more lively, engaging, and concise if you use the active voice whenever possible.

Being Consistent

Avoid mixing active and passive constructions in the same sentence.

NOT   A letter was written by the homeowners saying the weeds would be cleared when they (the homeowners) were good and ready.

BUT   The homeowners wrote a letter saying they would clear the weeds when they were good and ready.

Exercise 18.4

Change passive constructions to active constructions where appropriate. If the passive voice is preferable, write **C.** Be prepared to defend your choices.

1. The light changed to amber before the intersection was reached by Oliver.

2. The municipal swimming pool was opened for the summer last week.

3. My directions were completely misunderstood by Burt.

4. After much lengthy debate, the meeting was finally adjourned.

5. The milk was spilled, but Marietta made no effort to wipe it up.

6. The building site has been shut down until all safety hazards have been eliminated.

7. Marcia was hurt by Sarah's careless remark.

8. After the lawn was trimmed and raked, we weeded the front flower bed.

9. Before setting out to write my exam, I searched for my good luck pen, but it couldn't be found anywhere.

10. The newspaper was delivered late again this morning.

Weblinks

• Online English Grammar, which has useful information on grammar and writing topics.

    www.edufind.com/english/grammar/index.cfm

• This handy list of irregular verbs is provided by OWL.

    owl.english.purdue.edu/handouts/esl/eslirrverb.html

- The OWL's explanation of verb tenses.

  owl.english.purdue.edu/handouts/esl/esltensverb.html

- Exercises on Subject-Verb Agreement from *Grammar Bytes*.

  www.chompchomp.com/exercises.htm#Subject-Verb_Agreement

- An explanation of subject-verb agreement and link to interactive exercises.

  grammar.ccc.commnet.edu/grammar/sv_agr.htm

18f

Understanding
and Using the
Active and
Passive Voice

CHAPTER 19

Proofreading: Pronouns

Pronouns substitute for nouns or other pronouns. The word to which the pronoun refers is called its **antecedent.**

My **grandmother** goes bowling every Wednesday. Then **she** eats lunch at **her** fitness club. [*Grandmother* is the antecedent of *she* and *her.*]

We will discuss the five most common types of pronoun problems:

- pronoun shifts
- pronoun case errors
- possessive pronoun errors
- pronoun agreement errors
- pronoun reference errors

19a PRONOUNS OF ADDRESS

Just as you must choose what verb tense to use in a writing composition, you must choose what pronoun of address to use and stick with it. You establish your relationship to your reader by the **pronouns of address** you use (or don't use) in your first paragraph.

If you want your readers to focus on you—your ideas, your experiences—use first-person pronouns (*I, me, my, mine*). If you want your readers to consider how your subject relates to them directly (as in sermons, advertisements, directions), use second-person pronouns (*you, your, yours*). If you use only nouns and third-person pronouns (*he, she, it, they*), you will encourage your readers to focus on your subject.

These sentences illustrate the different relationships you might establish with your readers in an article about word processors.

FIRST PERSON	When I first began to use a computer, I lost several files.
SECOND PERSON	When you first begin to use a computer, you may lose a few files.
THIRD PERSON	When they first begin to use computers, most people lose a few files.

Once you have established the basic pronouns of address for a piece of writing, do not shift abruptly and without reason to another set of pronouns.

NOT   When **you** first begin to use a word processor, **one** may lose a few files. [shift from second person to third person]

NOT   When **most people** begin to use a word processor, **you** may lose a few files. [shift from third person to second person]

Confusing pronoun shifts may occur *between* as well as *within* sentences.

NOT   When **I** began to use a word processor, **I** lost several files. **You** find it hard at first to master the sequence of commands. [shift from first person to second person]

These shifts disrupt your relationship with your reader and make your writing hard to follow.

Correcting Pronoun Shifts

In the following example, the perspective shifts from the third person, *Conrad (his)*, to the second person, *you.*

Conrad has invested **his** money wisely because, as an oil rig worker, **you** always face the possibility of seasonal unemployment.

There are two ways to correct this error.

• Replace *you* with *he.*

Conrad has invested **his** money wisely because, as an oil rig worker, **he** always faces the possibility of seasonal unemployment.

• Rephrase the sentence to eliminate the use of the pronoun.

Conrad has invested his money wisely because oil rig workers always face the possibility of seasonal unemployment.

Exercise 19.1

Revise the following sentences to eliminate pronoun shifts. Where there are several possibilities, be prepared to explain your choice. If the sentence is correct, write **C.**

1. I dislike asking Pauline for help because you never know whether she will keep her promise.

2. Even when you are knowledgeable and competent, many sales associates find dealing with a difficult customer to be an unnerving experience.

3. When you see Simon, you will be surprised at the changes in his appearance.

4. The owners claim that you can hear their ancestor's ghost on his nightly tour of the old mansion.

5. Colin has agreed to have a root canal rather than an extraction because you don't want to lose a tooth that can be saved.

19b

Pronoun Case

Exercise 19.2

Revise the following paragraph to eliminate all pronoun shifts.

Participants will get a more effective workout in your next fitness class if you follow this advice. Novice participants should position themselves near the instructor so you can see and hear clearly. The participant near the front is also less likely to be distracted by other participants. We should give the class our full attention, so don't spend your time worrying about whether other people are watching you or whether you put enough change in the parking meter. Although one might be tempted to compensate for lack of ability with expensive exercise clothes, don't spend a fortune on exercise accessories. All participants really need is a T-shirt, shorts, running shoes, and a willingness to devote an hour to their own good health.

19b PRONOUN CASE

The **subject pronouns** (*I, we, you, he, she, it, they,* and *who*) are used as the subject of a sentence or a clause—who or what is performing the action. The **object pronouns** (*me, us, you, him, her, it, them,* and *whom*) are used as the object of a verb or a preposition—who or what is receiving the verb's action, either directly or indirectly. The most common error in pronoun case is confusing the subject and object pronouns.

Subject Pronouns

Use subject pronouns in the subject position in the sentence. Don't be confused when the pronoun is part of a compound subject.

NOT   Frances and **me** went to the Farmers' Market on Saturday to buy vegetables.

BUT   Frances and **I** went to the Farmers' Market on Saturday to buy vegetables.

Don't be confused when the subject pronoun is followed by an explanatory noun (*we home owners, we students, we smokers*). The pronoun is still in the subject position.

NOT   **Us** residents are presenting a petition to city council.

BUT   **We** residents are presenting a petition to city council.

Use subject pronouns after comparisons using *than* or *as*.

NOT   Peter is as tall as **me.**

BUT   Peter is as tall as **I (am tall).**

NOT   No one was more surprised than **her.**

BUT   No one was more surprised than **she (was).**

Use a subject pronoun as the subject of an embedded subordinate clause. Be especially careful with *that* clauses.

NOT   Ramesh said that **him** and his wife would be glad to help.

BUT   Ramesh said that **he** and his wife would be glad to help.

Object Pronouns

Use object pronouns as the direct or indirect object of a verb.

NOT   The manager assigned Loretta and **she** to work a double shift.

BUT   The manager assigned Loretta and **her** to work a double shift.

NOT   Please let your mother or **I** know when you will be home.

BUT   Please let your mother or **me** know when you will be home.

Use object pronouns in prepositional phrases.

NOT   Between you and **I,** there is something strange about our new neighbour.

BUT   Between you and **me,** there is something strange about our new neighbour.

NOT   The city replied to **we** home owners.

BUT   The city replied to **us** home owners.

Note: Don't use a **reflexive pronoun** (the pronouns that end in *self/ selves*) as a substitute for a subject or object pronoun. A reflexive pronoun reflects on the subject or completes the meaning of the verb; it can be used only when there is a subject pronoun in the sentence.

OK   She asked **herself** if she was ready to go on stage.

OK   He allowed **himself** another trip to the buffet table.

NOT   My family and **myself** will be going to Nova Scotia for a camping holiday.

BUT   My family and **I** will be going to Nova Scotia for a camping holiday.

NOT   Ms. Chang asked that all inquiries be directed to **herself** rather than to Mr. Morgan.

BUT   Ms. Chang asked that all inquiries be directed to **her** rather than to Mr. Morgan.

Who and Whom

Who is a subject pronoun. Use it to refer to a subject noun or pronoun.

> Helen is the candidate. She is sure to win.

> Helen is the candidate **who** is sure to win. [*Who* replaces *she*.]

Whom is an object pronoun. Use it after prepositions and to refer to an object noun or pronoun.

> **To whom** do you wish to speak?

> He is a lawyer. We can trust him.

> He is a lawyer **whom** we can trust. [*Whom* replaces *him*.]

Possessive
Pronouns

Exercise 19.3

In these sentences, correct all pronoun case errors. Mark **C** for the correct sentences.

1. Us workers must stand firm in our demand for safer conditions.
2. Him and me agree on hardly anything.
3. Todd is no more likely to know the answer than her.
4. Can you tell me who to contact about this insurance claim?
5. Please let Mrs. Wallace or I know your vacation plans.
6. James said that you can get additional copies of the newsletter from Serena or he.
7. Adrilla and myself share the same birthday.
8. Michael, Stephen, and him will be working for the same tree planting company this summer.
9. Olga told me that her and her sister haven't seen each other in years.
10. She is the kind of person who isn't afraid to express an unpopular opinion.

19c POSSESSIVE PRONOUNS

Use **possessive pronouns** (*my, mine, our/ours, your/yours, his, her/hers, its, their/theirs, whose*) to show ownership or possession. Pay especially close attention to the following points.

• Don't confuse the possessive pronoun *its* with the contraction *it's* (*it is*).

POSSESSIVE   The committee has tabled **its** report.

CONTRACTION   Don't call me unless **it's** an emergency.

- Don't confuse the possessive pronoun *your* with the contraction *you're* (*you are*).

POSSESSIVE	Did you bring **your** books?
CONTRACTION	**You're** late.

- Don't confuse the possessive pronoun *whose* with the contraction *who's* (*who is*).

POSSESSIVE	I didn't hear **whose** name was announced as the winner.
CONTRACTION	I don't know **who's** calling.

- Don't confuse the possessive pronoun *their* with the contraction *they're* (*they are*) or the adverb *there*.

POSSESSIVE	The Séguins are attending **their** family reunion in Regina.
CONTRACTION	**They're** staying with Cousin Denis and his family for two weeks.
ADVERB	They hope to see the whole family **there.**

- Do not use apostrophes with *hers, his, ours, yours,* and *theirs.*

The battered canoe tied to the dock is **theirs.**

This sweater must be **yours.**

- Add *'s* to indefinite pronouns.

Everyone's assignments have been returned.

Someone's keys were turned in to the receptionist.

Exercise 19.4

Correct all errors in the use of possessive pronouns in the following sentences.

1. It is anyones guess why Greg didn't show up for the interview.
2. Who's piece of chocolate cake is on the table?
3. I know that the suitcases are identical, but I'm certain this one is your's.
4. There's is the most beautiful garden in the neighbourhood.
5. The dog bared it's teeth and growled menacingly.

Exercise 19.5 Review of Pronoun Case and Possessive Pronouns

Correct all errors in pronoun case and possessive pronouns. If the sentence is correct, write **C.**

1. Please tell Nigel or myself if you need a ride on Saturday.
2. Dale promised that him and his brothers would vacuum the pool before the barbecue.

3. No one is happier than me that you and her have won the scholarships.

4. The Vachons sold most of there furniture and moved into a condominium.

5. Do you know who's limousine is stopped at the light?

6. Justine claims that the idea was entirely her's.

7. Between you and I, she is not giving Ian his share of the credit.

8. Put everything back in its proper place.

9. The earliest that Dave and me can be there is noon.

10. Evangeline hopes that her boyfriend and herself are accepted by the same university.

Exercise 19.6 Review of Pronoun Case and Possessive Pronouns

Correct all errors in pronoun case and the use of possessive pronouns in the following passage.

Last February Peter and me decided to get married. We wanted to get married in June, so their were four months to plan the wedding. Although our wedding cost only $2,000, it turned out beautifully. Here's how we did it.

First we made a list of everything we could do ourself. Me and my sister spent two weeks shopping every chance we got in Value Village stores and all the second-hand vintage clothing shops. Luckily, I found the perfect dress for just under $50 and my sister found a gorgeous bridesmaid's dress for $100. I didn't mind that her's cost twice as much as mine because she said that her and her boyfriend might get married theirselves and she would wear that dress to the wedding. Peter was able to borrow his dad's dark suit, which his dad said looked better on Peter than it did on he. Peter's brother Tom had just gotten married, so he had a dark suit he could wear as best man. Having dealt with the clothing issue, we went to a pawnshop and bought two gold rings for $50 each.

Now we had to find a place to get married. We have a friend who's parents own a cottage near a local lake. They agreed to lend us there place for the weekend. For $200 we could rent canopies and tables to put on the lawn. Then I persuaded my mother to let Peter and myself raid her garden for lilacs, tulips, and daisies. They made lovely bouquets for all the tables.

Peter's Uncle Ted said that him and his friend, an amateur photographer, would take all the photographs. If we supplied the film, which cost about $100, he would print the photos with his own computer.

Now we had to find someone to marry us. We contacted a local marriage commissioner and discovered that the usual gratuity is $50. We had to give her another $50 to cover her travelling expenses. The marriage licence cost $50. So far, we had spent $700.

Its probably not surprising that food and liquor were our biggest expense. Because so many of our guests had allergies or were on special diets, we decided on a simple meal of chili, homemade cornbread, and huge salads, with beer and wine. For dessert, we had soy ice cream and a vegan wedding cake made by my father and I. Buying the food and liquor, and renting cutlery, glasses, and dishes cost about $700.

Of course, what's a wedding without music and dancing? No one knows more about the local music scene than Peter and myself, so we hired a band for $300. We didn't need to provide any of the sound equipment because the band said they would bring their's. Naturally, there were a few more miscellaneous expenses, but the total cost of our wedding was well under $2,000. Between you and I, the wedding couldn't have suited we thrifty folks better if it had cost $20,000.

19d PRONOUN AGREEMENT

Errors in pronoun agreement, just like errors in subject-verb agreement, occur when you don't match a singular pronoun with a singular noun or a plural pronoun with a plural noun. Pronoun agreement errors occur most frequently in the following situations.

Agreement with Singular Nouns

Pronoun agreement errors often involve using a plural pronoun to refer to a singular noun. Most often, the noun names a type of person (the alcoholic, the mature student, the typical worker) rather than an individual, as in the following example:

ERROR   The **alcoholic** may blame **their** drinking problem on unsympathetic family members.

There are four ways to avoid this kind of agreement error.

1. *Use a singular possessive pronoun.*

   The **alcoholic** may blame **his** drinking problem on unsympathetic family members.

Although this version is grammatically correct, the use of *his* is unappealing because it implies that all alcoholics are men.

2. *Use the phrase* **his or her.**

   The **alcoholic** may blame **his or her** drinking problem on unsympathetic family members.

This correction works well in single sentences but becomes cumbersome when repeated frequently. Avoid using *he/she, s/he,* or *him/her* in any piece of writing.

3. ***Make the noun plural.*** Pluralizing is often the simplest and most effective way to ensure pronoun agreement.

    Alcoholics may blame **their** drinking problems on unsympathetic family members.

4. ***Alternate masculine and feminine pronouns.*** If you were writing about types of people, such as the teacher and his or her students or the doctor and his or her patients, you could alternate masculine and feminine pronouns by referring to the teacher or doctor as *he* in one paragraph and as *she* in the next paragraph. Alternating masculine and feminine pronouns paragraph by paragraph is much less confusing and distracting than alternating them within a single paragraph.

Exercise 19.7

Revise the following sentences to make antecedents and pronouns agree.

1. Every manager has been asked their opinion of the merger.
2. A new immigrant generally suffers from culture shock, no matter how well they have prepared for the move.
3. A daycare worker must ensure that their qualifications in basic first aid are current.
4. It is not unusual for even an experienced actor to suffer from stage fright before they begin a performance.
5. A customer service representative needs to remain calm and polite in their dealings with the public.

Agreement with Collective Nouns

Collective nouns are words such as *jury, team, band, audience, group, family, committee, congregation, herd,* and *flock* that refer to people or things taken together.

When a collective noun refers to people or things acting as a single unit, the collective noun takes singular verbs and singular pronouns.

The **jury was** unanimous in **its** verdict.

The **band was** doomed without **its** leader.

When a collective noun refers to people or things acting as individuals, the collective noun takes plural verbs and plural pronouns.

The **jury were divided** in **their** judgment of the defendant.

The **band were arguing** over **their** next number.

When a collective noun is followed by a prepositional phrase, be careful to match the pronoun with the collective noun and not with the noun inside the prepositional phrase.

A small **group** of hecklers made **its** impact on the meeting.

The stranded **herd** of horses lost **its** way.

Agreement with Indefinite Pronouns

Singular Indefinite Pronouns

The following indefinite pronouns are always singular. They take singular verbs, and any pronouns referring to them should also be singular.

everyone	*anyone*	*no one, one*	*someone*	*either*
everybody	*anybody*	*nobody*	*somebody*	*neither*
everything	*anything*	*nothing*	*something*	*each*

Here is a typical example of an agreement error with an indefinite pronoun:

Everyone in the office had put in **their** request for time off at Christmas.

Here *everyone,* which is singular, and *their,* which is plural, do not agree.

You could correct this error by using the strategies suggested above for singular nouns. Alternatively, you could rephrase the sentence to eliminate the pronoun altogether.

Everyone in the office had requested time off at Christmas.

Don't be misled by prepositional phrases. If a singular indefinite pronoun is followed by a prepositional phrase ending with a plural noun (*of the children, in the houses, under the benches*) the verb and any pronouns referring to the subject are still singular.

Neither of the drivers has contacted **her** insurance agent.

In this sentence, the antecedent of *her* is *neither.* Because *neither* is singular, the pronoun referring to it must be singular.

Plural Indefinite Pronouns
(*Many, Few, Several, Both*)
The indefinite pronouns *many, few, several,* and *both* take plural pronouns.

Both of the drivers filed claims with **their** insurance companies.

Singular or Plural Indefinite Pronouns
(*All, None, Some*)
The indefinite pronouns *all, none,* and *some* are matched with singular pronouns when they are followed by a prepositional phrase that contains a singular noun.

None of the furniture has been moved from **its** original position for years.

These pronouns are matched with plural pronouns when they are followed by a prepositional phrase containing a plural noun.

None of the chairs have been moved from **their** original positions for years.

Exercise 19.8

Revise the following sentences where necessary to make antecedents and pronouns agree. If the sentence is correct, write **C.**

1. Everyone purchasing these selected products is eligible to submit their name for the grand prize in the draw.
2. None of the witnesses on shore were prepared to risk their own safety to rescue the drowning man.
3. Each of the crafters is selling their best creations at the fall fair.
4. Neither of the men left their names when they called this morning.
5. Anyone interested in joining the canoe trip should send his or her payment to Harriet by the end of the month.

Agreement with *Either/Or, Neither/Nor, Or, Nor*

Singular nouns joined by *either/or, neither/nor, or,* and *nor* are matched with singular pronouns.

Neither Farida nor Barbara has contacted **her** lawyer.

Either Mark or Craig will lend you **his** truck for the move.

Plural nouns joined by these conjunctions take plural pronouns.

Neither the students nor the teachers had time to collect **their** belongings when the fire alarm sounded.

When mixed singular and plural nouns are joined by these conjunctions, put the plural noun last and use a plural pronoun.

Neither the lead singer nor **the dancers** have been fitted for **their** costumes.

Exercise 19.9

Revise the following sentences where necessary to make antecedents and pronouns agree. If the sentence is correct, write **C.**

1. Neither the employees nor the supervisor believed that their position was wrong.
2. Either Sheryl or Jennifer will lend you her bicycle for the outing.

3. The herd of cattle left their grazing area and wended their way home.

4. Next week the safety committee will publish the results of their investigation.

5. If you need help with opening night at your restaurant, either Matt or Richard will offer their services.

6. The municipal government has issued their recommendations on property tax increases.

7. The weary group of tourists finally arrived at their hotel.

8. The class were packing their books in anticipation of the bell.

9. A family of bats has made their home in our attic.

10. I know you are curious, but neither Pierre nor Antoine wants me to tell you their plans for the weekend.

Exercise 19.10 Pronoun Agreement Review

Revise the following sentences where necessary to make antecedents and pronouns agree. If the sentence is correct, write **C.**

1. An experienced writer considers their readers' needs.

2. Neither of the suspects has confessed their involvement in the embezzlement.

3. The congregation is unanimous in its support of the new minister.

4. No one in the office has submitted their ideas on the proposal.

5. Some of the passengers stowed their baggage in the overhead bins.

6. After dissecting a frog in biology class, neither Stacey nor Veronica could eat their lunch.

7. A gambling addict may go deeply into debt to finance their habit.

8. All of the stolen money has been returned to its rightful owner.

9. An army marches on their stomach.

10. Everyone is expected to be on their best behaviour.

11. The band began its Canadian tour in Halifax.

12. Either Sandra or Brianne will give their oral presentation on Friday.

13. Neither of the two lost little boys knew their home address.

14. Every winner will have their picture in the newspaper.

15. Mr. Warden is a man who does their work without complaint.

Exercise 19.11 Pronoun Agreement Review

Revise the following paragraph to eliminate all errors in pronoun agreement.

A PowerPoint presenter arranges words and pictures into a series of pages that they project from a laptop computer onto a screen. Each of the screens typically has their heading followed by bullet points: six or seven words a line, six or seven lines a slide. Paragraphs and even sentences have too many words for a PowerPoint presentation, so the presenter must reduce their most complex ideas to little phrases. Of course, the bullet points eliminate the need for transitions, such as *because* or *on the other hand,* that might help a viewer understand connections among these phrases. The typical presenter hasn't noticed the absence of transitions. They have been so caught up in the technical features of PowerPoint that they have concentrated on the appearance of the text and the accompanying graphics. Never mind, if there are enough snappy visual aids, neither the viewers nor the presenter may notice that their presentation has the intellectual substance of a kindergarten show and tell.

19e PRONOUN REFERENCE

When you are speaking, you can usually make yourself understood even if you use pronouns rather vaguely. When you are writing, however, you don't have the opportunity to point to things or to explain vague ideas to your reader; thus, you need to make the connections between pronouns and nouns clear. When this connection is unclear, you have made an error in pronoun reference.

Here are some of the most common errors in pronoun reference.

Confusing Pronoun References

This problem is most likely to occur in sentences containing indirect speech.

VAGUE   When Kevin told Ali that he was being laid off, he was very upset.

CLEAR   Kevin was very upset when he told Ali, "I'm being laid off."

CLEAR   Kevin told Ali, "You are being laid off." Ali was very upset.

Vague Use of *They* and *It*

Avoid using *they* if it doesn't refer to a specific noun in your writing.

VAGUE   **They** say that a number of western democracies are shifting politically to the right.

CLEAR	**Respected commentators** say that a number of western democracies are shifting politically to the right.

You can see a similar problem with *it* in this sentence.

VAGUE	I spent hours working out a detailed budget, but **it** didn't solve my financial problems.

This sentence leaves your reader wondering what didn't help and what, exactly, *it* refers to: the time you spent working on your budget? Or the budget itself?

CLEAR	I spent hours working out a detailed budget, but **this effort** did not solve my financial problems.
OR	I spent hours working out a detailed budget, but **the budget itself** did not solve my financial problems.

Vague Use of *That, Which,* and *This*

In vague sentences, *that, which,* or *this* can refer to several different ideas.

VAGUE	The cousins fought on different sides in the war, **which** tore their family apart.

What tore their family apart—the fact that they fought on different sides? the exploits? the war? A clearer version might read like this.

CLEAR	The family was torn apart by the cousins' **decision** to fight on different sides in the war.

Exercise 19.12

Revise the following sentences to clarify vague pronoun references.

1. They say that nightmares are caused by anxiety.
2. Why do you tease your sister and call her names when you know it upsets her?
3. Natalie was disappointed when Nicole told her that she didn't get the job.
4. I rested and drank plenty of fluids, but it didn't make me feel better.
5. Maxine wanted to subscribe to the newspaper, but they said that home delivery was not available in her neighbourhood.
6. The cash register stopped working because a customer's child had turned off the main switch, but at the time Giselle didn't know it.
7. Raul added too much water to the dough and beat it mercilessly, which is why the pie crust is tough.

8. Rex is lazy, immature, and irresponsible, but that doesn't bother his friends.

9. I heard that Candace left her husband and children and ran away to Tahiti to paint. This greatly surprised me.

10. Mr. Carlson applied too much weed killer and overwatered the grass, which ruined the lawn.

Exercise 19.13

Revise the following paragraph to eliminate all vague and ambiguous pronoun references.

Vegans do not eat any animal products. This means that many of the foods most people enjoy, such as ice cream, mayonnaise, bacon and eggs, even toast with honey, are off limits. Because most prepared foods contain some animal products, eating out can be a real challenge, which is why many vegans cook at home and bring food with them when they go out. Of course, vegan cooking presents its own difficulties. When I became a vegan, I bought a cookbook with lots of delicious-looking recipes, but it didn't help. They put so many exotic ingredients in each recipe that I had to dash to the health food store before I could begin. Despite these obstacles, I'm glad to be a vegan. Now that they talk about so many diseases carried by cows, fish, and birds, who would want to eat meat even if they were killed more humanely?

Weblinks

- More explanations of pronouns from Charles Darling.
  grammar.ccc.commnet.edu/grammar/pronouns1.htm

- A convenient handout on pronoun case from OWL.
  owl.english.purdue.edu/handouts/grammar/g_proncase.html

- Pronoun Agreement and Reference Exercises from *Grammar Bytes*.
  www.chompchomp.com/exercises.htm#Pronoun_Agreement

20a KEY TERMS TO KNOW

Adjectives modify nouns and pronouns (that is, they describe the physical, mental, and emotional qualities of the people, places, and things named by nouns and pronouns). Words that end with *ful, ish, less, like* (*thankful, foolish, helpless, childlike*) are usually adjectives.

> The quick brown fox jumped over the lazy dog. [*Quick* and *brown* modify *fox; lazy* modifies *dog.*]

Adverbs modify verbs, adjectives, and other adverbs; they describe the manner or degree of the actions or qualities named by verbs, adjectives, and other adverbs. Many descriptive adverbs end in *ly* (a few adjectives, such as *friendly* and *lovely,* also end in *ly*). Some common adverbs, such as *very, always, not, well,* and *often,* do not end in *ly.*

> The cat stretched lazily in the sun. [*Lazily* modifies the verb *stretched.*]

> Dr. Lucas' lecture on the shortage of clean water in Ghana was extremely interesting. [*Extremely* modifies the adjective *interesting.*]

> The car went by too quickly for me to see who was in it. [*Too* modifies the adverb *quickly.*]

20b COMPARATIVE FORMS OF ADJECTIVES AND ADVERBS

Most adjectives and adverbs have degrees of comparison (*pretty, prettier, prettiest; interesting, more interesting, most interesting*). If you are not sure of the comparative form of a particular adjective or adverb (should it be *clearer* or *more clear*?), consult your dictionary. Avoid using double comparisons, such as *more happier* or *most fastest.*

Some adjectives (such as *unique, perfect, empty*) express absolute concepts. One piece of pottery cannot be *more unique* than the rest, one math test cannot be the *most perfect* in the class, and one glass cannot be *more empty* than another.

20c TROUBLESOME ADJECTIVES AND ADVERBS

■ *Good, well*

Good is an adjective.

> I haven't seen a **good** movie for ages.

Well is usually an adverb.

NOT   Declan **ran good** in the last race.

BUT   Declan **ran well** in the last race.

Well in reference to health is an adjective.

Jane hasn't been **well** since her bout of mononucleosis.

■ *Bad/badly, real/really*

Bad and *real* are adjectives.

This is a **bad** photograph of me.

The huge boulder looks **real,** but it is actually made of papier-mâché.

Badly and *really* are adverbs.

NOT   The roof was damaged **bad** in the hailstorm.

BUT   The roof was **badly** damaged in the hailstorm.

NOT   Ben is **real** eager to begin his new job on Monday.

BUT   Ben is **really** eager to begin his new job on Monday.

■ *Less and fewer*

Though they are both adjectives, *less* and *fewer* are used differently. *Less* (the comparative of *little*) is an adjective used with items that cannot be considered as separate objects: *less* food, *less* kindness, *less* snow. *Fewer* (the comparative of *few*) is an adjective used with things that can be counted individually: *fewer* students, *fewer* courses, *fewer* responsibilities.

NOT   **Less** students have enrolled than we expected.

BUT   **Fewer** students have enrolled than we expected.

■ Adjectives ending with *ing and ed*

If your first language is not English, you may find it confusing to decide on the correct meaning and appropriate ending for adjectives formed with an *ing* ending (present participle) or an *ed* ending (past participle of a regular verb).

She is **exciting.** [meaning that she causes others to feel excitement; *exciting* is an adj.]

She is **excited.** [meaning that she herself feels excitement; *excited* is a verb here.]

A good dictionary should help you decide on the correct ending.

■ Articles (*a, an, the*)

Many languages do not have articles, so learners of English often find this aspect of the language difficult. These guidelines may help:

1. Use the article *a* or *an* (before vowels) to indicate a noun in general terms (*a* meal, *an* orange).

2. Most proper nouns do not use an article. *The* is used with some plural proper nouns to indicate specific people (*the* Smiths) and geographical designations (*the* Rockies). *The* is also used with collective proper nouns referring to countries or groups (*the* United States of America, *the* United Kingdom, *the* CFL).

3. Use *the* to indicate a particular noun or one that has been mentioned earlier. (*The* photograph of *the* moon that I referred to is on page ten).

Exercise 20.1

Revise the following sentences so that adjectives and adverbs are used correctly.

1. He looked at me serious and began to speak.
2. The engine still runs good, but the body is badly rusted.
3. Less players have registered for hockey camp this summer.
4. The supervisor is real interested in your opinion of the proposal.
5. Clarence gets good grades in physical education, but he doesn't do so good in the chemistry.

Exercise 20.2

Revise the following sentences so that adjectives and adverbs are used correctly. If the sentence is correct, write **C.**

1. Lynette is the most liveliest member of my aerobics class.
2. You will feel considerable better after you have taken this medication.
3. The play went good in rehearsal, but opening night was a disaster.
4. Since landing a full-time job, Satpal has been able to afford more dressy clothes, but she has less social occasions on which to wear them.
5. The milk bottle in the refrigerator is completely empty.
6. Of the two reports, which is the more informative?
7. Eric answered all of the questions as honest as he could.
8. Although the hikers were real tiring, they decided to press on.
9. The door opened more easily after Jack adjusted the hinges.
10. Max is less happier living on his own than he was living at home.

20d MISPLACED MODIFIERS

One morning, I shot an elephant in my pajamas. How he got into my pajamas, I'll never know.

— Groucho Marx, *Animal Crackers*

As the above example suggests, comedians have long known the humour of the misplaced modifier, the grammatical error in which a modifier (adjective, adverb, or phrase or clause acting as one of these) is in the wrong place in the sentence. The misplaced modifier can create a *confusing* and unintentionally *amusing* sentence.

Mr. Kowalski saw a horse by the side of the road on his way home from work.

Because Mr. Kowalski is more likely to be on his way home from work than a horse is, the prepositional phrase *on his way home from work* should be placed closer to *Mr. Kowalski* in the sentence.

On his way home from work, Mr. Kowalski saw a horse by the side of the road.

A misplaced modifier often calls up a ridiculous image in the mind of the reader, such as in the sentence below.

Hanging from the ceiling, I noticed a large chandelier.

In this sentence, the participial phrase (*Hanging . . . ceiling*) modifies the "I" of the sentence. But because it is unlikely that the speaker is hanging from the ceiling, the phrase should be in a different location so that it modifies the noun *chandelier*.

I noticed a large chandelier hanging from the ceiling.

Words such as *only, hardly, barely, nearly,* and *almost* are especially troublesome because they can easily be misplaced.

NOT   She was almost pregnant every year.

BUT   She was pregnant almost every year.

NOT   I **only want** a minute of your time.

BUT   I want **only a minute** of your time.

Note: Do not use *hardly* and *barely* with *not.*

NOT   I **can't hardly** hear you.

BUT   I **can hardly** hear you.

NOT   She **couldn't barely** hear the faint sound coming from the basket on the front steps.

BUT   She **could barely** hear the faint sound coming from the basket on the front steps.

Misplaced
Modifiers

20d

20e SPLIT INFINITIVES

An **infinitive** is *to* + a verb: *to think, to walk, to breathe*. A **split infinitive** occurs when a modifier (usually an adverb) is misplaced between *to* and the verb (*to quickly run*). It is best to avoid splitting an infinitive, especially when the resulting construction is awkward. You can correct a split infinitive by rephrasing the sentence.

SPLIT INFINITIVE   Marjorie needed time to **mentally prepare** for the exam.

REVISED   Marjorie needed time to **prepare mentally** for the exam.

Sometimes, however, a split infinitive sounds less awkward than when the modifier is relocated in the sentence.

The diners asked the man at the next table **to please stop** smoking his cigar. [Putting *please* anywhere else in the sentence would be clumsy.]

Exercise 20.3

Revise the following sentences to avoid split infinitives and to fix misplaced modifiers.

1. Soak the shirt in cold water with the spaghetti sauce stain.
2. Sonia could almost run ten full circuits around the field.
3. Preserved in formaldehyde, the students examined the jar of tapeworms.
4. I promise not to unfairly judge you.
5. I had difficulty hearing the conversation standing by the band.

Exercise 20.4

Revise the following sentences to avoid split infinitives and to place modifiers as close as possible to what they modify. If the sentence is correct, write **C.**

1. The singer's fans couldn't hardly wait for the concert tickets to go on sale.
2. Properly cooked, you can eat hamburger without fear of food poisoning.
3. I want to thoroughly consider all my options before making a decision.
4. Greg has only enough money to cover this month's rent.
5. Seeing the accident ahead, the car pulled to the side of the road, and Tran got out to investigate.
6. We enjoyed the beautiful lawn and gardens eating our lunch on the patio.

7. You must be ill; you only ate half the pizza.

8. Jim heard the phone ring with his mouth full of toothpaste.

9. There is a family picture of our trip to Nassau on the hall table.

10. I asked him one final time to please stop pestering me.

20f DANGLING MODIFIERS

Participial and infinitive phrases at the beginning of a sentence normally modify the subject of the main clause. As you learned in Chapter 17, **participial phrases** are formed with the present or past participle of a verb.

Twisting in the wind, the kite rose higher.

Driven from their homes, the villagers set up camp in the hills.

Sometimes the introductory phrase suggests a participial form rather than stating it directly.

While [travelling] **in France,** we visited many wineries.

Infinitive phrases are formed with an infinitive (*to* + verb).

To swim well, you need to coordinate your stroke with your breathing.

To mend the tire, she had to find the leak.

Recognizing Dangling Modifiers

An introductory phrase that does not modify the subject of the following clause or that has no logical subject to modify is called a **dangling modifier.**

DANGLING   Driving down the mountain, three bears were seen.

DANGLING   **To run a marathon,** endurance must be built up gradually.

Notice that if you expand these phrases into clauses, the subject is not the same as that of the following sentence: *We* were driving down the mountain. *Three bears* were seen.

Notice too that the verbs in the main clause are in the passive voice: *were seen, must be built up.* Introductory phrases are more likely to dangle when the verb is in the passive voice.

NOT   After discussing the case for days, a verdict **was** finally **reached** by the jury.

BUT   After discussing the case for days, the jury finally **reached** a verdict.

When you put the verb into the active voice, the phrase no longer dangles because the subjects are now the same (*the jury*). (For more on active and passive voice, see 18f.)

Exercise 20.5

Underline the dangling modifiers below. If the sentence is correct, write **C.**

1. Before signing a contract, a lawyer should go over it with you.
2. In the middle of the night, we were awakened by police sirens screaming down the street.
3. To reduce conflicts with their children, better listening skills are needed.
4. When in Rome, the social customs of the Romans should be followed.
5. Because they arrived early, the Chans had good seats for the concert.

Correcting Dangling Modifiers

When an introductory phrase dangles, you can revise the sentence in one of two ways. You can either expand the dangling phrase to a subordinate clause or revise the main clause so that the introductory phrase logically modifies its subject.

NOT Intending to finish the report by the end of the day, my plan was to work through lunch and coffee breaks.

BUT Because I intended to finish the report by the end of the day, my plan was to work through lunch and coffee breaks.

OR Intending to finish the report by the end of the day, I planned to work through lunch and coffee breaks.

You could correct the dangling modifier in the next sentence by changing the prepositional phrase to a clause, with the subject clearly stated.

NOT After being honoured by sports writers and fellow athletes, the retired hockey star's name was inscribed in the Hall of Fame.

BUT After the retired hockey star was honoured by sports writers and fellow athletes, his name was inscribed in the Hall of Fame.

Sometimes, however, it is necessary to revise a sentence extensively to eliminate the dangling modifier.

NOT Upon learning about the budget cutbacks, it was difficult for Ruth to hide her concern that her position would be abolished.

BUT When Ruth learned about the budget cutbacks, she found it difficult to hide her concern that her position would be abolished.

Exercise 20.6

Correct each dangling modifier. If the sentence is correct, mark **C.**

1. Walking into the room, a strange sight caught my eye.

2. While in high school, George's father was promoted and the family moved to Vancouver.

3. Exhausted by a heavy work schedule, a complete rest was recommended by the doctor.

4. To make a perfect omelette, the freshest ingredients are required.

5. After pleading earnestly, the curfew was extended to midnight.

6. Hoping to catch the final inning of the baseball game on television, Michael left the office early.

7. Driven by arrogance and greed, Joe's friends were soon alienated from him.

8. After working so hard on the committee, our gratitude is definitely deserved.

9. To extend your cable service, you may call any time during office hours.

10. While reading Stephen King's *Cujo,* my dog began barking in the backyard.

11. Driving on the highway, Hank's car engine suddenly seized.

12. Staring intently at the small print, spots began to swim before my eyes.

Exercise 20.7

The following paragraph contains errors in the use of modifiers. Revise the passage to correct these errors.

Nineteenth-century workers couldn't hardly survive without spending long hours at demanding jobs. Farm workers and outside workers in the summer toiled from sunrise to sunset. Working shorter hours in the winter, less money was made. Shop employees were treated equally bad. To effectively meet the needs of their customers, shops stayed open real long hours—often fourteen to sixteen—with the same employees. The most dreadfulest conditions were in the factories. Treated as part of the machinery and forced to work at the pace of the machine, there was no time for talking or joking with other workers. Children as young as seven worked twelve-hour shifts and slept in factory dormitories. In England by the middle of the nineteenth century it was illegal to employ children under nine in textile factories, but most children were working full-time by the time they were thirteen or fourteen in 1900.

- This useful page is from the University of Ottawa's writing centre.

  www.uottawa.ca/academic/arts/writcent/hypergrammar/
  modifier.html

- Charles Darling's page on modifier placement and associated online exercises.

  grammar.ccc.commnet.edu/grammar/modifiers.htm

- OWL'S *very* useful handout on understanding and fixing dangling modifiers.

  owl.english.purdue.edu/handouts/grammar/g_dangmod.html

20f

**Dangling
Modifiers**

CHAPTER 21

Proofreading: Punctuation and Mechanics

21a COMMAS

When you are proofreading for comma errors, remember the following two principles:

- **Single commas** are used to separate the items in a series of words, phrases, or clauses and to set off elements at the beginning or end of the sentence.
- **Pairs of commas** are used to enclose parts of a sentence.

Key Terms to Know

A **series** consists of three or more similar grammatical constructions, whether they be words, phrases, or clauses.

> To complete grade twelve, Petra needs **English, chemistry,** and **physics.** [a series of nouns]

> Before leaving for the lake, Simon needs to **buy groceries, pack the camper,** and **pick up his children.** [a series of phrases]

> **If you can meet the entrance requirements, if you can find a sponsor,** and **if you can arrange your own transportation,** you can run in this year's marathon. [a series of clauses]

A **phrase** is a group of words without a subject and a verb (*around the corner, looking out the window, to finish the test on time*).

A **clause** is a group of words with a subject and verb.

A **main clause** can stand on its own as a sentence (*Bob walked his ferret*).

A **subordinate clause** cannot stand alone as a sentence (*After Bob walked his ferret*).

Using Commas to Separate

Separating Items in a Series

Use a comma to separate words, phrases, or clauses in a series. Although usage varies, we recommend putting a comma before the *and* or other conjunction that joins the last two items in the series, both to provide emphasis and to prevent misreading:

■ *Words in a series*

> I forgot to buy **orange juice, milk, bread, peanut butter,** and **jam.**

Note 1: Without the comma, the sentence would read ". . . peanut butter and jam." Because you can buy peanut butter and jam mixed together, you need this comma between the last two items to clarify whether you are buying one item or two.

Note 2: However, do **not** put a comma between pairs of items considered a single unit.

> The Prime Minister said that full employment, regional development, and **law and order** are the chief priorities.

■ *Phrases in a series*

> The frightened puppy raced **through the door, down the hall,** and **under the bed.**

■ *Clauses in a series*

> **Mohammed handles the budget, Judy handles customer complaints,** and **Philip handles the advertising.**

Setting Off Main Clauses

Use a comma before the coordinating conjunctions *and, but, or, nor, for, yet,* and *so* when they join main clauses.

> The company sold off its unprofitable subsidiaries, **and** its shares had doubled in value.

> The greyhound can run at least 40 mph, but it prefers to rest on the couch.

However, the comma is often omitted before *and* and *or* if the clauses are short.

> You stand in line and I'll find a table.

To prevent misreading, always use a comma before *for, so, yet* when they are used as coordinating conjunctions because these words have other uses.

> The dog limped, **for** it was old. [coordinating conjunction]

> The dog limped **for** the door. [preposition]

Setting Off Introductory Subordinate Clauses

Use commas after introductory subordinate clauses, which begin with subordinating conjunctions, such as *although, because, after, when, before, since,* and *while.*

> **Before anyone could stop the baby,** she had grabbed the edge of the tablecloth and pulled the dishes to the floor.

> **Because there has been so much rain,** the mosquitoes have been bad this year.

Exercise 21.1

Add all necessary commas to the following sentences.

1. Lorraine packed two suitcases called a cab and headed for the airport.
2. The secret ingredients in my stew are eye of newt toe of frog wool of bat and tongue of dog.
3. We have agreed to put the armoire in the master bedroom the console in the hall and the pine desk in the study.
4. We'll need bread cheese cold cuts fruit and sodas for the picnic.
5. The diner complained that the meat was underdone the vegetables were soggy and the wine was sour.
6. We must go now for our ferry leaves exactly at noon.
7. Freida knocked down the wall and David hauled away the rubble.
8. Liam is a painstaking editor yet a few small errors escaped even his sharp eye.
9. The Richardsons knew that they must replace the worn linoleum and repaint the walls a neutral colour or the house would never sell.
10. When Fiona first began working as a cashier she thought that she would never remember the PLU's for produce but she had soon memorized dozens of codes.

Setting Off Other Introductory Elements

■ *After introductory phrases of more than five words*

Sitting patiently beside my neighbour's woodpile, Brutus stood vigilant guard over escaping field mice.

■ *After introductory transitional words and phrases*

The usual practice is to put a comma after transitional phrases such as *for example, on the other hand, in contrast.* Also, put a comma after conjunctive adverbs of more than two syllables: after *nevertheless,* but not after *thus.*

On the other hand, many prairie grain farmers are in desperate straits.

Nevertheless, people were optimistic that the economy would improve.

Thus we need to work out a new system to deal with rural bankruptcies.

Note: Do **not** confuse subordinate conjunctions with introductory transitional words; do not put a comma after subordinate conjunctions but after the entire clause.

NOT   **Although**, she wanted to leave the party, she was afraid of being rude.

BUT   **Although** she wanted to leave the party, she was afraid of being rude.

■ *After introductory interjections*

Use a comma after mild interjections (*oh, well, my goodness, my*), and after *yes* and *no*.

My, what an ugly baby.

■ *After any introductory element to prevent misreading*

In the evening, darkness settled over the town.

Setting Off Elements at the End of a Sentence

Use a comma to set off a word, phrase, or clause at the end of a sentence that qualifies, contrasts with, or questions what comes before. Don't, however, put a comma in front of all subordinate clauses.

A puppy is a perfect pet, **if you have lots of patience.** [qualifying clause]

I ordered the chicken, not the squid. [contrasting element]

You'll give me a hand, **won't you?** [question]

Exercise 21.2

Add all necessary commas to the following sentences.

1. For example pizza has ingredients from all four food groups but it can also be high in fat.
2. During his years at university in Calgary Louis never took the opportunity to visit Banff or Lake Louise.
3. When Bret dropped the iron skillet on the tile floor he heard a sharp crack.
4. High above the planes flew in precise formation.
5. No I don't remember your lending me ten dollars.
6. It's best to feed a cold and starve a fever isn't it?
7. Time and tide wait for no man if you catch my drift.
8. Music has its charms to soothe the savage breast not the savage beast.

Using Pairs of Commas to Enclose

Enclosing Interruptions in the Sentence

Use a pair of commas to enclose words, phrases, or clauses that slightly interrupt the flow of the sentence but add no essential meaning. Such expressions include parenthetical remarks (*of course, indeed, for example*), transitions (*however, therefore*), interjections (*well, oh*), and nouns of direct address (*Henry, Mother*).

I will, **as I have already told you,** investigate the matter fully.

The events described in this story are true. The names, **however,** have been changed to protect the innocent.

I'd say he weighs about, **oh**, 80 kg.

This decision, **Kevin,** is for you to make.

Enclosing Nonrestrictive Phrases and Clauses

Use a pair of commas to enclose a nonrestrictive phrase or clause. These phrases and clauses function as adjectives, but they are unessential; they supply additional information and can be removed without changing the sentence's meaning. These clauses and phrases usually modify **proper nouns**—nouns that name a person, place, or thing.

NONRESTICTIVE PHRASE	Bob Edward, publisher of *The Calgary Eye-Opener*, was an influential and controversial figure until his death in 1922.
NONRESTRICTIVE CLAUSE	Clarence's Uncle David, who is an accomplished seaman, is planning to sail around the world.

In formal writing, clauses beginning with *which* are nonrestrictive; clauses beginning with *that* are restrictive.

NONRESTRICTIVE CLAUSE	In "The Lottery," which is about a seemingly ordinary village lottery, the horrifying nature of the prize is not revealed until the draw is made.
RESTRICTIVE CLAUSE	I've lost the book that I intended to lend you.

Note: Do **not** use commas to enclose a restrictive phrase or clause that provides essential information in the sentence.

RESTRICTIVE	All customers who install a smoke detector are eligible for a discount on insurance premiums. [Only customers who install a smoke detector are eligible.]
INCORRECT	All customers, who install a smoke detector, are eligible . . . [If you write the sentence this way, you are saying that all customers are eligible.]

Exercise 21.3

Add all the necessary commas below. If the sentence is correct, write **C**.

1. Thank you Mr. Sutherland for booking your vacation trip through our travel agency.

2. The people who live next door are covering their entire backyard in artificial grass.

3. Punch Dickins who won the Distinguished Flying Cross in World War I gained fame as a bush pilot in the 1920s.

4. Monty's python which hasn't eaten in a month has escaped from its cage.

5. Monty promised us however that we had nothing to fear.

- Use a comma to set off direct speech and quotations from the rest of the sentence.

Alice remarked, "The lights are on, but no one seems to be home."

We see Hamlet's growing awareness of the burdens placed upon him when he says, "The time is out of joint. O cursed spite / That ever I was born to set it right!"

21a

Commas

Note: Do **not** use a comma when a quotation is introduced with *that*.

We see Hamlet's hostility when he says that Claudius is "A little more than kin and less than kind."

- Use a comma to separate the day of the month from the year. Canada celebrated its centennial on July 1, 1967.

Note: Do **not** use a comma when only the month and year are given.

Canada celebrated its centennial in July 1967.

- Use a comma to separate the elements in geographic names and addresses.

Architect Douglas Cardinal designed the Museum of Civilization in Hull, Quebec.

The couple were married at St. Joseph's Basilica, 10044 113 Street, Edmonton, Alberta.

- Use a comma after the salutation in personal or informal letters and after the closing in all letters.

Dear Aunt Margaret,

Yours truly,

Sincerely yours,

Exercise 21.4 Comma Review

Add all necessary commas and delete unnecessary commas in the following sentences. If the sentence is correct, write **C**.

1. However I always counter "Look before you leap."
2. After Christmas the family ate turkey sandwiches turkey casserole and turkey croquettes for a week.
3. Repairing the defective component after the warranty has expired Mr. Fortino is not our responsibility.
4. When the signal on the microwave sounded Ted poured the wine and called his guests to the table.
5. The Sandersons are the only people who did not contribute money to the Victoria Day fireworks display.

6. Whenever we go camping Father always says "If you don't fish where the fish are you'll be having hot dogs for supper."

7. Albert opened the window took a deep breath and composed his thoughts.

8. The one novel that I didn't read, was the basis for the essay question on the English exam.

9. Lucy Maud Montgomery the author of *Anne of Green Gables* was born in Clifton Prince Edward Island on November 30 1874.

10. Well you have certainly chosen a deep subject for your research paper.

11. To put the matter into its proper perspective I want you to consider the following factors.

12. Yes we do have that shoe style in your size.

13. I decided that Howard would bring the food Cliff would bring the drinks and you would bring the music.

14. The snow blockaded the door in deep drifts and icicles hung like spears from the roof.

15. Here is my estimate of the cost of paving your driveway. Taxes of course are not included.

16. Even during the day light could not penetrate the canopy of leaves.

17. Mr. Ramondo said "We're a few bricks short of a load but I think we have enough to build the firepit."

18. Anyone who is caught stealing money will be fired immediately.

19. On a dark stormy night I like nothing better, than to curl up with a good novel.

20. Cynthia went back to university to study engineering, because she discovered, that her BA in linguistics was not highly marketable.

21b SEMICOLONS

If the comma and period were to have a child, that child would be the semicolon. The semicolon creates a pause that is stronger than a comma, but it is usually used after a complete sentence, like a period.

Use a semicolon in the following ways:

• By itself to join two clauses that are sharply contrasted or closely related

The storm struck with a destructive fury; the ship was broken by the violent wind and waves.

- With a conjunctive adverb (*nevertheless, however, otherwise, consequently, thus, therefore, then, meanwhile, moreover, furthermore*) or with a transitional phrase (*in addition, as a result, for example*) to join main clauses

  The advertisement states that applicants with a degree in a related area are preferred; **nevertheless,** applicants with a diploma and relevant experience will be considered.

- With a coordinating conjunction (*and, but, or, nor, for, yet, so*) when the main clauses contain internal commas. Use this rule carefully and sparingly.

  Already late for work, I dressed hurriedly, ran out of the house, and jumped into the car; but when I turned the key, I heard only the ominous clicking sound of a dying battery.

- Instead of a comma between items in a series when the items themselves have internal punctuation

  The lottery prize includes the dream home, custom-built by a leading home builder; custom-made draperies, professional interior decorating, and exclusive furnishings; and free cleaning for one year.

Note: Semicolons can be useful, but use them cautiously. They should be used sparingly throughout your paper, not sprinkled like salt but like a fine spice that adds flavour and flair to your writing. If you're becoming addicted to the semicolon, you're probably relying too heavily on coordination to join your ideas, or you may be using this punctuation mark improperly, as in the examples below.

Unnecessary Semicolons

Note 1: Never use a semicolon to join a subordinate clause to a main clause.

NOT   Although it had snowed heavily during the day; the roads were clear by midnight.

BUT   Although it had snowed heavily during the day, the roads were clear by midnight.

Note 2: Avoid using a semicolon as a kind of big comma for emphasis.

NOT   Horrified, Nelson watched the tidal wave approach; knowing that his tiny boat could never withstand its force.

BUT   Horrified, Nelson watched the tidal wave approach, knowing that his tiny boat could never withstand its force.

For more information on joining sentences effectively, see Faulty Subordination (17i).

Exercise 21.5

To the following sentences, add any necessary semicolons and replace any unnecessary semicolons with the correct punctuation. If the sentence is correct, mark **C**.

1. Emilio wanted to be a famous astronaut he ended up operating the Ferris wheel at the amusement park.

2. When John graduated from university, he was fortunate to get a junior management position with an accounting firm; he then began setting aside money to repay his student loan.

3. The variety show will feature Vox Populi, a well-known local band, the Crazy Bones, a hilarious comedy act, and the Tumbling Turners, an acrobatic troupe.

4. Zack thought that he had enough money in his account to pay for the new jeans however, his direct debit payment was not approved.

5. When the smoke had cleared from the oven, Lucas was afraid to open the door but, fortunately, a quick glance showed that the roast still looked edible.

6. Ashley is going camping with her family Erica has therefore agreed to take over the paper route for a week.

7. Even though the skater was disappointed with the poor marks for artistic interpretation; he was pleased with the high marks for technical merit.

8. There was a heavy frost in the night as a result, farmers are concerned about the peach crop.

21c APOSTROPHES

Because plurals, possessives, and contractions that end in *s* sound the same, your ear is not a reliable guide for when and how to use an **apostrophe.** Instead, you need to know which of these forms you intend to create so that you can use the apostrophe appropriately. Remember, too, that if you're unsure of how to use an apostrophe, you are as likely to put it in the wrong place as to omit it in the right place. The apostrophe, because it is so abused and misused in our culture (check out the signs in your neighbourhood) might take you a while to figure out. But if you return regularly to this section, you can use it properly and not contribute to widespread apostrophe abuse.

- A **plural noun**, which is usually formed by adding *s* or *es*, indicates that more than one person, place, or thing is being discussed. Do not add an apostrophe when you wish to indicate a plural. Be especially careful with proper nouns.

PLURAL   All the **Joneses** congratulate you on keeping up with them. [The plural of *Jones* is formed by adding *es*.]

POSSESSIVE   The **Joneses'** car is in the garage. [The apostrophe indicates that the car belongs to the Joneses.]

- A **contraction** indicates the omission of one or more letters. The sense of the sentence will indicate whether the apostrophe signals possession or a contraction.

CONTRACTION   Your **report's** already three weeks late. [*report's = report is*]

POSSESSIVE   Your **report's** recommendations are out of line with current department policy. [The apostrophe indicates that the recommendations belong to the report.]

- **Possessive pronouns** (*yours, hers, its, ours, theirs*) do not take apostrophes. Only nouns and indefinite pronouns (*someone, something, somebody, everyone, everything, everybody, no one, nothing, nobody, anything, anybody*) take an apostrophe to show possession.

NOT   These problems are **their's** to solve.

BUT   These problems are **theirs** to solve.

- *Its* is a possessive; *it's* is a contraction.

POSSESSIVE   The dog buried **its** bone in the garden.

CONTRACTION   **It's** a serious problem.

Making Nouns and Indefinite Pronouns Possessive

- To make an indefinite pronoun possessive, add '*s*.

This is **nobody's** business.

Everyone's assignments have been marked.

- To make a singular noun that does not end with *s* possessive, add '*s*.

The **child's** bike lay abandoned on the driveway.

The **horse's** saddle is hanging on a nail in the barn.

- To make a singular noun that ends with *s* or *ss* possessive, add '*s* if the word is one syllable. Add only an apostrophe if the noun is more than one syllable.

James's gloves are lying on the hall table.

The **boss's** instructions are on her desk.

The next **witness'** testimony is crucial to the defence.

The **actress'** hopes were raised by the screen test.

* To make a plural noun that ends with *s* possessive, add only an apostrophe.

All **students'** marks will be posted by the main office.

There will be a meeting of the **girls'** hockey team on Wednesday.

* To make a plural noun that does not end with *s* possessive, add *'s*.

Men's suits are on sale this week.

The **children's** story hour has been cancelled.

* To make a compound noun possessive, add *'s* to the last word.

Mario borrowed his **father-in-law's** lawn mower over the weekend.

* To indicate that two or more people own one thing (joint possession), add *'s* to the last name.

Carmen and Roberta's restaurant opened last month.

* To indicate that two or more people own things separately (separate possession), make all the names possessive.

Ralph's and **Howard's** cars are in for repairs.

Note: Possessive nouns do not always refer to people. They can also refer to animals or objects.

The **sun's** rays are very strong today.

Today's news is better.

This **society's** children have special needs.

Other Uses of the Apostrophe

* To form the plural of letters, add *'s*. Italicize or underline the letter but not the *s*.

Pay particular attention to the long *o***'s** in this poem.

* To form the plural of words referred to as words, add *'s*. Italicize or underline the word but not the *s*.

There are five *a lot***'s** in this one paragraph.

* To form the plural of abbreviations, add *'s*.

She has two **MA's,** one in English and one in history.

* You have a choice in forming the plural of numerals and dates. Add *'s* or *s* alone.

His family emigrated from Scotland in the **1920's** [1920s].

What are the chances of rolling nothing but **2's** [2s] in a dice game?

Exercise 21.6

Add all necessary apostrophes to the following sentences.

1. Helens and Stephanies projects both won honourable mentions at this years science fair.

2. Several patrons cars were vandalized in the mall parking lot.

3. Nobodys pecan pie is as good as yours.

4. For some reason, I can never remember that *vacuum* has two *u*s and only one *c*.

5. Its important to respond to your hostess invitation promptly and courteously.

6. Lester and Marys puppy chewed up three pairs of shoes in less than a week.

7. Justins parents cottage is badly in need of a new roof.

8. I need to buy some apples and bananas for the childrens lunches.

9. Short pauses in your oral presentation are perfectly acceptable. Dont fill the space with *ums* and *uhs*.

10. Wont you have more tea and another of Grandmother Mildreds ginger snap cookies?

21d COLONS AND DASHES

The **colon** and the **dash** can both be used to introduce a phrase or clause that explains or illustrates what precedes it. Whereas a colon is more formal, a dash is less formal.

> After the tenth day without food, the subject began to exhibit psychological debilitation: he had trouble concentrating and slept much of the time.

> I still love listening to the Beatles—they remind me of the sixties.

A pair of dashes can also be used to enclose parenthetical comments that slightly disrupt the flow of the sentence. By using dashes rather than commas or parentheses, you can set off these comments more emphatically from the rest of the sentence.

> The relationship between father and son—never very good—worsened as the son began to assert his independence.

Be careful not to overuse the colon and the dash. Too many sentences containing colons will make your writing too formal and stilted, and, as Lewis Thomas says, make your reader feel like he or she is being ordered around. Too many sentences containing dashes will make your writing look too choppy and informal.

Colons

Use a colon in the following situations:

- To introduce a list or series preceded by a complete main clause. You will need the following equipment: a small tent, a sleeping bag, and a camp stove.

- In a sentence introducing a list of items, you can use a colon after a verb when *as follows* or *the following* is **strongly implied,** as in this example:

  Our report includes:

  1. background information about the problem
  2. an analysis of its causes
  3. recommendations for solutions
  4. a detailed budget

Note: Do **not** use a colon with *such as* or *for example.*

NOT   The Robinsons brought back a number of souvenirs, such as: a red plush cushion with "Visit Niagara Falls" emblazoned on it, a slightly pornographic calendar, and two incredibly ugly beer mugs.

BUT   The Robinsons brought back a number of souvenirs, such as a red plush . . .

- To introduce a concluding explanatory phrase

  She dedicated her research to one goal: finding the link between Einstein's theory of relativity and the theory of quantum mechanics.

- To join main clauses when the second clause restates, explains, summarizes, or emphasizes the first

  The movie was a complete waste of time: the plot dragged, the characters were boring, and the special effects were silly.

- To introduce a formal quotation. Both the sentence introducing the quotation and the quotation itself must be grammatically complete.

  In Alice Munro's short story "Boys and Girls," the narrator gradually becomes aware of the full implications of being a girl: "A girl was not, as I had supposed, simply what I was; it was what I had to become. It was a definition, always touched with emphasis, with reproach and disappointment. Also it was a joke on me."

Note: Do **not** use a colon when the sentence introducing the quotation ends with *that* or is otherwise incomplete.

NOT   Hamlet shows a new acceptance of death when he says that: "There is a special providence in the fall of a sparrow."

BUT   Hamlet shows a new acceptance of death when he says that "There is a special providence in the fall of a sparrow."

- In biblical references (John 3:16)
- In time references (9:45, 12:05)

- Between the title and the subtitle of an article or a book

  A Harvest Yet to Reap: A History of Prairie Women

- After the salutation in a business letter

  Dear Business Manager:

  Dear Editor:

  Dear Ms. Bennett:

Dashes

Use a dash in the following situations:

- To indicate a sudden interruption or change of thought

  I left my briefcase—I remember it distinctly—right here by the front entrance.

  And then she said—but I see you've already heard the story.

- To emphasize parenthetical remarks

  Antonia worked hard—perhaps too hard—in spite of her illness.

- After a series at the beginning of a sentence

  Sports figures, entertainers, politicians—all have been invited to the wedding.

- To set off a series that comes in the middle of a sentence

  It had everything—power, grace, beauty—that Chantal wanted in a car.

- To emphasize an expression that explains or illustrates

  Philip worked tirelessly toward his goal—an A in English.

Exercise 21.7

Add colons and dashes where appropriate to the following sentences. Where either is possible, be prepared to explain your choice. If the sentence is correct, write **C.**

1. Mae West offers an interesting perspective on making moral choices "When choosing between two evils, I always like to try the one I've never tried before."

2. I have registered in the following courses for the winter term Basic Calculus, Fluid Dynamics, and Introductory Drafting.

3. I am convinced I say this without reservation that Luke and Laura will never get back together.

4. None of the suspects Winken, Blinken, or Nod knew that they were under surveillance for stealing the sleeping pills.

5. My cat Puck is an excellent companion he is intelligent, affectionate and infinitely patient.

6. He had no means of escape all of the exits were blocked.

7. When Herb boasted that he was a "self-made man," Vernon replied, "That's the trouble with cheap labour."

8. Weaving and willow furniture all will be for sale at the spring craft show.

21e PARENTHESES AND BRACKETS

Both **parentheses** and **brackets** serve to set apart certain information in a sentence or a paragraph, but they are used in different circumstances.

Parentheses

Use parentheses in the following situations:

- To set off supplementary material that interrupts the flow of the sentence

  The council finally agreed (but only after a heated debate) to the proposed amendments.

Note 1: Parentheses, dashes, and commas can all be used to set off nonessential information. When you enclose material in parentheses, you signal to your reader that it is relatively unimportant. Dashes tend to emphasize its importance, whereas commas will give it approximately equal weight.

Note 2: Do **not** use parentheses to enclose important information. In the example below, the parentheses are misleading because they suggest that essential information is incidental.

Although he was only fifteen, Victor was sentenced to nine months in a juvenile detention centre. (This sentence was the result of his fifth conviction for theft over $1,000 in two years.)

- To enclose explanatory material, such as bibliographical citations, brief definitions, and pieces of historical information

  The Celsius (centigrade) thermometer was invented by the Swedish astronomer Anders Celsius (1701–1744).

  For information on in-text citations, see appendices B and C.

- To enclose letters or numerals in a list of items

  Each oral presentation will be graded on (1) delivery, (2) voice, (3) content, and (4) language.

Resist the temptation to use parentheses too often. Information enclosed in parentheses interrupts the flow and meaning of a sentence. Too many of these interruptions will make your writing sound haphazard and your ideas irrelevant, as in the example:

Headhunting (often called an executive search) is the practice of seeking out (sometimes through advertising, sometimes through more direct approaches to individuals) senior, specialized employees (when no one with sufficient expertise is available within an organization) for business.

Rewritten with only one pair of parentheses, the paragraph reads much more smoothly.

Headhunting (as executive searches are often called) is the practice of seeking out specialized senior employees for business firms when no one with sufficient expertise is available within an organization. Headhunters may advertise these positions or approach prospective candidates directly.

Using Other Punctuation with Parentheses

- If the parenthetical remark is a sentence within another sentence, the parenthetical sentence does not begin with a capital or end with a period.

  The baby was sleeping (at least his eyes were closed) when I peeked into the room.

- If the parenthetical remark is a complete separate sentence, capitalize the first word and put the end punctuation inside the closing parenthesis.

  After weeks of dull, cloudy weather, the first snowflakes began to fall on Christmas Eve. (The children had been convinced that Christmas wouldn't be Christmas without snow.)

- If the parenthetical construction within a sentence requires a question mark or exclamation mark, that punctuation goes inside the closing parenthesis.

  It is important for students to learn how to think (who can deny that necessity?), but they also need facts and information to think about.

21e

Parentheses and Brackets

Brackets

Use brackets in the following ways:

- To enclose explanatory material inserted into a quotation. These square brackets tell your reader that the material was not part of the original quotation.

  In the essay "Grace before Meat," Charles Lamb says, "I hate a man who swallows it [his food], affecting not to know what he is eating. I suspect his taste in higher matters."

Note: The punctuation of the original sentence (the comma after *it*) goes outside the material enclosed in brackets.

- To show that you have changed a word (usually a verb or a pronoun) in a direct quotation so that it will fit grammatically with your sentence

  Old King Cole [is] a merry old soul/And a merry old soul [is] he.

- With the word *sic* (Latin for *thus*) to indicate that an error in spelling, grammar, or fact is part of the original quotation

  The newspaper headline read "Affects [sic] of cutbacks not yet known."

21f QUOTATION MARKS

The main purpose of **quotation marks** is to acknowledge that you have used someone else's words. Use quotation marks in the following situations:

- Whenever you quote more than **three consecutive words** from any printed material. (For how to document your sources, see Appendices B and C.)

  Many primatologists and psychologists believe that "chimpanzees have the capacity for self-awareness, self-consciousness, and self-knowledge."

- When you include comments made by someone you have interviewed. (For how to document interviews in a research paper, see Appendices B and C.)

  According to Sharon Bush, records clerk in the registrar's office, "The completion rate for this course averages about 30 percent."

- When you include dialogue in a personal narrative or a short story. Indent the words of each speaker as you would indent separate paragraphs.

  "Do you have any plans to publish your autobiography?" the critic asked the novelist.

  "Actually, I was saving the best till last," remarked the author. "I might even arrange to have it published posthumously."

  "The sooner, the better," replied the critic.

Note: Remember that quotation marks set off direct speech. Don't use them with indirect speech.

DIRECT SPEECH	The clerk asked the customer, "Will you pay cash, or shall I charge this purchase to your account?"
INDIRECT SPEECH	The clerk asked the customer whether she wanted to pay cash or charge the purchase to her account.

- Use single quotation marks to indicate a quotation within a quotation.
- The witness testified, "I was present when the accused said, 'She'll pay for what she did to me!'"

Other Uses of Quotation Marks

- Put quotation marks around the titles of short works that have not been published separately, such as titles of chapters, short stories, articles, and most poems.

  His favourite Poe story is "The Fall of the House of Usher."

- When you want to draw your reader's attention to a word used in a special way, you can either underline/italicize the word or put quotation marks around it.

  It's quite acceptable to begin a sentence with *because*.

  It's quite acceptable to begin a sentence with "because."

- Do **not** use quotation marks or italics merely to draw attention to slang or irony.

NOT   My sister has become a real "couch potato."

NOT   Our "paperboy" is at least fifty years old.

Exercise 21.8

Use quotation marks appropriately in the following sentences. If the sentence is correct, write **C**.

1. Two negatives make a positive, explained Ludwig. However, two positives don't make a negative.
2. Yeah, right! replied Noam.
3. Heather said that she would pick Katie up from work and save Mother the trip.
4. According to an old Russian proverb, When money talks, the truth keeps silent.
5. I wish you would stop saying like and basically in every sentence. That habit drives me crazy, you know.
6. Virginia Woolf's essay The Death of the Moth is a thoughtful meditation on the nature of the life force.

Using Other Punctuation with Quotation Marks

When you close a quotation, you might be uncertain whether the end punctuation goes inside or outside the quotation marks. Follow these guidelines:

- As a general rule, commas and periods go inside quotation marks; colons and semicolons go outside.

  Staring in disgust at the cans of escargots in the specialty section of the grocery store, Mr. Johnson remarked to his wife, "Let's can all the snails from the garden. We'll make a fortune." [The period is inside the quotation marks.]

  Facing Mr. Waters squarely, William replied, "That, sir, is not your concern"; he then walked resolutely out of the room. [The semicolon is outside the quotation marks.]

- When a quotation is a question or an exclamation, the question or exclamation mark goes inside the quotation marks.

  "Where are the snows of yesteryear?" she asked pensively.

  "Get out of my way!" the enraged customer bellowed as he pushed through the crowd.

- When the entire sentence containing the quotation is a question or an exclamation, the question or exclamation mark goes outside the quotation marks.

What does it mean to say, "A stitch in time saves nine"?

The Great China Circus is now truly "the greatest show on Earth"!

- When a quotation ends a sentence, whatever punctuation is inside the quotation mark also ends the entire sentence. Don't add any other punctuation.

Jane listened with growing horror as the voice from the attic screamed, "Please let me out!"

When you have a parenthetical citation, the end punctuation goes after the citation.

In *The Jazzonians,* Graff writes, "Ballroom dancing is art set to music" (103).

21f

Quotation
Marks

Exercise 21.9

Use quotation marks and other punctuation appropriately in the following sentences. If the sentence is correct, write **C**.

1. No, I won't move my car shouted the irate driver.
2. Aunt Eva is fond of saying that no one is responsible for making another person happy.
3. Was it Archimedes who said Give me a firm place to stand, and I will move the earth
4. The term portmanteau word refers to a word combining the sounds and meanings of two other words. For example, the word smog is a blending of the words smoke and fog
5. In today's English class we explored the attitudes to war expressed in Wilfred Owen's poem Dulce et Decorum Est and Randall Jarrell's poem The Death of the Ball Turret Gunner
6. What did Mother mean when she said The acorn never falls far from the oak tree
7. If fifty million people say a foolish thing noted Anatole France it is still a foolish thing
8. Hearing the familiar bell, the children ran into the street yelling We all scream for ice cream
9. The words chimpanzee, gorilla, and zebra all came into English from African languages.
10. Sitting alone in the darkened room, Steve morosely hummed the tune to Sam Cooke's Sad Mood

21g ITALICS AND UNDERLINING

Use **italic** script in typeset and word-processed material, or **underlining** in handwritten or typed material, **for each of the following cases:**

- For the titles of books, newspapers, magazines, pamphlets, plays, films, television and radio series, works of art, albums, or long musical compositions

    The city library has purchased two sets of *The Canadian Encyclopedia*.

    The police drama *Homicide: Life on the Streets* steadily gained popularity during its first few years.

- For the names of airplanes, ships, trains, and spacecraft

Note: Do not italicize or underline *the* or abbreviations that come before a name.

    Captain James Cook commanded the H.M.S. *Resolution* on his second Pacific voyage.

- For foreign words and phrases that have not been accepted as English terms

    Examples of these expressions include the following:

    bon vivant (a person who enjoys food and drink)

    casus belli (an event that brings about war)

    tête-à-tête (an intimate conversation between two people)

    Weltanschauung (a comprehensive concept of the universe and the relationship of humans to it)

- For words referred to as words, letters referred to as letters, and numerals referred to as numerals

    The one word on the test that I couldn't define was *dipsomaniac*.

    Don't forget to cross your *t*'s.

    Is this an *8* or a *3*?

- For emphasis and clarity

    I asked *who* you are, not *how* you are.

    Late papers will *not* be accepted.

Note: Be cautious whenever you are tempted to use italics for emphasis. Like exclamation marks, italics lose their effectiveness if overused.

21h HYPHENS

Hyphens are used as part of some compound words (*father-in-law, trade-in*). Other compound words are written as one word (*hairbrush, stepmother*) or as two words (*lawn bowling, token payment*). Because there is no pattern for forming compound words, and because compound words are constantly changing, your best source of current information is an up-to-date dictionary. You may even find that dictionaries disagree on compound forms. If they do, choose one spelling and use it consistently.

Use a hyphen in the following ways:

- With two-word numbers from twenty-one to ninety-nine

  There are **ninety-nine** bottles of beer on the wall.

- With numbers used as adjectives

  Is the tank **three-quarters** full?

  Atsuko, a **thirty-four-year-old** musician, made her television debut last night.

- With the prefixes *self* (*self-satisfied*), *ex* (*ex-husband*), and *all* (*all-purpose*); with prefixes that come before proper nouns (*anti-Catholic*); and with the suffix *elect* (*minister-elect*).

- To avoid an awkward combination of letters or to prevent misunderstanding: *re-cover* (cover again)

- To indicate that two or more prefixes or words share a common root

  Both **pre-** and **post-natal** classes are available.

  This course covers **eighteenth-** and **nineteenth-century** drama.

- To join two or more words that function as a single adjective conveying a single concept: *well-written essay, reddish-brown hair*

Note 1: If these constructions come after the noun, they are **not** hyphenated.

The essay is well written.

Her hair is reddish brown.

Note 2: If the group of words contains an *ly* adverb, do **not** hyphenate: *poorly conceived plan, frequently used reference book.*

Hyphenating Words at the End of Lines

It's best to avoid dividing words at the end of a line if possible. Occasionally, however, you may not be able to squeeze all the letters on the line you are writing. Here are the guidelines to follow:

- Always hyphenate a word between syllables. The first part of the word must contain at least three letters. Try to divide the word in two approximately equal parts that convey the sense of the whole word (*butter-fly* not *but-terfly*).

- Include a single-letter syllable with the first part of the word (*regu-late* not *reg-ulate*).

- When a double consonant occurs at the end because you have added a suffix (*ing, ed*), divide between the two consonants (*let-ting not lett-ing*). If the root word ends in a double consonant, divide between the root word and the suffix (*bill-ing* not *bil-ling*).

- Do **not** hyphenate one-syllable words or words of five or fewer letters (regardless of the number of syllables). If possible, avoid hyphenating words of six letters.
- Do **not** hyphenate figures ($21.36, 123,000), dates (Dec. 10, 1926), abbreviations (UNICEF), or proper names (Albert Einstein, Calgary).
- Do **not** hyphenate the last word of more than two consecutive lines.
- Do **not** hyphenate the last word in a paragraph or the last word on a page.

Exercise 21.10

Add, change, or take out hyphens as necessary in the following sentences.

1. This neutral carpet can serve as an allpurpose floor-covering in any room.
2. You are looking particularly selfsatisfied after winning the job over twenty three equally-qualified candidates.
3. If you want to use gender neutral terms, use "workers" rather than "work-men" and "humanity" rather than "man-kind."
4. The ninety year old woman made her first parachute jump on the week-end.
5. Julia's ex boyfriend returned all the compact-disks she had given him as presents.

Exercise 21.11

How would you hyphenate each of the following words if it appeared at the end of a line? If the word should not be hyphenated, write **C**.

1. iconoclast
2. crybaby
3. wrapping
4. faded
5. CUSO
6. railroad
7. thrilling
8. jimjams
9. memorize
10. radio

21i ABBREVIATIONS

Abbreviations are appropriate in scientific and technical writing and in footnotes and bibliographies. In most other kinds of writing, use abbreviations sparingly. If you wish to abbreviate a term that you intend to use repeatedly, write the term out in full the first time you use it, and then use the abbreviation.

American Sign Language (ASL) is the first language of many deaf children. Because ASL has a different grammatical structure from English, deaf children who use ASL must learn English as a second language.

The following guidelines cover the appropriate uses of abbreviations in nontechnical writing.

Names of Dates and Times

• Write out the names of months and holidays.

Hanukkah comes in the darkest part of December.

• Use *a.m.* (*ante meridiem*) to refer to exact times before noon and *p.m.* (*post meridiem*) to refer to exact times after noon. Note that these abbreviations are not capitalized.

The meeting began at 9:07 a.m. and concluded at 5:31 p.m.

• Use *BC* (Before Christ) to refer to dates before the birth of Christ. Put *BC* after the date. Use *AD* (*Anno Domini*) to refer to dates after the birth of Christ. Put *AD* before the date. Stop using *AD* when you can assume that your reader knows that the event did not take place before the birth of Christ, usually for any date after AD 500.

Julius Caesar, who unified the Roman Empire under his dictatorship, was assassinated in **44 BC.**

Hadrian's Wall, completed in **AD 123,** was constructed to prevent northern tribes from invading Roman Britain.

If you prefer, use *BCE* (Before the Common Era) and *CE* (Common Era). Both of these abbreviations follow the year.

Units of Measurement

Write out metric words such as *gram, metre,* and *kilometre* when you use them without numerals.

Speed limits are now given in **kilometres** per hour.

Abbreviate these words when you use them with a numeral. Don't put a period after the abbreviation.

Combine **10 g** flour with **1 l** milk.

Scientific and Technical Terms

Some commonly known scientific and technical terms are usually abbreviated.

DNA (deoxyribonucleic acid)

DDT (dichlorodiphenyltrichloroethane)

AIDS (Acquired Immune Deficiency Syndrome)

Common Latin Terms

Although it's useful to know the following Latin abbreviations, it's usually better to omit them or replace them with English equivalents. If you use them, note the periods.

e.g.   *exempli gratia* (for example)

i.e.   *id est* (that is)

etc.   *et cetera* (and so forth)

Be especially careful with *etc.* Using it at the end of a list suggests that you have run out of ideas. Instead, end the list with an inclusive phrase like "and other . . . ." or begin the list with the phrase *such as* or an equivalent expression.

NOT   The Niagara region grows apples, peaches, pears, **etc**.

BUT   The Niagara region grows apple, peaches, pears, **and other fruits**.

OR   The Niagara region grows fruits **such as** apples, peaches, and pears.

The Ampersand (&)

Never use this symbol in general writing. Use the ampersand only when you are copying the name of an organization or following APA documentation style.

He works the night shift at the local **A&W.**

Maccoby, E. E., **&** Jacklin, C. N. (1974) . . .

21j CAPITALIZATION

All proper nouns are capitalized. A proper noun names a specific person, place, or thing.

Meet me at the main entrance of **The Bay.**

Use capitalization in the following way:

- For kinship terms such as mother, father, brother, sister when they are part of a name (as in *Mother Teresa, Grandfather McGregor*) or when they are used as a substitute for the proper name. Do not capitalize kinship terms preceded by a possessive adjective (*my, our, your, her, his, their*).

Is **Baba Kostash** going to the dance?

Is **Grandfather** going to the dance?

We are going with our father and mother.

- For titles used as part of a person's name

I have a meeting with **Professor Qureshi** this afternoon.

I get along well with two of my **professors** this term.

21j

Capitalization

- For the names of directions (*north, south, east, west*) when they are part of a proper name or refer to a region

It has always been his ambition to travel to the **North.**

The house faces **north.** [*North* names a direction, not a region.]

- For the names of planets, stars, and other heavenly bodies. Do not capitalize *sun* and *moon*. Do not capitalize *earth* when it is modified by *the*.

The astronauts saw **Earth** from their spaceship.

Unless we act now, all the waters of **the earth** will be polluted.

- For the names of institutions, organizations, political parties, and branches of government. Do not capitalize words such as *party, college,* or *university* unless you are using the term as a shortened version of the full name.

Faryl has a **university** degree in biology.

Tim will complete his final year at **Capilano College** this spring.

- For nationalities, languages, religious groups, religions, sacred and religious names

Canadian, Cree, Protestant, Taoism, the Qur'an, the Bible

- For days of the week, the months, holidays, events. Do not capitalize the names of seasons.

Monday, January, New Year's Eve, the Middle Ages, summer, winter, spring, fall

- For the names of specific courses. Do not capitalize the names of general subjects, except languages.

Psychology 101, **Chemistry** 400

I studied **English, French, drama, math,** and **sociology** in my first year of university.

21j

Capitalization

Other Occasions for Capitalization

- Capitalize the first word in a quotation if the quotation is a complete sentence. If the quotation is not a complete sentence, do not capitalize the first word.

The instructor turned to me and said, "Please give me your views on the opening scene in *Macbeth.*"

Susan remarked that she would rather be "poor and healthy" than "rich and sick."

- Capitalize *all* words in the titles of books, short stories, plays, poems, articles, newspapers, magazines, movies, and musical compositions *except* conjunctions and prepositions of fewer than four letters and articles. However, you must capitalize *any* word that immediately follows a period, colon, or dash or is the first or last word in a title.

"Back in the USSR"   *River of the Brokenhearted*

"To an Athlete Dying Young"   *The Globe and Mail*

21k NUMBERS

Numerals are appropriate and preferred in scientific and technical writing. In general writing, however, certain conventions determine the use of numerals or words to express numbers.

Numerals

Use numerals in nontechnical writing in the following cases:

■ *To provide a series of numbers*

> In 1986, **250** children were involved in the school lunch program. By 1987, the number had increased to **300** children. Last year, **350** children were eating lunch at school.

■ *To express a number that would take more than two words to spell out*

> Last year the shelter for battered women helped **259** women and their children.

■ *To express exact times of the day and with* a.m. *and* p.m.

> We'll begin the meeting at **9:15** sharp.

> The plane from Toronto will arrive at **8:03 a.m.**

■ *To express exact sums of money*

> This wonderful car can be yours for only **$2,999.99.**

■ *To express dates.* Years are always expressed in numerals; centuries should be written out.

> The events between **1939** and **1945** affected the rest of the **twentieth century.**

You can use *st, nd, rd, th* with numerals in dates if you do not give the year, but these abbreviations are not essential.

> The concert is scheduled for August 20th [or August 20].

■ *To express addresses*

> 2939 107 Street; #976, 10098 Elm Street; P.O. Box 12

■ *To express percentages and decimals*

> 29%, 87 percent, 3.9 cm

■ *To express page, line, verse, act, and scene numbers in literary works.* See Appendix B for more information.

> Act 3, Scene 2, lines 23–38 **or** 3.2.23–28

> John 1:1–5; 1 and 2 Corinthians

Words

Use words in place of numerals in these instances:

- *For numbers that can be spelled out in one or two words*

  At least **fifty** people were invited to the party.

- *To express approximate numbers used with money, times of the day, and measurements.* In these cases, the whole of the round number should be expressed in words. If the number is VERY large, a combination of numerals and words can be used.

  I used to be able to buy a huge bag of candy for less than **ten cents.**

  Every day she gets up at around **five o'clock** to do her homework.

  By the end of this century, **10 billion** people will compete for the earth's resources.

- *When you begin a sentence with a number*

  Thirty percent of first-year students need some form of financial assistance.

Note: Use a combination of words and numerals as necessary to prevent confusion.

NOT   He ordered **2 10 cm** pieces of wood.

BUT   He ordered **two 10 cm** pieces of wood.

Exercise 21.12

Correct all errors in the use of numerals or words to express numbers in the following sentences. If the sentence is correct, write **C**.

1. He bought 4 250-page packages of binder paper at the beginning of the term.
2. 15 percent of those polled responded that they were still undecided about how they would vote in the election.
3. At least 20 customers have returned the sheets because they were labelled the wrong size.
4. Including the PST and GST, the chocolate bar costs $1.14.
5. Some sports analysts say that Wayne Gretzky was at his peak playing with the Edmonton Oilers in the nineteen eighties. Gretzky retired from professional hockey in nineteen ninety-nine.

Weblinks

- Guide to Grammar & Writing, Capital Community College—links to word- and sentence-level topics, among others; includes interactive quizzes.

  www.ccc.commnet.edu/grammar

- UBC Writing Centre Online Resources—links to Purdue University On-Line Writing Lab; The Rensselaer Writing Center; University of Victoria Writer's Guide; Rutgers University Guide to Grammar and Style.

  www.writingcentre.ubc.ca/online_resources.html

- UBC Writing Centre's Writers' Workshop—links to dictionaries, grammar and composition resources, general writing references.

  www.writingcentre.ubc.ca/workshop/reference.htm

- University of Maine Writing Center—links to grammar and mechanics guide, writing resources, dictionaries, thesauruses, foreign language dictionaries, citation format guides, ESL resources, composition and rhetoric resources.

  www.ume.maine.edu/wcenter/

- Hypergrammar, University of Ottawa Writing Centre—online grammar handbook.

  www.uottawa.ca/academic/arts/writcent/hypergrammar/

- Useful Writing Links, Queens University Writing Centre—links to grammar resources, ESL-related resources, dictionaries, reference resources, among others.

  qsilver.queensu.ca/~wcentre/usefulinks.html

- Advice on Academic Writing, University of Toronto—links to style and editing resources, grammar and punctuation resources, ESL answers, among others.

  www.utoronto.ca/writing/advise.html

- University of Wisconsin-Madison Writing Center, Writer's Handbook—links to resources on grammar and punctuation, improving your writing style, among others.

  www.wisc.edu/writing/Handbook/index.html

21k

General Writing Resources

Numbers

If you log on to www.altavista.com and type "online writing" in the SEARCH box, you will find dozens of sites for online writing resources.

PART 6

READINGS

BECOMING AN ATHEIST
Michael O'Shaughnessy

1   It is difficult to pinpoint the exact moment when I became an atheist. I was raised Catholic, in a devout family environment. My father is Irish by descent—from the Catholic parts of the island, not the "occupied counties"—and a Quebecer by birth. My mother is an immigrant from the Philippines. My family not only attended weekly mass and all days of obligation, but also a lay prayer group affiliated with a group called Charismatic Catholics, which is Catholic in theology but borrows liberally from Protestant Pentecostal denominations (including an emphasis on the real presence of the Holy Spirit, lively music, and speaking in glossolalia).

2   I often got the chance to interact with my priest, a Jesuit and accomplished scholar who was working on his doctorate while in Canada. As such, not only was I emotionally enraptured by the religion, but intellectually engaged as well; I would often sit in on theological debates conducted by my priest—discussions ranging from the obstacles to ecumenical union with the Anglicans and Eastern Orthodox churches to the possible theological implications of Earth's being visited by extra-terrestrial creatures. (As a nine-year-old, guess which one I enjoyed more?)

3   At some point, however, it all began to ring hollow. My priest finished his doctorate and left for the Philippines. Meanwhile, the songs and glossolalia became familiar, and somehow less real.

4   I remember going to a Youth Encounter, which aimed to give adolescents an "encounter" with the Holy Spirit, and sitting through all the usual prayers and songs. At the end of the service came the anointing with Holy Oils. The aim of this consecration was to prepare one for their encounter with the Holy Spirit.

5   As in a scene out of a televangelist's infomercial, when the people in front of me in line were anointed, they lost strength in their bodies and had to be helped to the ground to lie down, so overwhelmed were they by the experience. So I waited with some degree of anxiety for my turn, and when it came? nothing. I felt nothing.

6   I searched for the sensation of oneness with the world, of the sagging of strength in my legs that I assumed would come, but nothing came. I simply had an oily forehead. A bit embarrassed, I faked the sagging of strength and lay down with the rest of the children, and then it occurred to me: Could all these people be faking too?

7   It was all downhill from there, as the saying goes. My parents had raised me as a devout Catholic, but they had also encouraged my intellectual curiosity. I was raised to question everything, and to argue well. (For as long as I can remember, if I could challenge a house rule and present a valid case for it being changed, it would be changed.) I had believed that it was impossible to know whether or not God is real, but had always accepted His existence on faith. Eventually, I came to abandon that, as I realized that the argument in favour of God was not particularly strong.

8   Though all good theoretically came from God, I didn't feel particularly evil now that I was denying his existence. Why did I not cheat on tests, skip class or lie to my parents if there was no God to watch over me and threaten me with punishment? Why did I bother being a good person at all? Though I wrestled with these questions, I never behaved in an amoral way. I concluded that my moral compass was not given to me by God but by my parents. I came to believe that "right" and "wrong" were based around the suffering of other people, and that morality can be summed up very succinctly in the words of Hippocrates: "First, do no harm."

9   I came to appreciate how the universe operates on its own, without any outside interference, and came to see how humanity evolved through a slow, incremental process over hundreds of millions of years, from the simplest single-celled organism, to the dinosaur, to the ape who carves great cities out of the earth. And eventually, in the midst of all this, I came to the

conclusion that while there was nothing directly contradicting the existence of God—He could possibly be sitting in His divine director's chair watching this all happen—there was nothing to confirm it, either. So why believe it at all? And so I became an atheist.

10   It was lonely, at first. Even terrifying. But eventually I realized it meant I was free.

LOOK AT US. SUDDENLY WE'RE ALL CELEBRITIES
John Intini

1   Michael Tyas's Hollywood experiment lasted eight long months. "I was an intern on a reality TV show in L.A., and was hating it with a passion because it wasn't reality," says Tyas, who prefers not to reveal the name of the show. "I logged all of the original footage—about 500 hours—so I saw the real story, and then I saw the fantasy story they made out of it." So the 23-year-old free-lance photographer, now back in his parents' Shelburne, Ont., home, did what thousands from his generation have done: he turned the camera on himself.

2   Tyas began a vlog—an online video diary of his life. "I always thought it would be cool to get my face in front of hundreds of people." He's unapologetic about building a site around his remarkably ordinary existence—his first post was a six-minute tour of his filthy L.A. apartment; more recently he's included a clip of his trip to the Ontario Science Centre, and another just hanging out at a friend's apartment. "I make narcissism look good," says Tyas, who has made $8.49 in ad sales on his site since April 2005. "It's a very positive thing to like yourself and think you're marketable enough to put your face out there."

3   His confidence, cultural observers point out, is not an anomaly. "This is the Barney Generation," says Alison Hearn, an assistant professor of information and media studies at the University of Western Ontario. "These kids have grown up in a world in which they've constantly been told they're special." This age of narcissism has spawned an industry that's all about you and me. And now, a few years into the Me Media revolution, an array of professional-grade vanity products and services have cropped up to meet the new narcissists' needs. "They're all ways of defining yourself," says Hearn. "Creating an image of yourself and then falling in love with it."

4   Anyone interested in a bit of immortality? No problem. For a fee ranging from $15,000 to $80,000, London, Eng.-based eDv, which bills itself as the "personal motion picture company," gets professional filmmakers to sort through your old home videos, conduct and tape interviews with your family, and edit together a high quality biography. If that seems too commercial or too much work, try buying your way into the pages of a book by a favourite author. This is often done through charity auctions. Last September, John Grisham, Dave Eggers and Stephen King put the names of upcoming characters on the block (a Florida woman paid US$25,100 for the right to put her brother's name to a character in King's new book).

5   There are many other ways of making yourself a star. One website, based in the Netherlands, allows users to create their own soap opera by posting messages, pictures and video from their own lives. While it

doesn't much resemble your typical mid-afternoon guilty pleasure, that hasn't stopped people from posting and visitors from checking in and voting for their favourites. The highest ranking "stars" can win prizes, including a celebrity magazine feature (the site is run by a magazine publisher). Then there's Playstation 2's EyeToy—a digital camera that literally places gamers within a video game. In *Kung Fu,* users can show off their martial arts skills by taking on the bad guys with their very own digitized hands and feet.

6   Technology is in part to blame. It's helped us meet these needs—and create them. The affordability of digital cameras, for instance, has sparked a surge in the popularity of self-portraits. Most young people are perfectly comfortable taking their own pictures—a key part of their Internet egos on MySpace and the like. Some change their photo almost every day. "It's an image economy," says Hearn. "It's all about branding yourself."

7   Some, like Erica Morgan, have devoted entire websites to self-portraiture—a form in which one can be a star on *both* sides of the camera. Since February 2003, Morgan, who was born in South Carolina and now lives in Sydney, Australia, takes a photo of herself every day and posts it on her site (1,111 at last count). "At first I was a little concerned about obsessive strangers," says the 27-year-old photographer. "And a little self-conscious about pulling out my camera and turning it in my direction." Apparently, she got over it.

8   These days—again thanks to technology—you can pretty much get your likeness plastered on anything. This business niche hearkens back to those booths at shopping malls that would print your picture on a coffee mug or a T-shirt. By contemporary standards, that old personalized fare appears like cave art. Today, fond parents can get a replica doll made of their children for US$139. To create a 23-inch Mini Me, parents can go on *mytwinn.com* and build the doll themselves, or send in a photo of junior and have the toy specialists do the legwork. The doll is an exact likeness; freckles and birthmarks are hand-painted at no additional cost. A couple of years ago, a California-based firm started selling personalized confetti—your digital images were turned into tiny paper scraps. Before they shut down, the company had sold 30,000 bags—starting at US$17 each—to people who wanted to be the life of the party.

9   Our look-at-me industry has even found its way into the art world. Send about $400 and a saliva sample to Ottawa-based DNA 11, and you'll receive an 18 x 24-inch portrait (available in one of eight colours) of your very own personal genetic code. "Before we started, we thought that everyone with a big ego would want one of these hanging in their offices—and we have lots of CEOs, power-brokers, investment brokers and venture

capitalists that own our artwork," says co-founder Adrian Salamunovic, whose company has shipped art to 30 countries and sold more than 1,000 prints since last July. "But moms and grandmas have done it too. For most, ego doesn't play a factor." In celebration of its one-year anniversary, the company is unveiling this week a new twist on the original: fingerprint portraits. "What we do is not in-your-face narcissistic—like say an oil painting of my face over the fireplace," says Salamunovic, 30. "This is highly personal art—it's one of one. And you're a collaborator."

10   The proliferation of personalized services may just be a logical next step for a society in which everything—from weddings to funerals—is hyperpersonalized. For several years now, thanks in large part to the reality TV craze, we've been told that we can be stars. Now we're starting to act like it. At the extreme end of the spectrum, people, desperate for the rock-star treatment, can hire an entourage—complete with a bodyguard, faux-friends and paparazzi photographers to greet them climbing out of a limo at the hottest club.

11   An effect of all this is the elevation of the completely ordinary. The clearest model may be YouTube, the video-sharing website with the narcissistic "Broadcast Yourself" tag line, which is getting 70 million video views a day. YouTube has hundreds of thousands of clips from rock concerts and old TV shows, but the very random—and sometimes humorous—videos of regular people doing boring stuff has also played an integral role in the site's success. We're not just finding ways to share our very mundane lives, we're also tuning in to watch other people's. One recent trend involved users posting videos of themselves watching other youtubers watching YouTube.

12   Or consider the six-month-old vlog of Dan O'Rourke, a provincial government policy worker in Halifax, who says that making himself the star is simply a product of necessity. "I'm the only actor I can afford," says the 26-year-old, who spends as many as 10 hours a week working on his vlog. "I just do things that I think will turn out interesting without a target audience in mind." Road trips, he says, usually make for the best posts, but, much to his own surprise, his most popular clip so far—which has attracted more than 1,000 views—was a 30-second spot during which he pours out a container of spoiled chocolate milk.

13   People seem to be going to greater heights in the pursuit of real reality—and they aren't exactly succeeding. "Authenticity is a very hazy construct," says Marc Ouellette, who teaches English and cultural studies at McMaster University. "In the race for distinction, everyone ends up ultimately looking the same." And often, he suggests, we end up using the modes of mainstream and celebrity culture, even when we think we're being original.

"I'd like to think that it's totally their voice, but I don't," he says. "There are so many forces. It's not purely narcissistic since it's almost always attached to some pre-existing cultural and celebrity icon."

14   In fact, more than narcissism, Ouellette believes many of us today suffer from solipsism—the inability to recognize the existence of another viewpoint. "Solipsism is supposed to end by mid-adolescence, but I don't think it's disappearing at the same stage in the cognitive process that it used to," he says. "Most people get to a point in their lives when they recognize that others have a viewpoint that is just as valid as their own. With adolescence starting earlier and ending later, some never get to that stage. It ultimately comes down to always thinking, 'what's in it for me?'"

GETTING AWAY WITH MURDER: A SHORT COURSE ON MYSTERY WRITING

Janice MacDonald

1   Here is a quick and easy introduction to the formula of mystery fiction in general. This is akin to a recipe for no-fail brownies. While you will turn out brownies each time with this formula, in order to win the bake-off, you're really going to have to add something of your own. The only warning is, don't tinker too much with the recipe. One or two tweaks per product will work, too many and you may end up with a bodice-ripping western, or (oh, the horror) a mainstream novel.

2   There are two ways to raise your genre novel out of the morass of all that has gone before. Create a believable and fascinating *detective* (your hero, and the character with whom your readers will identify) and conjure up a vision of a new *setting* in which to situate your plots. Plots themselves are secondary (when all is said and done, they've all been done before). This is not necessarily a bad thing. Your reader knows what to expect, is already halfway to becoming your "ideal reader" and is more able to jump right into your world as a result. What follows are some of the ingredients essential to the recipe.

The detective

3   Your detective should be/have:

a)   a loner

4   This is necessary to ensure the believability of your mystery. For one thing, the detective must necessarily be the "other" to allow him/her objectivity on the scene. There will also come a time when your detective will need to put himself in grave personal physical danger. You will lose your reader's sympathy immediately if your character is walking into a bullet at the same time she is supposed to be picking the kids up from an after-school program. If you *have* to give your detective a spouse, make sure the significant other has a good job, so that if you detective dies in the line of action, her husband will mourn, but not starve.

b)   curious

5   The best way to show that your detective is the curious sort, the terrier type of person who just *has* to know the answer, is to put her in a job/career that seems to attract curious types. Make your detective a photojournalist, a scientist, a researcher, a librarian, a graduate student, a trained reader of some sort . . . you get the idea. Not only will readers accept your detective as

the sort who will pursue the quest; these jobs will also often lead to interesting plots.

c) abilities and resources

6   Consider your detective's *job*. Will it allow time out to go solve a puzzle? Is the mystery on site? Can the mystery take place over a weekend? Or a summer holiday? Is your detective independently wealthy? There is so much that is distinctly "unbelievable" in mystery novels (how many people trip over seven bodies a week?) that anything you can centre in reality is a great comfort for your readers.

7   Your detective has to be *strong*. She will be in great personal danger at some point in the novel. Make her strong, healthy, in shape. If you have her jogging regularly, or taking a dance course, the suggestion that she can endure a swim in icy water, or high kick a gun away, or wriggle out of constraints will be easier to absorb.

8   Think of hobbies and skills that will help. Is he a computer whiz? Can she read lips? Does he understand Latvian? Not all these traits will be necessary in each novel, but laying the groundwork now can be helpful.

9   Friends of your detective will be useful. All detectives should have one pal in either the police or Department of Motor Vehicles. Lawyers and research librarian friends also come in handy. If you want a really violent world, a doctor may be a good person to include.

f) a sense of morality

10   This doesn't mean they have to volunteer to teach Sunday School. However, in the words of Chandler, your detective has to be the "best man for his world, and a good enough man for any world." We have to know that, if offered a bribe by the bad'uns, she won't accept it.

g) needs to find the solution

11   To avoid your detective being seen as some sort of snoopy voyeur, you need to find a means by which he is impelled to find the solution. In police or private eye novels, this is easy: detectives are hired to do the job. They need the money, and have to move forward.

12   If your detective is a "gifted amateur," then the best way to have him continue is to make him either a suspect, or have someone he cares for be a suspect. If the police have determined that they have "who dunnit," then no one else is looking for the real culprit. Alternatively, if the detective or someone she cares about is in danger, then she has to proceed with the investigation regardless of the danger.

h) intelligence

13   This character is going to solve a puzzle. Help people believe that he *can* do it. There is a curious paradox involved in reading mysteries whereby, while the readers want to solve the puzzle, they don't want to solve it themselves. If the detective is an idiot but solves a tremendously complex puzzle, it insults the readers' intelligence (this is *not* a good thing if you want to sell more books). This is often why there are sidekicks for the principal character, to give the reader someone to feel superior to (e.g. Watson, Hastings, Archie, Bunter).

The victim

14   There are three possible victims to create.

15   **1.** The victim should be someone the reader cannot stand. Snarky Uncle George who arrives at the family reunion, insults seventeen people in fifteen pages and then appears dead—face down in the fruit punch in chapter three. The reader can then say, "Tut tut, the game's afoot," and get on with the puzzle at hand. No mourning required.

16   **2.** The victim should be someone likeable but not too well-known. The reader isn't given time enough to identify with the victim, although she likes him/her enough to want vengeance/justice. Grief levels are moderately low.

17   **3.** The victim must never be a child. This is a mystery, not a slasher novel. If you want to write horror, kill seven children immediately and float them down a sewer drain. Kill a child in a mystery, and you risk losing your audience immediately. The concept of "game" goes out the window and your reader just gets sad. If your plot requires that you *must* kill a child, do it third or fourth in a long line. Ensure it comes well after your reader has identified with your detective and trusts him to return justice to the land.

The villain

18   In most cases, your villain will be the murderer. If by chance you decide that your murderer is a victim of society, give your detective someone else to truly hate in the narrative. An idiotic boss or overlord of some sort.

19   **1.** The murderer should be intelligent. He/she, after all, is presenting a seemingly insurmountable puzzle for your detective and reader. Make your villain worthy of the conundrum.

20   **2.** Decide early on whether your villain is amoral or immoral. This may dictate how many bodies you stack up. Remember, an immoral person knows that something is wrong, but decides to do it anyway.

An amoral person (serial killer, for instance) believes that rules are made for others, and just does whatsoever he or she pleases.

21   **3.**   Somehow, you should present a flawed ego in your murderer. They might seem meek and mild, but they always press their trousers just so, or wear a flower in their lapel, or polish the undersides of their shoes. After all, it is the most egotistical thing in the world to consider taking another's life . . . this has to appear somewhere in their psychological makeup to help the reader believe they are capable of the crime.

The clues

22   The etymology of the word "clue" comes from a Greek fable wherein Ariadne gave Theseus a "clew" of thread (one of those huge spools like they use on sergers) to tie to the opening of the Minotaur's labyrinth and reel out as he went in order to find his way back. That is what we give our readers, a maze to find their way through. However, we needn't (and this is a failing of novice mystery writers who are terribly intent on "playing fair") light the clues in neon for our readers. In fact, our readers really wish we wouldn't. The best place to salt a lot of clues is right at the beginning, when the reader is still trying desperately to find our rhythm, learn the characters' names, and determine the "lay of the fictional land."

23   Dot clues sporadically, especially if your detective is communicating in the first person to the reader. Make it look like she is getting somewhere. The very best place to put a clue is upside down, hidden in a cluttered drawer, right next to a juicy "red herring" (see below). Remember though, play fair . . . the clues should all be there.

The red herrings

24   Here is some more fascinating etymology that you can cast out at the next boring dinner party, where I can guarantee that you will be met with some amazing rejoinder like, "Pass the cauliflower, please."

25   Whatever. "Red herring" is the term used for false clues.

26   Centuries ago, when the gentry decided to call several dozen close personal friends down to their country estates, they would hold a Hunt as part of the lavish entertainment. Now, most of the countryside would be informed of this event beforehand so they could be hired in as extra help. The evening before the Hunt, reynardophiles (fox lovers) would wander about the countryside armed with three-day-old (or "red") fish, wiping said fish on trees, rocks, pathways, etc. The next morning, the hounds would get confused by the scent and go baying off in all directions, and the fox would be safe for another time.

27   Red herrings in mystery novels are either gloriously shiny and interesting "things" found next to rather drab real clues, or they are other suspects in the plot. Face it, everyone will have something to hide and, if pressed, at least half will lie about it. People don't lie just because they are murderers. Sometimes they just have something innocuous to hide like a predilection for countryside animals. However, if a person's caught out in a lie, there is a very good chance your reader is going to finger that suspect as the murderer and follow his trail as your detective wanders off to corner the real fox . . . I mean killer.

28   Red herrings can be a great deal of fun, but remember, you have to explain everything away to the reader's satisfaction by the end of the narrative, so don't get too carried away.

The setting

29   This is the second-most-important part of your contribution to the genre. In mystery novels there are two forms of *setting* to consider. The first is the locale in which you situate your detective, the territory which you stake out as your own. (Hint: the Navaho Reservation, Alaska, and northern Alberta are all taken . . . go find your own.)

30   The second form of setting you need to consider is a closed environment. This is essential to a mystery novel and why so many have been located on trains, airplanes, cruise ships, and snowed-in ski resorts. You needn't limit yourself to these tired ways of corralling your villain though. Today, you can look to a specialized field of endeavour. If only seven people in the city could have committed the crime with their knowledge of a mass spectrometer . . . and one of them has winged it to Brazil, chances are you know who the killer is. Closed environments make for a better read, giving the readers inside knowledge of a world they might ordinarily not be privy to.

31   And, most of all, never apologize or get flustered when someone accosts you and says, "When are you going to write a real book?" Agatha Christie, bless her li'l cotton socks, still outsells Saul Bellow.

WHY ARE WE DRESSING OUR DAUGHTERS LIKE THIS?
Lianne George

1   In his most recent visual tome, *Katlick School,* the famed American fashion photographer Sante D'Orazio examines the titillating power of the Catholic schoolgirl uniform—a fetish, his publishers write, "as psychosexually resonant as the black motorcycle jacket or the nurse's uniform." The book chronicles the coming of age of Kat, a "beautiful Latina schoolgirl," whose sexual curiosity grows increasingly outsized for her pleated skirt and bobby socks. (It's not the most original idea, maybe, but it's a crowd-pleaser.) Kat's unraveling begins with flashes of Snoopy underwear. In a matter of pages, she's traded in her pressed plaid uniform for nothing but a pair of thigh-high spike-heeled boots. "I was experimenting with a symbol of virginity, the untouched, the ideal, the romantic notion of the pure," says D'Orazio, who famously enshrined Pamela Anderson in the canon of erotic coffee-table literature in 2005 with *Pam: American Icon.* "That is what the uniform signifies."

2   The book also signifies something rather less high-minded—it's a lascivious ode to the cultural muse of the moment, the Lolita. Shortly after it was launched last month, the Catholic League for Religious and Civil Rights registered its disgust in the *New York Post* (after which, not coincidentally, sales of Katlick School spiked). And yet, the response was not entirely honest. Because if there is one iconic symbol of the girl-about-to-go-wild, it's the schoolgirl uniform—and the Catholic community is well aware of it.

3   Even before Britney Spears paired a kilt with pigtails and a midriff-baring blouse in the 1998 video that launched her career, the kilt was a source of deep discomfort for Catholic schoolteachers, administrators and parents. Rules evolved to control its power: it should be three inches from the knee—no higher—and one Canadian uniform manufacturer even patented the X-Kilt, with built-in shorts to prevent girls from transforming them into miniskirts. So far, in Ontario alone, at least seven Catholic schools have voted to phase out the garment altogether. "It always has been an issue," says Ron Crocco, principal of St. Augustine Catholic High School in Markham, Ont., where the kilt was banned in 2003. "As a male, it's difficult to enforce, to say: your kilt is too short. Because then, why am I looking there?" In a post-Britney era, it seems, the kilt is just too sexy for school.

4   How, then, to explain the low-slung jeans, sequined halter tops and lacy miniskirts that so many young girls are wearing to class? In fact, in the broader universe of children's clothing, "Why am I looking there?" has become an increasingly pressing question. Streetwear for little girls has

never been more overtly provocative. Girls as young as 6 are adopting the external cues of womanhood, adorning themselves not only with lip gloss and nail polish, but also body sprays, skin glitters and spa lotions. Club Libby Lu, a Saks Fifth Avenue spinoff with 62 outlets across the United States, invites "super fabulous girls" ages 6 and up to book "sparkle spa" makeover parties for their friends.

5   North American retailers like La Senza Girl, Abercrombie & Fitch and Limited Too sell fishnet stockings, skinny jeans, message panties and padded "bralettes" in micro-sizes. In 2002, Abercrombie & Fitch launched its infamous kiddie thong collection, arguing that girls as young as 10 "are style-conscious and want underwear that doesn't produce a Visible Panty Line." (They have since dropped the line.) Earlier this month, the New York designer Marc Jacobs, having his pick of every grown-up bombshell in Hollywood, tapped 12-year-old Dakota Fanning, star of the newly released *Charlotte's Web*, to be the face of his latest womenswear collection.

6   Meanwhile, in an odd inversion of the Lolita trend, women old enough to vote are embracing the trappings of girlhood, with varying degrees of tongue-in-cheek. Victoria's Secret's lingerie collections have innocent, girlie names like "Angels" and "Pink." Starlets such as Paris Hilton and Britney Spears tote around miniature dogs in tutus—called Tinkerbell and Bit Bit— as though they were cuddly stuffed animals. In her latest video, "Fergalicious," the musician Fergie is dressed in a sexed-up Brownie uniform, surrounded by a troupe of bootie-popping Brownie dancers. Last month, the British retailer Tesco landed in hot water over a pole-dancing kit for sale on its website. The kit, packaged in a pink plastic tube, featured an illustrated Barbie-type character and bubble letters that read: "Unleash the sex kitten inside." It was inadvertently placed on the site's children's toy section, where it looked so entirely at home that none of the Web designers questioned it. Perhaps most creepily, we're in a moment when one of the latest celebrity "trends"—exemplified by Spears and Lindsay Lohan—is to expose one's privates, completely waxed to look like a 10-year-old's, from the backseat of a car.

7   The eroticization of girlhood—once the stuff of Russian literature, Atom Egoyan films, Japanese comic books and good old-fashioned American porn—has been seeping ever more into the larger culture. Now it is one of our dominant aesthetics. In a Lolita-tinged culture, whether the sell is "my body is underdeveloped, but I am precocious" or "my brain is underdeveloped, but I am stacked," the message is the same: exploit me. "For adult women, that notion of being kind of girlie and innocent and sexually pure, as well as very

sexy, has been in men's magazines forever," says Lyn Mikel Brown, co-author of *Packaging Girlhood: Rescuing Our Daughters from Marketers' Schemes.* But whether it's because of the pornification of culture or the extreme worship of youth, the trend has migrated to ever younger age groups. Add this to the fact that the physiological onset of puberty itself keeps inching downward, and the definitions of "girl" and "women" have become moving targets. Which raises the question: what does it mean for little girls when the very things of their lives—kilts, puppies, angels, pink, princesses—become fetishized to the point of rendering them obscene?

8   In stores marketing to young girls, a phenomenon that the authors of *Packaging Girlhood* have termed "the pink wars" is easy to discern. There's the sweet, innocent "princess" girl (baby pink) and the saucy, naughty "diva" girl (hot pink). The two aesthetics are clearly delineated in the selection of novelty T-shirts on offer. A "princess," for instance, would wear one of these scrawled across her chest: *Sweet Treats, Angel, Daddy's Girl, Official Cheer Bunny.* While a "diva" would gravitate toward: *Trouble-maker, Drama Queen, You Will Do What I Say,* and of course, Paris Hilton's idiotic tag line, *That's Hot.* But T-shirts are just the beginning. It is the "total girl" marketers are after, write Brown and Sharon Lamb in *Packaging Girlhood.* " 'xTotal girl' to marketers means finding every inch of their body to adorn," they write. "Expanding one's market means not just reaching down to the lower ages for products introduced to the older ages, but finding new parts of their bodies to colonize or own. The tiniest parts, the forgotten parts, such as nails, which should be dirty after a day of play." Implicit in the various products available is a sexy wink that has never before been associated with children so young.

9   Or so we think. The idea of children as innocent is a relatively modern one. "Children are the great vessels of fantasy," says Anne Hollander, a New York-based clothing historian and author of the classic 1978 text *Seeing Through Clothes.* Historically, a mother saw a little girl as a smaller, unspoiled version of herself, and so a daughter should be formed in her mother's image—and through most of history, she was. Up until the late 18th century, children, both male and female, were outfitted like little adults. Labourers' children dressed like labourers, and society children dressed like their elders, in garments designed for their pomp and rigidity to encourage socially appropriate behaviour. Moreover, says Hollander, royal children were dressed to look sexually attractive so that heads of state in other countries might look at their portraits and think, hmm, maybe I'd like to marry that sweet thing. "Girls of 6 wore low-cut dresses and very fetching hairdos," she says. "You can see it in the paintings, all

meant to be sent off to Louis XV or some such. They don't have any breasts yet, but never mind."

10   It was only with the advent of the Romantic period in the late 1700s that modern notions of childhood arose, inspired largely by the sentimental writings of the Swiss-born philosopher Jean-Jacques Rousseau. "As the 18th century took on its second half," says Hollander, "you have an idea that children are a separate marvellous, terribly fragile, impressionable, innocent kind of creature that needs freedom and liberty of all kinds. There was the sense of nature infusing everything. They get to play and have a wonderful time and move all of their parts." And so, for the first time, girls were dressed differently from their adult counterparts—in a simple chemise with a sash.

11   As the Victorian age crept in, there was a stiffening of everybody's clothing, but girls and women remained sartorially distinct. "It was very, very important that the girls wore short dresses and the ladies wore long dresses," says Hollander. "Girls wore their hair down in curls or braids and put their hair up at the time they got long dresses—whenever they were supposed to be marriageable. The idea was that children are innocent. They don't have any sexuality, so don't worry."

12   What we're seeing now, she says, is a reversion to pre-Enlightenment days, a time before children were innocent, when they were nothing but smaller versions of ourselves in every way. "We are back in the 17th century," she says. "We're dressing little kids like adults and adults are dressing like little children. There is no distinction once again. A girl is a woman by the time she's 8 and a woman remains a girl until she's 80."

13   For many parents, there's nothing wrong with this. Kids are always trying to be more like teenagers, and the precocious fashions are kind of sweet and funny in the way those Anne Geddes photos of kids kissing are. "There is a mistaken sense that kids don't get the joke or the meaning so it's okay for them to wear sexualized slogans," says Susan Linn, an instructor in psychiatry at Harvard Medical School and a co-founder of the coalition Campaign for a Commercial-Free Childhood.

14   But even for parents who do have a problem with these off-the-rack identities, there is tremendous pressure to buy in. For one thing, they are susceptible to the "everyone is doing it" argument, and they don't want their kid to be ostracized. For another, it's often the least of their concerns. "They are in the middle of numerous commercially created battles with their children," says Linn. "Battles about junk food, violent media, expensive brands and all sorts of things. It's hard, if not impossible, to say no all of the time."

5   The popular marketing spin—which, incidentally, is supposed to reassure parents in some way—is that it is kids who are "getting older younger," a theory called age compression, brought on by the fact that young people have never had access to so much information. But what we're really seeing, says Linn, is marketers exploiting the natural tendency of young girls to want to emulate older girls, who appear to them to have more independence and social prestige.

6   In the end, then, it's not really a kid problem, but a grown-up problem. Because girls, looking the way they look, are only aping grown women, which serves to remind us of the turmoil and confusion surrounding what we currently believe a woman should be. The New York-based writer Ariel Levy documented this phenomenon, which she dubbed "raunch culture," in her 2006 book *Female Chauvinist Pigs*. The idea is that, in a post-feminist universe, a woman can be the agent of her own objectification and still be empowered. And so we see a boom in trends inspired by porn culture: pole-dancing and striptease lessons, boob jobs and Brazilian waxes. "A tawdry, tarty, cartoonlike version of female sexuality has become so ubiquitous, it no longer seems particular," writes Levy. "What we once regarded as a kind of sexual expression, we now view as sexuality." More recently, the *New York Times* columnist Bob Herbert, inspired by an Abercrombie & Fitch T-shirt he came across that read *Who Needs A Brain When I Have These?*, addressed what he calls a "disrespectful, degrading, contemptuous treatment of women" that has become "so pervasive and so mainstream that it has just about lost its ability to shock."

7   "This is some sort of response to the feminist movement," says Hollander. In fact, it's part of a trial-and-error continuum. In the '70s, as women prepared to invade the workplace en masse, the most overt manifestation of this new societal phase was sartorial. "It meant throwing out the skirts and certainly girdles and dressing so that you couldn't tell the difference between a man and a woman, except very small things," she says. "The masculine wardrobe was entirely co-opted by women. Suits and shoulder pads denied curves. Breasts and behinds and hips were not in fashion."

8   The current hyper-feminine aesthetic, one could argue, is an overcorrection of this correction—an almost fanatical reclaiming of pink and frilly. But what may have been born of a spirit of defiance has lost its revolutionary edge, and now young girls are learning the not-so-progressive lesson that their primary value lies in their worth as sex objects. "Just because we are post doesn't mean we are feminists," writes Levy. "There is a widespread assumption that simply because my generation of women has the

good fortune to live in a world touched by the feminist movement, that means everything we do is magically imbued with its agenda."

19	The trickle-down effect we're now seeing among very young girls has resulted in a Junior Miss version of raunch culture. Watching kids adopt these same behaviours is like looking at the larger culture through a funhouse mirror. On the body of a six-year-old, the diminishing aspect of an *Eye Candy* T-shirt is amplified and twisted—and entirely devoid of any of the irony that makes it pseudo-radical coming from a twentysomething pop star. "The problem is that girls are acquiring the trappings of maturity," Linn says, "but there's no indication that their social or emotional development is keeping pace." In fact, the aspiring-up trend preys upon and heightens the particular insecurities of kids in this age group. "Will she be popular? Will she be invited somewhere? With what group does she belong?" write Brown and Lamb. "Before a girl has half a chance to reflect on issues of belonging and desirability, she is being confronted with a market that tells her she should be concerned about this—even when she's as young as 8."

20	We tell girls that, in wearing these things, they are somehow expressing themselves in an essential way. "If Ts expressed who a girl is," write Brown and Sharon Lamb, "you'd think she'd be wearing the T she got at the summer camp she went to, the music festival she attended or the Humane Society where she volunteers to walk the dogs. But instead they express 'attitude' rather than interests, skills, concerns, and hobbies." Worse still, in their very construction, these clothes prescribe behaviours that are hard to describe as empowering. A micro-mini, for instance, is a great disincentive to playing on the monkey bars. A halter top and tight, low-rise jeans make it rather more challenging to run and jump. "Every message to a preteen girl," write Brown and Lamb, "says that it's preferable to pose on the beach rather than surf, to shop rather than play, to decorate rather than invent."

21	But for marketers, it's not about grooming girls to be the next generation's cast of *Girls Gone Wild*. It has much more to do with grooming them to be promiscuous consumers. "Marketers are not setting out to sexualize little girls," says Susan Linn. "They are setting out to make a profit selling clothes to and for children and don't care what the consequences are." Girls themselves don't necessarily understand the clothing as sexual, she says, but "what they do comprehend is that they get a lot of attention by dressing in a particular way."

22	Female power has always been inextricably linked to ornamentation. When a woman comes of age, the convention is that she takes on a series of external cues to indicate sexual readiness: bright red lips that signal arousal, high heels that show off shapely legs, clothing that hugs fertile curves. This is what it means to be a sophisticated, mature and, to some extent, a powerful woman. But these things no longer correspond to any sort of biological turning point. Instead, they signify a claiming of personal economic autonomy. Call it consumer readiness. And as far as marketers are concerned, girls are never too young to be ready.

23   In fact, the most important identity of all for girls to cultivate is their identity as shoppers. For example, the educational toy brand International Playthings has a product called My First Purse, marketed to girls two years old and up. It's pink, purple and plush, and it includes play accessories, among them a wallet, debit card, lipstick, keys, mirror, and cellphone. (No, they don't make oversized baby-blue billfolds for boys to wedge in the back of their diapers.) Likewise, Mattel's Barbie Bank-with-ME ATM machine for girls 3 and up that takes bills and coins and displays their balance on the screen. The debit card activates sound effects and banking commands from Barbie. Anyone for a game of "Transfer funds"?

24   Ultimately, it is the "play" aspect of aspirational products that seems to have evaporated. Young girls have always loved to play dress-up—to trip around the house in their mother's heels and pearls. Playing mom, playing house, playing glamour girl or doctor was about little girls creating safe spaces for themselves in which to experiment with grown-up female identities. The difference is you can turn play off. Play time is confined and varied. Whereas now, taking on a womanly identity is incorporated into girls' everyday lives. They don't see it as a pretend purse, it's *their* purse. Wearing a halter top is not for dress-up, it's for show. "There's a seriousness to it that there wasn't," says Brown. "Now, it's really not about fantasy play. It's about adopting something that's out there for them. It's like practice for something very specific, to be like Jessica Simpson."

25   The latest dolls for girls offer not-so-subtle reinforcement of the same ideas. Twenty years ago, popular collections including Cabbage Patch Kids and Strawberry Shortcake had big floppy hats, pudgy limbs, and silly clothing. They were cartoonish—with bright colours and scents created to appeal to kids' imaginations. In 2001, MGA Entertainment launched the Bratz dolls with the tag line: "The girls with a passion for fashion." These toys, says Linn, are a "ratcheted up male fantasy of what women should look like—big eyes, big lips, big breasts, an anorexic waistline and very long legs." Soon, the Bratz dolls—who do nothing but shop and socialize—were outselling even Barbie, grossing roughly US$2 billion per year. Mattel fought back with a sluttier, more urban line of Barbie dolls called the My Scene collection. "That kind of plastic sexuality seems to be normalized for younger and younger kids," says Linn. We used to worry about Barbie, with her improbable proportions and dismal math skills. Now we long for Barbie. Not

the new Bling Bling Barbie, but the old one with the job. At least she tried to do math.

26   It is no coincidence that the Lolita moment is surfacing now, at a time when boys are supposedly in crisis, says Brown. "Twenty years ago, we were talking about girls and loss of voice and self-esteem and there were all these empowerment programs," says Brown. "Now we have girls and women more likely to go to college, getting better grades, being really out there and claiming more power. What women are doing is challenging the status quo, and when that happens, things tighten up. It's an anxiety, a collective response."

27   And so, while adults try to navigate all of these complicated, fragmented ideals about gender, childhood, empowerment and sexuality, girls have become our ideological guinea pigs. And they're being taught some pretty unappealing lessons. "You can learn a whole lot of very serious narcissism by being brought up to be looked at constantly," says Hollander. "That was Marie Antoinette's upbringing, who was scheduled to be the queen of France since she was born." And we all know how that one turned out.

28   Unless we are prepared to see six-year-olds in garters, then it would seem we're ready for another backlash. Already, the boundaries of what the public will put up with are beginning to constrict. Religious and family groups, media critics, feminists and other concerned citizens have teamed up to halt production of certain products deemed too outrageous—including a line of Bratz bras for little girls, and a line of Hasbro dolls aimed at six-year-olds based on the Pussycat Dolls, a burlesque troupe turned singing group. Now, advocacy groups have their sights set on a new line of clothing for babies called Pimpfants. "It's a kid thang," the company's slogan says. But when you see a six-month-old child in a *M.I.L.F.* onesie, even the most permissive grown-up has to stop and ask herself, whom is this really about?

LEGACY OF BETRAYAL: THE TROUBLE WITH FILM ADAPTATIONS OF VIDEO GAMES

David Annandale

1   Presented, for the reader's consideration: a study in contrasts. Two bigger than life characters, iconic in their respective art forms. Both are fabulously wealthy and based in gigantic mansions. Both are adept at hand-to-hand combat. They are both haunted by the death of parents, and the only constant relationships in their lives are the ones they have with their loyal domestic help. Both, finally, are the stars of big-budget film franchises, and here lies the crucial distinction. One character is Batman, and his most recent film, Christopher Nolan's *Batman Begins* (2005), was characterized, among other things, by the intelligence of its script and the seriousness with which it treated its character. The other figure is Lara Croft, and *Lara Croft: Tomb Raider* received a lot of attention for its coals-to-Newcastle strategy of padding Angelina Jolie's bust, but was otherwise consigned to the dustbin of mediocrity. These two high-profile productions encapsulate the current state of affairs with regards to the film industry's approach to adapting comic books and video games. Maturity and a respect for the source are no longer unheard-of characteristics of comic book adaptations. Video games should be so lucky.

2   Cinema, which has always drawn inspiration from the other arts, has been adapting plays and novels virtually since its inception (Edison filmed snippets of plays, and a version of Victor Hugo's *Hunchback of Notre-Dame* appeared as *Esmeralda* in 1906), and it has continued to draw inspiration not only from those sources and from its cousin, television, but also from music—*Fantasia* (1940)—and even painting—*Isle of the Dead* (1945). However, cinema's relationship with that youngest of art forms, the video game, is much more problematic. Despite some glimmers of hope, most cinematic versions of games have been neither good adaptations nor good films. The reasons why the films are bad are legion, but I would submit that most of them come down to one bedrock issue: a fundamental lack of respect for the source material.

3   This lack of respect should not be a surprise, given the attitude of society at large toward video games. After all, the vast majority of literature about games has been obsessively devoted to their nefarious effects on players. The first studies considering them as an art form are only now beginning to appear.

4   A comparison with comic book adaptations is instructive, in that filmmakers only began to get the adaptations right when they stopped regarding comics as a debased art form. Superheroes have been turning up

in the movies for decades. The 1940s saw serials starring the likes of Captain Marvel (*Shazam!*) and Batman. Spirited fun as these efforts were, they were also strictly juvenile fare. But comics matured, though the film industry did not, it seems, receive the memo. Consider the case of Batman. The campy television show (which begat an equally campy movie in 1966) has essentially remained the touchstone until *Batman Begins*. Despite their darkness, even Tim Burton's *Batman* (1989) and *Batman Returns* (1992) were as much comedies as they were dramas.

5   But the last ten years have seen something of a revolution in comic book adaptations. Apart from Nolan's film, audiences have seen a plethora of films that are faithful to the spirit, themes, and storylines of the comics inspiring them. The *Spider-Man* and *X-Men* films and *Hellboy* (2004) are the obvious examples here, but attention should also be paid to the non-super-hero adaptations such as *Ghost World* (2001), *Road to Perdition* (2002), *A History of Violence* (2005), *V for Vendetta* (2005) and even the problematic *From Hell* (2001). These are films, some highly regarded, of whose comic book origins, it is safe to say, are unknown to a fair proportion of the viewing audience. The films do not scream "comic book" to viewers in no small part because they show no hint of condescension. The stories are treated as important and deserving of a respectful translation to the new medium, which is exactly how the best novel adaptations come to be.

6   What then, is happening with video game adaptations? Like comic books, video games suffer from the outside culture's perception that they represent an art form that is, at best, in a state of arrested adolescence, aimed exclusively at children. The hair-pulling, chest-beating, sputtering outrage directed at games from various State Legislatures and other political organs (institutions which, when it comes to informed and mature debate, have themselves not succeeded in moving beyond daycare, let alone adolescence) is more than slightly reminiscent of the fulminations directed at comics in the 1950s. Then, as now, an extremely popular art form largely alien to, and therefore feared by, the ruling classes was denounced as a Corruptor of Youth. The same thing, of course, happened when movies were new, and also when novels were, well, "novel." Then, as now, the charge against the art form was led by a crusader as voluble as he was hysterically inaccurate in his claims. In 1954, Dr. Fredrick Wertham, in his book *Seduction of the Innocent*, made the unassailable claim (please note sarcasm) that comics led to juvenile delinquency. Today, lawyer Jack Thompson announces to all within earshot that video games are training the Sociopaths of Tomorrow.

7   If we consider *PONG* as the moment when the video game proper was born, then the form has only been around for about 35 years. When

cinema was that age (circa 1930), it had only just entered the sound era. Film theory had come into being only a few years earlier. In other words, the idea that films were a legitimate art form was a new one. Games are at a not-dissimilar stage of development. In their first three decades, movies moved from Edison's kinetoscope peep shows and the Lumière brothers' short glimpses of daily life to the likes of *Intolerance* (1916), *Battleship Potemkin* (1925), and *Metropolis* (1928). In a like manner, games, quite apart from enormous technological advances in their audio and visual presentations, have reached a level of narrative and thematic sophistication undreamed of in the arcades of yore. Players today encounter everything from the scalpel-sharp social satire of the *Grand Theft Auto* series, to the political commentary of *Raze's Hell* (whose science fiction setting barely disguises an attack on George W. Bush's war in Iraq), to the serious engagement with issues of survivor guilt and incest in *Silent Hill 2: Restless Dreams*. Have games had their *Battleship Potemkin* yet? The question is a difficult one, and I do not want to postulate too close a developmental relationship. The point, though, is that along with narrative sophistication, games are finally beginning to receive serious critical attention.

8   By and large, these developments would be very hard to know about if one's knowledge of games was based solely on the movies they inspire. Granted, there are some very significant challenges that confront any game-to-film adaptation. One is length: a game that runs under ten hours is considered short, and the likes of *The Elder Scrolls IV: Oblivion* can last hundreds. Compressing these experiences to approximately two hours is no simple task. However, if comic narratives arcing over dozens of issues and novels spanning 500 pages or more can be successfully brought to the screen, length should not be an insuperable obstacle.

9   The other, bigger problem is linked to the deceptive similarity games and movies share. Both are narratives that are experienced on a screen, appealing primarily to the same senses. They also share talent, with actors, music composers and writers moving back and forth between the two forms. But these similarities run the risk of blinding the filmmaker to the fundamental difference: the game is interactive. A recurring complaint regarding adaptations is that watching the film is like watching someone else play. As soon as a film creates *that* unfortunate experience, it has failed to substitute the visceral effects of one medium with equivalent (but *different*) effects in the other.

0   This problem is never more apparent than in the first-person sequence in *Doom* (2005). This is the scene that comes closest to capturing visual look of the game, but is also a significant moment of failure on the part

of the film. The game is a seminal example of the FPS (First-Person Shooter), but that genre of game is so successful precisely because the interactive nature of the experience gives the player a visceral sense of being in the scene, of personally taking action or being in danger. The game structure moves toward invisibility. The opposite is true in film, where first-person sequences in general, far from rendering the director's style invisible, draw attention to it. This is a technique that pulls viewers out of the narrative as they become extremely conscious of the camera. And this is exactly what happens in *Doom*. The visual aping of the game is so obvious that the sequence works only at the level of a joke, and indeed, viewers tend to react with laughter as they recognize the imitation. Of course, if any suspension of disbelief were still operating, it collapses completely at this point. The film is mocking any notion that it is attempting real suspense, or taking its story at all seriously.

11   Evidence of the lack of respect the film has for its source material does not end here. Certainly the film's drab steel interiors are far less visually appealing than the vivid greens, reds and blacks of the *Doom 3* game. But the biggest problem by far lies with the script, which guts the game's fundamental premise. Instead of marines arriving on Mars to discover the opened gates of Hell, now the encountered monstrosities are the results of that most tired of all sci-fi/horror conventions: genetic engineering.[1] Yes, the game's main idea is more than slightly absurd, which *Doom 3* acknowledges with some sly winks (a pre-cataclysm e-mail from an employee demands to know by what bureaucratic tangle a shipment of chainsaws was sent to treeless Mars), but never to the degree of undermining the tension. The story and its dangers are played straight. And while the notion of Hell on Mars may be ridiculous, it also has a delicious directness and simplicity, which is testified to by the enormous success of the game franchise, a staple since the first game became a defining early FPS. Although most FPS's have similar control schemes, and, at a very basic level, are close to being interchangeable, the worlds in which they take place are not. The *Doom* games may not have the fully fleshed-out universe and complex religio-political contexts of *Halo*, but their blend of industrial science fiction and extreme supernatural horror creates an atmosphere and environment that is most distinctive, and is a defining

---

[1] A student of mine has argued, quite persuasively, that this deviation is not that grievous a betrayal. Because, he argues, the plot of the game is fairly minimal, serving primarily as the excuse to have monsters popping out of the darkness to attack the player, as long as the core action remains (guns versus monsters), the rationale for the action hardly matters. I disagree.

characteristic of the franchise. Remove this world and the film becomes nothing more than another dreary series of gunfights in corridors.

12   In summary, the film *Doom* attempts to bring over the wrong elements of the game (the camera perspective), thus failing to properly distinguish between the strengths of the two different media, and ignore what could well have made the transition from game to film very successfully: the world of the game.

13   The question of respect for the source material plays out differently in the careers of two filmmakers who have made a speciality out of game adaptations: Uwe Boll and Paul W. S. Anderson. The less said about the former, the better. He is responsible for *House of the Dead* (2003), *Alone in the Dark* (2005) and *BloodRayne* (2005), and is threatening hapless audiences with forthcoming adaptations of the likes of *Dungeon Siege* and *Far Cry*. His films are terrible by any standard of measure, and are even worse adaptations, bearing little, if any, resemblance to the games whose titles they share. Anderson, on the other hand, has directed *Mortal Kombat* (1995) and *Resident Evil* (2002), and has produced *Resident Evil: Apocalypse* (2004), *DOA: Dead or Alive* (2006) and the forthcoming *Resident Evil: Extinction*. None of these titles are anything approaching masterworks. The *Resident Evil* films are, however, among the most successful game adaptations (barring the much more expensive Lara Croft films), and benefit from Anderson's acknowledged familiarity with, and love for, the games themselves. The degree to which the individual films hew to the letter of the games varies. Thus, Alice, the protagonist of the *Resident Evil* films, is not a character in the games, and the films are less gothic and doom-laden, and more explosion-happy than the games. But they are still taking place in a universe that is recognizably that of the games, and do not treat their sources of inspiration as disposable objects of ridicule.

14   So respect helps make Anderson's films better than Boll's (as does a certain basic ability), though they are still far from perfect. Neither fully action nor fully horror, the *Resident Evil* films, for example, are somewhat unsatisfactory hybrids, and thus not entirely successful movies in their own right. A further ray of hope can be seen in 2006's *Silent Hill*, directed by Christophe Gans. The film's storyline is recognizably derived from the first game in the series. Visually, the film's artistic design is the game world made flesh. Its monsters are accurate cinematic representations of their virtual counterparts. Even the score is largely that of the game. Nothing is played for camp value. The film is not an unqualified success (its incorporation of the puzzle-solving elements of the game is forced and out of place), and it did disappoint some fans of the game series. Nonetheless, *Silent Hill*

represents a committed effort to bringing a gaming world intact to the screen. Significantly, its primary audience appears not to have been the gaming community as such, but the horror audience. Many of the complexities of the world of Silent Hill itself are left unexplained in the film, as they are in the games. This ambiguity may thus have baffled some audience members. However, *Silent Hill* does appear to be arguably the closest example yet to a film that, while staying true to its source, is simultaneously a film that works as a horror movie in and of itself.

15   We are still a long way from the likes of David Cronenberg's *A History of Violence.* In other words, video game adaptations have yet to produce a work that is outstanding cinema in its own right, a film that audiences without prior knowledge would not tag as deriving from games, but that is still a respectful translation of its source. In fact, the only completely artistically successful game-related film to date remains Cronenberg's own *eXistenZ* (1999). Though not based on any individual game, it not only recreates the intense gaming experience in perfectly cinematic terms, but, with its tale of characters struggling to understand what, exactly, constitutes reality once the virtual world is indistinguishable from the physical one, rigorously investigates the ontological questions that the very experience of gaming raises. With the character of superstar game designer Allegra Geller (Jennifer Jason Leigh), Cronenberg not only acknowledges the arrival of new, completely viable art form, he embraces it. He is the first filmmaker of power to do so. It is vital to the health of both media that he not be the last.

BRAINS, BRAWN, AND BEAUTY: A PLACE FOR FEMINIST ACADEMICS IN AESTHETIC BODY SPORTS, OR WORKING TOWARDS A PHYSICAL FEMINISM

Carolyn Ives

1   Imagine that you are at a bodybuilding show. You watch as the tanned, oiled up athletes take the stage and then start their posing. For some reason, the bodybuilder who is third from the left strikes you as oddly familiar. Then it hits you: that bodybuilder is one of your university teachers!

2   Now, when I said "bodybuilder," you probably imagined a man—I'll bet you didn't imagine a woman. Herein lies a connection: while women fought so hard to be recognized as serious academics[1] in universities over the past several decades, so have they fought to be recognized as serious competitors in the physique sport arena. Add the fact that aesthetic physique sports[2] are marginalized even by the rest of the athletic world (there is no Olympic event, and even Arnold Schwarzenegger is trying to distance himself from his bodybuilding past), and female physique athletes are left trying to sort out where they fit in. It's no wonder that some women competitors use or even abuse steroids to try to appear more masculine—and then get breast implants to appear more feminine. Even more of a paradox is that both figure and fitness athletes are expected to wear glittery posing suits and stilettos on stage, traditionally feminine apparel, sometimes with sexual connotation, while sporting bodies that many would call masculine in their levels of muscularity.

3   Now, if that woman athlete is also an academic, the room for controversy may be even greater, as neither her colleagues nor her students will likely understand or respect her sport, perceiving her as being too overtly sexual, of being—ironically—anti-feminist. Somehow, disciplining the mind still is valued more highly than disciplining the body. It's no surprise, however, that women sometimes have to challenge social norms of what is considered "appropriate" in order to succeed, not just in academia, but in other arenas, also. This leaves me to question what place, if any, can exist for women, both in and out of universities, who wish to use their brains and

---

[1] The term "academic" in this context refers to university teachers and researchers.

[2] These include bodybuilding, fitness, and figure. Bodybuilding competitors may be men or women; competitors are judged on muscularity, leanness, symmetry, and posing. Fitness and figure competitions include only women in Canada (through the Canadian Bodybuilding Federation, or CBBF), although some organizations in the USA include male fitness competitors. Figure athletes are judged on physique and general appearance, but they do not have to be quite as large or as lean as the bodybuilders. Fitness athletes are also judged on physique, but they must also perform a fitness routine, which includes several strength and flexibility moves combined with dance and gymnastics.

brawn (and, depending on the physique sport, perhaps also their beauty, however problematic that may be) in an attempt to overcome barriers and dispel misconceptions.

4   Now, even before these competitors ever hit the stage, they must negotiate the arena that is the gym. There have been numerous studies and interviews that examine the place for women within the gym, but as Sassatelli explains that "the toned body has become a commercial icon" (228), she also argues that within the site of the gym, "a place which has its own rules and where a vast array of meanings and identities are negotiated" (229), the fit body represents "a conspicuous sign of personal worth" (244). However, in the experiences of many women weightlifters, that worth has been relegated to men only. Indeed, many men at my gym become resentful when we local women physique athletes use equipment that traditionally only men use, or when we lift as much as they do. In fact, Dworkin points out that "The proportion of men to women in the weight room at any given time is approximately 80/20 or 90/10" (132). She also discusses the women she's interviewed who "dare" to lift weights: "it is clear that there is a rejection of femininity when it is perceived as the equivalent of frailty or dependency. Words such as "power," "strength," "independence," and even outright "rebellion" are often used to describe weightlifting" (144).

5   This sense of rebellion, however, pervades more than the gym: some women in physique sports sometime go to extremes to get noticed both on and off stage as well. Apparently confused about their identities, they scatter their energies in many directions: they want to be athletes, but often they resort to "adult" modeling to fund their sport. In fact, some well-known Canadian bodybuilders are even more famous for their porn sites. This misdirection creates difficulties for those competitors who hold professional positions and want to be taken seriously as athletes. The lines between body sport and body exploitation become blurred, but this line must be clearly drawn for women physique athletes in professional positions: for an academic, for example, there must be no suggestion of overt sexuality. I'll give you a personal example. Our local newspapers often feature local athletes from various sports. When our bodybuilders and figure competitors are preparing for competition, they often appear in the newspaper with explanations of their training schedule and details about the competition. For one such interview, the photographer asked us to put on our posing suits and lie across a car. His request wasn't completely unreasonable, as our posing suits are regulation competition attire, and the car was one from our sponsor, whom we wanted to publicly thank.

Still, I could not bring myself to pose in a bikini in the local paper, nor could I lie across the hood of the sports car. Therefore, covered completely in my workout gear and sitting neatly on the car, I didn't look much like a physique competitor, but I worried less about what my colleagues and students would think.

6   However, on the positive side, these same women who expose their bodies for fame and money outside of their sport are at the same time challenging societal expectations of femininity: they are muscular, and they are strong—traditionally masculine qualities. Still, they pose in rhinestoned bikinis and stilettos, and they often undergo breast implant surgery to appear more feminine, more physically balanced on stage and in photos. In fact, the sport of figure has been recently criticized as becoming a muscular beauty pageant, an accusation that damages the credibility of the sport and the sensibilities of the competitors who train for hours a day and follow strict diets all year in order to challenge and sculpt their bodies to be able to stand on stage with pride. In their search for a feminist theory of physical liberation, Roth and Basow explain that "the masculine ideal is one of physical strength, large size, and aggressiveness. The feminine ideal, on the other hand, is beautiful, small, thin, and perhaps most importantly, weak" (249). However, women who compete in physique sports combine the positive attributes of both the masculine and the feminine, potentially reconstructing a new, stronger feminine ideal, exactly what Roth and Basow want, but by allowing themselves to be reduced to sexual objects, these competitors and their bodies' feminine aspects become imminently exploitable. Since competing is costly, many of these women believe they have no choice. Also, since social norms dictate that a female body is a sexual body, for some it seems a reasonable compromise to allow that sexual objectification to justify their masculine physiques.

7   How, exactly, did women's bodybuilding get here, in this precarious and problematic position? Just as early feminists were, early women bodybuilders were pioneers, often enduring harassment and abuse from men at the gym. The main difference, as Jagger points puts, is that while early feminists strove for equality of rights, physical bodies and physical strength never entered into the equation (qtd. in Roth and Basow 246). Women physique athletes strove to find their place in society, both in and out of the gym (Klein Ch. 7). They challenged social perceptions of femininity and built strong, muscular bodies—and in competition, they were judged on muscular size, shape, symmetry, and overall aesthetics, just as the men bodybuilders were. Over the decades, however, in order to win, those bodies had to become

even bigger. This drove many to steroid abuse in order to achieve that. As the general public became less interested in these competitions, claiming that these new bodily constructions were "unnatural" and not attractive, a new physique competition gained popularity: figure. Figure athletes tend to be smaller, sometimes less genetically gifted in terms of muscle-building. Some women start with figure and work their way to bodybuilding as they develop more mass; others turn to figure when they are too injured for fitness or want a different look than that of the bodybuilders. Surprisingly, though, the main difference between figure and bodybuilding, however, isn't size, at least at the amateur level (at some novice competitions here in BC, there are women who compete in both categories)—the real difference is in presentation. While bodybuilders traditionally pose in plain suits and bare feet, figure athletes are required to wear stiletto heels, and they are judged not only on their physiques, but also on their overall presentation, including decorative suits, hair, and make-up. This competition has ballooned in numbers, as the average woman sees it as a more attainable look, and, most importantly, it's more socially acceptable for women to look like figure athletes than it is for them to look like bodybuilders. While women bodybuilders have the potential to be subversive within the male-dominated sport, figure athletes instead reinforce (not while working out in the gym, but while made up on stage) the social norms that prevent equality, both physical and otherwise.

8   The popularity of figure has made people within the sport question is validity, which is somewhat unfair, as many figure athletes train just as hard as bodybuilders, but it has also dramatically increased ticket sales. It's worth noting that since the inception of the figure competition, women bodybuilders have begun wearing prettier suits and paying more attention to their hair and make-up as well. Increasingly, the figure competitors have also become bigger, like the bodybuilders, raising concerns within the sport about steroid abuse, even to the point that in an unprecedented move, the International Federation of Bodybuilding (IFBB) announced in December 2004 that it wanted to see women physique athletes in all fields of competition come in approximately 20% smaller, starting the following year. Although this proclamation has since disappeared from the IFBB website as the site has been updated several times since then, it still exists on Wikipedia under "Female Bodybuilding"; furthermore, discussion about it remains on several bodybuilding discussion boards where it has been hotly debated. Some posters defended the move, arguing that the IFBB is only looking out for the best interests of those competitors who might abuse supplements

and harm their health in order to win, while others complained that the move is clearly sexist, arguing there would have been total outrage if the IFBB had made the same proclamation for the men.

9   Whatever the reasons for the ruling, we saw evidence of its effects in the CBBF Canadian Fitness and Figure Nationals just this year (July 2007). Several of the class winners were smaller than many of the winners from previous years, and many spectators claimed to be surprised by some of the judges' choices. In a few figure classes, previous winners did not even place in the top five. Therefore, women are allowed to compete on the same stage as the men, but they aren't allowed to get "TOO big." The men, however, are praised for looking as big and freaky as they can. Only in the world of bodybuilding is the term "Freak" a compliment, again challenging social perceptions of beauty. Shara Vigeant, an Alberta bodybuilder, argues that this inability to easily categorize women physique athletes is partially responsible for the general public's discomfort (Vigeant, para 3).

10   I suspect that the other part of the problem, perhaps even the main problem with the place for women in physique sports, is that while society has begrudgingly accepted that women are equal to men in terms of intellectual capability, at least in principle, society is not ready to accept the physical equality of women. People who are uncomfortable with women bodybuilders say they are unattractive because they look unnatural. It wasn't that long ago that women's voting was unnatural, that women working was unnatural, that women in the academy were unnatural. It's probably worth noting that this same cry for what's "natural" and "biologically right" is the root of homophobia and other types of discrimination, also. Social constructions of normalcy are keeping women from reaching their true potential in the gym, in much the same way it kept women out of the work force for decades, and then out of the academy, etc. In fact, I can't count the number of times when I have been training a woman who won't lift more than five pounds because she is afraid of getting too big, of looking too strong. Are we going to ever be prepared to accept physically strong women as natural? If the federations who govern aesthetic body sports can allow women to get past the beauty pageant element of the competitions, then perhaps women physique athletes will be able to carve out new identities for all women—so it will be okay for women to be smart and strong, and women academics won't have to be "closet" physique athletes for fear of losing professional respect. And a "strong woman" will be more than just a metaphor.

Works Cited

Dworkin, Shari L. "A Woman's Place is in the . . . Cardiovascular Room?? Gender Relations, the Body, and the Gym." *Athletic Intruders: Ethnographic Research on Women, Culture, and Exercise.* Ed. Anne Bolin and Jane Granskog. Albany, NY: SUNY, 2003. 131–158.

Klein, Alan M. "Sally's Corner: The Women of Olympic." *Little Big Men: Bodybuilding, Subculture, and Gender Construction.* Albany, NY: State UNY, 1993. 159–193.

Roth, Amanda and Susan A. Basow. "Femininity, Sports, and Feminism: Developing a Theory of Physical Liberation." *Journal of Sport and Social Issues.* 28.3 (2004): 245–265.

Sassatelli, Roberta. "Interaction Order and Beyond: A Field Analysis of Body Culture within Fitness Gyms." *Body Modification.* Ed. Mike Featherstone. London: Sage, 2000. 227–248.

Vigeant, Shara. "Female Bodybuilding." Alberta Bodybuilding. Retrieved October 7, 2006, from <http://www.albertabodybuilding. com/abffeature8.htm>.

APPENDIX 1

ESSAY AND CITATION FORMAT

A1 FORMATTING: WRITING ASSIGNMENTS

The presentation of any writing assignment creates your reader's first impression and ensures that your ideas are clearly communicated. Take time to proofread and format your paper properly, using the following guidelines.

■ *Typing*

Strive to produce a clean, professional-looking paper. Most instructors prefer papers to be typed and some insist on it. (Publishers accept only typed material.) If you are allowed to submit handwritten papers, use blue or black ink.

Make sure you have chosen an acceptable font, such as Times New Roman or Arial. Avoid fonts and typographical devices that create a cluttered look. Avoid last-minute problems by testing your printer long before the essay is due.

Proofread your final hard copy and, if necessary, make neat corrections in ink.

■ *Paper*

Use standard white computer paper or, if you are handwriting, lined paper of approximately the same size (216 mm x 279 mm or 8½ x 11 in.). Use only one side of the page.

■ *Word-processing functions*

Become familiar with your computer's default settings and the functions with which to change paragraph format (indenting, spacing), to insert automatic page numbers, to sort and format works cited or reference entries, and so forth.

■ *Spacing*

Always type double-spaced to allow room for comments. Many readers prefer handwritten work to be double-spaced for the same reason. Others prefer handwriting single-spaced on wide-lined paper.

■ *Margins*

The default margins on most word-processing programs are adequate. If you need to set margins, leave 4 cm (1½ in.) on the top and left sides and 2.5 cm (1 in.) on the bottom and right.

- *Title*

Your title should make your paper's main point clear to your reader. An essay's title is often a short form of the thesis. Don't use labels such as "Essay #1" or "Personal Essay."

- *Title page*

Determine the documentation style you will use for your essay. Then see Appendix B (MLA) or Appendix C (APA) for title-page guidelines and sample title pages.

- *Pagination*

In both the MLA and APA documentation styles, all pages are numbered at the top right corner. See Appendices B and C to see how these right headers differ.

- *Bibliography*

End your paper with your list of references (APA) or works cited (MLA), if required. Be sure to number these pages.

- *Fastening*

Use a staple or paper clip to fasten the pages. (Some instructors and editors object to staples; all object to straight pins and other hazardous devices.)

- *Copies*

If you are using a word processor, make two backup copies: one on your hard drive and one on a disk or memory key. Set your computer's back-up function to ten minutes or so, and overwrite revisions as necessary. If you are handwriting, photocopy your original.

- *Compatibility*

Be aware of possible incompatibilities between the word-processing program you use at home and those of other computers you may be using to print or submit your work. Computer labs often don't allow disks or memory keys to be brought in from the outside because they might spread viruses; consider emailing your essay to yourself to print it at school. If you submit work electronically, through a course tool such as WebCT or by email attachment, ensure that your instructor will be able to convert your documents.

A2 DOCUMENTATION: GENERAL GUIDELINES

Whenever you use quotations, facts, or ideas from other sources, whether in a research paper or any other kind of writing, you must clearly indicate what you have borrowed, and you must do so in **two places.** Use parenthetical references (called *in-text citations*) to acknowledge your sources within your paper, AND include a list of those sources at the end of your paper to provide more complete bibliographical information.

Documenting your sources is important for two reasons. First, it enables your reader to check statements that you have made or to look up more information on your subject. Second, it ensures that you do not take credit for information that is not your own. (See Taking Notes and Avoiding Plagiarism, 13f, and Documenting Sources, 13g.) For these reasons, knowing what to document is just as important as knowing how to do it.

- You **don't** need to document the source of commonly known pieces of information, such as the fact that the earth is the third planet from the sun, or the source of familiar quotations, such as Homer Simpson's infamous "D'Oh!"

- You **do** need to document quotations from primary and secondary sources.

- You **do** need to document the source of all facts, ideas, and opinions that you have taken from other sources *whether or not* you have quoted directly. Be especially careful to acknowledge the source of statistics. Don't make the mistake of thinking that you can avoid having to acknowledge the source of your information by changing the wording slightly. Failure to cite your references in this situation is still **plagiarism.**

There are two main systems of documentation. The Modern Language Association of America (MLA) is the accepted authority for documentation in the humanities (for example, English, film studies, or philosophy). The American Psychological Association (APA) is the accepted authority for documentation in education, the social sciences (for example, psychology, sociology, or anthropology), and many fields in the physical sciences. See Appendices B and C, respectively, for more information on these documentation styles.

A3 QUOTATIONS: GENERAL GUIDELINES

Although you need to acknowledge all sources of information you use, you don't always need to quote your sources directly. In fact, in non-literary essays, avoid quoting unless the exact wording seems important. Alternatives are paraphrasing and summarizing. (For more information, see Chapter 13, Research Papers.) When you analyze works of literature, however, you should use quotations to support each point you make.

It takes skill and practice to use direct quotations effectively. Here are some general points to remember.

■ *Use brief quotations to support points.*

Make all the major points in your own words and use brief quotations to support them. Do not rely on the quotation to make the point for you; your reader may interpret the quotation quite differently from the way you do. Often you can shorten a quotation by expressing most of it in your own words and quoting only the crucial part.

■ *Use quotations in context.*

Do not take quotations out of context and use them to mean something other than what the writer intended, as in this example.

Original Text

"The movie was entertaining, but it simplified the more interesting complexities of the novel."

Misleading Extract

"The movie was entertaining . . . [creating] interesting complexities."

■ *Clarify the context for quotations.*

Introduce each quotation with a sentence clarifying its context. Identify the speaker and the circumstances of the comment. Don't string several quotations together; introduce each one separately. Make sure that the quotation fits grammatically with the sentence introducing it.

Weak Example

"It is a truth universally acknowledged, that a single man in possession of a good fortune must be in want of a wife" (1). This quotation is a good example of Jane Austen's irony because single women need to marry, not single men.

Weak Example

The opening sentence of *Pride and Prejudice* is ironic because "It is a truth universally acknowledged, that a single man in possession of a good fortune must be in want of a wife" (1).

Strong Example

The ironic opening sentence of Jane Austen's *Pride and Prejudice* introduces the central concern of the novel—the economic necessity for women to marry: "It is a truth universally acknowledged, that a single man in possession of a good fortune must be in want of a wife" (1).

■ *Punctuate quotations appropriately.*

Pay close attention to punctuation before the quotation. If the introductory material ends with *that,* use no punctuation. Do not capitalize the first word of the quotation.

> The editorial in this morning's paper states **that** "if the Canadian dollar rises, exporters suffer; if it falls, importers suffer" ("Chasing the Dollar," *Daily Express,* Nov. 24, 2003, A13).

When the introductory material ends with words such as *states, says, argues, remarks,* and so forth, use a comma. Capitalize the first word of the quotation.

> The editorial in this morning's paper states, "If the Canadian dollar rises, exporters suffer; if it falls, importers suffer" ("Chasing the Dollar," *Daily Express,* Nov. 24, 2003, A13).

Finally, use a colon after a grammatically complete sentence introducing a quotation that is also a complete sentence.

> The editorial in this morning's paper captures the dilemma of the Canadian economy: "If the Canadian dollar rises, exporters suffer; if it falls, importers suffer" ("Chasing the Dollar," *Daily Express,* Nov. 24, 2003, A13).

Notice that the end punctuation always follows the parenthetical citation.

These rules for introducing quotations apply to all documentation styles; what differs in MLA and APA is the content of the parenthetical citations.

A3

APPENDIX B

Documentation: MLA System

As previously mentioned, the main system of documentation in the humanities is the one developed by the Modern Language Association of America. The material in this appendix is a summary of the most common items required for MLA documentation. Your college or university library may have printed and electronic summaries; there are also numerous internet sites that post style sheets for MLA users. For more advanced work, consult the explanations in the most current edition of the *MLA Handbook for Writers of Research Papers* or check the updates in www.mla.org.

Please note that your instructors might have specific preferences or additional guidelines for you to follow. Be sure to consult with them if you have any questions about MLA format.

The MLA website states that although computers can create italic type, underlined roman type may be more exact in student papers. Check which style your instructor prefers.

B1 FORMATTING YOUR ESSAY

The guidelines for formatting (Appendix A) apply to essays in MLA style. Unless your instructor asks for a separate title page, prepare the first page of your paper as follows.

- Create a header that includes your last name and an automatically inserted page number. (This header will appear on all pages of your essay.)
- Beginning on the first line of double-spaced text, and flush with the left margin, type your name.
- On the next and subsequent lines, type your instructor's name, your course number, and the date.
- On the next line, centre the title of your essay.
- Immediately below the title, begin your essay text.

Here is a scaled-down example of the first page of an essay in the MLA style.

Lin 1

Carol Lin

Professor Smith

English 101 (XXX)

8 October 2008

Language and Structure in Sharon Olds's "The Victims"

Sharon Olds's poem "The Victims" plays with forms of the verb "to take." The infinitive and its forms have multiple meanings, but two distinct ones resonate throughout Olds's poem, helping to structure the

---

B2 IN-TEXT CITATIONS

In-text citations provide enough information for your reader to locate full bibliographical references in your Works Cited list; they give page numbers (or, for some electronic sources, paragraph numbers) for quoted, paraphrased, and summarized material.

- The basic format consists of putting the last name of the author(s) and the page or paragraph number(s) in parentheses immediately after the quoted or paraphrased material.

  In the world of Alice Munro's short stories, no one is innocent (Caplan 23).

- If you have included the name of the author(s) in your introduction to the quotation or paraphrase, give only the page or paragraph number(s) in parentheses.

  Caplan argues that in the world of Alice Munro's short stories, no one is innocent (23).

- If you refer to more than one work by the same author, include a shortened version of the title in the parenthetical citation.

  In a recent article, Caplan argues that the question of identity is central to Munro's fiction ("Self-Creation" 77).

- For works with two or three authors, give the last names in the order they appear on the title page. For works with more than three authors, give only the first author's last name and add *et al.* (meaning "and others").

  The development of the bourgeois family can be traced in the novels of the nineteenth century (Seligman and Urbanowitz 112–113).

  The editors of this anthology provide helpful comments on prosody (Beaty et al. 2004).

- For works without an author, use the title or a shortened form that begins with the word under which the entry appears in the list of works cited.

> A *Daily Express News* editorial calls the film "a gross distortion of history" ("Crusade").

Sample In-Text Citations

In the following entries, pay special attention to punctuation surrounding the passage and the in-text citations.

Quotations

■ *Short quotations of prose (author not previously identified)*

If the quotation is four typed lines or less, incorporate it into your sentence. Do not change the capitalization. If the quotation is obviously incomplete, do not put an ellipsis (three spaced periods) before or after it. Put the in-text citation after the quotation, followed by the end punctuation for the sentence.

> Elizabeth's pride in her own intelligence is obvious in her remark that she would "never ridicule what is wise and good" (Austen 50).

■ *Short quotations of poetry (author previously identified)*

Incorporate three lines or less of poetry into your sentence. Punctuate exactly as in the original. Use a slash, with a space before and after it, to indicate line divisions. Put the line reference in parentheses after the quotation. If you are quoting from a play with act, scene, and line numbers, give these in your reference.

> Claudius realizes that Hamlet is neither lovesick nor mad: "Love! His affections do not that way tend, / Nor what he spake, though it lacked form a little, / Was not like madness" (3.1.156–158).

■ *Long quotations of prose or poetry*

For quotations over four typed lines, start on the next available line, double-space, and indent the whole quote 2.5 cm (1 in.) from the left margin. Do not use quotation marks unless the quotation includes dialogue. Put the parenthetical citation **after** the final punctuation at the end of the long quotation. However, avoid long quotations unless you will be making detailed commentary on the passage.

> John Donne begins "The Sun Rising" by complaining that the sun has awakened him and his beloved:
>
> > Busy old fool, unruly sun,
> > Why dost thou thus,
> > Through windows, and through curtains, call on us?
> > Must to thy motions lovers' seasons run? (1–4)

■ *Quoted words inside secondary sources*

In this example, notice the single quotation marks around two words that, in the original passage, were emphasized by double quotation marks.

> As James L. Johnson points out, "Tom's world is one in which 'adventure' replaces 'experience'" (51).

In the example below, the student is directly citing the words of one source (Singer) that were found in another secondary source written by Holmes. Because she does not have the original Singer source, she must be honest and cite the source she has.

> According to Singer, "Canada is catching up to American obesity rates" (cited in Holmes 299).

Paraphrased or Summarized Material

■ *Paraphrase or summary from primary text (author not previously identified)*

This excerpt is from an essay that refers to more than one work by Margaret Atwood.

> A severe thunderstorm passing directly overhead reminds Iris of the advice that Reenie would give the girls: every piece a dire warning calculated to instill fear (Atwood, *Blind Assassin* 135).

■ *Paraphrase or summary from secondary source (author not previously identified)*

> Tom is not changed by his encounters with Muff Potter, Dr. Robinson, and Injun Joe, even though encounters such as these would ordinarily affect how a person sees the world (Johnson 51).

B3 LIST OF WORKS CITED

At the end of your paper, on a separate sheet entitled Works Cited, present a list of sources. Your list of works cited should include only the works you have actually cited in your paper. If you consulted a reference, but did not cite it, do not include it on the list.

- Make sure every reference is in a form your readers can find. If you have cited an essay in an edited collection, for instance, the bibliographical entry should appear under the name of the author of the essay, not under the name of the editor.

- List the entries alphabetically according to the author's last name. If a work has more than one author, keep the names in the order they are given and alphabetize according to the first name in the list.

- If the author is not given, alphabetize according to the first word in the title (Do not count the articles: *The, A,* or *An*).

- Double-space within the entry but not between entries. The first line of each entry should start at the left-hand margin. Use the hanging indent function on your computer to indent subsequent lines by five spaces. Do not number bibliographical entries.

In the following examples, note both the order of information and the punctuation.

Sample Works Cited Entries
Print Sources
■ *Article*

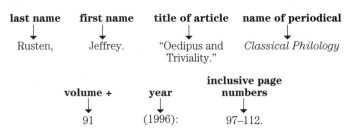

If each issue in the volume starts with page one, give the issue number as well: 91.1 (1996).

■ *Book*

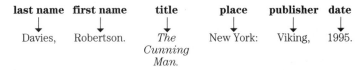

Note 1: If the city of publication is not well known or could be confused with another city of the same name, add the abbreviation for the province, state, or country (Paris, TX). If several places are listed, give only the first.

Note 2: Give only a short form of the publisher's name (McClelland, not McClelland and Stewart Inc.).

Note 3: Some instructors may prefer that you underline titles rather than italicize as shown here.

■ *Part of a book*

Put the editor's name (if applicable) after the title and the inclusive page numbers of the part you are citing at the end.

Cohen, Leonard. "Suzanne Takes You Down." *The HBJ Anthology of Literature.* Eds. Jon C. Stott, Raymond E. Jones, and Rick Bowers. Toronto: Harcourt, 1993. 632–33.

Ellman, Richard. "The Critic as Artist as Wilde." *Oscar Wilde.* Ed. Harold Bloom. New York: Chelsea House, 1985.

Atwood, Margaret. "Uglypuss." *Bluebeard's Egg.* Toronto: Seal, 1984. 67–93.

■ *Subsequent work by the same author*

Type three hyphens in place of the author's name. Continue as for the appropriate entry.

- - -. "Unearthing Suite." *Bluebeard's Egg.* Toronto: Seal, 1984.
   240–58.

■ *Multiple authors or editors*

Invert the order of the first name only.

Barnet, Sylvan, and Hugo Bedau. *Critical Thinking, Reading, and Writing: A Brief Guide to Argument.* 4th ed. New York: Bedford-St. Martin's, 2002.

When there are more than three names, use only the first name and *et al.*

Beaty, Jerome, et al., eds. *The Norton Introduction to Literature.* 8th ed. New York: Norton, 2002.

■ *Reference books*

If the article is signed, the author's name comes first; if not, the title of the article comes first. If the reference work, such as an encyclopedia, is well known, omit the place of publication and the publisher, but include the edition (if given) and the year. If the work is arranged alphabetically, omit the volume number and the page number.

"Biological Effects of Radiation." *Encyclopaedia Britannica,* 1998 ed.

Electronic Sources

The format for citing material you access through a portable electronic database (such as a CD-ROM), through an online database, or through the internet does not differ much from other citations. You include everything you would give for the print version of your source along with some additional information.

1. *The publication medium*—This information is important because versions of the same material published in various media (CD-ROM, diskette, magnetic tape) may not be identical.

2. *The name of the vendor*—This is required if the information provider has released different versions of the data to more than one vendor.

3. *The date of the electronic publication*—For an online database, indicate both the date of its publication and the date you looked at it, since material online may be changed or updated frequently.

You may not be able to find all of the required information. Cite what is available.

■ *CD-ROMs and other portable databases*

Portable databases are electronic media that you can carry around, such as CD-ROMs, diskettes, and magnetic tapes.

1. *Periodically published databases on CD-ROM*—Many periodicals (scholarly journals, magazines, and newspapers) and reference works such as annual bibliographies are now available on CD-ROM as well as in print versions. Begin your entry by following the guidelines for citing the print version. Then give the title of the database, the publication medium, the name of the vendor (if relevant), and the electronic publication date.

   Feaver, William. "Michelangelo." *Art News* 94 (1995): 137–38.

database	medium	vendor	electronic pub. date
↓	↓	↓	↓
Art Index.	CD-ROM.	SilverPlatter.	1995.

B3

2. *Books on CD-ROM*—Cite these publications as you would the print version, but add the medium of publication.

   medium
   ↓
   The Oxford English Dictionary. 2nd ed. CD-ROM. Oxford UP, 1992.

3. *Publications on diskette or magnetic tape*—Cite these publications as you would books, but add the medium of publication.

   Kriya Systems Inc. *Typing Tutor III with Letter Invaders for the IBM PC.* Diskette. New York: Simon and Schuster, 1984.

■ *Online databases*

Electronic databases are available online (MedEffect Canada, TAC Library Catalogue) and by subscription through your college or university library. Give all the information you would for the appropriate print version. Then add the name of the database, the name of the computer service or network, and the date you accessed the material. Your instructor might also request the website for your academic institution.

Strommen, Linda Ternan, and Mates, Barbara Fowles. "Learning to Love Reading: Interviews with Older Children and Teens." *Journal of Adolescent & Adult Literacy.* 48.3 (2007): 188–200. Academic Search Premier. Grant MacEwan College. 1 June 2007.

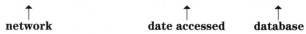

network	date accessed	database

Be sure to check with your instructor and the library staff at your educational institution about preferences for citing online databases. Your local library's URL, for example, will be easier to access than the originating library, as prescribed by the *MLA Handbook*.

■ *Internet sources*

When you obtain research materials directly through your favourite search engine, include as much of the usual information as you can, the date you accessed the website, and the URL (Universal Resource Locator) or electronic address.

URL Access—Professional or Organizational Home Page

Literary Landscapes. Home page. Collect Britain Putting History in Place. 18 Sept. 2003. <http://www.collectbritain.co.uk/galleries/litlandscapes/doorway.cfm?author=wordsworth>.

URL Access—A Page on a Website

"How to Make Vegetarian Chili." *eHow.com.* 10 May 2006 <http://www.ehow.com/how_10727_make-vegetarian-chili.html>.

URL Access—Articles in Online Periodicals

Sinopoli, John. "A Pact with God, A Pact with the Devil." Rev. of *Mercy Among the Children,* by David Adams Richards. *Varsity Review.* 18 Sept. 2003. <http://www.varsity.utoronto.ca/archives/121/oct16/review/apact.html>.

An email

Smith, Graeme. "Transgenics" E-mail to Brian Caplan. 2 June 2007.

B4 OTHER MATERIAL

■ *Film or video recordings*

Include the title, the director, the distributor, and the date. Add any other information that is relevant to the discussion (such as the principal actors) just before the distributor and the date. For videocassettes and similar recordings, give the original release date and put the medium (videocassette, filmstrip) before the name of the distributor.

Anne of Green Gables. Dir. Kevin Sullivan. Perf. Megan Follows and Colleen Dewhurst. Videocassette. Sullivan Films, 1986.

If, instead of the film itself, you are citing the work of a director, actor, or screenwriter, begin your entry with that person's name.

■ *Interview*

Give the name of the person interviewed, the type of interview (personal, telephone, email), and the date.

Brandt, Di. Personal interview. 3 Feb. 1996.

APPENDIX C

Documentation: APA System

The system of documentation developed by the American Psychological Association (APA) is the accepted authority for research papers in education, health care, the social sciences (psychology, sociology, anthropology, and so forth), and many fields in the physical sciences. Students in a wide range of disciplines use this system of documentation for their papers.

The material in this appendix is a brief summary of the most common items required for documentation in APA. Your college or university library may have printed and electronic summaries, and there are numerous internet sites that post style sheets for APA users. For more advanced work, consult the explanations and examples in the current 5th edition of the *Publication Manual of the American Psychological Association.*

Please note that your instructors might have specific preferences or additional guidelines for you to follow. Be sure to consult with them if you have any questions about APA format.

C1 FORMATTING YOUR RESEARCH PAPER

The general guidelines for formatting (Appendix A) also apply to student papers using the APA system of documentation. More rigorous formatting and stylistic requirements apply to papers that will be published in professional journals.

- All pages of your paper should include a header, referred to as the **manuscript page header.** Include one or two of the most significant words in your title, as well as the computer-generated page number, in this automatic text. This header will appear on the title page and on all subsequent pages of your paper, including the references page.

- The next item is the **running head.** At the top-left margin, type *Running head:* followed by an abbreviated version of your title in ALL uppercase letters. The running head, which can be a maximum of 40 characters, appears only on the title page.

- Centre the rest of the information on the title page both horizontally (centre align) and vertically (use print preview to judge). The official APA format calls for the writer's affiliation, but student papers usually include course information as in our sample below. Present this information in double-space format:

- the title of your paper
- your name
- the course and section number
- the instructor's name
- the date

Here is a scaled-down title page for the sample APA research essay that appears in Chapter 13.

Male Volunteers 1

Running head: MALE INVOLVEMENT IN VOLUNTEER PROGRAMS

Male Involvement in Social Services and

Healthcare Volunteer Programs

Sharon Cornelius

ENGL 108 Section 999

Jane Professor

April 18, 2008

C2 IN-TEXT CITATIONS

The basic information to be documented is the last name(s) of the author(s), the date, and the page or, for unpaginated electronic sources, the paragraph number.

- Place parenthetical references to your sources immediately after quoted or paraphrased material.
- When you are paraphrasing an idea, give only the author's last name and the year of publication at the end of your sentence. However, APA guidelines also encourage you to give the page numbers of paraphrases.

  A recent study suggests that although depression and substance abuse are associated, it is not necessarily the depression that comes first (Wu, 2002). OR (Wu, 2002, p. 198).

- If you include the author's name in the sentence introducing the reference, put the year of publication immediately after the author's name.

  In another study, Wu (2002) reports that although depression and substance abuse are associated, it is not necessarily the depression that comes first.

- If you are quoting directly, put the page number after the year in the parenthetical citation, with *p.* or *pp.* For electronic text, paragraph numbers identified by the symbol ¶ may be used in place of page numbers.

(Wu, 2002, p. 45)

(Hardy & Srinivasan, 2002, ¶3)

- If you are citing a work that is discussed in another work, name the original work; then cite the source you consulted and give the date for that source.

Singh's study (as cited in Robertson, 2000) . . .

. . . (Singh, as cited in Robertson, 2000).

- If you are repeating the same source in the same paragraph, omit the year of publication and include only the author's name in parentheses for the second and subsequent citations.

- If you will be referring to more than one work written in the same year by the same person, use the year of publication and a lowercase letter that identifies the order of the work in the references.

(Gibaldi, 2001b)

- If the work has two authors, cite both names every time you refer to the work.

   If the work has three to five authors, cite all the authors in your **first** in-text citation, but in subsequent references, include only the surname of the first author followed by *et al.* and the year. (In the references page, however, list all of the names of the authors.)

   If the work has six or more authors, in the first and subsequent citations, cite only the surname of the first author followed by *et al.* and the year. (In the references page, provide the first six authors' surnames and initials and indicate the remaining authors with *et al.*)

- If the author of the work is not identified, give a short version of the title in your in-text citation.

- When using internet sources, you should clearly direct the reader to the source of your information. In your parenthetical citation, name the group or person responsible for the information. Direct your reader to the exact location of your information by using the the paragraph symbol ¶.

- Spell out the name of corporate authors in every in-text citation.

   If a source has no date, use the abbreviation **n.d.** in place of the date: (Martin, n.d., p. 89).

(National Film Board, 1996)

   You can find more detailed information on parenthetical references in the 5th edition of the APA style manual; also, check to see if your library provides a summary of APA style.

C2

Sample In-Text Citations

The following examples demonstrate various ways of integrating material from common sources into your APA paper.

Quotations

■ *Short quotations*

If a quotation is short (40 words or fewer), incorporate the quotation, with regular (double) quotation marks around it, into the text of your paper. Put the final punctuation for the sentence after the parenthetical citation. This example uses ellipses to indicate words omitted, and square brackets to indicate changes. The original passage includes a quoted portion; in the example, these words are enclosed with single quotation marks.

> A research question may be difficult or easy to answer directly; an example of a research question with a "final, definitive answer . . . [is] 'How does penicillin destroy bacteria?'" (Troyka, 2004, p. 131).

■ *Long quotations*

Use a long quotation only when the original passage contains ideas or statistics that cannot be paraphrased easily. Do not enclose the passage in quotation marks. Indent the quotation 2.5 cm (1 in.) from the left-hand margin. Check whether your instructor prefers double- or single-spacing quotations. Put the citation in parentheses after the final punctuation at the end of the quotation. Introduce the quotation appropriately, as in the following example.

> F. C. Donders, a Dutch physiologist (1818–1889), invented mental chronometry, a method of measuring mental processes. Early psychologists eagerly adopted this new technique.
>
>> Precisely because it was a quantitative method, [mental chronometry] helped to ensure the scientific stature of experimental psychology as apart from qualitative philosophical psychology. It took the mind out of the armchair and into the laboratory. (Leahey, 2000, p. 225)

■ *Quotation from a professional article*

This quotation is taken from a full-text article retrieved from a database. The document was saved as a pdf file, preserving the original pagination.

> Lonsdale (2002) reminds us that a 1943 experiment found that "marginal thiamine deficiency produced bad behavior that would be traditionally thought of as psychological in character if it occurred spontaneously" (p. 86).

■ *Indirect quotation*

When you quote a passage that has been quoted in your source, be careful to indicate both writers clearly. Give the page number from your source (in this example, Leahey's book) and list this source in your references.

> Ulric Neisser (as cited in Leahey, 2000) considered computer models of cognition as "simplistic" and not "satisfactory from the psychological point of view" (p. 505).

Paraphrased or Summarized Material
■ *Paraphrase or summary*

Often it is preferable to paraphrase a writer's ideas or shorten a passage. Name the author (with date) to make it clear that the paraphrased or summarized material reflects another writer's, and not your own, ideas. The *APA Manual* encourages but does not require the page (or paragraph) reference for paraphrased or summarized passages. You can't go wrong if you include it as a courtesy to your reader. The examples below are, respectively, an appropriate paraphrase and summary of the quotations above.

Paraphrase

Lonsdale (2002) reminds us that a 1943 experiment found that bad behaviour can be caused by a slight thiamine deficiency. Prior to this discovery, it was thought that sudden, unexplained bad behaviour was related to a psychological problem (p. 86).

Summary

F. C. Donders, a Dutch physiologist (1818–1889), invented mental chronometry, a method of measuring mental processes. As Leahey (2000) explains, early psychologists were keen to use Donders' technique because it allowed mathematical, empirical inquiry and thus gave them the status of scientists rather than philosophers (p. 225).

C3 LIST OF REFERENCES

At the end of your paper, on a separate sheet entitled References, present a list of all the works you have cited.

- Alphabetize the entries according to the last name of the principal author (the one that appears first on the title page). Alphabetize government and corporate publications by the name of the government department, institution, or business where they originated, such as Statistics Canada, Royal Ontario Museum, or BC Hydro. For publications where no author is given, such as unsigned newspaper pieces and encyclopedia entries, alphabetize by the title, disregarding *A, An,* and *The.*

- Double-space within the reference and double-space between references. Begin the first line of each reference at the left margin; indent subsequent lines by one tab (use a hanging indent).

- For works that are NOT journals, such as a book, article, or webpage, capitalize only the first letter of the first word of a title and subtitle, the first word after a colon or a dash in the title, and proper nouns. Use italics for titles of books and other separately published works. Do not put quotation marks around the title of articles.

■ *Article*

Do not use *p.* or *pp.* for page numbers of journal articles, but do use them for magazine and newspaper articles.

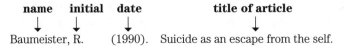

name	**initial**	**date**	**title of article**
↓	↓	↓	↓

Baumeister, R.   (1990).   Suicide as an escape from the self.

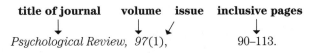

title of journal	**volume**	**issue**	**inclusive pages**
↓	↓	✓	↓

Psychological Review, 97(1),   90–113.

■ *Book*

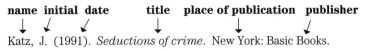

name	**initial**	**date**	**title**	**place of publication**	**publisher**

Katz, J. (1991). *Seductions of crime.* New York: Basic Books.

■ *Part of a book*

name   **initial**   **date**   **title of article or chapter**

Adam, K. (1994). Suicidal behavior and attachment. In M. B.

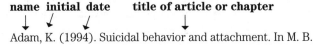

editor(s)   **title of book**

Sperling & W. H. Berman (Eds.), *Attachment in adults*

inclusive page nos.   **place**   **publisher**

(pp. 275–298).   New York: Guilford.

■ *Government documents and reports*

The basic elements are similar to other APA reference entries. If a government catalogue, report, or publication number is given, put it in parentheses after the title. Always cite a government department from the most general to the most specific (department>agency>division>committee>subcommittee).

Individual Writer Given

Day, D. M. (1995). *School-based violence prevention in Canada: Results of a national survey of policies and programs.* (Catalogue No. JS4-1/1994-2E). Ottawa: Solicitor General Canada, Ministry Secretariat.

Department as Author and Publisher

Statistics Canada. (2002). *Human activity and the environment, annual statistics.* Ottawa: Statistics Canada, Environment Accounts and Statistics Division, System of National Accounts.

◼ Subsequent work by the same author

If you have used more than one source by the same author, arrange the works by year of publication, starting with the earliest. Arrange two or more works by the same author in the same year alphabetically by the title (disregard *A*, *An*, or *The*). Add lowercase letters beside the year, within the parentheses.

> Freud, S. (1963a). *An autobiographical study* (J. Strachey, Trans.). New York: W. W. Norton. (Original work published 1925.)
>
> Freud, S. (1963b). *A general introduction to psycho-analysis* (J. Riviere, Trans.). New York: Simon & Schuster. (Original work published 1920.)
>
> Bowlby, J. (1977). The making and breaking of affectional bonds. *British Journal of Psychiatry, 130,* 201–210.
>
> Bowlby, J. (1980). Attachment and loss. Vol. 3, *Loss, sadness, and depression.* New York: Basic Books.

◼ Multiple authors

Give last names followed by initials for all authors, in the order they appear in the publication. Use a comma and an ampersand to join the last two authors in the entry.

> Wharf, B., & McKenzie, B. (1998). *Connecting policy to practice in the human services.* Toronto: Oxford.

◼ Reference books

If no author is given, begin with the title of the entry.

> Dinosaurs. (1993). *Collier's Encyclopedia.* New York: Collier.

Electronic Sources

◼ CD-ROMs and other portable databases

1. If there is a print version that's the same as the electronic version, cite the print version.

2. If there is no print equivalent, start with the author, date, and title as for print versions.

3. Put the type of medium (CD-ROM, electronic data tape, computer program) in square brackets after the title.

4. If you are citing a bibliographic database, give the location and name of the producer and distributor.

◼ Articles Retrieved from Online databases

Give the author, date, article title, journal title, and volume and issue number as for a print version. Follow with the date of retrieval and the database name. If the author is not given, begin with the title followed by the date.

> Lonsdale, D. (2002). High calorie malnutrition. *Journal of Nutritional and Environmental Medicine, 12*(2). Retrieved September 17, 2003, from MasterFILE database.

Anorexia nervosa—Part 1: How the mind starves the body, and what can be done to prevent it. (2003, February). *Harvard Mental Health Letter, 19*(8). Retrieved September 26, 2003, from Health Reference Center Academic database.

■ *Internet sources*

When you obtain materials directly through your favourite search engine, begin with the usual information, and then state the date you accessed the website and the URL (Universal Resource Locator), or electronic address. When giving an electronic address or URL, do not end with a period, for stray punctuation will interfere with retrieval. Here are some other pointers for documenting internet sources:

- Check your URL to make sure that it works; you want your reader to be able to easily locate the source that you cited.

- Direct readers as closely as possible to the cited information; reference specific documents or sections of the website rather than the homepage.

- If your instructor wants no hyperlinks on your References page, make sure that you carefully type out the website address instead of cutting and pasting it.

Daily Newspaper Article Retrieved Through an Internet Search
Waters, M. (2007, August 06). Doting doggie parents converge on Calgary. *Calgary Herald.* Retrieved August 6, 2007, from http://www.canada.com/calgaryherald

Document Created by a Private Organization
MADD Canada. (April 23, 2003). *Checklist shows little done to fight impaired driving.* Retrieved September 30, 2003, from http://madd.ca/news

Section in an Internet Document
Statistics Canada. (2006, July 6). Overview of Canadians' eating habits. In *The Daily.* Retrieved August 4, 2007, from http://www.statcan.ca/Daily/English/060706/d060706b.htm

Section of an Internet Site
Statistics Canada. (2007, August 2). History of the Census of Canada. In 2006 Census: Reference Material. Retrieved August 2, 2007, from http://www12.statcan.ca/english/census06/reference/info/history.cfm

Other Material

■ *Films, videotapes, audiotapes, slides, charts, works of art*

Give the titles of the originator and primary contributors in parentheses after the name, and the medium of publication in square brackets after the title.

originator   **and/or primary contributors**
↓   ↓
Kilbourne, J. (Writer), & Lazarus, M. (Producer/Director).

medium
↓
(1987). *Still killing us softly* [Videorecording].

■ *Interview*

In APA documentation, personal communications—letters, interviews, email—are cited parenthetically in the text and *not given* in the list of references.

For a model of the APA system of citations and references, see the sample research paper, "Male Involvement in Social Services and Healthcare Volunteer Programs" (13i).

For more information and references not covered here, see the official publication manual on APA Style. For updated changes to the APA Manual, see "What's New" or changes to the 5th edition of the APA Publication Manual at www.apastyle.org/whatsnew.html.

C3

APPENDIX 2

BUSINESS WRITING

Basics of Business Writing

D1 THE PURPOSE OF BUSINESS WRITING

Although some business writing aims to convey or request information, most business writing has both an explanatory and a persuasive purpose. Suppose you want to form a committee to plan for graduation celebrations. You will need to send a memo to your classmates with specific information about the work and time commitment of being on a committee, but you will also want to give them some good reasons to participate. Thus your memo would have both an explanatory and a persuasive purpose.

D2 THE BASICS OF BUSINESS STYLE

Business writing, like all writing, should be written in a language that is clear and easy to follow. Here are some practical suggestions:

- *Make sure your letter or report is complete, accurate, and precise.* Include all the background information (*who, what, when, where, why, how*) your reader will need to understand the context of your subject. Check all facts and figures. Telling your insurance agent that *The car skidded twenty metres* is more precise than saying *The car skidded a short distance.* In a report, include all the factual information and analysis required to support your conclusions and recommendations.

- *Make your writing clear and businesslike.*
  - Keep the proper tone by avoiding outdated expressions, such as *with regard to your inquiry;* contemporary bureaucratese, such as *prioritize our objectives* (set our goals) and *implement procedures* (act); and slang, such as *take one for the team.*
  - Use short, familiar words to increase readability; use *find out,* not *ascertain,* and *use,* not *utilize.*
  - Avoid "tion" nouns such as *implementation* and *facilitation.* Reword the sentence and use verbs instead.
  - Use active verbs instead of passive verbs, unless you have a reason for choosing a passive verb.

- *Foster goodwill by keeping your tone friendly.*
  - Consider everything you write from the reader's viewpoint. Use *you* and *yours* more often than *I* or *we.*
  - Reflect on the benefits of what you say or propose for the reader, and include the reader's benefits in your message.

- Be positive. Avoid drawing unnecessary attention to negative messages by using words such as *unfortunately, blame,* or *insist.*

■ *Keep your sentences and paragraphs fairly short.* Average sentences in business writing are about twenty-two words, and paragraphs do not exceed eight to ten lines. Avoid using very short paragraphs, though, which can make you sound scattered.

- Although you can put main points in short sentences, avoid long strings of short sentences, which can create a monotonous or aggressive tone.
- Use lists with numbers (specific order) or bullets (no specific order) whenever they are appropriate. Introduce lists with a clear lead-in sentence. Be sure your list has parallel structure (see Faulty Parallelism, 17h).

D3 BUSINESS LETTERS

Requesting information, making complaints, and sending special messages (such as thank-yous, sympathy, and congratulations) are common reasons for writing letters.

Business Letters: Format

Like other kinds of writing, business letters have their own conventions that raise particular expectations in a reader. By adhering to these conventions, you create a favourable first impression—one suggesting that you know what you are doing and should be taken seriously. Even if your handwriting is perfectly legible, type all business correspondence.

Here is the standard format for business letters. Left-justify all the parts of the letter, do not indent paragraphs, and leave a space between paragraphs. Every business letter should have the first six components.

1. **Your address and the date**
Place this information in the upper left corner, single-spaced. If you are using personal or company letterhead stationery that includes the address, leave a space and type the date below it. Do not include your name with your address.

123 Juniper Drive

Thompson, MN R7N 2K8

April 26, 2003

2. **Your correspondent's name and address**
Place this information on the left margin, single-spaced. It should include everything you would type on the envelope.

3. **The salutation (Dear . . .), followed by a colon (:)**
If you do not know the name of the person to whom you are writing, use the title of the individual or department (*Dear Editor:* or *Dear Customer Relations Department:*) or the name of the organization (*Dear*

Starbucks:). If you can, find out the name of a contact person and use it. Thanks to the internet, this information is now easily available.

4. *The body of the letter*
Your business letter will normally consist of three or four paragraphs. Business letters are seldom more than one page. If you need a second sheet, place the page number at the top. Never use the back of a page.

5. *The complimentary closing*
Use *Yours truly* for more formal letters and *Yours sincerely* or *Sincerely* for less formal letters. Capitalize the first word of the closing. Place a comma at the end.

6. *Your signature*
Type your name below the signature.

7. *Enclosures*
Draw your reader's attention to any enclosures, such as a brochure or a cheque, by typing either *Enclosure* or *Enc.* beside the left margin after the signature. Indicate more than one enclosure like this: *Enc. 2.* Name an especially important enclosure in this way: *Enc.: contract.*

8. *Copies forwarded*
Use the notation *c* or *copy,* followed by either a colon or a period, to indicate that copies of the letter are being sent to other people:

  c: Mrs. Elizabeth Nelson

  copy: Dr. F. D. Schmidt

Sample Business Letter

In the following business letter, the numbers correspond to the eight components discussed above.

Centre for Applied Language Studies   ①
Carleton University
Ottawa, ON K1A 6B6

October 30, 2008

Dr. Salim Singh
English Department
Mount Saint Vincent University   ②
Halifax, NS B3M 2J6

Dear Dr. Singh: ③

Thank you for responding so fully and promptly to our questionnaire on computer-assisted learning programs for second-language English students. Your detailed critique of several popular software packages was especially useful.   ④

Please find enclosed our latest issue of *Carleton Papers in Applied Language Studies*. We would be especially interested in your response to self-assessment as a guide to placing second language students.

I look forward to talking with you again at our summer retreat in July. Don't forget to bring your fishing tackle.

Sincerely, ⑤

Black ⑥

Alison Black

Enc. *Carleton Papers* ⑦
c: R. B. McKim, Editor, *Carleton Papers* ⑧

D4 MEMOS

Memorandums, or memos, are the usual form of communication between members of the same organization. Follow the guidelines for letter writing to organize the content of your memorandum. The format conventions are illustrated below. Notice that memos are not signed. Add your initials (by hand) after your name.

Sample Memo

DATE: July 23, 2008
TO: Susan Schnell, Franchise Manager [name and title of the person to whom the memorandum is sent]
FROM: Carmen Ditopa [name of the writer] CD
SUBJECT: Bunk Bed Safety [precise statement of the main focus]

Last week I received a letter from the Consumers' Advocates of Sarnia reporting complaints about the safety of children's bunk beds. These complaints included concerns about ladders that became detached from the bed frames and bunks that were not securely bolted together.

The most serious problems, however, occurred when sleeping children were caught between the guard rail and the mattress. The enclosed safety guidelines from Consumers' Advocates clearly show how a child can suffocate.

Please use these guidelines to check your stock and warn all sales personnel of the dangers posed by the models listed in the second enclosure. Sales staff should alert prospective buyers to the risks bunk beds may pose to children under six years of age.

Enc. 1.: safety guidelines
Enc. 2.: list of bunk bed models

D5 EMAILS: FORMAT

Emails are frequently used for communication within an office or between offices in the same company. Once used only internally, emails are increasingly used to communicate with clients quickly. Many emails are printed and filed, and they may be seen by others. Be sure your emails look as professional as your letters and memos. Each one needs careful proofreading.

Warning: Because business workers are becoming inundated with emails, consider whether or not your email is necessary or whether a phone call would be preferable.

Although you may be used to sending and receiving email, here is some protocol:

1. *Copies*
Fill in the address of anyone receiving a blind or carbon copy.

2. *Subject line*
Make the subject line clear and specific so that the receiver knows what the message is about. Each email should only address one topic so emails can be filed appropriately.

3. *Style and Readability*
Emails should be written in professional, clear business language, and not the style of text messages to your friends. Use upper and lowercase letters as all caps are hard to read. Use bullets or numbers for lists, and leave a space between paragraphs.

4. *Salutation and Closing*
You may use a salutation such as *Hello Latisha,* or *Dear Andrew:* or you may lead into the first sentence by using the receiver's name followed by a comma. Emails that are sent externally will look more professional with a salutation. Although signing is optional, most do sign emails after a close such as *Cheers, Best,* or *Regards.* Many writers include a signature block with their full name and contact information below it.

Sample Email

To: "Ivy Leung"
From: "Crystal Lucas"
Cc:
Sent: November 15, 2008

Subject: My talk with your students

Dear Mrs. Leung:

Yes, I will be happy to speak with your students about college life. I will tell them about residence life as well.

Will you please give me the following information so I can begin to prepare?
1. How many students do you expect?
2. Have they expressed any particular concerns?

3. Do you have a video projector available?
4. Which Friday in January will be best for you?

I look forward to seeing you again.

Best,

Crystal Lucas

D6 REPORTS

The term **report** can refer to many kinds of communication, from an informal discussion over the telephone to a lengthy, formal document with a title page, table of contents, and bibliography. In most work situations, you will be given detailed guidelines for the content and the form of the reports you are expected to write. You can then adapt the more general information in this text to your particular task.

All reports are based on factual information presented in an organized form. The two general categories of reports are **informational** and **analytical.**

The information report provides details and data, such as weekly sales reports or progress reports on specific projects. It does not analyze any of the information presented. In contrast, analytical reports evaluate information in order to make recommendations, provide options, or attempt to solve problems.

Regardless of their purpose, reports come in four forms:

1. fill-in-the-blank forms for routine reporting
2. memo reports for reports written within an organization
3. letter reports for reports written to another organization
4. manuscript reports for reports that stand alone with a title page and an accompanying letter or memo

The first three reports are generally short, informal reports. Manuscript reports are formal reports of three or four pages or longer.

Use headings to identify major sections of your report for the reader.

Analytical Problem-Solving Reports

As its name suggests, a **problem-solving report** is appropriate when you want to analyze a problem and suggest ways to solve it. Specifically define the problem you want to solve; instead of discussing a general subject, such as security problems, discuss the *30-percent increase in locker room thefts in the last six months.*

A problem-solving report usually has three sections:

1. *Background*
Provide enough information to give the context and the importance of the problem. How often does the problem occur? When and where does it

occur? How many people are affected? What are the costs in money, efficiency, safety, prestige, morale?

2. *Analysis*

Develop this section of your report through causal analysis. Make a list of all the factors contributing to the problem. Be sure to include both immediate causes (inadequate supervision contributes to theft by employees) and more remote causes (employees are dissatisfied with their wages and benefits, and therefore some feel entitled to steal).

You can organize this analysis as a list of independent causes or as a chain of interdependent causes (low wages cause employee dissatisfaction; this dissatisfaction causes resentment against the employer; this resentment causes employees to steal). If your problem is complex, you may want to combine both methods of developing a causal analysis. Make sure you connect your analysis with the background information.

3. *Recommendations and implementation*

For the problem, suggest solutions that follow logically from the analysis section. If you are suggesting a number of possible solutions, indicate which one is best and explain why. If appropriate, describe how the recommendations could be implemented.

Sample Problem-Solving Report

TO: Peter de Jong, Manager of the Marco Polo Restaurant
FROM: Lindsey Tomlinson, Dining Room Supervisor
DATE: January 31, 2008
SUBJECT: Serving Staff Injuries

Introduction

Since September 1, 2007, five of our fifteen servers have been injured on the job. Four of these injuries were minor (mostly cuts and burns), but one server sprained her wrist after falling on a wet floor. Although these injuries are certainly not life-threatening, they are distressing and they seem to be increasing. We need to find ways to reduce them.

Analysis

Not surprisingly, most injuries occurred during our busiest times: the 11:30–1:30 lunch rush and the 5:30–8:30 dinner rush. Young and inexperienced staff find these times especially stressful, so they are more likely to make mistakes and get hurt. When I asked serving staff, both new and experienced, for their thoughts on the causes of injuries, they made the following observations:

1. Staff who have worked in other restaurants may not be as well trained as they say or assume they are.

2. When we are very busy, we ask staff to help out by doing jobs they are not adequately trained for. A new busboy, for example, may be asked to serve hot dishes.

3. Angry and demanding customers, as well as those who leave without paying, upset serving staff who are then less careful about handling dishes, cutlery, and trays.

4. The ice machine leaks, so the floor around it is always slippery.

Recommendations

This feedback suggests that staff are well aware of safety problems and interested in helping to solve them. Here are some specific recommendations to consider:

1. Provide new servers with two training shifts whether or not they claim to be experienced. Focus on the most frequent causes of injuries: slips, spills, cuts, burns, and back strain.

2. Hold monthly safety meetings to give staff opportunities to voice their concerns and to learn safety tips from each other.

3. Remind all serving staff to ask for help if they don't know how to do a job or are having problems with customers. Provide staff with more opportunities to do a variety of jobs so they can help out when we are short-staffed.

4. Appoint a server to inspect the dining room for safety hazards (such as the leaking ice machine) at the beginning of each shift. Alert all serving staff to potential problems.

5. Repair or replace faulty equipment and furnishings promptly.

D7 BROCHURES AND FLYERS

You may be one of the thousands of Canadians who create and run their own businesses at some point—to earn money for your education, to freelance after you have gained experience, or to earn post-retirement income. Despite the invasion of television advertising, most businesses still rely on written communication to promote their products and services. Newspaper and magazine ads, promotional letters, brochures, and flyers are the most common types of persuasive pieces.

With only a limited budget and eager volunteers, you can, in three stages, produce a brochure or a flyer.

Stage 1: Creating a Framework

Before you begin to write, answer the following questions to provide your framework:

1. What do you want the brochure to do for you (inform existing customers, find new customers, give information about new products or services, advertise a sale)?

2. Who is your target audience (households, other businesses, specific income levels or age groups)?

3. What needs does your product or service fill?

4. How will you use this piece (mail-out, drop-off, handout, leave-behind)?

5. What format will be most effective (full-page text, 6-panel–2 folds, half-page fold-over)?

Once you've answered the who, what, how, where, and why, you will know whether a brochure or a flyer is more appropriate, and you will be ready for the next stage.

Note: A flyer is either a full- or half-size, unfolded sheet (8 ½ x 11 in.) with all the text on one side of the page. A brochure has one or two folds in the paper with text printed in columns on both sides of the page (8 ½ x 11 or 8 ½ x 14 in. are the typical sizes).

Stage 2: Writing the Contents

In her book *Persuading on Paper* (Haverford, PA: Infinity Publishing, 2001), Marcia Yudkin outlines five steps to creating your piece:

1. ***Brainstorm ideas.*** For at least a week, jot down all ideas, using a thesaurus to generate more thoughts. Allow enough extra time for these ideas to take shape.

2. ***Craft an attention-getting opener.*** This important first line helps you capture your readers' attention. These grabbers can be in the form of questions, news headlines, promises, or results (testimonials).

    Ever Wondered How to Get More for Your Money?

    Wake Up and Smell Our Coffee!

3. ***Spell out the offer or the action readers should take. Be simple and direct.***

    This is a limited offer. Book your appointment by calling . . .

    Take advantage of our gift with purchase.

4. ***Select and arrange supporting facts and ideas gathered in Step 1 above.*** Provide details about your product or service that explain why people should buy from you. This is your chance to persuade your readers.

5. ***When you have produced a rough draft, get an unbiased second opinion.*** Make changes and then proofread carefully.

Stage 3: Designing the Format

Gather samples of other brochures and ads, and decide what you like and don't like. Visit your local copy shop and ask to see samples of paper. Pick out suitable paper in the weight and colour you think will get your message across.

D7

The format needs to align closely with the tone and intent of the brochure. Choose the fonts, graphics, and layout that most closely match the content. It's a bit like choosing the right frame for a beautiful picture—isn't your content worthy of a great frame?

Although a typical graphics package offers many choices, keep it simple. A clean, uncluttered look will be more eye-catching than too much text or too many graphics.

Sample Flyer

TOO MANY CHORES & TOO LITTLE TIME FOR FUN?

Give yourself a summer break—
Let Handy Hammers do those jobs for you!

Plagued by weeds?
Worried about your plants during vacation time?
Frustrated with a falling-down fence?
Tired of spring cleaning?
Bored with tending your garden?
Concerned about leaky eavestroughs?

GIVE US A CALL

At your service, Shandy, Harry, June, and Ahmed are all eager to fix pesky problems and reduce those tiresome tasks so you'll have time for sun, surf, and relaxation. Our dedicated staff has a combined total of over 12 years' experience in household and yard maintenance. We guarantee our work—if you're not satisfied, we'll make it right!

FREE CONSULTATION & ESTIMATE
SPECIAL PRICES FOR SENIORS
REASONABLE RATES

CALL 555-6677 NOW & GET YOUR JUNE DISCOUNT

Handy Hammers Home & Garden Care
123 Elm Street, Parkerville, ON M3C 1X1
Phone: 555-6677; Fax: 555-5544

D7

Business Writing: Getting a Job

When applying for a job, you need to present yourself, both on paper and in person, in a professional, businesslike manner. This appendix provides you with guidelines for creating the following documents: résumé, cover letter, and list of references. Here, you will also find tips for preparing for interviews.

E1 RÉSUMÉS

A résumé is a one- or two-page summary of your work experience and educational background, tailored to fit the requirements of the position you are applying for.

Simply type your choice of résumé, save it on disk, and modify it as needed, using the "cut and paste" feature of your computer.

Although professionally prepared résumés look impressive, they are costly and they sometimes inflate the applicant's abilities. In an interview, employers look for a match between the person they have seen on paper and the one facing them. Any discrepancy will raise questions about suitability. If you get help creating your portfolio, just be sure the words and descriptions fit with your personality and experiences. Just like any other piece of writing, make the résumé your own.

Contents of a Résumé

1. **Personal information**
At the top of the page, type your name, address, phone and fax numbers, and email address. Make sure these numbers are not temporary; you want to be reached.

2. **Objective or summary of skills**
If you're applying for a part-time or summer job, this statement is optional. However, if you are searching for a job experience to reinforce your career path, include this information. Briefly describe your career goal, stating the skills and abilities you will use.

> To broaden my administrative responsibilities in the health care field while relying on my experience in nursing and my effectiveness in dealing with people.

Alternatively, you may begin with a bulleted list of four or five key skills or abilities that your employer needs. Be sure your list is in parallel structure.

3. **Work experience and educational background**
These are the most important parts of the résumé. How you present this information depends on the kind of résumé you are writing (see below), but your main purpose is to demonstrate that you can do the job you are applying for. Instead of merely giving your job title, emphasize your achievements and the range of your responsibilities. List both work experience and education in reverse chronological order, listing the most recent first. List responsibilities in parallel structure, using past (or present) tense verbs. Include the names of the institution(s) you have attended and the degrees or certificates you have received. If you are a college or university student, you can omit information about your high school education.

List any work-related workshops, training sessions, and non-credit courses you have completed, because they indicate your enthusiasm. Indicate computer programs you use and any languages you speak. If your grades are high, list your GPA.

4. **Interests, activities, recognition, and awards**
This personal information is optional in a résumé. You can include sports, hobbies, and awards to indicate that you have diverse skills and interests (some of which might be relevant to the job). These items may also indicate qualities that an employer would value, such as courage or perseverance. This information should be current, so don't include everything you have ever done. Also, your interests may provide an interviewer with an opening topic in an interview.

5. **References**
List names, addresses, and phone numbers of three people willing to provide references. Include their job titles and their relationship to you. Be sure to ask referees' permission before you include their names.

For references, pick the people who can provide the best information about you for the job you're applying for—former employers, supervisors, and teachers. When you have an interview scheduled, you may want to alert your referees, so they are prepared to comment on your abilities, such as your reliability, performance, and teamwork.

A frequently asked question about references is whether to include them on your résumé or just provide them when asked. Because most interviewers check references only after an interview, you may wish to take the references list to the interview. If you have room on your résumé, you may prefer to include them. If you have copies of favourable letters of recommendation, you can include one or two with your résumé.

Three Types of Résumés

There are three types of résumés: the *chronological*, the *functional*, and the *combination* résumé. Each has advantages and disadvantages.

The Chronological or Traditional Résumé
This style of résumé, which presents your work experience and educational background in a chronological sequence from most to

least recent, is easy to read and prepare. Use this format if you have a consistent work record and steady employment. However, if you are new to the job market, haven't worked for some time, or have gaps in your work history, this type may quickly reveal your potential weaknesses.

The Functional Résumé

Headings for the functional résumé focus primarily on specific skills and accomplishments related to the prospective job, rather than the chronological listing of education and work experience. If you've been away from the job market for a while, have an erratic work history, or have gained most of your experience from volunteer activities, this format may best emphasize your strengths. Use headings that emphasize the skills required in the position you are applying for. The major disadvantage of the functional résumé is that some employers find it dense and hard to follow. Even in this résumé, it's a good idea to include a brief employment history.

The Combination Résumé

As its name suggests, this résumé combines the features of the chronological résumé and the functional résumé. As in the functional résumé, you use skills and accomplishments as the major headings, but within these headings, you list the relevant information chronologically. The major advantage of a combination résumé is that you can present a more complete picture of yourself. The major disadvantage is that it is harder to organize. It may also be difficult to restrict to the maximum two pages.

E2 SAMPLE CHRONOLOGICAL RÉSUMÉ

Monique Tremblay

#3, 10032–119 Street, Calgary, Alberta T5K 1M9
Home: 555-228-2910

Summary of Skills
- Experience in a variety of public relations settings
- Strong writing and organizational skills
- Enthusiastic team player
- Creative problem solver

Education

2005–2006	**Bachelor of Applied Communications (Public Relations)** Mount Royal College, *Calgary, Alberta*
2000–2003	**Public Relations Diploma** Algonquin College, *Ottawa, Ontario*

Work Experience

January 5– **April 30, 2006** **P/T**	**Account Coordinator, Shandwick Canada,** *Calgary, Alberta* **(Practicum Position)** • Wrote memoranda to clients. • Booked a community tent throughout the summer for a city realtor, requiring research and correspondence with clients. • Interpreted and entered marketing data. • Planned program extensions for existing programs.
January 3– **April 25, 2006** **P/T**	**Administrative Assistant, Alberta Motion Picture** **Industries Association (AMPIA),** *Calgary, Alberta* **(Practicum Position)** • Kept track of all AMPIA Award entries (approx. 200), and silent auction donations in the database. • Organized the silent auction with a committee. • Assisted in preparing the program information.
September 2004– **September 2005**	**Marketing and Communication Assistant,** **The Alberta College of Art & Design,** *Calgary, Alberta* • As part of a team, organized and planned a major fundraising event. This involved taking ticket orders, organizing the silent auction, booking entertainment, planning party rentals, mailing out invitations, and working with a committee. • Maintained a fundraising database of approximately 8,000 names. • Planned/distributed an internal monthly newsletter. • Organized monthly President Luncheons promoting the College programs.
May 5– **August 24,** **2002**	**Public Relations and Sponsorship Liaison,** **Fringe Theatre Adventures,** *Edmonton, Alberta* • Arranged opening day ceremonies with a focus on the trade show and parade. • Compiled over 100 individualized artist packages. • Worked on Angels of the Fringe campaign, a fundraising venture with a $60,000 goal.

Professional Development

• Understanding of Microsoft Word and the internet.
• Working knowledge of computer programs such as Raiser's Edge database program, PowerPoint, and Excel.
• Creative writing workshop certificate from Mount Royal College.
• Assistant Stage Manager of a Calgary theatre production, *Possible Worlds* (February and March 2005).

Personal Development

• Outdoor activities—skiing, softball, hiking
• Live theatre, music
• Travelling—travelled for four months to Thailand, Malaysia, and Australia

References and Portfolio upon Request

Monique Tremblay used this résumé to get her first position in public relations after completing her degree at Mount Royal College in Calgary.

E3 SAMPLE FUNCTIONAL RÉSUMÉ

A social worker changing jobs might prepare a résumé like this one.

Jason Singh
1235 Elm Street

Halifax, NS B3M 3J6

Ph: (555) 429-7854 Fax: (555) 429-7725
email: jsingh@iconn.com

Objective:
Personnel manager in a major retail firm where problem-solving, communication, and administrative skills would be assets.

Communication Skills:
- Set up and provided editorial assistance for an information newsletter for people on welfare. Achieved a readership of over 10,000 in the Halifax area.
- Delivered talks and lectures on family problems, organizational dynamics, and liaisons with government agencies. Considered an interesting and informative speaker.
- Wrote proposals for projects requiring provincial government funding. Succeeded in securing an annual grant of $30,000 for special services to runaway teenagers.

Administrative Skills:
- Set up and directed a special project to assist runaway teenagers. Provided assistance to over 100 young people and their families.
- Hired, supervised, and assisted recent social work graduates in their first year of employment. Improved the efficiency and effectiveness of all employees.

Employment Highlights:
- Worked with a caseload of 150 families for five years.
- Counselled and provided practical assistance to parents and children.
- Known for offering skilled assistance to families in economic and emotional crisis.

Education:
- Bachelor of Social Work (Dalhousie University, 1999)
- Bachelor of Arts (major in sociology and English, Mount St. Vincent, 1997)
- Certificates from workshops in group dynamics, crisis intervention, and effective management skills

Activities:
- President, Toastmasters Club, 2004; member 2000–present
- Treasurer, Mount Pleasant Community Assoc., 2001–2006

Recognition and Awards:
- Volunteer Service Award, Westside United Church, 2001

References:

Dion Harris, Director
Youth Emergency Shelter
1310 Glengarry Avenue
Halifax, NS B5J 2P4
(555) 429-422l

Simone Hornby, Editor
Scotia Times
Box 1341, Postal Station B
Halifax, NS B2N 1J7
(555) 429-0000

Alice LaPointe, Supervisor
Families in Transition
123 Boat Harbour Drive
Halifax, NS B2R 3P6
(555) 429-2957

E4 SAMPLE COMBINATION RÉSUMÉ

Sarah Daniels prepared this résumé for her first job in the travel field. She targeted areas of interest to her employer.

SARAH DANIELS
1920 Oak Street, Sudbury, ON L5S 0M9
Telephone: (555) 489-0715 email: sdaniels@compusmart.ca

Objective	A position in sales and marketing of tours and holiday packages

Education

September 2004 to September 2005	**Travel and Tourism Certificate** *Cambrian College, Sudbury, ON* *Courses completed: September 13, 2005* *Practicum: August 9–September 12, 2005* *Cumulative Grade Point Average: 3.45*
December 2002	**Front Page 2001 Advanced Workshop** *Humber College, Toronto, ON*
September 2000 to August 2002	**Computer Information Systems Diploma** *Humber College, Toronto, ON*
September 1997 to April 1998	**Electrical Engineering Technology Certificate** *Cambrian College, ON*

Skills

- Proficient with the Apollo computer reservation system
- Familiar with Sabre computer reservation system

- Adept with Global/Matrix accounting system
- Skilled with word processing software such as Microsoft Office and Lotus 1-2-3
- Accomplished with graphics software such as Paint Shop Pro and CorelDRAW
- Trained at balancing bank deposits, bookkeeping, and administrative work
- Experienced in customer relations and retail store opening and closing procedures
- Capable of office machinery operation

Travel Experience

- Tour of northern AB and the winter road from Ft. MacKay, AB, to Yellowknife, NWT
- Exploration of Yellowknife, NWT, and area (including activities such as snow-shoeing and dog-sledding)
- Independent travel through ON, PQ, NB, and NS
- Organized a weekend skiing trip for 50 to Banff, AB
- Cruised from Los Angeles, California, to Ensenada, Mexico

Work History

Administrative Assistant, Brown Family Dayhomes, Sudbury, ON
October 2003 to June 2004
- Completed bookkeeping and administrative duties
- Increased efficiency of administrative processes
- Introduced a new computer system
- Improved administrative file organization

Web Page Designer, Shell Canada Limited, Toronto, ON
January 2002 to June 2003
- Examined and evaluated Human Resources department information
- Developed Human Resources department intranet pages for employee use
- Collected and summarized process flow data
- Created an interactive process flow website for internal and external use

Children's Entertainer and Balloon Artist, Just Clownin' Around, Sudbury, ON
September 1997 to December 2001
- Developed programs and performed at children's events and festivals
- Trained new employees and supervised others

Memberships

President, Cambrian College Travel Club	2004–2005
Council Member, Shell Web Council	2002–2003
Publicity Director, Humber College Campus Student Association	2001–2002
Editor, *The Chronicle,* Humber campus newspaper	2001–2002

Interests and Volunteer Work

Interests:
- travelling
- bicycling
- kayaking
- skiing (cross-country and downhill)

Volunteer Work:
- S.P.C.A. Walk A Dog participant
- Red Cross volunteer staff
- Head of Red Cross Blood Clinic organizing committee
- Travel Information Night organizing committee member and participant

E5 COVER LETTERS

The cover letter accompanies your résumé when you apply for a job. Your aim in both pieces of writing is to create enough interest to secure an interview.

In your letter, you create interest principally by showing how your qualifications meet the position's requirements. To achieve this purpose, you need a clear sense both of what your qualifications are and of what the job demands. Preparing your résumé will give you a good sense of your qualifications. To figure out what the job demands, first examine the job ad carefully. Note any particular skills and abilities required, such as a driver's licence or experience with a particular computer program. Second, find out as much as you can about the company and the position. Talk with anyone you know who has had a similar job or worked for the same employer and research the company/organization on the internet. You may have to visualize yourself in the position and think through its demands. Then try to tailor your qualifications to the job requirements. Make sure to anticipate the questions of your prospective employer.

You also create interest by how you present yourself. Convey those aspects of your personality that are most appropriate for the job—enthusiasm, initiative, personal warmth, experience. But don't get carried away; this is a business letter. Choose your words carefully so that you don't sound too gushy, too pushy, or overly casual.

Warning: Proofread carefully. Mistake-ridden letters end up in the trash!

Contents of the Cover Letter

Job application letters usually have three parts:

1. An **introductory paragraph** stating the position you are applying for and indicating where you found out about the job. If possible, establish a connection with the employer by naming the person who suggested you apply. Express enthusiasm for the aims of the organization you want to join.

2. A **summary of your skills,** knowledge, and characteristics most relevant to the specific requirements for this position. You may need more than one paragraph.

3. A **closing paragraph** referring to your résumé and indicating that you are available for an interview at the employer's convenience.

E6 SAMPLE COVER LETTER

Cindy Chow's cover letter helped her gain employment upon completing her diploma.

2093 Granville Street
Vancouver, BC V6H 4D1

July 8, 2008

Jennifer Ormsbee
Manor Home Improvement Centre
300 Robson Street
Vancouver, BC V3H 5K1

Dear Ms. Ormsbee:

Working with London Drugs for nearly eleven years, I have developed a solid understanding of the sales industry. This environment has provided me with a strong background and knowledge of retail and its dynamics. I am very interested in applying my sales and customer service experience, along with my college education, in a challenging, varied, and demanding role as an employee for Manor Home Improvement Centre. I read of your need for a Junior Marketing Consultant on your website.

I will complete a two-year Management Studies Program at Capilano College in September of this year. In addition, I possess a bachelor of education from the University of British Columbia. I possess excellent interpersonal skills, communicating effectively with individuals at all levels. Throughout my work experience, I have demonstrated my willingness and ability to familiarize myself quickly with applications, procedures, and policies, and to establish positive relationships with colleagues, managers, customers, and suppliers.

In my present role, a management training position, I have been responsible for overseeing stock personnel and cashiers while maintaining the smooth operation of the store. By listening and communicating with customers and other staff, I have developed a keen understanding of the sales industry. As you can see on my attached résumé, I am energetic, resourceful, and committed to both company objectives and personal growth. I offer your team of professionals a highly motivated and professional approach to customer service and to the promotion of the home improvement industry.

I look forward to the opportunity to present further details of my qualifications in an interview. You may call me at (604) 514-9749.

Sincerely,

Cindy Chow

Cindy Chow

Enclosure

E7 LETTERS OF RECOMMENDATION

In addition to your résumé and cover letter, it's a good idea to include one or two letters of recommendation. If you make a habit of collecting them when you leave a job or complete a course, they will be readily available as attachments.

E8 THE JOB INTERVIEW

Finally you get a call for an interview. You will need to prepare for it by finding out all you can about the company and the position. You will need to anticipate what questions you will be asked, as well as what questions you will need answered. And finally, you will need to practise for the interview to show yourself in the best light.

First, research the company. Check the company's website or annual report, or ask other employees of the company as long as they are not in the area you are applying for. You may call the receptionist, the Human Resources department, or the interviewer. Know how the company differs from its competitors.

Second, consider what skills the company wants. Analyze the position carefully, considering the technical and the interpersonal skills needed. Match your skills to those requirements. Consider difficult situations that could arise. If you are aware of areas of weakness or inexperience, consider how you would compensate or learn new skills.

Third, think of what you need to know about the position and the company. You may want to know about when the job will begin, training or mentoring, benefits, wages, or the dress code. Asking questions shows your interest and curiosity, so you want to be sure to ask a few. You will probably be asked if you have any questions toward the end of the interview. If you're not, tell the interviewer you have some questions. You want to be sure you will be happy with the position if you are offered it.

Lastly, consider the structure of the interview. It will probably be like a formal conversation with a new acquaintance: you will begin with some general and light comments—the weather, common interests, the decor in the building or office, or even the traffic. You will then get to know each other better to see how your needs mesh. In an interview, most questions fall into general categories—questions about yourself, your strengths and weaknesses, past experience, and your handling of past experiences. You may get a question that will make you squirm, or you might be asked about a specific scenario. Relax, think, and then speak. The interview will likely end with a summary, and either a plan to speak again or a time when you can expect the outcome.

Prepare for an interview by anticipating all details. The following guidelines will help:

1. Get a good night's sleep before the interview.
2. Plan what you will wear. Be sure your clothes are clean, conservative, and comfortable. Dress one notch above what you

believe employees generally wear at the job. Avoid large dangling jewelry, heavy make-up, and strong perfume, which look unprofessional and which may bother your employer, if he or she has allergies.

3. Review your résumé and take two extra copies with you. Take samples of your work in a portfolio.

4. Plan where you will park or how to get there. Arrive at least five minutes early.

5. Shake hands firmly when you are introduced, smile, and make direct eye contact with each interviewer.

6. Don't ask for the position, but stress how you are suitable for it.

7. Think before you speak.

Weblinks

- Community Learning Network Career Resources—a collection of online resources on résumé writing, interview skills, success in the workplace, rights in the workplace, and Canadian career and job search centres. See Hunting Jobs; Writing Resumes and Cover Letters.

  www.cln.org/themes_index.html

- The Rensselaer Writing Center offers a variety of online handouts, including information on résumés and cover letters.

  www.rpi.edu/dept/llc/writecenter/web/handouts.html

- The Riley Guide: Employment Opportunities and Job Resources on the internet.

  www.rileyguide.com

APPENDIX 3

GRAMMAR

Glossary of Grammatical Terms

Adjective
A word modifying a noun or pronoun. An adjective can express quality (*red* balloon, *large* house, *young* child) or quantity (*one* apple, *many* peaches, *few* pears). Other words, phrases, and clauses can also function as adjectives, including present and past participles (*skating* party, *torn* shirt), phrases (Memphis is the dog *in the red coat*) and subordinate clauses (the woman *who is chairing the meeting*).

Adjectives change form to show degrees of comparison—positive, comparative, superlative (*clean, cleaner, cleanest*).

Adverb
A word that modifies or describes a verb (run *quickly*), an adjective (*extremely* heavy), or another adverb (eat *very* slowly). Adverbs usually answer the questions *how, when, where,* or *why.* (They whispered *how*? They whispered *quietly.*)

Phrases (walked *into a room*) and clauses (He couldn't speak *because he was angry*) can also function as adverbs.

Adverbs change form to show degrees of comparison—positive, comparative, superlative (*quickly, more quickly, most quickly*).

Antecedent
The noun to which a pronoun refers. It usually, but not always, precedes the pronoun.

The **dancers** [antecedent] are rehearsing **their** [pronoun] routine.

Appositive
An explanatory word or phrase that follows a noun or pronoun, further describing it.

Martha, **my closest friend,** is visiting from Halifax.

Auxiliary Verb
A verb that helps to form the tense or voice of another verb (*have been* practising, *should have* phoned, *was* consulted).

Case
The form of a noun or pronoun that shows its relationship to other words in a sentence.

Possessive case [nouns and indefinite pronouns]: **Bill's** car, **nobody's** business.

Subject case [personal pronouns]: **She** and I left early.

Object case [personal pronouns]: Give the message to **him** or **me.**

Clause

A group of words containing a subject and a verb. **Main clauses** can stand on their own as grammatically complete sentences.

He didn't finish dinner.

Subordinate clauses, sometimes called dependent clauses, often begin with subordinating conjunctions such as *because, although, while, since, as, when.* These function as adverbs, answering why, how, when, or where.

Because he was in a hurry, he didn't finish dinner. (Why didn't he finish dinner?)

Other subordinate clauses begin with relative pronouns, such as *who, which,* and *that.* These subordinate clauses function as adjectives or nouns, answering who or what.

The man **who didn't finish dinner** is in a bad mood. [adjective clause] (Who is in a bad mood? *The man who didn't finish dinner.*)

She wished **that the ordeal would end.** [noun clause] (What did she wish?)

Comma Splice

A sentence structure error in which main clauses have been joined by a comma alone, or by a comma and a conjunctive adverb.

The party is over, everyone has gone home.

The party is over, **therefore** everyone must go home.

Complex Sentence

A sentence containing one main clause and one or more subordinate clauses. See *Clause.*

If we can't fit everyone in the car, and if we can't get the truck, we'll take the bus.

Compound Sentence

A sentence containing two or more main clauses. See *Clause.*

We can't fit everyone in the car, so we'll take the bus.

Compound-Complex Sentence

A sentence containing two or more main clauses and one or more subordinate clauses.

Before the storm broke, Mary put away the lawn chairs, and Shistri closed the windows.

Conjunction

A word or phrase that joins words, phrases, or clauses. See *Conjunctive Adverb, Coordinating Conjunction, Correlative (Paired) Conjunctions,* and *Subordinating Conjunction.*

Conjunctive Adverb

An adverb used with a semicolon to join main clauses in a compound or compound-complex sentence. Some common conjunctive adverbs are *therefore, however, nevertheless, otherwise, thus, furthermore, moreover*.

I must hurry; **otherwise**, I'll be late for class.

Coordinating Conjunction

A word used to join ideas of equal importance expressed in the same grammatical form. The coordinating conjunctions are *and, but, or, nor, for, yet, so*.

He was down **but** not out.

The weather was good, **but** the facilities were terrible.

Coordination

The stylistic technique of using coordinating and correlative conjunctions to join ideas of equal importance. See *Coordinating Conjunction* and *Correlative (Paired) Conjunctions*.

The battery is dead **and** all four tires are flat.

Neither the fridge **nor** the stove is working.

Correlative (Paired) Conjunctions

A pair of conjunctions used to join ideas of equal importance expressed in the same grammatical form. The correlative conjunctions are *either/or, neither/nor, both/and, not only/but also*.

These apples are **not only** expensive **but also** tasteless.

These apples are **both** expensive **and** tasteless.

Dangling Modifier

A modifying phrase that is not logically connected to any other word in the sentence.

Turning green, the pedestrians crossed the street.

Driving down the highway, the moose ran in front of our car.

Definite Article

The word *the*, which specifies the noun it is describing: *the* book, *the* baby, *the* opportunity of a lifetime.

Fragment

A phrase or subordinate clause punctuated as if it were a complete sentence.

And last, but not least.

Although it seemed like a good idea at the time.

Fused Sentence (also called *Run-on Sentence*)
An error in which two main clauses are joined without punctuation.

It's cold today my ears are freezing.

Indefinite Article
The words *a* and *an,* which do not specify the nouns they describe: *a* book, *a* breakthrough, *an* amazing feat.

Infinitive
To + a verb: *to run, to walk, to think.* See *Split Infinitive.*

Interjection
A word or phrase thrown into a sentence to express emotion or add style.

"Oh great, we're going on a picnic!"

Some interjections can stand on their own as complete sentences.

"Wow!" "Ouch!" "Hurray!" "D'oh!"

Misplaced Modifier
A modifying word, phrase, or clause in the wrong place in the sentence.

Hanging from the ceiling, I noticed a large chandelier.

Mixed Construction
(also called an *Awkward Sentence)*
An error in which a sentence begins with one grammatical structure but switches to another. It often results from improperly combining two sentences.

An example of this is when she daydreams constantly.

The more he learns, **he doesn't seem to remember much**.

Modifier
A word, phrase, or clause changing or qualifying a noun, pronoun, or verb.

Restrictive modifiers provide essential information and are not enclosed in commas.

Teenagers **who take drugs** need help.

Nonrestrictive modifiers provide additional information and are enclosed with commas. They can be removed from the sentence.

Susan, **who has been taking drugs for several years**, needs help.

Mood
The form of the verb showing whether the speaker is stating a fact (indicative mood: He *wants* some food), giving a command or making a request

(imperative mood: *Give* him some food), or suggesting a possibility or condition (subjunctive mood: If we *were to give* him some food).

Noun

A word that names a person, place, thing, quality, idea, or activity. A **common noun** is not capitalized and refers to any one of a class: *woman, cat, city, school.* A **proper noun** is capitalized and refers to a particular person, animal, place, thing: *Linda, Fluffy, Guelph, Westlane Elementary School.* A **collective noun,** such as *herd, flock, family, community, band, tribe,* is considered singular when the group is acting as a unit and plural when the group members are acting as individuals.

The band is on an extended trip.

The band are unpacking their instruments.

Object

A word, phrase, or clause that receives the action of the verb or that is governed by a preposition.

Stephen lent me his pen. [*Pen* is the direct object (what is being lent) whereas *me* is the indirect object (who will eventually receive the pen).]

She has already left for work. [*Work* is the object of the preposition *for.*]

Parallel Structure

A construction in which ideas of equal importance are expressed in the same grammatical form.

His analysis is **precise, thorough**, and **perceptive**. [parallel adjectives]

What he says and **what he means** are completely different. [parallel clauses]

Participle

A verb form that can function as a verb or as an adjective. Present participles are formed by adding *ing* to the present tense. Past participles of regular verbs are formed by adding *ed* to the present tense.

When combined with an auxiliary verb, participles become the main verb in a verb phrase (*is laughing, has been dancing, could have finished*).

As adjectives, participles can modify nouns and pronouns (*smiling* face, *running* water, *chipped* tooth, *sworn* testimony; *frowning*, he addressed the assembly).

Parts of Speech

Types of words, such as nouns, verbs, and adverbs. See *Adjective, Adverb, Conjunction, Interjection, Noun, Preposition, Pronoun, Verb.*

Preposition

Prepositions include such words as *by, between, beside, to, of,* and *with.* A preposition, its object (usually a noun or a pronoun), and any words that describe the object make up a prepositional phrase (*toward the deserted beach*). These phrases can function as adjectives (the man *with the red beard*) or adverbs (walked *down the road*).

Pronoun

A word that substitutes for a noun.

Indefinite pronouns *everybody, everyone, everything, somebody, someone, something, nobody, no one, one, nothing, anybody, anyone, anything, either, neither, each, both, few, several, all*

Personal subject pronouns *I, we, you, he, she, it, they*

Personal object pronouns *me, us, you, him, her, it, them*

Possessive pronouns *my, mine, our, ours, your, yours, his, her, hers, its, their, theirs*

Reflexive/Intensive pronouns *myself, ourselves, yourself, yourselves, himself, herself, itself, themselves*

Relative pronouns *who, whom, which, that, what, whoever, whomever, whichever*

Pronoun Agreement

The principle of matching singular pronouns with singular nouns and pronouns, and plural pronouns with plural nouns and pronouns.

The **committee** forwarded **its** recommendations.

Everyone has made **his or her** views known to the nominating committee.

Pronoun Reference

The principle that every pronoun must clearly refer to a specific noun. See *Antecedent.*

Tom told Hussein that **he** had won the scholarship. [pronoun reference unclear]

Tom told Hussein, "**You** won the scholarship." [pronoun reference clear]

Pronoun Shift

The error of shifting abruptly and with no logical reason between personal pronouns.

I didn't like working in the complaints department because **you** were always dealing with dissatisfied customers.

Split Infinitive

A form of misplaced modifier in which an adverb is placed between *to* and the verb.

> to **quickly** run

Subject

The word or group of words interacting with a verb to establish the basic meaning of a sentence or clause. Subjects are nouns, pronouns, or constructions acting as nouns.

> **Costs** are rising.

> **To argue with him** is a waste of time.

> **Cleaning the garage** is not my idea of a pleasant way to spend the weekend.

Subject-Verb Agreement

The principle of matching singular subjects with singular verbs and plural subjects with plural verbs.

> **He has** his work cut out for him.

> **They have** their work cut out for them.

Subordinating Conjunction

A word used to begin a subordinate clause—a clause that expresses an idea of subordinate or secondary importance. Subordinating conjunctions include words such as *although, because, before, since, while, when, if, until*. See *Clause*.

Subordination

The expression of less important ideas in subordinate clauses and phrases.

> **Although I am angry with you**, I am still willing to listen to your side of the story.

Tense

The form of the verb that shows its time (past, present, future).

Tense Shift

The error of shifting abruptly and with no obvious reason between verb tenses.

> Hamlet **was** angry when he **confronts** his mother.

Verb

A word that indicates action (*run, jump, breathe*), sensation (*feel, taste, smell*), possession (*have, own*), or existence (*are, were, seem, become*). A verb phrase consists of a main verb (a past or present participle) and one or more auxiliary verbs. For more information on verb phrases, see *Participle* and *Auxiliary Verb*. For more information on verbs, see *Tense, Mood, Active Voice, Passive Voice,* and *Subject-Verb Agreement*.

Verb voice can be active or passive:

Active Voice: A construction in which the subject performs the action of the verb.

Lightning **struck** the enormous tree. [subject + active verb + object]

Passive Voice: In the passive voice, the **true subject** is receiving the action of the verb.

The enormous tree **was struck** by lightning. [object + passive verb + subject]

F

Answer Keys

Chapter 17 PROOFREADING: SENTENCE STRUCTURE

Exercise 17.1

1. prepositional phrase, prepositional phrase
2. gerund phrase
3. gerund phrase, appositive phrase, prepositional phrase
4. infinitive phrase
5. participle phrase, infinitive phrase
6. absolute phrase

Exercise 17.2

1. you must not falsify data or ignore contradictory evidence
2. Clarence cut the questioning short
3. Karen wound up for the pitch
4. Gavin admired his handiwork
5. Hans scrubbed at the large blue stain; he couldn't get it out

Exercise 17.3

1. that live submerged = adjective clause
2. which get up to only 5 cm long from snout to tail = adjective clause
3. Even though these frogs are tiny = adverb clause
4. that remove heavy metals = adjective clause
5. That they need variety in their diet = noun clause
6. Although they spend most of their time swimming = adverb clause
7. because they are easy to maintain and entertaining to watch = adverb clause

Exercise 17.4

1. simple
2. complex   <u>who had no cognitive impairment</u>
3. simple
4. compound-complex   <u>When these 482 people were . . . . levels</u>
5. complex   <u>that 40 percent of the people . . . . them</u>
6. complex   <u>that . . . . response, which . . . . memory</u>
7. compound

Exercise 17.5

Answers to this exercise will vary, but you should make sure that your paragraph has a variety of simple, compound, complex, and compound-complex sentences as well as a variety of short and long sentences.

Exercise 17.6

Answers for this exercise will vary.

Exercise 17.7

1. Wendell **drove** around in circles, unable to find his date's house in the maze-like neighbourhood.
2. According to *The Hitchhiker's Guide to the Galaxy*, forty-two **is** the answer to the meaning of life, the universe, and everything.
3. After getting up to change channels himself because the remote control battery was **dead, Brad** sank back exhausted onto the couch.
4. Lydia **is** the last person I expected to quit school.
5. **The driver was** angry at the parking attendant for writing up a ticket because the meter had expired.

Exercise 17.8

1. **He was** always quick to judge others, but he bridled at even the mildest criticism.
2. **C**
3. The fans **cheered** wildly as the defenceman raced down the ice.
4. **C**

5. **She is** a woman with fierce pride and a determined spirit.

6. The reason for the fire **was** a pot of hot oil left burning on the stove.

7. **C**

8. **She tore** open the envelope and nervously **removed** the transcript of her final grades.

9. Although I could detect movement inside, no one **answered** my knock.

10. Because he didn't phone in or show up for work, **Garry lost his job.**

Exercise 17.9

In life and in literature, people create alternate versions of reality to avoid facing the unpleasant aspects of the lives they actually live or just to make their lives more exciting. In "Spy Story" by Filipino writer Jose Y. Dalisay, for example, Fred has convinced himself that he is a secret agent for the US Embassy. **Thinking that everyone around him is a spy and up to no good, Fred creates some excitement in his otherwise boring job as a chauffeur.** It's clear to most readers that Mr. Sparks, Fred's boss, is running a prostitution ring **and forcing** Fred into the role of a pimp. But Fred imagines that Mr. Sparks is entertaining high-ranking American contacts to foil dangerous espionage activities. **As well as commenting on our capacity for self-deception as individuals, "Spy Story" has a significant political dimension.** By setting his story in a seedy bar in the Philippines during the Cold War of the 1950s, Dalisay comments on the distortions of reality widely shared during this time of propaganda, spies, and secrets.

Exercise 17.10

1. **C**

2. **SPL**

3. **C**

4. **SPL**

5. **C**

Exercise 17.11

Because sentences containing comma splices can be corrected in a number of ways, these sentences suggest only one of a number of possible revisions.

1. A loud crackling sound alerted Gerta to the fact that she had left the foil cover on the dish; both the meal and the microwave oven were ruined.

2. Alicia offered to replace my shift; when I called to confirm the arrangement, however, she had changed her mind.

2. Although Gina used the proper amount of bromine and shocked the pool regularly with chlorine, the pool sides were still covered with algae.

3. The pilot light in the basement fireplace frequently goes out when snow blocks the outside vent.

4. Because Todd forgot to include his charitable receipts in his income tax return, his refund was delayed.

5. If you want to buy a computer, call Roman, who is an expert on the best buys.

6. Although Craig isn't doing well in physics, he doesn't seem particularly concerned.

7. When I entered the building and heard the final bell, I knew I was late for class.

8. Even though Marina hates the taste of ketchup, she likes ketchup-flavoured potato chips.

9. Because I couldn't hear what he was saying, I asked him to speak up.

10. Everyone has been complaining about the heat since the air conditioner broke down.

Exercise 17.17

1. Geraldine asked her brother Ben how much longer he would be in the shower.

2. Because my dog ate my computer disk, my paper is late.

3. Portaging is carrying a boat overland between navigable lakes or rivers.

4. In his letter, Darrin explained why he resigned his position.

5. We cut our vacation short because it rained for a solid week.

6. Without more donations, the shelter will have to close.

7. Looking at his bank statement, Dominic wondered how he had spent so much money in only a month.

8. Mary shows her thoughtfulness when she cuts the lawn for her elderly neighbours.

9. The theatre program lists all the actors in the play.

10. The next day Frank finally thought of a snappy comeback to Vincent's insulting remark.

G2

Exercise 18.1

1. should have done	6. rang
2. have worn	7. has not written
3. **C**	8. **C**
4. had known	9. saw
5. The reason is	10. **C**

Exercise 18.2

It's important to see that Michael Henchard in Thomas Hardy's novel *The Mayor of Casterbridge* is a kind of Everyman figure. Like most of us, he is motivated by psychological forces that he **does** not recognize or understand. For example, he never seems to understand why he sells his wife and then **remarries** her. Henchard **is** also affected by external forces over which he, like the rest of us, has no control. During the 1840s when the novel **is** set, long-established agricultural practices were being modernized by machines and business practices **were becoming** much more complex. In addition to the forces of industrialization, Henchard, as a wheat trader, is especially vulnerable to natural forces such as the weather. After all, he **makes** his living by predicting the harvest yields. Finally, Henchard is affected by chance and coincidence. It just happens that Farfrae, the man with exactly the skills Henchard **needs, shows** up when he is looking for an assistant manager.

Exercise 18.3

1. sisters/are	6. goldfish/makes
2. team/has	7. **C**
3. Neither/is	8. jury/has
4. **C**	9. Each/has
5. Fear/is	10. Nothing/seems

Exercise 18.4

1. The light changed to amber before Oliver reached the intersection.

2. **C** [The agent opening the pool is unknown or unimportant.]

3. Burt completely misunderstood my directions.

4. **C** [The agent adjourning the meeting is unimportant.]

5. Marietta spilled the milk, but she made no effort to wipe it up.

6. **C** [The agents shutting down the site and eliminating the safety hazards are unknown.]

7. **C** [if you want to emphasize Marcia's feelings]

8. After we trimmed and raked the lawn, we weeded the front flower bed.

9. Before setting out to write my exam, I searched for my good luck pen, but I couldn't find it anywhere.

10. **C** [The sentence emphasizes the late delivery.]

Chapter 19 PROOFREADING: PRONOUNS

Exercise 19.1

1. because I never know

2. Even when they are knowledgeable and competent,

3. **C**

4. The owners claim that they can hear [**Or** visitors can hear]

5. because he doesn't want to lose a tooth that can be saved.

Exercise 19.2

You can write this paragraph in either the third person (participants/they) or the second person (you). Both versions are shown below.

You will get a more effective workout in your next fitness class if you follow this advice. **If you are new,** position **yourself** near the instructor so you can see and hear clearly. **If you are near the front, you** are also less likely to be distracted by other participants. **You** should give the class **your** full attention, so don't spend your time worrying about whether other people are watching you or whether you put enough change in the parking meter. Although **you** might be tempted to compensate for **your** lack of ability with expensive exercise clothes, don't spend a fortune on exercise accessories. All **you** really need is a T-shirt, shorts, running shoes, and a willingness to devote an hour to **your** own good health.

Participants will get a more effective workout in **their** next fitness class if **they** follow this advice. **Novices** should position themselves near the instructor so **they** can see and hear clearly. **Those** near

G3

the front **are** also less likely to be distracted by **others. All partic-ipants** should give the class **their** full attention **rather than** wor-rying about whether other people are watching **them** or whether **they** put enough change in the parking meter. Although **some peo-ple** might be tempted to compensate for lack of ability with expensive exercise clothes, **no one needs to** spend a fortune on exercise acces-sories. All participants really need is a T-shirt, shorts, running shoes, and a willingness to devote an hour to their own good health.

Exercise 19.3

1. We workers
2. He and I
3. than she
4. whom to contact
5. or me
6. or him
7. Adrilla and I
8. Michael, Stephen, and he
9. that she and her sister
10. **C**

Exercise 19.4

1. anyone's
2. Whose
3. yours
4. Theirs
5. its

Exercise 19.5

1. Nigel or me
2. he and his brothers
3. than I that you and she
4. their furniture
5. whose limousine
6. hers
7. Between you and me
8. **C**
9. Dave and I
10. she and her boyfriend

Exercise 19.6

Last February, Peter and **I** decided to get married. We wanted to get married in June, so **there** were four months to plan the wedding. Although our wedding cost only $2000, it turned out beautifully. Here's how we did it.

First we made a list of everything we could do **ourselves.** **My sister and I** spent two weeks shopping every chance we got in Value Village stores and all the second-hand vintage clothing shops. Luckily, I found the perfect dress for just under $50 and my sister found a gorgeous bridesmaid's dress for $100. I didn't mind that **hers** cost twice as much as mine because she said that **she** and her boyfriend might get married **themselves** and she would wear that dress to the wedding. Peter was able to borrow his dad's dark suit, which his dad said looked better on Peter than it did on **him**. Peter's brother Tom had just gotten married, so he had a dark suit he could wear as best man. Having dealt with the clothing issue, we went to a pawnshop and bought two gold rings for $50 each.

Now we had to find a place to get married. We have a friend **whose** parents own a cottage near a local lake. They agreed to lend us **their** place for the weekend. For $200 we could rent canopies and tables to put on the lawn. Then I persuaded my mother to let Peter and **me** raid her garden for lilacs, tulips, and daisies. They made lovely bouquets for all the tables.

Peter's Uncle Ted said that **he** and his friend, an amateur photographer, would take all the photographs. If we supplied the film, which cost about $100, he would print the photos with his own computer.

Now we had to find someone to marry us. We contacted a local marriage commissioner and discovered that the usual gratuity is $50. We had to give her another $50 to cover her travelling expenses. The marriage licence cost $50. So far, we had spent $700.

It's probably not surprising that food and liquor were our biggest expense. Because so many of our guests had allergies or were on special diets, we decided on a simple meal of chili, homemade cornbread, and huge salads, with beer and wine. For dessert, we had soy ice cream and a vegan wedding cake made by my father and **me.** Buying the food and liquor, and renting cutlery, glasses, and dishes cost about $700.

Of course, what's a wedding without music and dancing? No one knows more about the local music scene than Peter and **I,** so we hired a band for $300. We didn't need to provide any of the sound equipment because the band said they would bring **theirs.**

Naturally, there were a few more miscellaneous expenses, but the total cost of our wedding was well under $2,000. Between you and **me,** the wedding couldn't have suited **us** thrifty folks better if it had cost $20,000.

Exercise 19.7

1. manager/his or her [**Or** all managers/their]

2. immigrant/he or she [**Or** new immigrants/they]

3. daycare worker/his or her [**Or** daycare workers/their]

4. actor/he or she [**Or** actors/they]

5. customer service representative/his or her [**Or** customer service representatives/their]

Exercise 19.8

1. Everyone/his or her
2. **C**
3. Each/his or her
4. Neither/his/he
5. **C**

Exercise 19.9

1. supervisor/his **or** supervisor/her [**Better:** Neither the supervisor nor the employees/their]
2. **C**
3. herd/its/its
4. committee/its
5. Matt/Richard/his
6. government/its
7. group/its [**Or** the hotel]
8. **C** [class acting as individuals]
9. family/its [family acting as unit]
10. Pierre/Antoine/his [**Or C**]

Exercise 19.10

1. writer/his or her [**Or** writers/their]
2. Neither/his
3. **C**
4. No one/his or her
5. **C**
6. Stacey/Veronica/her
7. addict/his or her [**Or** addicts/their]
8. **C**
9. army/its
10. Everyone/his or her
11. **C**
12. Sandra/Brianne/her

13. Neither/his

14. winner/his or her

15. who/his [*Who* is singular because it refers to *man.*]

Exercise 19.11

PowerPoint presenters arrange words and pictures into a series of pages that they project from a laptop computer onto a screen. Each **screen** typically has **a** heading followed by bullet points: six or seven words a line, six or seven lines a slide. Paragraphs and even sentences have too many words for a PowerPoint presentation, so **presenters** must reduce their most complex ideas to little phrases. Of course, the bullet points eliminate the need for transitions, such as *because* or **on the other hand,** that might help a viewer understand connections among these phrases. **Typically, presenters haven't** noticed the absence of transitions. They have been so caught up in the technical features of PowerPoint that they have concentrated on the appearance of the text and the accompanying graphics. Never mind, if there are enough snappy visual aids, neither the viewers nor the presenter may notice that **the** presentation has the intellectual substance of a kindergarten show and tell.

Exercise 19.12

1. Experts say

2. when you know your behaviour upsets her?

3. when Nicole told her, "You [or I] didn't get the job."

4. but my efforts

5. the customer service representative said

6. but at the time Giselle didn't know what had caused the problem.

7. The pie crust is tough because Raul added too much water to the dough and beat it mercilessly.

8. but these qualities don't bother his friends.

9. Her actions greatly surprised me.

10. Mr. Carlson ruined the lawn by applying too much weed killer and overwatering the grass.

Exercise 19.13

Vegans do not eat any animal products. This **dietary limitation** means that many of the foods most people enjoy, such as ice cream, mayonnaise, bacon and eggs, even toast with honey, are off-limits. Because most prepared foods contain some animal products, eating out can be a real challenge, **so** many vegans cook at home and bring food with them when they go out. Of course, vegan cooking presents its own difficulties. When I became a vegan, I bought a cookbook with lots of delicious-looking recipes, but **these recipes** didn't help. **Each recipe contained so many exotic ingredients** that I had to dash to the health food store before I could begin. Despite these obstacles, I'm glad to be a vegan. Now that **stories about so many diseases carried by cows, fish, and birds are in the news,** who would want to eat meat even if **animals** were killed more humanely?

Chapter 20 PROOFREADING: MODIFIERS

Exercise 20.1

1. seriously
2. runs well
3. fewer players
4. really interested
5. do so well, in chemistry

Exercise 20.2

1. liveliest
2. considerably better
3. went well
4. fewer social occasions
5. is empty
6. **C**
7. as honestly
8. really tired
9. **C**
10. less happy

Exercise 20.3

1. Soak the shirt with the spaghetti sauce stain in cold water.
2. Sonia could run almost ten full circuits around the field.
3. The students examined the jar of tapeworms preserved in formaldehyde.
4. I promise not to judge you unfairly.
5. Standing by the band, I had difficulty hearing the conversation.

G4

Exercise 20.4

1. The singer's fans could hardly wait . . .

2. You can eat properly cooked hamburger . . .

3. I want to consider all my options thoroughly . . .

4. **C**

5. Seeing the accident ahead, Tran pulled the car to the side of the road and got out to investigate.

6. Eating our lunch on the patio, we enjoyed . . .

7. . . . you ate only half the pizza.

8. With his mouth full of toothpaste, Jim heard . . .

9. On the hall table there is a family picture . . .

10. **C**

Exercise 20.5

1. Before signing a contract

2. **C**

3. To reduce conflicts with their children

4. When in Rome

5. **C**

Exercise 20.6

1. Walking into the room, I saw a strange sight. **Or**
   When I walked into the room, a strange sight caught my eye.

2. While George was in high school, his father was promoted and the family moved to Vancouver.

3. Because Maurice was exhausted by a heavy work schedule, the doctor recommended a complete rest.

4. To make a perfect omelette, you require the freshest ingredients.

5. After Theresa pleaded earnestly, her parents extended her curfew to midnight.

6. **C**

7. Driven by arrogance and greed, Joe soon alienated his friends.

8. After working so hard on the committee, Bernard definitely deserves our gratitude.

9. **C**

10. While I was reading Stephen King's *Cujo,* my dog began barking in the backyard.

11. While Hank was driving on the highway, his car engine suddenly seized.

12. As I stared intently at the small print, spots began to swim before my eyes.

Exercise 20.7

Nineteenth-century workers **could hardly** survive without spending long hours at demanding jobs. **In the summer,** farm workers and outside workers toiled from sunrise to sunset. Working shorter hours in the winter, **they made less money.** Shop employees were treated equally **badly. To meet the needs of their customers effectively,** shops stayed open **really** long hours—often fourteen to sixteen—with the same employees. The most **dreadful** conditions were in the factories. Treated as part of the machinery and forced to work at the pace of the machine, **factory workers** had no time for talking or joking with their mates. Children as young as seven worked twelve-hour shifts and slept in factory dormitories. **By the middle of the nineteenth century it was illegal in England** to employ children under nine in textile factories, **but in 1900** most children were working full-time by the time they were thirteen or fourteen.

Chapter 21 PROOFREADING: PUNCTUATION

Exercise 21.1

1. two suitcases, called a cab, and headed for the airport.

2. eye of newt, toe of frog, wool of bat, and tongue of dog.

3. to put the armoire in the master bedroom, the console in the hall, and the pine desk in the study.

4. bread, cheese, cold cuts, fruit, and sodas

5. the meat was underdone, the vegetables were soggy, and the wine was sour.

6. We must go now, for our ferry leaves exactly at noon.

7. Freida knocked down the wall, and David hauled away the rubble.

8. Liam is a painstaking editor, yet a few small errors escaped even his sharp eye.

9. The Richardsons knew that they must replace the worn linoleum and repaint the walls a neutral colour, or the house would never sell.

10. When Fiona first began working as a cashier, she thought that she would never remember the PLU's for produce, but she had soon memorized dozens of codes.

Exercise 21.2

1. For example, pizza/groups, but
2. in Calgary, Louis
3. on the tile floor, he
4. High above, the planes
5. No, I don't remember
6. fever, isn't it?
7. no man, if you catch my drift.
8. the savage breast, not the savage beast.

Exercise 21.3

1. Thank you, Mr. Sutherland,
2. **C**
3. Punch Dickins, who won the Distinguished Flying Cross in World War I,
4. python, which hasn't eaten in a month,
5. promised us, however, that

Exercise 21.4 Comma Review

1. However, I always counter, look
2. turkey sandwiches, turkey casserole, and turkey croquettes
3. has expired, Mr. Fortino, is not
4. microwave sounded, Ted
5. **C** [no commas]

G5

6. Whenever we go camping, Father always says, "If you don't fish where the fish are, you'll be having hot dogs for supper."

7. opened the window, took a deep breath, and composed

8. The one novel that I didn't read was the basis for the essay question on the English exam. [no commas]

9. Lucy Maud Montgomery, the author of *Anne of Green Gables*, was born in Clifton, Prince Edward Island, on November 30, 1874.

10. Well, you

11. perspective, I

12. Yes, we do

13. Howard would bring the food, Cliff would bring the drinks, and you

14. deep drifts, and icicles

15. Taxes, of course, are

16. Even during the day, light

17. Mr. Ramondo said, "We're a few bricks short of a load, but I

18. **C** [no commas]

19. dark, stormy night, I like nothing better than

20. to study engineering because she discovered that

Exercise 21.5

1. astronaut; he

2. **C**

3. The variety show will feature Vox Populi, a well-known local band; the Crazy Bones, a hilarious comedy act; and the Tumbling Turners, an acrobatic troupe.

4. pay for the new jeans; however, his

5. open the door; but, fortunately, a quick glance

6. family; Erica has therefore agreed (or has, therefore, agreed)

7. interpretation, he was pleased

8. night; as a result, farmers are

Exercise 21.6

1. Helen's/Stephanie's/year's

2. patrons'

3. Nobody's

4. *u*'s

5. It's/hostess'

6. Mary's

7. Justin's/parents'

8. children's

9. Don't/*um*'s/*uh*'s.

10. Won't/Mildred's

Exercise 21.7

1. choices: "When choosing

2. term: Basic Calculus, Fluid Dynamics, and Introductory Drafting

3. convinced—I say this without reservation—that Luke

4. suspects—Winken, Blinken, or Nod—knew

5. companion: he

6. escape: all [**Or** escape—all]

7. **C**

8. furniture—all

Exercise 21.8

1. "Two negatives make a positive," explained Ludwig. "However, two positives don't make a negative."

2. "Yeah, right!" replied Noam.

3. **C**

4. proverb, "When money talks, the truth keeps silent."

5. "like" and "basically" [**Or** *like* and *basically*]

6. "The Death of the Moth"

Exercise 21.9

1. "No, I won't move my car!" shouted the irate driver.

2. **C**

3. said, "Give me a firm place to stand, and I will move the earth"?

4. The term "portmanteau word" refers to a word combining the sounds and meanings of two other words. For example, the word "smog" is a blending of the words "smoke" and "fog." [period goes inside the quotation marks]

   [Or portmanteau word/smog/smoke/fog.]

5. "Dulce et Decorum Est" and Randall Jarrell's poem "The Death of the Ball Turret Gunner." [period goes inside the quotation marks]

6. said, "The acorn never falls far from the oak tree"?

7. "If fifty million people say a foolish thing," noted Anatole France, "it is still a foolish thing."

8. yelling, "We all scream for ice cream!"

9. "chimpanzee"/"gorilla"/"zebra" [**Or** *chimpanzee/gorilla/zebra*]

10. Sam Cooke's "Sad Mood."

Exercise 21.10

1. all-purpose floor covering

2. self-satisfied/twenty-three/equally qualified

3. "workmen"/"mankind"

4. ninety-year-old/weekend

5. ex-boyfriend/compact disks

Exercise 21.11

1. icono-clast
2. cry-baby
3. wrap-ping
4. **C** [no hyphen]
5. **C** [no hyphen]

6. rail-road
7. thrill-ing
8. jim-jams
9. memo-rize
10. **C** [no hyphen]

Exercise 21.12

1. four 250-page
2. Fifteen percent
3. twenty

4. **C**
5. 1980s **or** 1980's/1999

Index

Note: Page references in *italics* are glossary entries.